Lever Action

Lever Action

Essays on Liberty

By
L. Neil Smith

A Mountain Media Book

Lever Action
Essays on Liberty

Published by
    Mountain Media
    P.O. Box 271122
    Las Vegas, NV 89127
    email at vin@lvrj.com

ISBN 0-9670259-1-5

Cover Design — Scott Bieser
Page Design — Kathy Harrer

Thanks to Christoph Kohring, founder of pro LIBERTATE Society for Individual Liberty (Switzerland), a division of the International Society for Individual Liberty (ISIL), and Freeman Craig Presson for their help with the backcover copy.

CONTENTS

೧♥ ೧♥ ೧♥ ೧♥ ೧♥

AUTHOR'S NOTE

My Purloined Letters
ᐆ ᐆ ᐆ ᐆ ᐆ

It's with mixed feelings that I come to the keyboard for a final time in connection with this project. On the one hand, these writings should speak for themselves and require no introduction. On the other, I could regale my readers for hours with the triumphs and tragedies they represent, have caused me to endure, or have even gotten me out of.

(If you're curious, I've had more hate mail because of my analysis of Lincoln and my defense of smokers than from anything else I've ever written.)

On the third hand (I *am* a science fiction writer, after all), maybe it'll do to fill you in on the background or consequences of a few of these pieces, and save the rest of my war stories for the lectern on occasions where I have to speak for an hour on a half-hour subject.

The volume you hold in your hands is the illegitimate offspring of 25 years of stealing time from my real work as a novelist to write articles, speeches, and letters to the editor. There's no adequate way to express what it's like to see them all in print together, between the covers of a real book. It's a dream — or a nightmare — come true.

I say that, not to annoy my esteemed editor, Deke Castleman, or my esteemed publisher, Mountain Media, to both of whom I owe a debt of gratitude, but because some of these columns spring from moments of the blackest fear and/or the reddest anger I've experienced in my adult life. In the last 20 years, whenever I felt helpless, frustrated, or outraged by events around me I had no power to change, I wrote about them.

And it helped.

You see, I'm sort of a comic-book American. I grew up in a white, middle-class, Protestant, Ozzie and Harriet family. My mom was a den mother; my dad was a scoutmaster. He was also a World War II veteran, a former prisoner of war, and a bombardier-navigator in Strategic Air Command. My younger brother and I were Cub Scouts, Boy Scouts, and Explorer Scouts by turn. I won a translator's bar (German), the God and Country Award, was tapped for the Ordeal and Brotherhood levels of the Order of the Arrow, and became an Eagle Scout with 23 merit badges.

I can't recall exactly when I became aware that things weren't the way they were supposed to be in America. It may have been just after the flight of Sputnik, the first artificial satellite — a *Russian* artificial satellite — scared the American political and education satrapies spitless, shitless, and even more witless than they were already.

I was in seventh grade when they gave us the IQ tests. I must have done pretty well, because I was summoned to the principal's office (a fairly scary experience in those days), grilled about my college plans (I didn't have any; hell, I was in seventh grade!), and lectured on the Vital Importance — to the country, not to me — of living up to my potential, the first of at least a hundred living-up-to-my-potential or not-living-up-to-my-potential lectures I would get during the next seven or eight years. But in 1957, it was clear I wasn't an individual in this pucker-assed chairwarmer's eyes, but a superweapon in the Cold War.

I didn't like it a bit, and it was all downhill from there. I had learned about bureaucracy when my father was punished for blowing the whistle on instructors in a SAC training school who were selling the answers to exams. Dad thought it might

2

be good if the guys flying around with H-bombs in their hip pockets actually knew what they were doing. For his trouble, he got shipped off to an Arctic base (where many other such miscreants had been stashed already) and finally retired after 30 years' service as a major when he should have been a colonel.

Then came the Kennedy-King-Wallace-Kennedy shootings, the murderous stupidity of Vietnam, the Kent State shootings, and Watergate. That I drew somewhat different lessons from these events than the media and most of my fellow beings does not mean they didn't affect me. My head had already been turned by the writings of Robert A. Heinlein and Ayn Rand.

I'd also had one extremely strange experience in fourth grade. One day, walking to school in an age and place (tiny Gifford, Illinois) when parents could feel safe letting their fourth graders walk to school, I had sort of an epiphany. Something about the quality of the golden morning light, something about the early September frost on the leaves and grass, *something*, I don't know what, told me that I was living in the last days of a great but rapidly declining civilization — I knew a lot about Rome even then — and that it was my job to stop it.

I know how that sounds. Make of it what you will.

Gradually, I learned the real history of America. I learned the Great Depression had been caused by the very system that was supposed to have prevented it. I learned that it was greatly exacerbated by a sick, twisted, vestigial fealty to England that caused the Roosevelt government to ship American gold overseas by the ton in an attempt to support the pound at five dollars when it was worth perhaps fifty cents.

I learned that World War II had been caused by Allied bungling at the end of World War I. I learned that the Roosevelt administration, desperate to escape an economic disaster that its policies had made vastly worse, not better, had just as much to do with — and was equally guilty of — the vicious sneak attack on Pearl Harbor as the Japanese.

And then, as if the terror, suffering, privation, and sacrifice of the Second World War weren't enough, just as the veterans returning from Europe and the Pacific were settling into civilian life, many of them were called again to fight an even more stupid and pointless war in Korea. Luckily, by the time my dad had finished training, the war was over.

I was determined now to do something about the sorry condition the country of Jefferson and Paine now found itself in. I didn't know what it would take. I didn't know how much I could do. But I would do ... *something*.

It was clear, from the outset, that the source of the problem was the 20th century superstate. Never in history had there been so much government; never in history had there been so much misery and death. So I picked the issues that energized me most and started writing articles and short stories and letters to the editor and eventually novels (of which, at this writing, there are twenty-one), each aimed at increasing individual liberty and decreasing the power of the state.

You hold part of that effort in your hands, and you may well ask, have I had any great success? I haven't the slightest idea. The state is bigger, stronger, and vastly more evil now than when I began. That often makes me feel like an abject failure; it isn't nice to feel that you've wasted your life since you were fourteen (that's when I first read *Atlas Shrugged* and became a *real* nuisance to my family and neighbors).

By contrast, there are vastly more people out there, now, who know their unalienable individual, civil, Constitutional, and human rights. And they're better armed as individuals right now than ever before in history. It's also harder today for government to pull off crimes like nationalizing health care or confiscating privately owned military weapons. And I believe the fact that they keep trying so desperately indicates that they know their days of running our lives for us are numbered.

Hey, I predicted the collapse of the Soviet Union, the Internet as we now know it, the laptop computer, the digital watch, and the fact that Y2K would come to zilch. Could it be that I'm right about this, too?

Whether I am or not, there are always small victories along the way. I was gratified to learn from a Paul Harvey broadcast, many years later, that the angry parents of a different school district had molasses-and-feathered my seventh-grade principal and run him out of town.

It was a schoolboy's wish come miraculously true.

L. Neil Smith
Fort Collins, Colorado
September, 2000

INTRODUCTION

My Willingness to Be Drafted
to Run for President
∞ ∞ ∞ ∞ ∞

September, 1999

Over the past 20 years, I've produced two dozen books upholding not just the concept, but the *practice,* of individual liberty.

In those 24 books, and in innumerable articles and speeches, I've made successful predictions — the Internet, laptops, even digital watches — demonstrating my understanding of history, human nature, and the way civilization works. In the process, I've brought thousands upon thousands of people into the libertarian culture.

I've also had my part in launching an historic movement to *arm* individuals, which — despite its authoritarian detractors — is rapidly bringing an end to a horrific era of runaway violent crime their policies spawned over the past 50 years.

Last July, borrowing an idea from former President Aquino of the Philippines, I chose the 223rd anniversary of American freedom to announce that, if those who want me to do it could convince me I'm not wasting everybody's time and energy, I'd run for President in 2000. Naturally, I thought long and hard before making that announcement.

Long ago, when I was my 10-year-old daughter's age, I calculated that I'd be 53 years old when the year 2000 arrived. I envisioned a brilliant colorful future, based on the science fiction I was reading and various possibilities I'd learned to imagine for myself. (I never considered the possibility that we'd be *less* free than we were in the 1950s.) I assumed we'd all be flying to work in personal helicopters or even on flying belts, visiting with each other by videophone, living in undersea domes, and vacationing on the Moon or Mars.

Aging and disease would be wiped out.

Instead, over the next 40-odd years, most possibilities like that (and many more I failed to foresee) were eaten up by taxes to support the "welfare-warfare state" and by regulations that were both insane and unconstitutional. State terrorism began turning my daydreams into nightmares, having begun (although I didn't know it at the time) with Operation Keelhaul and the persecution of Wilhelm Reich (just to pick two examples), and climaxing (but certainly not ceasing) with Ruby Ridge and the butchery we witnessed at Mount Carmel near Waco in 1993.

Don't ask me when it's *going* to happen; America is a police state *now*. At this point, instead of a brilliant colorful future, it's likelier to be a future resembling Beirut at the grimmest of the fighting there, or Dachau at the worst moment of the Holocaust. All of my adult life, since I was a politically precocious 14, I've struggled to *prevent* that kind of future, and a bitter bloody civil war — a civil war both Republicans and Democrats seem hell-bent on provoking — that many of my wisest friends are now convinced is inevitable.

But I still want *my* 21st century, not Gore's or Bush's or Bradley's or McCain's. I believe you want it, too, or I wouldn't be doing this. I want it for myself, my wife, and most of all for my little girl. Like me, she writes. I want her to write, while she's a child, about sunshine, butterflies, and flowers, not machineguns, razor wire, and Ferret missiles. I want her to live as an adult and raise her own children amidst the peace, freedom, progress, and prosperity I grew up believing were the birthright of every American.

Over the past decades I've personally tried many approaches — and observed many more — to reclaiming our

Revolutionary heritage and advancing, once again, the cause of liberty. Every one has failed and we are worse off at this moment than when we started so long ago. From that disappointing experience, I've come to believe the best "flag" to rally round is the one left to us by our 18th century ancestors.

Indeed, I've often said in print and at the lectern that any difference between a society created by the most radical Libertarian Party platforms I was proud to help write in the 1970s, and the society that would arise from stringent enforcement of the first ten amendments to the Constitution, would merely be a matter of "fine tuning."

The first ten amendments to the Constitution.

The Bill of Rights.

My platform is *enforcement* of the Bill of Rights.

This single policy would eradicate every last trace of socialism from America and eliminate at least 90 percent of government.

My first act as President would be to order the arrests of Bill Clinton, Janet Reno, and Webster Hubbell for their vile crimes at Waco, round up everybody who had a part in what happened there, and, within view of the whole world, put them on trial for their lives.

I'd invite Michael New, the young soldier who refused to obey United Nations commanders, to the White House, give him a medal, and appoint him to oversee our disentanglement from NATO and the UN — which would be given 24 hours to pack up and get out of the country.

I'd empty America's prisons by turning the White House into an Executive Clemency *factory* with legal forms stacked to the ceiling, until the War on Drugs, 25,000 gun laws, and all other victimless crime laws were repealed, nullified, or otherwise disposed of.

Like the ancient Roman senator Cato the Elder, who demanded after every speech that "Carthage must be destroyed," I would end my every public utterance, no matter what else it had been about, by reminding potential jury members across the country of their 1,000-year-old right and duty to judge the law itself, as well as the facts of the case.

I want to make it clear — some folks have seemed confused by my correct identification of objective reality — that I don't believe I'll be sleeping at 1600 Pennsylvania Avenue any time soon. I won't be. Get over it. Nor am I willing to make myself a liar or sound like a lunatic by claiming the contrary — I have to look my little girl in the eye every day, and she's a harsh judge. My goal, a realistically achievable one, is to prove publicly, beyond a shadow of a doubt, that there is a constituency for the Bill of Rights too large to ignore — or to abuse any further.

Rely on me to tell the truth and remain within the principles that have guided my life for nearly 40 years. There's no mythical "Great Unwashed" to be fooled or coddled here, no "gentle sensibilities" to be protected. It's too late for that. There's no need for "outreach" in any conventional sense. All we have to do in order to change the course of history — although it's a huge task — is to find and gather together everyone who already basically agrees with us.

Let me make it "perfectly clear" that I'm not a candidate quite yet. The conditions I set last July, that would convince me to run, haven't been met. I'm still just a *potential* candidate (although I appear to be on the ballot in at least two states). The deal's the same as it was: If you want to see the Bill of Rights enforced, if you want the 21st century to be the Century of the Bill of Rights, *tell* me, tell *them*, tell the world, by endorsing my candidacy.

Editor's Note: The Arizona Libertarian Party ("Not Just Libertarian, Arizona Libertarian") broke ranks with the na-

INTRODUCTION

tional Libertarian Party and placed L.Neil Smith and Vin Suprynowicz (author of Send In The Waco Killers*) on the state ballot for president and vice president. They garnered 5775 votes, .39% of the total.*

I

LIBERTARIAN PHILOSOPHY

The LP's First Priority

Presented to the
Arizona Libertarian Party State Convention
May 21, 1994, Phoenix, Arizona

დ❀დ❀დ❀დ❀დ❀

Ladies and gentlemen, in spite of the millions of man-hours and billions of dollars spent each year to keep the American productive class safely in its place, essentially voiceless and deprived of an effective franchise, the era of its exploitation — by corrupt politicians and even more corrupt mass media — is coming to an end.

Few productive-class Americans understand — yet — that they stagger under a burden of taxes five times greater than that endured by their medieval serf ancestors.

What they do understand is that the harder they work the less they seem to have left.

And the less they have to look forward to.

Few productive-class Americans understand — yet — how it came about that their own grandparents managed to enjoy a spacious comfortable home, and they can't.

What they do understand is that, increasingly, they're compelled to live in tiny cardboard cracker-boxes or wheeled tin cans, so their Senator can have a limousine.

And his mistress.

Few productive-class Americans understand — yet — why

every year, year after year, a hangman's noose of red tape pulls tighter and tighter around their necks.

What they do understand is that in many respects life seems bleaker every day.

And offers fewer options.

Few productive-class Americans understand — yet — what the mass media have to gain from their degenerate, increasingly collusive partnership with government.

What they do understand is that somehow there's never any good news anymore, and that the newspapers and the TV constantly tell them that they're incompetent to live their own lives and their neighbors are all criminally insane.

And that somehow life never seems to get any better.

Few productive-class Americans understand — yet — how their natural, fundamental, and inalienable human, individual, civil, and Constitutional rights have been systematically gnawed away by the politicians elected to protect them.

What they do understand is that more and more, their rights are treated as trivialities.

And that everything they do or like or want seems to be against the law.

Few productive-class Americans understand — yet — how the Federal Election Commission, a phantom "News Election Service," and the League of Women Voters rig elections more effectively than in any South American banana republic.

What they do understand is that their ballot never seems to count for anything.

And that if voting could change things, it would be illegal.

Few productive-class Americans understand — yet — the putrescently ancient evil inherent in the fundamentally un-American doctrine of Sovereign Immunity.

What they do understand is that the government always wins.

And that, somehow, they're always in the wrong.

Few productive-class Americans understand — yet — how their precious Bill of Rights has wound up being a one-sided bargain, interpreted and enforced by a single omnipotent entity, inimical to them, pretending to be divided powers.

What they do understand is that their country seems to have been overrun by lawyers.

And that somehow their rights never turn out to be quite what they thought they were.

******

Ladies and gentlemen, some productive-class Americans have come — regrettably — to blame it all on poor minorities, somehow forgetting that we're a nation entirely composed of minorities, most of whom arrived here without a penny.

Someday, sooner or later, they'll learn not to blame the average welfare mother with her pitiable child-support check, but the sixty-thousand-dollar-a-year public official whose non-productive way of life keeps everybody else destitute.

Some productive-class Americans have come — regrettably — to blame it all on immigrants, somehow forgetting that we're a nation of immigrants, and immigrants' children, many of whom fled the same tyranny and corruption we face today.

Someday, sooner or later, they'll learn not to blame people with funny names, funny clothes, funny customs, or a funny way of talking, but to look upon their own so-called "representatives" as the foreign despots they've all become.

Some productive-class Americans have come — regrettably — to blame it all on labor unions, somehow forgetting that for every gangster lounging at the top, a million workers only want an honest day's wages for an honest day's labor.

Someday, sooner or later, they'll learn not to blame the

workers, but the crooked union leaders and the tangled government regulations that make productive labor all but impossible in America today, and almost always unrewarding.

Some productive-class Americans have come — regrettably — to blame it all on the rich, somehow forgetting the all-important difference between making money and stealing it, and the way that the system always lets a few individuals get ahead for the same reason Las Vegas allows the occasional big winner.

Someday, sooner or later, they'll learn not to blame the miracle of individual achievement, but a system that more consistently rewards failure and punishes success, and loves to rub their noses in what they can never hope to have.

Some productive-class Americans have come — regrettably — to blame it all on the lunatic fringe, somehow forgetting that the mass media told them everything they think they know about such people, and that everybody is somebody else's lunatic.

Someday, sooner or later, they'll learn not to blame the unconventional individualist, but TV's well-groomed talking heads, and the officials they themselves elected.

******

Ladies and gentlemen, a Great Explosion is coming.

Productive-class Americans are sick and tired of being threatened by the very laws and regulations their parents naively thought were being created to protect them.

A Great Explosion is coming.

Productive-class Americans are sick and tired of being continually looted by well-fed politicians and bureaucrats with five- and six-figure salaries.

A Great Explosion is coming.

Productive-class Americans are sick and tired of being decimated by one senseless war after another, arranged, how very conveniently, one for almost every generation.

A Great Explosion is coming.

Productive-class Americans are sick and tired of being wooed and cast aside in two- and four- and six-year cycles by public figures they wouldn't trust alone with their children.

A Great Explosion is coming.

Doubtless the American productive class have made foolish choices in the past; doubtless they'll make them in the future; but in the end, the American productive class will triumph, because they *are* productive while their enemies are not.

A Great Explosion is coming.

And as usual, the politicians aren't listening.

But by this time in the 21st century, with the 20th century welfare-warfare state all but a forgotten nightmare, history may want to know what kind of idiots and weaklings in two of America's major political parties tried to sell out the American productive class at the very moment they began coming into their own.

Then again, history may not care.

******

Ladies and gentlemen, in a different part of the continent we share with nine other nations, the Fifth of May — Cinco de Mayo — has special historic and political meaning.

For us on the other hand, May 5th, 1994, will be celebrated, now and forever, as the day the Republican Party ceased to exist as anything other than the atrophied appendage to the Democratic Party we were always pretty sure it was, anyway.

May 5th, 1994, will be celebrated as the day this repulsive, voracious, tentacular, obscenely intermingled coalescent organism, the Demolican slime-monster, the Republicratic shoggoth, tried to shut the Constitution down without shutting down the State whose one excuse for existing derives from that very document.

May 5th, 1994, will be celebrated as the day 38 more Republicans joined their fellow Democrats in unzipping their flies and pulling out their tiny little ... atrophied appendages to pay dog-respects to the Bill of Rights — the Second Amendment in particular — inspired by a letter written for the occasion and signed by former Democratic President Jimmy Carter (well, what else would we expect of him?) and former Republican Presidents Gerald Ford and Ronald Reagan.

May 5th, 1994, will be celebrated as the day they handed the future over to us.

May 5th, 1994, will be celebrated as the day that the Libertarian Party crawled out of the baby-pool and became a shark, swimming in deep political waters.

Ladies and gentlemen, I've come to bring you your water-wings — and your jaws.

******

On September 3, 1993, at the Libertarian Party National Convention in Salt Lake City, Utah, I suggested that the first priority of the Libertarian Party should be "Putting the civility back into civilization through the most stringent enforcement possible of the highest law of the land, the first ten Amendments to the United States Constitution, commonly known as the Bill of Rights."

"I swear by my life, my fortune, and my sacred honor to uphold the first ten Amendments to the Constitution of the United States, popularly known as the 'Bill of Rights'."

The Bill of Rights is and ought to be (rather, I should say, "ought to be and is") the Ten Commandments of American political behavior, the one thing in life even Demolicans and Republicrats aren't allowed to lie about. Taking the oath of office is an absolute commitment to remember the Bill of Rights and keep it, wholly.

"I swear by my life, my fortune, and my sacred honor to uphold the first ten Amendments to the Constitution of the United States, popularly known as the 'Bill of Rights'."

I don't believe it's any accident that the first American President to be assassinated claimed to be fighting slavery — with conscripted soldiers — suspended habeas corpus, and instituted the first tax on income. I do believe a day will come when an American President can leave the White House and walk the land he shares with countless millions of other Americans, by himself, in perfect safety, because each and every American knows absolutely where he stands and that the President, and the government he leads, are a threat to nobody's rights.

"I swear by my life, my fortune, and my sacred honor to uphold the first ten Amendments to the Constitution of the United States, popularly known as the 'Bill of Rights'."

So the real question is what it has always been and always will be: How do we get there from here? Well, this may be one instance in which the truth really does set us free.

Libertarians are better informed than the average individual, and more sophisticated in their understanding of the basic philosophical concepts that make up the foundation and shape the political structure of this nation. Most of them are perfectly aware that their rights don't come from the government and that the Constitution explicitly acknowledges only a small number of the liberties that we all possess inherently, simply by virtue of having been born human. But it may come as a shock

— then again, it may not — to hear that the Bill of Rights doesn't apply to you or me; it hardly has anything to do with us at all.

The first ten amendments to the Constitution arose from a deal between the Federalists and the anti-Federalists; they were specifically required as a condition of ratification of the rest of the document by those who didn't want what civics textbooks call "a strong central government," but were willing to put up with it as long as certain limitations were imposed on its centrality and strength.

Those limitations were set forth in what we've come to call the Bill of Rights, but that's a misnomer, and a dangerous one. It should be called the "Bill of Limitations," because it doesn't apply to you, as I've said, or to me; it applies only to the State. As I've said, it's the Ten Commandments of American political behavior, a laundry-list of "Thou Shalt Nots," imposed upon the Federalist blueprint, that wouldn't make any sense at all, historically or logically, if it hadn't been intended — by both sides — to be absolutely binding.

No Second Amendment, no Bill of Rights.

No Bill of Rights, no Constitution.

No Constitution, no government.

No paycheck.

No power.

Any legitimacy politicians claim derives directly from the document they're trying to destroy. It's like sitting out on a tree limb and sawing it off. But politicians expect the tree to fall, leaving them and their limb hanging in midair. Well, life may feel like a cartoon sometimes — mostly thanks to them — but it isn't a cartoon, it's real. And if it were a cartoon, they'd be the coyote, not the roadrunner, because, in real life, they're the badguys.

No Second Amendment, no Bill of Rights.

No Bill of Rights, no Constitution.

No Constitution, no government.

No paycheck.

No power.

It's as simple as that; are you listening, Senator Moynihan, Congressman Schumer, Senator Feinstein? And the same thing goes for the President and the Supreme Court. Are you listening, soon-to-be former Senator Howard Metzenbaum and your ambulance-chasing son-in-law, soon-to-be Glorious People's Hereditary Senator Joel Hyatt?

Let's try it again, to make sure you get it straight.

No Second Amendment, no Bill of Rights.

No Bill of Rights, no Constitution.

No Constitution, no government.

No paycheck.

No power.

No you.

******

Now consider, ladies and gentlemen, why didn't we know these things already? Why did we have to learn them by joining the Sex, Dope, Guns, and Baby-killing Party, this collection of sociopaths and loonies we've come to know and love so well? Why didn't we learn them at our parents' knees, or in kindergarten?

We didn't learn them because of the miserable failure of two American cultural institutions — public education and the mass media — and the first thing you must understand clearly about this miserable failure is that, from their point of view, it represents an astonishing success. Their purpose all along — and if you believe for a minute that I'm mistaken in this, or merely exaggerating, I challenge you here and now to read the writings of John Dewey — was to keep you from learning the very things I've just told you about the Bill of Rights.

They've succeeded so well that now, after more than a century of effort, even most of *them* don't know the things I've just told you about the Bill of Rights.

I'm not really planning to speak further tonight about public schools. I've said many times that self-defense is a bodily function that cannot be delegated to another individual or group — and, more and more, I've begun to believe that precisely the same is true of educating our children. In any case, we know that the answer is separation of education and state, a process going on this very moment in America without much need of Libertarian help.

But what — to voice a question Libertarians ask themselves, usually in tones of anger and frustration, at least several times every day — can we do about the media?

We are far from alone.

Whatever else Americans may disagree about, everybody hates the mass media. Like you, I've never been involved in any event they managed to report correctly.

Socialist Nick Nolte makes a movie about the mass media and they're inevitably portrayed as some ineffable mixture of abhorrently evil and repulsively stupid.

Middle-of-the-roader Burt Reynolds makes a movie about the mass media and they're inevitably portrayed as some ineffable mixture of abhorrently evil and repulsively stupid.

Conservative Bruce Willis makes a movie about the mass media and they're inevitably portrayed as some ineffable mixture of abhorrently evil and repulsively stupid.

Libertarian John Milius makes a movie about the mass media and they're inevitably portrayed as some ineffable mixture of abhorrently evil and repulsively stupid.

This is not news to the abhorrently evil and repulsively —

I mean, to the mass media. They tell themselves (I've been there myself to hear them) that it's a sign they're doing their job right. They're so painstakingly accurate, so minutely unbiased, that nobody benefits unfairly and, as a natural consequence in this worst of all possible worlds, everybody hates them for it.

The trouble with this otherwise comforting theory is that they never entertain the simpler and likelier explanation that everybody hates them because, while the average profit margin in television, for example, is in the neighborhood of 80%, fewer than 12% of their "customers" believe they're doing a good job.

And besides, they're abhorrently evil and repulsively stupid.

American journalism has always gloried in its self-appointed role as the watchdog over the dignity and liberty of the individual. The sad truth is, that during its long self-congratulatory history, it's been a lot more like a cur, caught bloody-muzzled, savaging the very flocks it has been trusted to protect.

So what can we do about the media?

All my adult life, people like me have been seen and shown as criminals by those in the media who claim to speak for civilization, for exercising our rights under one of its basic rules, the Second Amendment. I know the media well, but I've never understood how they can be so smug about Southern whites of the 1950s, say, or Germans of the 1930s. They're certainly no better. They're small-minded, mean-spirited, frightened of their fellow human beings and the real world around them. They exemplify what Ben Wattenberg said is true of liberals in general, that they're afraid of "every known phenomenon." They're desperate to find somebody it's acceptable to feel superior to, acceptable to hate. People like me would be no better off in their hands than if we were blacks in the 1950s or Jews in the 1930s — except, of course, that we shoot back.

Which explains their position on one issue, anyway: Theirs is the same interest in suppressing private gun ownership as any bloated cartoon sheriff in mirrored sunglasses who wears a pillowcase over his head on weekends, or any goose-stepping yodeler of the Horst Wessel song. The idea of a Negro, or a Jew, or any member of the productive class with a gun is anathema to them. Especially since the self-discipline and focus on objective reality required to shoot effectively and safely themselves transcends their capacity for understanding.

So what can we do about the media?

We are, of course, limited, as Americans by the First Amendment, and as Libertarians by the Non-Aggression Principle. We can't blow up TV stations or burn them to the mudsills and sow salt on the ruins, as soul-satisfying as that might prove to be. And as much as they may deserve it, we can't roast the partially extracted intestines of anchorpersons or reporters over a slow fire while they watch. We are, unfortunately, limited, as Americans by the First Amendment, and as Libertarians, by the Non-Aggression Principle. That, of course, is exactly what the First Amendment and the Non-Aggression Principle are for.

It's also why it's such a bad idea — a dangerously terrible, horrible idea — for anchorpersons and reporters to undermine the Bill of Rights in any way. They're just too dumb to live, let alone understand how we all depend on the Bill of Rights. They believe that there's only one Amendment to the Constitution, anyway — the First Amendment — and that it only applies to them.

So what can we do about the media?

I'd like to propose an educational effort to be mounted across the country in every state, county, and city in which the

Libertarian Party is what we optimistically call organized. I propose a series of public debates — which those in the media will find themselves unable to ignore — between Libertarians and our conservative fellow-travelers (somebody with a ready wit and an ironic sense of humor, like G. Gordon Liddy, will be just perfect) who will take the affirmative, to wit: Resolved, that members of the news media be required by law to take a binding oath to uphold and defend the Constitution.

It goes without saying — although I'll say it — that we Libertarians, strong-principled upholders of the First Amendment and of the Non-Aggression Principle, will take the negative in these debates and defend the members of the news media in question, however much our enthusiasm may lapse as details of their century of systematic rape of the truth begin emerging in the heat of the forensics.

The point here, of course, is that we will set the terms and the tone of this series of debates, and the only real losers will be the media themselves — who (by some oversight they ought to be familiar with, having done it to others so many times themselves) will not be directly represented — and the real winners will be conservatives, Libertarians, and the battered bloody truth itself.

How's that for shouting "Fire!" in a crowded theater?

I even have an idea for an encore, if these debates prove successful. I have always opposed the death penalty, except at the scene and moment of the crime, at the hands of the intended victim. I have always believed that relying on the government — any government — for peace, justice, or civil order is like relying on government for bread or shoes: as any Russian can tell you, under central planning and a command economy, you wind up with bread that tastes like shoes, and shoes about as durable as if they were made of bread.

Which is pretty much the kind of peace, justice, and civil

order we've been getting lately.

But I am willing to make an exception. I am willing to abolish the death penalty in every instance — except for a single class of criminal and a single crime.

But not before we debate it publicly.

Resolved, that whenever a violation of the rights guaranteed Americans under the first ten Amendments to the Constitution results in the loss of a life they were written to protect, the politicians and bureaucrats responsible go to Death Row, there to await lethal injection, the electric chair, the gas chamber, the guillotine, or whatever else they had invented to intimidate the rest of us.

"I swear by my life, my fortune, and my sacred honor to uphold the first ten Amendments to the Constitution of the United States, popularly known as the 'Bill of Rights'."

The trouble is, if we exclude politicians and bureaucrats from these debates the way we did the media from the initial ones, who can we find to take the negative?

******

Ladies and gentlemen, if you're not a participant on electronic bulletin board systems, InterNet, CompuServe, GEnie, or what-have-you, then you don't know about "taglines." Taglines are little quips, aphorisms, or other flashes of wit, usually affixed to the ends of messages after a user's signature, that actually hearken back to 18th century literary forms, and may range from sage items like, "'Gun control' is a clear eye and a steady hand — what we're talking about here is 'victim disarmament,'" to the obvious, "Help stamp out taglines."

The most poignant of these was appended to a message I received from a Libertarian Second Amendment activist whose name some of you may be familiar with, Charles Curley. It read: "50 years of progress, 1943-1993: Warsaw to Waco."

Now I know it seems sometimes, especially when you look at Robert Reich, Donna Shalala, Steffie Stephanopolis, or the ever-popular Joycelyn Elders, that America is being ruled today by circus freaks and clowns. If Bill Clinton's moral impediments were physical, he'd need a ramp to get from the bare floor to the carpet. Argentina had Juan and Evita: We've got Evita and Bozo.

But have another look: If you were to take away Heinrich Himmler's charm and wit, Hermann Goering's refinement and self-restraint, and Joseph Goebbels' integrity and earnest regard for the truth, what would you have? James Carville.

The Clinton Administration is like something out of an old "Avengers" or "Batman" episode: a vicious gang of mass-murderers in baggy pants. That's why it's vitally important to take them seriously. Fortunately, the best way to take them seriously is to laugh at them, and get others to laugh at them, as well. And not on their own terms, for what they want you to believe is funny about them, and cute, but for what's genuinely funny about them — and pathetic. It's the best way to take away any dignity they have left, and any legitimacy.

As Rush Limbaugh could tell you — if he didn't have half his brain tied behind his back, which is all that keeps him from being a Libertarian — it's also the best way to get your own message across. It was the theory behind my novel, *The Probability Broach*: Because they like to laugh, because they need to laugh, people always pay closest attention when you're telling them something funny.

So let's give them something funny to pay attention to. How about a one-page document in proper form to be introduced as a Bill in the United States Senate and House of Representatives? Because it is a one-page document, it will also be in proper form for insertion into the "folk process" that office and factory workers use to spread officially unsanctioned ideas, most recently by Xerox and fax, from one end of the country to another in minutes, and keep it circulating in the culture for years. What it will say, in language clearly understandable to non-lawyers, is that, as of January 20th, 1997, every item of legislation enacted at the federal level since January 20th, 1993, is hereby null and void. This act officially erases the Clinton Administration, just as the face of Amenhotep IV was chiseled off the obelisks or Lenin's statue was given the bum's rush out of Russian parks and plazas.

To the enemies of liberty, this says that everything they've worked for, everything they've striven to accomplish all their lives, can be obliterated with the stroke of a pen. It gives them something to worry about for a change, something to make their stomachs churn, something to deprive them of a night's sleep no matter how absurd they tell themselves it is at a conscious intellectual level. It may even shorten their lives by a small but gratifying amount. In short, it does to them exactly what they've been doing to us for half a century.

To the friends of liberty, it's the welcome gift of a chuckle — and a glimmer of hope. It says that if we make it through the next couple of years, things will get better.

And here's the payoff: As co-sponsors, we'll write in "Your Libertarian Senator" and "Your Libertarian Congressman." The only way things will get better is if we convince enough voters that this time, if we make it through the next couple of years, they will be different, as well. We must stop being bounced like a Ping-Pong ball between the rackets of the Demolicans and the Republicrats.

The first priority of the Libertarian Party will be to put the "civility back into civilization through the most stringent enforcement possible of the highest law of the land, the Bill of Rights" — and that will make things very different, indeed.

"I swear by my life, my fortune, and my sacred honor to uphold the first ten Amendments to the Constitution of the United States, popularly known as the 'Bill of Rights'."

A handbill circulating this way automatically ties in to other efforts. In Colorado, we've begun urging people angry over increased and retroactive taxes, over Socialized Medicine or Else, and especially over the Brady Bill and the Feinstein Amendment, in what may eventually become an outright drive, to change their voter registration from whatever it was before — Demolican, Republicrat, Independent, United We Stand with our Big Floppy Ears Hanging Out — to Libertarian.

The badguys may suppress us in the media, they may even steal elections from us, but since we're talking to them, here, since they pay attention to things like changes in voter registration, our message will get to the people it's intended for.

To the Right, to the unclean thing that calls itself "Republican Party," the message is: You have fucked up big-time, and now you have to deal with us if you have any hope of cleaning up the mess you've made and saving your party from oblivion.

To the Left, to the Marxoid trash infesting the White House, the message is: We gave you your chance.

The National Firearms Acts of the 1930s were plainly unconstitutional, but the NRA dropped the ball, and somehow we learned to live with them. It was relatively easy, since you so-called liberals said it was all you wanted, anyway.

That was the covenant.

In 1968, while basically accusing productive-class gun owners of having murdered JFK and RFK, you illegally took more of our rights away. Again the NRA dropped the ball, and again we learned to live with the consequences. It was harder this time, but again you so-called liberals assured us it was all you wanted.

And again that was the covenant.

But this time, in 1994, because you so-called liberals got politically greedy and couldn't keep the covenant — because from the instant the Brady Bill passed, the instant Feinstein passed, you whimpered that they weren't enough — you will lose everything. Everything is up for grabs — Social Security, income taxes, the Federal Reserve, the United Nations, every vestige of the New Deal, every alphabetical agency, each of the 20,000 illegal victim disarmament laws in this country — and, as a bonus, you so-called liberals get to go to jail.

All because you so-called liberals couldn't keep the covenant that you, yourselves, insisted on, and because enough was never enough for you. This time, you've given us the leverage. This time you're up against a people who know their rights, a people who know the history and philosophy behind their rights. This time you're up against a political party, the Libertarian Party, that will strip every last federal agency of the weapons with which it wages constant war against the American people, and see each and every one of the Constitution's first ten amendments — the Ten Commandments of American political behavior — enforced for exactly what it is, the highest law of the land.

One thing for sure: Nobody's kids will ever be taken by the government again, nor will that threat be used to get somebody to do whatever government wants; any bureaucrat who tries will find herself in the deepest, darkest, dankest dungeon Leavenworth offers, having sunlight piped in on alternate leap years. If need be, we'll open Alcatraz again, just to make room for the social workers this aspect of Bill of Rights enforcement will ... shall we say, "impact"?

You so-called liberals have no hope; sooner or later, with or without Republican help — almost certainly without it — we will eradicate every last trace of socialism from this country, from the continent of North America, and from the world.

Let me say here and now that the second promise I'd make, if I were a Libertarian candidate for President, is that any Canadian province that ratified the American Bill of Rights by a 2/3 majority would be offered statehood.

Of course, the first promise I would make is this one: "I swear by my life, my fortune, and my sacred honor to uphold the first ten Amendments to the Constitution of the United States, popularly known as the 'Bill of Rights'."

And to the media, it says: Don't look to me, don't look to any exhibitionist who stands up in front of a crowd like this from time to time. I'm not the one who started it, you are. And it is individual members of the Libertarian Party who will finish it now, with or without my help, because their first priority is "Putting the civility back into civilization through the most stringent enforcement possible of the highest law of the land, the Bill of Rights."

And unlike their weak, whiny, hand-wringing, bed-wetting, opposite numbers on the Left or the Right, they do perfectly well, thank you, without a leader. With this outfit, it has always been ideas that counted, not personalities.

You may not realize it yet, you people in the media — you may not want to acknowledge it — but as an American, as a human being, you have a moral and political obligation to help them. If you're not up to it — if you're not "man" enough — at least don't get in their way while they're trying to save you from the consequences of your own abhorrent evil and repulsive stupidity.

******

Ladies and gentlemen, it all begins by telling your neighbor — who may be a conservative, turned off because the President is a moral cripple, that, as a protest that talks directly to

31

the system, one that doesn't have to wait until November to be felt, he needs to change his voter registration to Libertarian.

It doesn't mean he has to vote Libertarian, after all.

This is just a protest.

Tell him the words "conservative" and "Republican" are fully separable. Don't waste much effort explaining our positions on issues like abortion or the War on Drugs, and never make excuses or apologies for them. We're right and he's wrong.

And besides, this is just a protest.

How much better a protest if the Libertarian Party is known far and wide to take weird positions on all the issues of the day? Ask him what it says to the Republican leadership if its voters are willing to switch to something like that?

And this is just a protest, isn't it?

Tell your angry and disenfranchised conservative friend we're not asking him to marry us.

We're not asking him to have our baby.

We're not asking him to agree with us on every issue.

We're not asking him to become a Libertarian.

This.

Is.

Just.

A.

Protest.

We're not even asking him to join the Libertarian Party.

And even if it were more than just a protest, all we're asking is that he hire us to do a job — by consistently voting for Libertarian candidates — a job no other political party is willing to do: Put the civility back into civilization through the most stringent enforcement possible of the Bill of Rights.

Through Bill of Rights enforcement.

"I swear by my life, my fortune, and my sacred honor to

uphold the first ten Amendments to the Constitution of the United States, popularly known as the 'Bill of Rights'."

If it's the last thing you do, don't call what's happening now a police state. And don't say we've been taken over by commies or fascists. It may all be true, but even that grants the other side too much legitimacy, too much dignity.

Say that we've been a little careless the last couple hundred years, and now we have criminals in high office — we have a thousand Watergates going on, or ten thousand, or a hundred thousand — and that no matter how long it takes, these Nixonoid creatures from the damp underside of the political rock are going to jail.

Through Bill of Rights enforcement.

"I swear by my life, my fortune, and my sacred honor to uphold the first ten Amendments to the Constitution of the United States, popularly known as the 'Bill of Rights'."

About a month ago, at its annual convention in Sedalia, in the mountains west of Castle Rock, I told members of the Libertarian Party of my own home state that whenever they began to feel discouraged, I wanted them to visualize an old lady, twenty years from now, tall, stoop-shouldered, puffing at the stub of a cigar and wearing thick glasses and a dikey haircut. I wanted them to visualize her shuffling along with a canvas bag slung over her shoulder, one of those sticks in her hand, with a nail in one end, picking up odds and ends of paper trash as part of her 100,000 hours of public service, cleaning up America's shooting ranges.

Party on, Janet! And party on, Hillary, I said. America (or at least Joe-Bob Briggs) loves movies about "Bimbos Behind Bars." Let's see how they like the real thing!

To the enemies of liberty, this says that everything they've worked for will be obliterated — and on top of that, there's going to be a steep price to pay. It warns them all, from the cop on the beat to the President, not to be too zealous enforcing the Brady Bill or the Feinstein Amendment for the short time those laws are still on the books, because a higher law is going to be enforced against them.

To the friends of liberty, it's the welcome gift of a chuckle, a glimmer of hope, and a message that they needn't be too zealous complying with those or any other unconstitutional laws, because help is on the way. If we make it through the next couple of years, things will get better. A very great deal better.

"I swear by my life, my fortune, and my sacred honor to uphold the first ten Amendments to the Constitution of the United States, popularly known as the 'Bill of Rights'."

And if you really want to make it through the next couple of years, ladies and gentlemen of the Libertarian Party, if you really want things to get better, if you really want a chance to do that job no other party will do, so will you, ladies and gentlemen, you'll swear it, too, right now, right here, with me:

"I swear by my life, my fortune, and my sacred honor to uphold the first ten Amendments to the Constitution of the United States, popularly known as the 'Bill of Rights'."

Ladies and gentlemen, a Great Explosion is coming.

And it starts with you.

Thank you.

The Atlanta Declaration

WeaponsCon I, Atlanta, Georgia, September, 1987
Future of Freedom Conference,
Culver City, California, November, 1987

ᚙ ᚙ ᚙ ᚙ ᚙ

Every man, woman, and responsible child has an unalienable individual, civil, Constitutional, and human right to obtain, own, and carry, openly or concealed, any weapon — rifle, shotgun, handgun, machinegun, *anything* — any time, any place, without asking anyone's permission. Someday to demonstrate that principle — before I'm lying on my deathbed in a hospital with green plastic tubes up my nose, before arthritis sets in and I have to do it on crutches — I intend to walk the length of Manhattan Island with a handgun openly on my hip, unmolested by any freelance or official parasite.

The question is, how do I get there from here?

In the '80s we are witnessing the rise of a New Victorianism (the sort of mindset that prefers the word "limbs" to "legs") aimed not so much at human sexuality this time around (although that's happening, too) as the human capacity for violence.

Victorian times weren't characterized by sexual abstinence. Many of today's kinkier turn-ons originated in that era of repression, hypocrisy, sublimation, and guilt. Whenever any basic human function is repressed, behavioral distortions arise.

The claim today is that weapons are evil, that anyone dumb enough to try protecting himself will come to a bad end, that violence is always wrong, that non-violence is always and unquestionably right. Never was the persecution of a minority more persistent than that of gun owners, nor more hypocritical. Like any other law, gun control is enforced at gun point.

Lever Action

Those preaching non-violence are lobbying to license thugs for the purpose of imposing their views on others, unleashing against innocent people the deadliest weapon ever devised: government.

Repression never helps. Violence, like sexuality, is a morally neutral, perfectly natural capacity, linked with the survival of the species and the individual. A pseudo-morality of non-violence only serves the interests of established authority and other criminals by disarming the decent and making them helpless victims of evil. Charles Manson was a product of this pseudo-morality. So was Jim Jones. The only way to create a less violent society is to face the phenomenon honestly and openly, just as courageous thinkers like Havelock Ellis once did with sex.

History's most revolutionary ideas seldom blow bugles announcing their arrival. The work of Gregor Mendel, the first geneticist, went unnoticed for decades. And even otherwise well-educated individuals have trouble pointing to the time, place, and party responsible for the invention of the Scientific Method.

Likewise, another intellectual revolution has occurred in recent years that Dan Rather never told you about: The Non-Aggression Principle, a product of honest, open, courageous Libertarian thinking about ethics, states that "no one has the right, under any circumstances, to *initiate* force against another human being." This is all Libertarianism consists of, no more, no less. It's the most important thought ever generated by the mind of man. Those who act consistently with it are Libertarians, whether they realize it or not. Those who fail to act consistently with it are not Libertarians, regardless of what they may claim.

Recorded human history and what we can infer from archaeology goes back some eight thousand years. In all of those eighty centuries, the one question we see being fought over most bitterly and killed over most brutally and died over most horribly has always been, "Who shall have the power to tell others what to do?" To me, the answer has always been self-evident. Yet for me, growing up has largely consisted of becoming convinced that this was just one more way in which I differed from the people among whom I had to do that growing up.

From Rose Wilder Lane's *The Discovery of Freedom*, I first learned to confront an unplesant fact that no child of 20th century America is encouraged to find out for himself: The universe is a savage place where every natural force — and most man-made ones — are out to obliterate you. As Robert A. Heinlein pointed out, an unprotected human being, on the balmiest day of the kindliest season, standing unprotected in the temperate zone of the planet to which he was adapted by billions of years of evolution by natural selection, will die of sunstroke or hypothermia within hours. In addition to hailstorms, tornados, hurricanes, earthquakes, volcanos, meteor-strikes, poison oak, poison ivy, burning oleander leaves, the odd dire-wolf, cave bear, or saber-toothed timber rattler, *Homo sapiens* himself has proved capable of piling up a mountain-range of corpses to rival the Himalayas. Sixty million people died in World War II alone.

There never was any Garden of Eden. The legend (and its persistence is revealing in and of itself) is a transparent attempt to evade a profound and inescapable truth: That in the midst of a great and terrifying darkness, any little fuzzy-edged pools of light and warmth and love and hope that happen to appear in this horror-filled universe are purely artificial, established where they are, usually at an unspeakable cost, by the minds and hands of individual human beings.

Until you've absorbed this at the gut level, you'll never

understand the rest of what I'm trying to convey, nor anything important about your own life or those of your fellow naked apes: In the midst of a great and terrifying darkness, any little fuzzy-edged pools of light and warmth and love and hope that happen to appear in this horror-filled universe are purely artificial, established where they are, usually at an unspeakable cost, by the minds and hands of individual human beings.

Enjoying a strong hot cup of chocolate and cream-laced coffee with an English professor friend a while back, someone who knows and understands my work, teaches my books, and has followed my career from the start, I recently discovered yet another respect in which I differ from *my* fellow naked apes. With the preparation of this speech in mind, I stated the above thesis, which, although soft-pedaled at the preference of my first publisher, has always constituted the foundation for my stories. My friend was shocked: This was a grim, depressing world-view he hadn't discerned before. What surprised me was that he'd attempt to evaluate it in those terms. He couldn't challenge its validity; he'd be refuted by any history book, any newspaper, any TV show about nature and survival. The truth isn't anything you're entitled to form an opinion about.

My work and outlook are *not* grim and depressing at all, but optimistic. No less respected and generous a colleague than F. Paul Wilson has praised my books for their "positive sense of life," and I suspect that this is why other people read them, as well. Ayn Rand was pointing out a much-neglected but encouraging truth when she insisted that civilization isn't a natural feature of the universe, something that "just grew." In spite of the multitude of forces arrayed against them, those fuzzy-edged little pools of light and warmth and love and hope *exist*. They're what civilization — and life itself — are all about.

Of course, they come in all shapes and sizes, and they're dynamic in nature, not static. They arise, grow, diminish, and wink out of existence because — created as they are for the most part by unsystematic primitives — the conditions that must be satisfied to maintain them often fail to be met over a continuous range of time.

It's pleasant in the center of the pool of light and warmth and love and hope, enjoying a strong hot cup of chocolate and cream-laced coffee with a friend. It's easy to imagine that the center is all that exists. Americans are brought up to believe it. In their minds, the world's a giant theme park where they can pretend the edges of the pool don't exist, and they can safely ignore the dangers lurking out there. The edges, however, are the places that a rational individual watches. They're abstract in nature (a common mistake is to believe that they're geographic), but the entities slithering through the murk along the borders aren't. That's where bogey-things dwell: hail-storms, tornados, hurricanes, earthquakes, volcanos, meteor-strikes, poison oak, poison ivy, oleander leaves, dire-wolves, cave bears, saber-toothed rattlers, Huns, Tatars, Vikings, Communists, Nazis, Klansmen, burglars, muggers, and rapists.

I once heard the head of the Internal Revenue Service claim that taxes are the price we pay for civilization. In fact, it's the other way around — civilization is the price we pay, what we are required to sacrifice, in order to have taxes — and this creature of the outer cold and darkness wouldn't know what civilization is if it walked up and told him his fly was open. Among the slimiest and most voracious of the living nightmares at the pool-edge, he nourishes himself on the light and warmth and love and hope that others have created, steadily diminishing its circumference and intensity. He's the very reason that civilizations, having risen, fall. He may not be aware of his place in the order of things, but I intend to make certain that his grandchildren are.

Built right into that age-old question of who shall have the power to tell others what to do is the more fundamental and disturbing question of violence. Throughout history people have been offered only two alternatives. They could become pool-edge denizens themselves — muggers and IRS agents — or they could follow the pacifists and prophets whose advice, after their followers have run out of cheeks to turn, leaves them stripped naked, used for a humiliating purpose, and disposed of. Given the choice between becoming an animal or a victim, any rational individual will start looking for a third alternative.

I did. I began with the Non-Aggression Principle, one of those simple seminal concepts, such as Evolution by Natural Selection or Scientific Method, which will echo down the ages. The Non-Aggression Principle holds that no one has the right, under any circumstances, to *initiate* force against another person.

Without claiming that it proves anything, I've always thought it was a good sign that an individual can arrive at the Non-Aggression Principle from many different directions and accept it at many different levels. Some see it as a direct consequence or corollary of physical law. Others adopt it as a workable idea. Some assert it as an axiom, an arbitrary starting-point, or a metaphysical irreducible. Others carefully derive it from a variety of "first principles" ranging from Christianity to Objectivism. The encouraging thing is that, on an everyday basis, it doesn't seem to matter. Before I learned to call myself Libertarian, my orientation was scientific and science-fictional. I still sift new information through screens of evolutionary theory, physical anthropology, and the works — always taken with a grain of salt, of course — of thinkers like Louis Leaky, Robert Ardrey, Desmond Morris, and, yes, Elaine Morgan.

Some of my readers, Easterners, recoil in horror whenever they discover that I'm a gory-handed murderer of gentle limpid-eyed Bambi and Thumper. I believe they could learn important things about themselves, their species, and the nature of reality, the first time they found themselves standing over the half-dressed carcass of an animal their own size, with blood up to their armpits and the cloying scent of warm viscera in their nostrils. For me, it's crucial to recognize my natural identity as a killer-ape, not simply to accept it, but to rejoice in it. The alternatives are to spend your life trying, like the lion who choked on a head of cabbage in Mark Twain's *Letters from the Earth*, to deny nature or, out of a sense of cosmic embarrassment, to commit *seppuku*. Recognize it or not, accept it or not, rejoice in it or not, we *are* killer-apes.

Given my interests in evolution, anthropology, and hunting, my first appreciation of the Non-Aggression Principle was as one way that killer-apes might be able to live together without killing each other; individuals who agreed on nothing else could exchange values to their mutual benefit and perhaps even be friends. The Non-Aggression Principle was the most powerful tool ever forged for creating more and larger pools of light and warmth and love and hope — a discriminator not simply defining, in a categorical and succinct manner, the circumstances in which violence is wrong, but those in which it's justified.

This was the third alternative I'd been seeking. I purposed to explore it no matter where it took me, and that's how my first novel, *The Probability Broach*, got written.

The examination of violence within the context of the Non-Aggression Principle has occupied most of my professional time and energy ever since, but it hasn't won me many friends. Setting aside the predictable reactions of liberals and conservatives, within the Libertarian movement itself, plenty of individuals — otherwise highly principled but with certain phobias about accepting the responsibility for their own physical safety that contradict not just their political beliefs, but reality itself — haven't much liked the results.

But as Galileo, Darwin, or even Captain Kirk would tell you, personal integrity requires not letting others influence your search for something resembling the truth. Those years of inquiry have brought me to conclusions that *I* struggled against every step of the way. I was a limited statist when I began, and often wrote about the wonders of private security. However, like going to the bathroom, breathing, eating, sleeping, or making love, it turns out that self-defense is a bodily function one cannot safely or effectively delegate to a second party. The more I studied the proposition, the sillier it appeared.

Look: The police are like parents. They don't care about justice, all they want is *quiet.* They resent anyone disturbing what they conceive to be the peace, regardless of the reason. Anyone who reads newspapers or watches television knows that the one offense more serious than assaulting somebody is defending yourself. Numerous court cases over a period of time and a variety of jurisdictions have established that the police have no obligation to defend your life, liberty, or property. Individuals injured by criminals may not recover from the government for non-performance, whatever promises it may have made.

Perhaps that's just as well. According to civil rights attorney Don B. Kates, writing in the *Wall Street Journal* of January 10, 1986, civilians are attacked three times as often as police officers. Yet civilians are twenty-two percent more likely to succeed in driving off or wounding their attackers, and only one-fifth as likely to injure or kill the wrong person. Kates, a self-described liberal, validly concludes that civilians are more capable of maintaining their own well-being than the police are, and that this capability shouldn't be interfered with. But he spoils it with a contradictory non-sequitur to the effect that the capability should be regulated by government — rather like suggesting that the American Nazi Party should regulate the Jewish Defense League.

To me, it seems much less ridiculous to demand for the sake of public safety that a police officer at the scene of a crime be required to hand his gun over to the first civilian who happens along. The power of government agents to carry weapons at all derives from the individual right of self-defense, and is inferior to it.

Nor should the government be allowed to possess or use any weapon it forbids to civilians.

The police have no obligation to defend your life, liberty, or property. Aside from obvious questions raised by the government's refusal to guarantee services they collected for at gunpoint, there's a more profound consideration: In New York, to name a random location, the government has no obligation to protect you and at the same time it forbids you the means to protect yourself. In short, you're legally *required* to allow criminals to victimize you. Which explains why Ed Koch and Robert Morganthau were determined to get Bernie Goetz at any cost.

Many years ago, in my college psychology classes (which is no guarantee of anything, of course), I was told that police officers and career criminals display identical personality profiles. At about the same time, I heard Paul Harvey cite a study (once again, no guarantee of anything) demonstrating that Russian plumbers seem to get along better with American plumbers, despite the Cold War and the language barrier, than either do with their non-plumbing countrymen.

This makes perfect sense to me. We do tend to identify with those who earn their living the same way we do. It would make sense even if we didn't know that whenever a member of the American productive class stumbles — often through an innocent act of self-defense — into a system of "justice" that is in fact a homey burrow to both parasitic classes, they wind up being treated worse than the professional criminals with whom lawyers and judges (who also live on stolen money and the misfortune of others) naturally identify and sympathize.

Just to name a single example, the doctrine — which is utterly without basis in physical or ethical reality — that there are "degrees of force" is simply another trap for unwary self-defenders. Its proponents are responsible for rendering the productive class helpless against predation. Once physical force has been initiated, a *qualitative* barrier has been breached, and there is no going back — except, perhaps, as an act of mercy, which, as Ayn Rand pointed out, is not the same as justice, but in some respects its precise opposite.

All of this was borne out beyond the remotest shadow of a doubt when Koch began screaming for Goetz's hide. Koch, after all, "earns" his living in exactly the same way Goetz's so-called "victims" did. We thieves must stick together. How dare Goetz resist and injure the Mayor's screwdriver-wielding proteges!

Anyone who needs more evidence regarding the intelligence of relying on government protection should refer to the November 1986 *Voluntaryist*, reprinting an article about Amnesty International from the *Wall Street Journal*. What convinced me, as a young person, that the only *limited* government is an *abolished* government, was Operation Keelhaul at the end of World War II, when, under an agreement made at Yalta, two-and-a-half million Russian refugees were rounded up all over Europe and sent back in boxcars to Stalin and certain death — by the "civilized" government of the United States of America. The *Voluntaryist* underlines this by stating that, during the 20th century, while twenty-two people out of every ten thousand died as a result of war, three hundred forty-nine — *fifteen times as many* — died as a result of "other" government activity, meaning death camps, extermination marches, and artificial famines.

Now, remember that war itself is a government activity, and the grand average comes to three hundred seventy-one: Well over a hundred million murdered human beings. In the '60s, the Berkeley Free Speech Movement asserted that the only proper function for government is cleaning the streets. I'd add that it's a function for which the venal scum polluting our legislatures and council chambers are underqualified. Justice is a thin spotty film floating atop a cesspool of rule-by-coercion, and government is a greater danger — fifteen times greater — than anything it claims (and then denies) it protects us from.

The sad fact about private security is that it's forced to pay the very agency it competes with and (partly as a result) mostly hires minimum-wage employees. More than that, you have to understand the level of self-interest involved. Self-defense expert Jeff Cooper argues that bodyguards are subject to bribery and extortion, whereas you, presumably, are not. It was agreed by all sides of the Vietnam controversy that ten conventional soldiers must be fielded for every native guerilla. Robert Ardrey or Desmond Morris, I forget which, says that an animal defending its own territory is twice as effective as any aggressor. You're out to save your own life. Your bodyguard's out to collect a paycheck. The latter is an acceptable motivation, but it pales by comparison to the former.

But wouldn't chaos result if everyone defended himself? Aren't spouse murders the most frequent kind? Isn't there a ninety percent chance that a gun in the home will be used on a member of the household rather than an intruder?

Years ago, firearms manufacturer Bill Ruger appeared on television with a pack of gun-controllers making claims like that. He challenged them to name their source again and again, but they couldn't. The show went on. Now and then, Ruger would ask whether they'd remembered where they'd acquired their "facts" and they'd shy off. Like Carl Bakal's earlier self-admitted fiction that some eight hundred thousand Americans had died by gunshot since 1900, they'd made up another lie in a cause they considered virtuous, with the idea of concluding grandly that we're all potential murderers who need constant supervision and control — only to be caught at it by someone willing to make a scene.

In this connection, Second Amendment activist Neal Knox reports a study on the mythical "Wild West" that bears repeating. American cities of the 19th century East and West were paired by population and demographics. The macho one-industry whaling town of New Bedford, Massachussetts, for example, was compared with the macho one-industry mining town of Leadville, Colorado, both with populations of around ten thousand people. A decade of records from the height of the cattle-drive era shows that the only difference between them (and this was true of other paired cities, as well) was that nearly everyone in Leadville kept a gun, which was not true in New Bedford, and that murder and other violent crimes in New Bedford outnumbered those in Leadville by a hundred to one!

So much for the wild wild west.

As the National Rifle Association points out on its "Armed Citizen" page every month, the *presence* of a gun is enough to deter aggression seventy-five percent of the time.

Very well, then. If all the facts and logic martial themselves on the side of individual self-defense, and you know who the enemy is, where do you look for friends? Forget the American Civil Liberties Union, whose historic committment to the totality of individual rights is, in the most charitable interpretation, "flexible." Founded and financed by socialists, the ACLU says that your life is the property of society, and that you have no fundamental or inalienable right to remain unmolested by gun laws or any other expression of the collective need.

Most pro-gun pro-self-defense groups are politically conservative and practice typical conservative self-sabotage. They build their argument on the shifting sands of the politics of the day and social utility, rather than the rock of moral philosophy. Instead of pursuing productive strategies, they've been fighting a purely defensive holding action virtually since Wyatt Earp invented gun control.

Prolonged holding actions are doomed to failure.

Experience teaches us that there are natural Rebels and natural Tories. The latter defend the Establishment — whatever it happens to be — against the interests of the individual. All other things being equal, the former make better friends and are the kind of people our times and circumstances cry out for.

The sad fact is that gun people have never been able to distinguish very well between their friends and their enemies. They demonstrate a consistent disheartening proclivity to fawn over the police and the military. At least half of their magazine writers are active or retired enforcers of victimless-crime laws identical in structure to the very legislation that threatens them. They've forgotten that the Second Amendment was written to *intimidate* the government.

They have other skeletons in their closet, as well. Teddy Kennedy, for example, is America's greatest sporting-goods salesman. Every time he opens his dissolute cretinous mouth to push another gun law, uncounted thousands of individuals go out and buy a gun for the first time, just as I did, "before it's too late." Before 1968, I doubt that there were six million handguns in the whole country. The old rifle farts who dominated the shooting fraternity in those days regarded my passion for these "inaccurate toys" as perverse. Now, that many handguns get sold every year — thanks to Teddy. If he really wanted to reduce the number of handguns made and sold, all he'd have to do is shut up.

He knows it.

Both sides know it.

Nobody ever talks about it.

Too bad, because a fact like that might be used to silence anti-gunners forever.

Even more embarrassing is the average gun enthusiast's ignorance of the free-market system — as manifested by a recent "patriotic" flap over the advertising of Chinese guns in the pages of certain magazines. There's also a strong inclination in the field to try to limit the market, to disadvantage competition through regulation, because — just like automobile manufacturers who appear to believe that whining about Japan is an adequate substitute for honest goods at honest prices — so-called "stocking firearm dealers" believe they have a right to a profit whether they earn it or not. They abominate "basement" licensees who sell guns to their friends at cost, and would like to put them out of business through increased fees. They loathe the discount houses even more — Target, K-mart, Wal-Mart — but haven't yet thought of a way to deal with them.

Maybe worst of all, most firearms publications ooze editorial sanctimony over topics like weapons concealment, blathering that this holster featured in an article, or that gun, is — of course — suitable only for duly franchised citizen hoplites, when they know perfectly well their readers respect gun laws the same way they do speed limits. Their policies on national defense, land use, and conservation are undiluted socialist crap. To avoid the political heat, they used to talk a lot about the "legitimate sporting uses" of firearms, hunting and target-shooting, and have only recently taken a stance rooted in the individual right to self-defense. Even that remains disappointingly passive.

Thus, from this moment onward, we must begin to measure all persons and groups who claim to support our individual, civil, Constitutional, and human rights, not in terms of how well they *defend* those rights, but in terms of how well they *advance* them. If existing organizations won't take the offensive, then like any individuals with strong opinions and stronger principles, we've no choice but to adopt the most radical personal stance possible consistent with those principles, one that will compel others to disavow our position or follow along behind us.

At the barest acceptable minimum, principle demands unequivocal assertion of the following points:

● The individual right to self-defense is not collective in character, but an absolute inherent in the nature of each human being, indispensible to the individual right to life itself.

● The individual right to self-defense cannot be granted or denied by kings or constitutions, nor by any legislative or judicial act; neither is it subject to regulation or to the democratic process.

● The individual right to self-defense implies free access to, and uncoerced choice of, the physical means of self-defense: an unlimited right to obtain, own, and carry weapons of any kind.

● The individual right to self-defense especially includes the right of self-defense against government; power exercised by government derives from the individual right to self-defense and is inferior to it; any attempt on the part of government to deny or limit this right represents a conflict of interest.

● The individual right to self-defense demands the immediate repeal of any law that: requires the licensing or registration of weapons, manufacturers, gunsmiths, dealers, or owners; levies taxes on the ownership or transfer of weapons, parts, accessories, ammunition, or components; denies free individual choice concerning manufacture, price, acquisition, carrying, concealment or concealability, "social acceptibility," caliber, power or form of ammunition, design or configuration, "quality" or "safety," magazine capacity, or rate or mode of operation; interferes in personal, local, interstate, or international trade, transport, or transfer of any weapon or associated item; restricts the use of gas, electric, jointed, or edged weapons, impact-resistant clothing, or any other self-protective device; or permits the government or its employees to seize, retain, sell, or destroy weapons belonging to non-aggressive individuals.

● The individual right to self-defense requires that agencies responsible for the enforcement of such laws be abolished and their records destroyed; anyone ever arrested, under indictment, or convicted under such laws be granted immediate unconditional release, with full restitution to all previous rights and property; and employees of such agencies, rather than taxpayers compelled to support their activities involuntarily, be held responsible for such restitution.

Groups like the NRA, claiming to support the Second Amendment, that fail to endorse this minimal position should declare themselves morally bankrupt and shut up. Their approach has been a drawn-out failure because it addressed the basic concept of individual rights in the same piecemeal, contradictory, "flexible" manner as the ACLU — often threatening the very groups (gays and recreational drug users, for example) who might have been our allies. In the wake of this failure an inevitable rot has set in as corrupt leaders struggle over the power and wealth of an otherwise pointless organization. The real question is, are honest reformers — like Neal Knox — willing to acknowledge that failure, abandon their defensive posture, and try the Libertarian way, recognizing that the rights of others may be just as important to them as ours are to us?

The next time you have an opportunity to discuss these issues with your conservative friends, try putting it to them this way: "How much do you want to keep your guns?

"Would you agree to allow adults to pursue their own sexual preferences, homosexual, bisexual, or heterosexual, and to buy, sell, read, write, make, listen to, or watch any films, books, magazines, records, tapes, or live performances they want, no matter how pornographic, if they agreed to let you keep your guns?

"Would you agree to leave others alone, perhaps to ruin their lives with alcohol, nicotine, heroin, cocaine, marijuana, LSD, and other substances, if they agreed to let you keep your guns?

"Would you agree to respect the rights of anyone, no matter what their race or national origin, and to tolerate their practice of atheism, Buddhism, Islam, Scientology, Unitarianism, even Satanism, if they agreed to let you keep your guns?

"Would you agree to let women control their own bodies and reproductive processes — even to have abortions at their own expense — if they agreed to let you keep your guns?"

How much *do* you want to keep your guns?

No sane being would sacrifice the rights he considers most precious, just for the sake of imposing his tastes or opinions on others. And yet it seems that each of us disapproves of, and wants to outlaw, some one little thing that somebody else wants.

Little things add up.

With more than 250 million of us, all working for some kind of Prohibition or another, it's no wonder that government controls seem to ratchet tighter around our lives every day. Until now, it's been strictly a one-way process, with everyone winding up the loser — except for politicians, bureaucrats, and lawyers.

We can reverse the process with a committment to respect each other's rights no matter how much we personally disapprove of any particular exercise of them. The one limit is an obligation never to *initiate* force. Change the way we think about freedom and we can eliminate the power of politicians, bureaucrats, lawyers, and Prohibitionists to control the way we live, which means that every man, woman, and responsible child will be free to obtain, own, and carry, openly or concealed, any weapon — rifle, shotgun, handgun, machinegun, *anything* — any time, any place, without asking anyone's permission.

I challenge everyone interested in the Second Amendment to undertake that committment. Before I'm lying in a hospital bed with green tubes up my nose, before arthritis sets in and I have to do it on crutches, I intend to walk the length of Manhattan with a handgun on my hip, unmolested by parasites.

I will not settle for less.

Come along with me.

Bill of Wrongs
ဆ ဆ ဆ ဆ ဆ

Well, as the whole wide world knows by now, Bill Gates' Microsoft has been officially found guilty of violating the Sherman Antitrust Act.

That this is a completely meaningless judgment may not be quite as obvious to a younger generation. When I was young, just entering the freedom movement, there was a lot of talk —

and writing — about the Sherman Act, a body of blatantly unconstitutional pseudolaw many times more voluminous, twisted, contradictory, and arcane than the tax code.

Under its bizarre provisions — administered by bureaucrats and judges who don't have any more idea what it means than you and I do — corporations can be (and have been) convicted of having a monopoly when their share is openly admitted to be only a small fraction of the market. A corporation can be convicted of monopoly practices when they're alone in a market because nobody offers them competition. And that only scratches the surface of the insanities enshrined in this law.

The reason for the insanity is that this law was never meant to be enforced in any normal sense. It's almost certainly the law Ayn Rand was thinking of when she had a villain in *Atlas Shrugged* say that the real point of passing such a law is that it be *impossible* to obey, so that that government and its allies can "cash in on the guilt."

Others, revisionist historians and economists, point out that the Sherman Act and other legislative absurdities like it were not passed — the way we were taught in high school and college — by courageous crusaders-in-the-public-interest, to curb the vile excesses of greedy robber barons and Teddy Roosevelt's "malefactors of great wealth," but by politicians bought and paid for by the malefactors themselves, to make market entry and effective competition as difficult as humanly possible.

Every one of us has a fundamental, unalienable, individual, civil, Constitutional, and human right to be unmolested. As the great Robert LeFevre said, as owners of ourselves — as self-proprietors — we all have a right not to be involved *involuntarily* in relationships with other human beings. Basically, that's the only right there is. Every other right we commonly recognize is just a corollary to this one real right.

Lever Action

Unfortunately, we begin to get into a mess whenever we start to think of these corollary rights as somehow separable or divisible from one another. Everybody does it. To one degree or another, we've all gotten accustomed to thinking of them as rights in and of themselves, independent from any other rights or — and this is the real long-term historic tragedy — from any theory of the origin of rights that makes sense.

In part, this is an unavoidable consequence of a highly necessary division of labor within the freedom movement. Nat Hentoff and Wendy McElroy battle for free speech, Aaron Zelman and Larry Pratt battle for the right to own and carry weapons, Tom Sowell and Walter Williams battle to end the government's oppression of black people disguised as "help," Susan Wells and George O'Brien battle to end illegal property seizures, Vin Suprynowicz and I battle the raw, evil, insane stupidity today that places human dignity and the Bill of Rights in constant peril.

However, it often happens that an individual fails, inexplicably, to see that other people's rights are every bit as precious to them as his are to him. Or he may violently disapprove of other people's free exercise of their rights — while hypocritically demanding respect for rights of his own that stem from precisely the same philosophical source.

Just a few years ago, Bill Gates bankrolled a referendum in his home state of Washington, aimed at imposing yet another set of stupid, unconstitutional, Jim Crow-style laws on his gun-owning neighbors. The vote was an historic and humiliating defeat for the victim-disarmament crowd, spurring the gun-grabbers' current move to frivolous liability lawsuits. It's astonishing what autocrats the bigmouthed "democrats" are invariably revealed to be, whenever their schemes are thwarted by the Voice of the People they otherwise claim to revere as the Voice of God.

Gates' troubles with the Waco Willie Administration and Jackboot Janet Reno's Justice Department had only begun at that point, when TV journalists and picture magazines were pretending to be aghast at the seaside mansion he was building for his wife, and he'd begun throwing obscene amounts of money at politically correct causes, desperately trying to buy approval from a festering snakepit of parasitic vermin who spawn and devour their own in an endless cycle of cannibalistic depravity.

In reality, Gates was next on the liberal menu no matter whom he bribed.

I can't think of a better example of the indivisibility of rights. The simple fact is that if Gates had upheld the rights of others — instead of spending hundreds of thousands trying to take them away — then even as the most hated man on the Internet, he could have counted on millions of individuals, honorably willing to place principle above personality, to rush to his assistance. The same forces that got Rosie O'Donnell fired and stopped the infamous "Know Your Customer" bank spy scheme might have tipped the balance in Gates' struggle against the state.

Even now, were Gates to publicly endorse the idea of *full* Bill of Rights enforcement — denouncing victim disarmament and offering to make restitution to the gun owners he's helped to harrass — his situation could change dramatically, as millions made their disgust with the government's actions known. Especially in a future Republican administration he seems to be placing his hopes on, the case against his company would wither on the vine and blow away with the winds of change.

Like him or not, the only figure in world history comparable to Bill Gates is Henry Ford, an individual who was plenty unpopular in his own time. Ford didn't invent the automobile, but he put America — and humanity — on wheels. Gates launched America — and humanity — into cyberspace. In both cases America — and humanity — will never be the same, and they owe these unpleasant and unpopular figures a debt that's only been partially repaid by the enormous wealth they accumulated.

Gates should get together with the real civil rights leaders of the 21st century, with Larry Pratt of Gun Owners of America, Aaron Zelman of Jews for the Preservation of Firearms Ownership, and with a handful of uncompromising others, including Vin Suprynowicz and yours truly.

Forget the NRA. Talk is cheap — especially coming from the likes of Wayne LaPierre — and they're still the "loyal opposition," shills for the other side, until they prove otherwise by *deeds* rather than words.

Gates should stop wasting money on those who'll only turn and bite him in the assets. Let him endow GOA and JPFO to the tune of eight or nine figures. Let him underwrite semi-annual conferences to establish once and for all that the right to be unmolested — to do business without being hijacked by the Sherman Act — and to freely exercise the right to own and carry weapons are one and the same right, after all.

Together we could change the course of history.

What do you say, Bill?

A New Approach
to Social Darwinism
Presented to the
Boulder, Colorado, Libertarian Party,
Summer, 1987

❧ ❧ ❧ ❧ ❧

In terms of its social, economic, and political implications, Charles Darwin's monumentally historical theory of evolution by natural selection has been misinterpreted, almost certainly willfully; its actual mandate is for an open, pluralistic, "libertarian" society far "kinder and gentler" than most people living today — including former President George Bush — are capable of imagining.

I've been considering this new idea for several years, having developed it most fully in my wife Cathy's little magazine, *APAlogia: A Journal of Unanimous Consent*. Presently, I'm finishing the second volume of a science fiction trilogy about it — *Forge of the Elders* — for Warner books. The initial volume of that trilogy — *First Time The Charm* — hasn't yet been published. So, with a minor exception I'll get to in a moment, this will be the first time I've shared this new idea outside the narrow confines of the Libertarian movement.

I'll repeat it, just in case you didn't get it the first time around: In terms of its social, economic, and political implications, Charles Darwin's monumentally historical theory of evolution by natural selection has been misinterpreted, almost certainly willfully; its actual mandate is for an open, pluralistic, "libertarian" society far "kinder and gentler" than most people living today — including former President George Bush — are capable of imagining.

I share this new idea with trepidation, based on several

unfortunate experiences I've had sharing other items of leading-edge Libertarian thought with non-Libertarians. What I have to say this evening is introductory and tentative. This idea is new to Libertarianism itself. A long time may pass before it's generally accepted there, let alone in the wider world. A much longer time will pass before every ramification, consequence, and corollary is nailed down.

Libertarianism is an ordered collection of ideas about individual self-ownership and non-aggression which straddles the border between moral and political philosophy. I first became a self-conscious Libertarian in 1961, at the age of 14. Since then, for 28 years, I've been deeply concerned with achieving a successful social revolution based on that ordered collection of ideas.

One of the first things anyone should know about Libertarianism is that there's a Libertarian Party and then again there's a Libertarian intellectual Movement. The two have a considerable overlapping membership, but they are quite distinct. As an individual with a great deal of experience in both, I'd have to say that to any extent the Libertarian Party ever represented the ideas first set forth by the Libertarian Movement, it has never done it very well. Instead, Party members have often compromised, distorted, and watered down those ideas in a wrong-headed, unnecessary, and essentially futile attempt to make them more palatable to voters. And more importantly, to big-money contributors.

That's a topic for another evening. The reason I bring it up at all now is that I did learn one very important lesson working in the Libertarian Party — actually, I learned plenty of lessons from the Party, most of them negative — when I first helped with canvassing for its candidates. Canvassing is a process of going from door to door to acquaint potential voters with your candidate or party and to gain a rough idea of what support you can expect on Election Day.

I was told by seasoned veterans — all of them converts from other political parties — that you should never waste your time arguing with the people you contact in this way. At this stage, you're simply "gathering up" those who are already on your side. If you're successful at that, you may not need to convince the "hard cases." If you're successful, a surprising number of the "hard cases" will join the herd or jump on the bandwagon in the long run, anyway.

Some hard cases.

Unlike those converts from other political parties, I had never been anything but a Libertarian, almost from my first conscious political thought. To me, what they were handing out seemed like pretty cynical advice. It went against my grain as an idealist. It went against my grain as a natural-born teacher. And it went against my grain as an advocate of new ideas. That cynical advice was, however, to be confirmed by all my subsequent experience. And I've found it has a far broader application than simple political canvassing.

Some years ago, I was invited to speak to a group of people whose "first priority," their foremost professed concern, was the achievement of lasting world peace and the prevention of thermonuclear war. One reason I became a Libertarian in the first place was that I shared exactly the same concern. Furthermore, I was convinced (as I still am) that neither Left nor Right was competent in this area. In fact, I believed (as I still do) that their sad, shopworn, silly philosophies work exactly like horses in tandem, dragging us inexorably to the brink.

The Libertarian alternative — which I don't intend going into tonight, so you can relax — is straightforward, but it does require a willingness and ability to "think the unthinkable," to consider new ideas and discard old ones that haven't worked. Much more importantly, it demands sufficient personal integrity to slough off secondary agendas and irrelevant attitudes that have attached themselves over the years to the primary goal of achieving peace. In short, it takes about the same guts as telling the surgeon to "go ahead and amputate."

As far as this particular group was concerned, the willingness, ability, integrity, and guts simply weren't there. Most of them didn't show up, and those who did made it very plain that they'd rather go on whining to each other about how awful things were than do anything in the real world that might actually work.

In a classic exercise of left-wing knee-jerk bigotry, they didn't want to hear about peace from any Libertarian. I wasn't feeding them any of the conventional ideas they were used to hearing from one another — never mind that none of those ideas has ever worked. They were never able to overcome a false impression — which afforded them so much comfort I believe it had to be deliberate on their part — that I was some bizarre sort of conservative and therefore (in their view) I couldn't possibly be concerned with keeping the world from being incinerated. Instead, they wanted to waste my time ragging me about Libertarian positions on issues outside the scope of that night's presentation.

More recently, I've seen the same closed-mindedness, mental laziness, irrelevant nitpicking, and willful misunderstanding exhibited on computer bulletin boards. That's where I first began talking about this new idea — that, in terms of its social, economic, and political implications, Charles Darwin's monumentally historical theory of evolution by natural selection has been misinterpreted, almost certainly willfully; its actual mandate is for an open, pluralistic, "libertarian" society far "kinder and gentler" than most people living today, including former President George Bush, are capable of imagining — but I eventually gave up in disgust and stopped wasting keystrokes.

Ignorance is often bliss — to the ignorant. Slaves, in general, tend to cherish their chains. In any event, those upon whom enlightenment must be pressed are almost certainly never worthy of it. Those who must be persuaded to be free do not deserve to be. I'm still amazed that young minds can be so constipated — and more determined than ever that public schools be abolished, the buildings razed to the ground so that not one stone remains standing on another, and salt sown on the ruins. But that, too, is a topic for another evening.

I'm not here tonight to convert anyone to anything. I agree with Arthur Clarke's observation that old scientists (or anybody else) are almost never converted to new concepts. They simply die and make room for young scientists who grew up with the new concepts and are accustomed to them. (This is the only thing, by the way, that I agree with Arthur Clarke about.) If you have a religiously conservative objection to the theory of evolution, or if you want to talk about souls, this discussion isn't for you and you may go home. If you have a left-wing knee-jerk bigoted reaction to the term "Social Darwinism" that prevented you from noticing that I'm taking a brand new approach to it, you may go home. If you think Libertarians are a bizarre sort of conservative (or, as people do in California, some bizarre sort of liberal), go home. Open active minds are all I want to deal with tonight. I'm here to share some of my ideas, maybe answer the few questions afterward that strike me as honest — and then I'm going home.

I've always been interested in evolution. Politically, if we're trying to decide where we're going, it makes sense to have an idea where we came from, where we are now, and how we got from there to here. This is a very big subject — the very biggest there is — and I eventually found buried within it an even bigger idea: that in terms of its social, economic, and political implications, Charles Darwin's monumentally historical theory

of evolution by natural selection has been misinterpreted, almost certainly willfully; its actual mandate is for an open, pluralistic, "libertarian" society far "kinder and gentler" than most
people living today — including former President George Bush
— are capable of imagining. With regard to its meaning for
human beings, that idea is so big that it scares even me, and it
isn't often that happens.

Six hundred million years ago, life wasn't new to Earth. It
had already been around for some twenty-five hundred million
years. And yet the number of species living at the time was
only a tiny fraction of those living today. It appears that they
made their living very differently than most of the species we're
familiar with, absorbing the chemicals from the water around
them, taking their energy from the sun, scavenging the dissolving remains of other creatures that had died naturally. It all
sounds pretty boring, but this is what life was like — what life
had been like for those twenty-five million centuries — right
up to the dividing line between the "pre-Cambrian" and the
"Cambrian" eras.

Notice what was missing?

It was a time utterly without conflict, the very Utopia many
people urge on us today. There was no predation, no "exploitation," because, until now, it had never "occurred" to any organism that it might liven up its life (not to mention its diet) by
eating some other organism before it rotted away into its constituent chemicals. No living thing had ever eaten another living thing before.

Once this "Original Sin" had been commited, nothing
would ever be the same again. From that moment onward, all
life would be nourished, one way or another — and no matter
how you may feel about it — by the death of other life. Scientists call this moment the "Cambrian explosion," because suddenly — compared with the countless empty eons preceding it

— competition and progress increased a millionfold, along with the number of species we can find in the rocks of that time. No longer content to scrape the sludge from sea bottoms, animals (from the same root as "animation" — staying on the move was now a good idea) began to develop better ways to grab unwilling food, resist if they were on the menu, disguise themselves, or hide. They had no other choice, except to die. Life began to proliferate and differentiate, filling every available niche.

The first hammer-blow had been struck on what the Elders in my trilogy call "The Forge of Adversity."

The sparks are still scattering today.

Given the nature of language, which reflects the nature of our species, it's difficult to speak (or even to think) about the process of evolution-by-natural-selection without lapsing into "teleology." That is the implication, intentional or otherwise, that random motions of inanimate nature are meant to arrive at some predetermined goal. This difficulty is associated throughout history with every kind of conceptual absurdity, from belief in gods to motion pictures featuring talking animals. So as a preface, I want to make it clear that no matter how purposeful I may unintentionally make evolution sound, it isn't purposeful at all. It's simply the result of billions of years of random events operating within — that is, constrained by — a framework of natural law.

Likewise, contemplating a sweep of billions of years, it's difficult to remain focused on the heart of the process of evolution-by-natural-selection, which is brutally simple.

All living things are basically organic machines constructed according to the information contained within the nuclei of their cells. Packets of this information, long molecular chains of a protein called deoxyribonucleic acid or DNA, regulate the birth, growth, and (to one extent or another) behavior of the organic machines, which carry (and often exchange) the information prior to its self-replication.

That information is what it is — and not some other set of information — because, employing its organic carrier machine, it has managed to survive and replicate itself more successfully than competing information. If the nature of the machine is such that it carries the information long enough (and into the correct circumstances) for it to replicate, then it gives rise to yet another generation of machines. In short, machine/information combinations that survive produce offspring, which survive and produce more offspring, and so on.

In the interest of avoiding teleology, I'll stress that the information — which we call "genes" — doesn't care one way or another about its own survival. It's incapable of caring about anything and doesn't have anything to care *with*. It simply is what it is and does what it does. If a given organic machine fails to survive, replication doesn't occur. To any extent that the information it carried was responsible for that failure (having given rise to an inefficacious machine), then it's "erased" from the overall body of such information which we call the "gene pool." This is called "natural selection" — as one of my correspondents puts it, a chain of causation with feedback. One may not approve of the criterion involved, but it's fundamental to life, and complaining about it is like complaining that parallel lines never meet.

Many things (chemicals, radiation, microorganisms, systemic "glitches") may interfere with replication. When it occurs, it isn't always perfect. In most instances, alterations to the information (called "mutations") prevent the development and birth of the organic machine carrier altogether. In some rare instances, mutation doesn't affect the efficacy of the organism enough to prevent it from performing its "role." In even rarer instances, mutation actually enhances the organism's efficacy. Until recently, it was believed that this process occurred in tiny increments, as single molecules, perhaps even single atoms, of DNA were rearranged. However, evidence has accumulated that, for reasons still not understood, evolution occurs in larger steps as whole sections of DNA are knocked out, added, inserted in the "wrong" place, or turned end-for-end.

Nonetheless, the overall process of evolution is very slow. Unthinkably slow. After decades of reading, thinking, and talking about it, I believe that it's nothing more than an inability to conceptualize the gulf of time involved that keeps some people from accepting evolution for the scientific truth it represents.

Now, the question of an organism's "efficacy" can't be answered without reference to the environment in which it operates. Thus, a mutant polar bear without hair will almost certainly die at birth, whereas a hairless bear of a tropical species may survive to reproduce. And a hairless bear belonging to some hypothetical species already trending toward a marine existence (the path followed by porpoises and seals) may even enjoy an advantage over its "normal" fellows.

Some species, most notably our own, are capable of altering the impact of their environment to a greater or lesser extent. This strategem has proven so successful that, through feedback inherent in the phenomenon, the process of evolution has greatly accelerated in our species. On discovering fossil evidence of this acceleration, some observers have been tempted to doubt the theoretical basis of evolution. Better knowledge of biophysics, however (as well as the "unnatural" selective power of certain factors such as language use), has softened that trend.

But I'm getting ahead of myself.

Two hundred million years ago, three-quarters of all life on Earth, both marine and terrestrial species, died out overnight (whether on a geological timescale or literally remains unclear) for reasons that are still a source of mystery and controversy. This is called the "Permian-Triassic Extinction." There are plenty of theories that try to account for what happened: A nearby supernova bathed the planet in deadly radiation; a meteor or comet struck it, filling the air with particles that blocked the sun and plunging Earth into a century of winter; a great volcano erupted, accomplishing the same thing; the continents drifted together, spreading germs and eliminating enough coastline to alter the ecology.

What concerns us at this particular moment, however, is what happened afterward. The planet had once teemed with life in abundant variety occupying every possible environmental niche, making a living in every conceivable way. Now, most of it was gone, and a previously insignificant group of animals, suddenly deprived of natural enemies and competitors, began to proliferate and differentiate until, within a relatively short span, they filled all the empty niches.

We call them dinosaurs.

Nobody knows what killed their predecessors off. Nobody knows why they survived. The only safe surmise is that they were different in some way from the seventy-five percent of all life that died out. They had different habits, lived in different places, were awake at different hours, ate different things, needed different atmospheric gases, had different muscles, nervous systems, internal organs, or skin. Whatever it was, it kept them alive while almost everything else perished. Life on Earth went on precisely because they *were* different.

Some sixty million years ago, a significant fraction of all life on Earth died out overnight for reasons that still remain unclear: a nearby supernova; a meteor or comet; a great volcano; drifting continents. This is called the "Cretaceous-Tertiary Extinction" and it's the mysterious disaster that everybody likes to talk about, although on a grand scale it wasn't anywhere near as bad as the earlier Permian-Triassic Extinction.

This time the dinosaurs weren't so lucky. They died, while a previously insignificant group of animals, different in some way from those that perished, began to proliferate and differentiate the same way the dinosaurs once had, until, in a relatively short span, they filled all the empty niches.

Again.

We call them mammals, and they are us.

What these disasters teach us is that differentiation is the ultimate form of life insurance. Evolution has no plan. It proceeds through random genetic changes winnowed by harsh reality, just as if the output of a million typewriting monkeys were edited to eliminate the gibberish, leaving something that looks purposeful. It's a sort of optical illusion of the mind's eye, but it's what makes every generation, barring the occasional super-disaster, a bit harder to kill. Differentiation has preserved life itself, even through the super-disasters.

If there's an overall pattern to evolution or to the history of life on Earth in general, it might be expressed in a single "Commandment," the same sort of "optical" illusion, but one that explains all. That Evolutionary Imperative, if you will, is this: For life itself to prosper, living things must not only be fruitful, they must be as *different* from one another as possible.

You may be aware that Sherlock Holmes never really said, "Elementary, my dear Watson" or "Quick, Watson, the needle." You may be aware that Humphrey Bogart never really said, "Play it again, Sam." You may not be aware that evolutionary theory is *not* about "survival of the fittest," it's about "survival of the *fit*" — and that makes all the difference. The misquote is elitist, even fascist. The proper quote implies that anything that works is okay.

Now, if you've been told that, in the past, "Social Darwinism" served as an excuse to keep people in their places, or to justify the power and wealth of various types of aristocracy, then you may begin to see why I say that, in terms of its social, economic, and political implications, Charles Darwin's monumentally historical theory of evolution by natural selection has been misinterpreted, almost certainly willfully; its actual mandate is for an open, pluralistic, "libertarian" society far "kinder and gentler" than most people living today — including former President George Bush — are capable of imagining.

I've said that the Evolutionary Imperative is this: For life itself to prosper, living things must not only be fruitful, they must be as different from one another as possible. It isn't fashionable these days to assert that there are qualitative differences between human beings and other living things, but one of the most conspicuous of those qualitative differences is something I've heard many a zoologist talk about: There are more individual differences among human beings than between whole species of many other organisms.

What other organisms strive to accomplish as whole species, human beings tend to do as individuals. We live everywhere on the planet, almost from the South Pole to the North Pole, and from almost the highest mountaintop to the bottom of the sea. We eat everything that doesn't eat us first — and quite a number of things that try. We build every imaginable kind of shelter, wear every imaginable kind of clothing, practice every imaginable kind of marriage system and several different reproductive systems, indulge ourselves in every possible variety of religious and philosophical belief. Both literally and metaphorically, we try to fill every niche and be as different from one another as possible.

No two people agree with one another about everything. The fact is that I'm often surprised that two people can ever agree on anything at all. We all seem to possess a drive — and

I'm not sure that anyone has ever noticed it before — to differ with one another simply for the hell of it. And that drive appears far stronger to me than any contrary inclination toward conformity.

This is a good thing. This is a very good thing. At any moment, human beings are trying every possible survival strategy in terms of geography, topography, diet, habitat, clothing, custom, and belief. Since the universe is essentially random, no one can predict what disaster will next engulf the Earth. We're *way* overdue, statistically, for another big meteor strike. There's bound to be another supernova soon. Mt. Saint Helen's hardly compares with the great volcanic eruptions of the past. If we've each chosen our own survival strategy and, in aggregate, we've chosen a broad enough spectrum of survival strategies, then someone will survive, whatever happens, and human life will go on.

In terms of its social, economic, and political implications, Charles Darwin's monumentally historical theory of evolution by natural selection has been misinterpreted, almost certainly willfully; its actual mandate is for an open, pluralistic, "libertarian" society far "kinder and gentler" than most people living today — including former President George Bush — are capable of imagining.

The principal implication, to me, is that those human beings who wish to survive and who wish to see their species survive need to agree to disagree. In that context, the only system that makes political sense is a coalition for the mutual respect of individual rights, so that people can disagree without bashing each other's heads in, so that people can be as different from one another as possible and not try to force each other into choices they wouldn't otherwise have made.

Those human beings who wish to survive and who wish to see their species survive need to avoid or abolish anything that limits individual differences. Fascism certainly limits individual differences. Socialism limits individual differences. Democracy is probably the most dangerous of them all, because it limits individual differences — while giving its victims the illusion that they're free.

The only system I know of that doesn't limit individual differences is Libertarianism. Its philosophical heart — and the only limit of any kind it does impose — is the "Non-Aggression Principle," which holds that no one has the right to initiate force against another human being for any reason. That principle allows human beings to maximize their individual differences and thus guarantees — as much as anything can — the continued survival of our species on this planet.

And anywhere else we go in the universe.

The Tyranny of Democracy
Majoritarianism Versus Unanimous Consent
Prepared for the Boulder County Libertarian Party, 1989

For some time, I've meant to write various legislators, bureaucrats, and other sucklers at the public jugular to say, "Congratulations, assholes — beginning with the most decent livable culture in history, in just two centuries you've managed, with taxation, regulation, and conscription, to turn it into a prison whose best and brightest inmates, whatever disagreements they may cherish among themselves, are of a single mind when it comes to escaping from it." Everybody wants out: The condition's so uniform and universal hardly anybody sees it, let alone anything strange about it.

Even when they do, they miss its central significance.

Aerobics, alcohol, anorexia, bicycling, bird watching, board games, bulemia, celibacy, communes, communism, coca-cola, cocaine, country-western music, gambling, glue sniffing, gun collecting, hashish, heroin, hiking, horror stories, hunting, manic-depression, marijuana, medievalism, motorcycling, movies, neoNazism, nicotine, opium, overeating, pacifism, paramilitarism, premenstrualism, pornography, prohibitionism, promiscuity, psychotherapy, rock 'n' roll, role-playing, romance novels, satanism, science fiction, sexual deviation, soap operas, socialism, space colonies, spouse murder, suicide, survivalism, television, terrorism, tourism, vegetarianism, weird religion, and, as we can see in my 1986 novel *The Crystal Empire*, even weirder religion.

These are a few of my favorite things — each with its own advocates and detractors. As an enthusiatic practitioner of several, I'm not knocking any one in particular — at the moment. Each represents, to a greater or lesser degree, an attempt to stop the world and get off, if only for a few days, a few hours, a few minutes, or a few seconds.

Psychologist Nathaniel Branden speaks of a benevolent sense of life possible to those with rational productive values, vividly contrasted with the coercive parasitic group-culture of mystics and altruists we live in, where people all around you seem a burdensome annoyance, a threat to your survival. Having been told from childhood that life is a zero-sum game in which you owe everything to *others*, at some level you worry all the time that someday the bastards will collect. And collect they do, every April 15th. Why do you think they call it collectivism?

My experience with groups is much the same as yours: grade school, high school, the Air Force I grew up in, the Boy Scouts of America, the National Rifle Association, Students for a Democratic Society, Young Americans for Freedom, the Libertarian Party, every one seething with bickering and power struggles. Nobody ever seemed happy, but there were always plenty of excuses to fall back on to account for it: the inherent stupidity of mankind; the metaphysical futility of hope. Dumbest of all, although extremely popular in the military, the claim that, if people aren't complaining, that's when you should worry.

Another novelist once told me he spends half his life wanting to throw something through the TV. I can sympathize. Judging by what we see at the bottom of that "blue hole," the productive class is expected to show up at work, keep its mouth shut, accept what it's told, and tolerate being herded, milked, and slaughtered by a parasitic overclass and its freelance symbiotes. Yet, as I showed in my first novel, *The Probability Broach*, all that's necessary to achieve a kind of practical open-ended utopia is to understand that civilization is a machine whose purpose, like that of any machine, is to give back just a bit more than we put into it. In a technological society, that would be possible a thousand times over if it weren't for groups like the IRS whose function is to deny the average individual the benefits of the industrial revolution.

We've all taken a vow of poverty. It begins, "I pledge allegience to the flag ..."

As it still is at times, my progress toward something better than group culture, with all of its failures and excuses, was clumsy and faltering. Like the North American Confederacy to my fictional detective Win Bear, or the act of "detectiving" itself to Agot Edmoot Mav, of *Their Majesties' Bucketeers*, it was all new territory, where nothing was self-evident but the shortcomings of every other system of human organization. Puzzling out the answers one painful piece at a time, I often felt dim and stupid. Quantum leaps were few and far between.

Time and again I overlooked Sherlock Holmes' excellent advice that, once you've eliminated everything else, you must consider the impossible.

Nothing subject to majoritarianism ever gets better. "If voting could change things," goes an old anarchist saying, "it would be illegal." Set aside the fact that a voting majority always means a minority of the people. Set aside the fact that elections amount to no more than choosing between the scum that floats to the top of the barrel and the dregs that settle to the bottom. Even at majoritarianism's self-advertised best, there are always losers. Sometimes they constitute as many as just one less than half. As an individualist, it's hard for me to see even one percent as insignificant, especially since that one percent always seems to include me. Rather than accepting majority will, once the voting's over, a minority is inclined to skulk off, plotting to get even next time. In a culture where taxation, conscription, self-defense, capital punishment, and private lifestyles are considered legitimate public issues, where mental aberrations like religion and liberalism are given serious respect, it's even harder to view such a reaction as unreasonable.

Majoritarianism, as I argued in *Tom Paine Maru*, rests on two false assumptions and a cynical threat. It first assumes that two people are smarter than one person. Strength *is* additive, two people are stronger than one person, and this has been the primary source of tragedy throughout human history. Even stupidity seems additive somehow; possibly it's a phenomenon of interference that would explain a lot of that history. People, in fact, do possess certain attributes that are additive, and many that are not at all. Decency, kindness, integrity are all individual characteristics. Time is additive only in a limited sense: Two women can't have a baby in four and a half months. If you've ever observed a committee, you know that the highest intelligence in a room isn't the sum of its occupants' IQs, but simply that of the brightest individual — divided by the number of other people in the room. Just as gravity arises from the nature of space and mass, rights arise from our inherent nature as individual human beings. Rights aren't additive. Systems that assume they are labor under the false and dangerous assumption that two people have more rights than one.

Some claim that majoritarianism, despite its faults, is an alternative preferable to physical conflict. They're wrong: Majoritarianism *is* physical conflict. Elections are a process of counting fists, rather than noses, and saying, "We outnumber you — we could beat you up and kill you — you might as well give in and save everyone a lot of trouble." Majoritarianism, to put it straightforwardly, possesses the full measure of nobility manifested by any other form of extortion.

Based in fallacy and threat, majoritarianism is troubled by certain characteristic malfunctions. The lowest common denominator — Chelsea Bradford in *The WarDove*, Ron Paul representing himself as libertarian, any of the Democrats or Republicans running for president, their sharpened screwdrivers raised on high — the lowest common denominator is elevated to the most exalted position, a serious mistake in an ecology governed by natural selection. The multiple choices of the market are swept aside for the single coerced choice of politics. Less becomes more. "Might" is transubstantiated into "must." Winning votes and losing votes turns friends into enemies. Political and personal feuds arise of their own accord, to achieve the status of art for art's sake.

During my tenure in the Libertarian Party, when these malfunctions began occurring, I went so far as to write to other prominent libertarians, ask what was going on, and couldn't we stay friends? It didn't work. I don't mean to single out the LP, it's simply the place where I gained the bulk of my sad experience. It doesn't differ significantly from any other majoritarian group. If you think me unduly harsh, it's because you're hearing about ten years of mistakes that the LP failed to learn from, in about as many minutes. I'm determined that those presently investing their time, energy, and money in it, their hopes and dreams, learn from those mistakes sometime, somehow. If you know nothing of the LP, or don't care, think about any organization you ever belonged to where people vote on what to do, what not to do, what's right, and what's wrong, instead of looking and deciding for themselves as individuals.

Part of the problem was the LP's underwhelming political track record. Frustration inevitably became recrimination and soon afterward, pointless acrimony. Avoiding painful reminders of a real world they had aspired — and failed — to change, hearts and minds began to shrink, like Lando and Vuffi Raa in *The MindHarp of Sharu*, to fit an increasingly closed and microscopic subculture.

But more was going on than this could account for. The LP's majority-driven hierarchy was inappropriate to — incompatible with — any independent-minded individualist striving to maximize liberty. As my favorite character, Lucy Kropotkin, might put it, "It's hard t'ride an escalator in elevator shoes."

The LP's structure had been copied, without thought, from the Young Republicans, another group with its share of factionalism. Individual values soon became secondary to those of the organization. For our logo, we'd chosen the porcupine, a symbol of non-aggressive self-defense. But if it looks like an elephant, walks like an elephant, trumpets like an elephant, and smells like an elephant, it's an elephant, no matter how much you want to believe it's something else. Before long, people were jockeying to become "King of the Libertarians" simply, tragically, because a throne had been built into the structure by accident.

Lever Action

For me, the crowning blow came with the 1979 convention. Philosophers, educators, writers with their brains on hold led moronic floor demonstrations around the ballroom with plastic straw hats, personality-cult posters, New Year's Eve tooters, behaving exactly like the majority parties ours had been patterned after. Not only was the porcupine trumpeting like an elephant, it was braying like a jackass.

A nasty feeling of collectivism filled the air. Noise and motion had replaced thought and purposeful action. It was as if my little freenies from *The Nagasaki Vector*, forgetting that caffeine had turned them into intelligent beings, had sworn off coffee. And, as I feared, the spectacle warned of personal, political, and philosophical betrayals that became a hallmark of the subsequent Ed Clark campaign.

Not wanting to give up, believing that this was the one and only chance I had to be free, I kept thinking. Structure appeared to be paramount. What ethically acceptable alternative existed that might replace this majoritarian mess?

I'd first become aware of "hyperdemocratic" or "Unanimous Consent" theory during a 1972 seminar with Robert LeFevre. This is the familiar "blackball" system, where a group accepts new recruits only if no current member objects. Egalitarians detest this "no-objection" system, but far from being elitist as they claim, it takes all opinions into account better than majoritarianism, and can be used in making other decisions, as well. Helping the LP struggle for permanent ballot status, which, under the law, required admitting anyone — liberals, conservatives, Larouche types who didn't give a damn what we were supposed to stand for — I started thinking more and more about Unanimous Consent.

LeFevre had pointed out that the Declaration of Independence wasn't written for approval by one-over-half of the voters. My liberal college professors had regarded its failure to denounce slavery as a fatal weakness — the same clowns who supported the progressive income tax and compulsory national service. LeFevre claimed it was evidence of strength: The delegates at Liberty Hall were divided on the issue of slavery, yet they went ahead with what they did agree on, an unprecedented expression of individual sovereignty that even promised an eventual solution to the one problem they couldn't solve themselves.

Unanimous Consent was so important to them that they even *faked* it with the Constitution.

The free market, LeFevre proclaimed proudly, runs on Unanimous Consent. The canned-pears "issue" gets solved every day without debate, without TV pundits, without elections. If you don't like canned pears, you don't buy them. If you do, your choice isn't limited by political bosses in smoke-filled rooms. If your concern is cost, you buy generic. If you want savings *and* colorful pictures on the can, you buy housebrands. If you like a company because it has funny advertising or doesn't make its workers take urine tests, you buy name products. If you consider yourself above the common herd, you buy specialties — canned pears in garlic sauce — at specialty prices that don't penalize anybody else. Everyone — manufacturer, distributor, retailer, and consumer — gets what he wants. Unanimous Consent. Hyperdemocracy. Even crippled by taxation and regulation, quality steadily increases, while prices, in terms of real wealth, continuously fall. Satisfaction guaranteed or your money back.

Understanding that majoritarianism guarantees only dissatisfaction, I sat down to devise a new structure for the LP and wrote another letter to as many of its leaders as I could. The few who replied objected that nothing could get done under my plan. A common response was, "Ever see fifty people agree on anything?"

So, with the fresh insight that people who have to be persuaded to be free don't deserve to be, I finally gave up on the LP. Realizing also that intelligence is non-collective, I put everything I had into the kind of work that didn't depend quite so much on cooperation from others. Today, thanks to its majoritarian structure, a diminished LP is reduced to running a clone of Pat Robertson for president. Meanwhile, I've introduced a million readers to libertarianism, and receive letters and phone calls almost every day, thanking me, telling me I've managed to change the lives of countless individuals for the better.

Writing politically experimental books, such as *The Probability Broach*, *Tom Paine Maru*, and especially *The Gallatin Divergence*, I began acquiring the final puzzle pieces, although the picture is by no means complete even now. The most important piece arrived (as puzzle pieces often do) in a colorful cardboard box — steaming hot on a thick crust, with black olives, mushrooms, onions, sausage, pepperoni, green peppers, and extra cheese. Sitting in a room full of friends, I noticed how such a group makes decisions by the process of Unanimous Consent. They were hungry. Something got done because that's the way everybody wanted it. The idea of pizza met with unanimous approval, but the earth wouldn't have stopped if it hadn't. Whoever didn't want pizza wouldn't have to eat it. Or pay for it. Among libertarians, the individual is free, limited only by a non-aggression principle forbidding initiation of force, to do whatever he wishes, including going out for a hamburger. The crisis always centers on anchovies, but "pizzacracy," as I began to call it, seemed to be up even to that. Pizza could be had with anchovies on half its surface, although anchovies do tend to make their influence more widely felt than their little bodies are distributed. Two pizzas could be ordered, with and without, common practice even among non-libertarians.

But something else was happening. An anchovy-lover might consider his friends more important than dead fish on toast. His friends, seeing how he'd been deprived of anchovies since the McKinley administration, might decide, just this once, to suffer for the pleasure of his company. Nobody was campaigning, voting, or skulking off to plot revenge. Instead — and entirely unlike the majoritarian process — individual feelings seemed genuinely important to everyone. The Ordering of the Pizza had become among the most festive of American rituals.

As I demonstrated in *The Probability Broach*, the one principle that makes all of this possible is that an individual may opt out of group activity at any time, without negative sanctions. Without having to pay for what the rest of the group wants. As I discovered later, if this principle is stringently observed, there are rewards. The remainder of the group, thus "reconstituted," becomes unanimous all over again. The individual who opted out will likely rejoin for another later reconstitution. Even if he doesn't, everybody stays friends. The process is natural to human beings, if you wake them up in the middle of the night before they put on their majoritarian pretensions. It may resemble '60s-style consensus; it's also a transfer of the ethical processes inherent in the free-market system to all social endeavors. If it sounds simple, the best ideas are. How many moving parts are there in a lightbulb?

Some folks have an impression that, under Unanimous Consent, nobody does anything without everybody else's permission. On the contrary, no *group* does anything without the Unanimous Consent of its members, which is a different thing, indeed. But, I pretend to hear you asking, what about the claim that nothing can ever get done? To be absolutely truthful, with respect to the government, I wish to hell it were true. As my wife Cathy points out, when this objection is raised, it's a clear warning that something is about to happen that deserves scrutiny by everyone who values his life, liberty, and property.

The objection is also unfounded. As I tried to show in *The Venus Belt*, people live their everyday lives by Unanimous Consent. Yet I found that the process is so natural that it's transparent — invisible — in fiction unless you focus on its most political (and therefore least natural) aspects. Under the most absurd political handicaps, the Unanimous Consent system produces and distributes goods and services more broadly, more efficiently, and much more cheaply than any other economic system in human experience, giving us the highest standard of living anywhere in history, anywhere on Earth. The Declaration of Independence was written and ratified under Unanimous Consent. The Covenant of Unanimous Consent, centerpiece of my novel *The Gallatin Divergence*, was amended by its real-life Signatories to its present form by the same process:

A NEW COVENANT
Of Unanimous Consent

WE, THE UNDERSIGNED Witnesses to the Lesson of History — that no Form of political Governance may be relied upon to secure the individual Rights of Life, Liberty, or Property — now therefore establish and provide certain fundamental Precepts measuring our Conduct toward one another, and toward others:

== *Individual Sovereignty* ==

FIRST, that we shall henceforward recognize each Individual to be the exclusive Proprietor of his or her own Existence and of all Products of that Existence, holding no Obligation binding among Individuals excepting those to which they voluntarily and explicitly consent;

== *Freedom from Coercion* ==

SECOND, that under no Circumstances shall we acknowledge any Liberty to initiate Force against another Person, and shall instead defend the inalienable Right of Individuals to resist Coercion employing whatever Means prove necessary in their Judgement;

== *Association and Secession* ==

THIRD, that we shall hold inviolable those Relationships among Individuals which are totally voluntary, but conversely, any Relationship not thus mutually agreeable shall be considered empty and invalid;

== *Individuality of Rights* ==

FOURTH, that we shall regard Rights to be neither collective nor additive in Character — two Individuals shall have no more Rights than one, nor shall two million nor two thousand million — nor shall any Group possess Rights in Excess of those belonging to its individual Members;

== *Equality of Liberty* ==

FIFTH, that we shall maintain these Principles without Respect to any person's Race, Nationality, Gender, sexual Preference, Age, or System of Beliefs, and hold that any Entity or Association, however constituted, acting to contravene them by Initiation of Force — or Threat of same — shall have forfeited its Right to exist;

== *Supersedure* ==

UPON UNANIMOUS CONSENT of the Members or Inhabitants of any Association or Territory, we further stipulate that this Agreement shall supersede all existing governmental Documents or Usages then pertinent, that such Constitutions,

Charters, Acts, Laws, Statutes, Regulations, or Ordinances contradictory or destructive to the Ends which it expresses shall be null and void, and that this Covenant, being the Property of its Author and Signatories, shall not be Subject to Interpretation excepting insofar as it shall please them.

~~~~

Fundamentally, all rights are property rights, beginning with the right to control and dispose of your own life — as long as it doesn't conflict with anybody else's equal and identical right to control and dispose of his or her own life.

All rights are individual. Groups are simple aggregations of two or more human beings — like yourself, no more, no less — whose rights begin, as yours do, with a claim to ownership of their lives. Their rights cannot be any greater than your own.

Human rights are an aspect of natural law, a consequence of the way the universe works, as solid and as real as photons or the concept of *pi*. The idea of self-ownership is the equivalent of Pythagoras' theorem, of evolution by natural selection, of general relativity, and of quantum theory. Before humankind discovered any of these, it suffered, to varying degrees, in misery and ignorance. Where they are suppressed or disregarded today, people *still* suffer. When Pythagoras, Darwin, Einstein, Bohr, and Rand each made his or her uniquely valuable discovery about the way the universe works, mankind took another step away from savagery, toward lasting safety, comfort, pleasure, and convenience.

I explored the potential of Hyperdemocracy to see what weapons, if any, it might lend to those who wish to be free. So far, I've "discovered" one, the Covenant of Unanimous Consent. If it seems small, remember it's only the first, and it may be more powerful than it appears. At this moment it's being circulated in 40 countries and has signatories in more than 30 states and several Canadian provinces, and the number doubles every year. I wrote the Covenant to restore the machinery of civilization to the hands that built it and the uses it was intended for. I wrote it to start something that, like my books, didn't depend on others, progressed when I had the energy and could wait when I hadn't, didn't involve the stop-start-hurry-wait of politics, was effective whether the media were kind to it or not, and, although it was perfectly legal, operated outside the rules constructed by an establishment anxious to prevent change.

It wasn't my aim to create another faction in the struggle for liberty, but to eradicate the causes of factionalism. Without compromising anything I personally believe, I wrote the Covenant for natural rightists and non-natural rightists, religious libertarians and the non-religious, anarchists and non-anarchists — since the former can assume, accurately, that it's a first step toward abolishing government, whereas the latter can see, with the same degree of accuracy, an explicit contract establishing the systematic non-coercive order they desire. Under the terms of the Covenant, they amount to the same thing.

Whenever there's an election coming, especially a referendum, especially on taxes, which are not only a monkey wrench in the machinery of civilization — rent we're forced to pay on our own lives — but the very fuel of war itself, try suggesting — try demanding — of local Democrats and Republicans that it be settled in the only decent, moral, civilized way, by Unanimous Consent.

Hyperdemocracy.

Sure, they'll laugh at first. Later they'll scream and tear their hair. Never stop making their lives as miserable as they've made yours. If history demonstrates anything, it's that every lasting victory that the cause of liberty ever achieved was won for it by radicals. Every humiliation it ever suffered was inflicted, not by kings, dictators, or opposing parties, but by its own moderates and gradualists.

Shop Now and Avoid the Rush
ᴄᴥ ᴄᴥ ᴄᴥ ᴄᴥ ᴄᴥ

How often lately have you heard frightened conservatives — reacting to unmistakable evidence that their "revolution" is a fake — argue with Libertarians: "Why *can't* you be satisfied to work within the Republican Party? You're not gonna win. All you do is take votes from us and help Democrats. Want Bill Clinton for another four years?"

Which puts me in mind of something that happened recently in our family that may tell you what kind of people *we* are.

My wife Cathy has wanted a high-powered rifle a long while, to hunt antelope, mule deer, and elk. I knew less about rifle ballistics than the ballistics of handguns, so we made a careful project of deciding which gun — especially which cartridge — would be best, taking into account accuracy, power, the amount of bullet-drop at long range, reliability, recoil, her size and weight, ammunition availability, and, to some degree, aesthetics.

We decided on a bolt-action manufactured for .270 Winchester, the second or third most popular cartridge in America. We also decided that any of three different brands would fulfill our specifications: a Winchester Model 70 (preferably pre-1964), a Remington Model 700, or a Ruger Model 77. Because Cathy felt it was beautiful — and in spite of the stupid political views of corporation founder William B. Ruger —

she chose the Ruger, a model called "International" due to its long, graceful, "mountain" stock.

We were unable to afford a new rifle for her immediately, and because of Ruger's politics, she preferred to buy used, rather than pay him another cent (we own several Ruger firearms) to support his liberal-appeasing ways. Then last week, while we were in a local emporium after something else, Cathy asked the proprietor if she could look at rifles (a rite of passage for her; gun shops can be intimidating for women) and mentioned her preference for a Ruger Model 77 International, in .270 Winchester.

"Got one coming Monday," the proprietor told her (this was Friday), "from a guy who really needs the money. You oughta be able to get a deal."

Well, that was a *very* long weekend. Cathy had "gun fever" as badly as I'd ever seen it — not all that different from "car fever," which I've also seen, or "computer fever." Also known as the "wantsies," I've had it myself, many times, and she's suffered through it with me. This time, it was my turn.

Monday came and it turned out the guy wouldn't be in until Tuesday. When the calendar finally ground around to Tuesday, the proprietor, hoping for the best, told us he had the gun, it was, indeed, a Ruger Model 77 International, and in beautiful shape.

Trouble was, it was a .30-06, not a .270.

Cathy ... well, all weekend she'd been mentally sighting the damned thing in at 300 yards. I even looked into having it rebarreled, but these days, that costs about as much as a new rifle. So, we politely turned the proprietor down. He was disappointed — he'd wanted to make a sale and help his friend — but being a rifleman himself, he understood. The .30-06 just wasn't what she wanted.

We're still looking. And ever since, I've been thinking

about what it would have been like if Rush Limbaugh had been behind the counter, unhappy with Cathy's decision.

"I just don't understand," he would say. "Thirty-ought-six, two-seventy — what's the difference? Why can't you be happy with what's available? Why do you have to hold out for what you can't get?"

"You mean what you don't have in stock?" Cathy would reply. "Because it's what I *want*, Rush. Because my husband and I did our homework: thirty-ought-six won't do all the things I expect from a two-seventy."

"But it's such a *tiny* difference! The primer's the same, the powder's the same, even the cases are *almost* the same. Three-hundred eight thousandths minus two-hundred seventy-seven thousandths (the true diameters in question). That's only thirty-one measly thousandths of an inch!"

"Yes, and because of that measly thirty-one thousandths, I can shoot farther and flatter, and with only about half the recoil; thirty-ought-six *hurts* when it goes off in a light sporting rifle, and doesn't kill game as cleanly. It was designed for war, where the object is to wound the enemy, not kill him, so he uses up more of the other side's resources."

"You're just too picky," Rush would pout. "Thirty-ought-six is the only game in town. You keep insisting on what you want, rather than accepting what you can get, you'll hafta wait a long time — and you may not get what you want, at all."

"Listen, if I can't get what I want, I don't *want* anything else. What would be the point? I'm willing to wait, even take the risk of not getting what I want, because — if I buy what *you've* got to sell, Rush — I won't be getting what I want *any-way*. Will I?"

"Okay, lady," Rush would scowl at my wife, "that's *it* for you. You've *failed* the kook test!"

Rush never will get the point because, besides being a

political wussie, he's a gun wussie, too. Maybe I should have written this about expensive cigars, but I stopped smoking three years ago, and don't know anything about them. Maybe accepting only one percent of what you want — along with another ninety-nine percent of what you *don't* want — is okay where cigars are concerned.

But the inconvenient truth is that Republicanism is *not* what Libertarians want. It won't abolish taxes or economic regulations, it won't end the War on Drugs, it's getting *worse* about abortion and censorship, and, deep inside, it's just as terrified of privately owned weapons as Democrats are.

Libertarians want something else, as different from the policies of Republicans as from those of Democrats. Libertarians want control of their own lives, something Republicans and Democrats *claim* they want, but have *demonstrated* that they hate and fear. So, no matter how much Republicans whimper — even if it means Democrats may win — *real* Libertarians will go on voting for *real* Libertarians.

Because we're willing to wait for what we *really* want. Really.

II

LIBERTARIAN POLITICS

Lever Action —
Accept No Substitutes

Delivered at the Libertarian Party National Convention
Salt Lake City, Utah, September 3, 1993

Good morning, Comrade Libertarians.

I am the author of *The Probability Broach*, *The Venus Belt*, *Their Majesties' Bucketeers*, *The Nagasaki Vector*, *Tom Paine Maru*, *The Gallatin Divergence*, *Lando Calrissian and the MindHarp of Sharu*, *Lando Calrissian and the FlameWind of Oseon*, *Lando Calrissian and the StarCave of ThonBoka*, *The WarDove*, without Lando Calrissian, *BrightSuit MacBear*, *Taflak Lysandra*, *Contact and Commune*, *Converse and Conflict*, *Concert and Cosmos*, *The Crystal Empire*, *Henry Martyn*, and *Pallas*, 18 novels — and I've always wanted to do that — 16 of which have found their way into print with publishers like Random House/Del Rey, Berkley/Ace, Avon, Warner Communications, and Tor/St. Martin's Press.

Many of them have been published in Europe.

Pallas is forthcoming this November.

And *Concert and Cosmos* was canceled by its publisher for political incorrectness. (What publisher? That was Warner Communications. For what it's worth, *Pallas*, forthcoming in November, was very nearly canceled for the same reason.)

I have written stories and articles for publications including *Stellar Science Fiction Stories, Alternatives, New Libertarian, Marvel Comics, Guns, Nomos, Laissez Faire, LP News, Colorado Liberty, Reason-Frontlines, APAlogia*, and *The Orange County Register*. And yes, I am an unsung, but ridiculously well-paid, source of gags for cartoonists like "Frank & Ernest"'s Bob Thaves, "Ziggy"'s Tom Wilson, Bunny Host of "The Lockhorns" and *Parade* magazine, Doug Sneyd of *Playboy*, Chon Day of *The New Yorker* ... and our own Rex F. May, better known as "Baloo," of *Liberty, National Review*, and *The Wall Street Journal*.

It's a fact that I'm known primarily as a science fiction writer, and a fact like that is likely to be regarded differently by different people, mostly depending on whether they read SF themselves or not. One thing science fiction writers are known for, justifiably or not, is an ability to predict the future. This ability, if it exists, doesn't rely on tea leaves, Ouija boards, or crystals, but on identifying and extrapolating significant historical, technological, social, political, and economic trends.

Sometimes SF writers do a very bad job. In the '60s, for example, *Star Trek* predicted genetic wars and interstellar travel by 1996 — although it *is* more common for science fiction writers to err on the conservative side. Science fiction writers failed to predict meteor craters on Mars, for example, although in retrospect it should have been obvious that the planet would be lousy with them. While forecasting commuter aviation and the video telephone for decades, neither of which have fully materialized yet, they failed to predict the invention and subsequent cultural importance of the pocket calculator.

Future-predicting is not an SF writer's primary job; accurate prediction may be the *last* thing he really wants. It's clear that *Brave New World* and *1984* represent predictions Aldous Huxley and George Orwell hoped would never come true. They hoped making predictions like that would *prevent* them from coming true. Nevertheless, when they make predictions, and their predictions are on target, science fiction writers can be forgiven if they take pride in what they've done, especially if some *method* was involved, rather than mere random shots in the dark.

In the first story I ever wrote, I predicted the invention of the digital watch. Regrettably, by the time the story sold ... 10 years later ... digital watches were old news.

In my second novel, *The Venus Belt*, I predicted the violent turn recently taken by the "right-to-life" movement.

And in my fourth book, *The Nagasaki Vector*, pursuing a line of reasoning anyone familiar with Ludwig von Mises would recognize, I predicted the collapse of the Soviet Union and the kind of fighting we're seeing now in Yugoslavia, the former Soviet Georgia, and other places. My Random House editor, a conservative "expert" on Soviet affairs, dismissed this prediction at the time as "wishful thinking."

A few years ago, at the height of his public approval as the remote-control hero of "The War to Make the World Safe for Backward Middle Eastern Monarchies" (formerly known as "The War to Reelect the President"), I predicted the electoral defeat of George Bush in an article that eventually found its way, something like my first short story, into *LP News*. I also predicted that his defeat — rather the foolish failure of principle that was the *cause* of his defeat — would place a third party on the political map.

I never imagined for a moment that the third party would not be ours, but that of a miniature Mussolini like Ross Perot.

******

It's possible that you've surmised by now that I'm about to offer you some political advice. And, quite aside from my ability as a soothsayer, in which you should place no great stock because I don't myself, you may be wondering about my political credentials. Well, I've been a Libertarian for 32 years, since 1961, when I was 14 and I committed myself to what I estimated then would be a 75-year struggle to liberate America from the clutches of "mysticism, altruism, and collectivism."

One reason I evolved the strategy I plan to advocate this morning is that gun ownership brought me into the Party. Not the movement — that was Ayn Rand's novels — but watching the legislative steamroller derby that followed the killing of Bobby Kennedy. I saw what was coming and was sickened by the way people allow themselves to be herded by corrupt media and collectivist politicians willing to use *any tragedy*, even the murder of one of their own (or *especially* the murder of one of their own), as a stepping-stone to advancing their agenda. As soon as I heard there was a Libertarian Party, I was in.

Now in 1993 when I am 47 and that 75 years isn't quite halfway over yet, although I get just as discouraged as you do at times, my general view is that considering what's at stake, and the sheer inertia of a society of more than 250 million people — and despite many recent setbacks (which I think represent hysteria on the part of our enemies who *know* that time is running out for them) — we're doing respectably well in all the areas that count. And in fact, my original three-quarter-century estimate may have been a trifle pessimistic.

Although I've held responsible positions internal to the LP at county, state, and national levels, I've run for public office only once, in 1978, for the Colorado House of Representatives. My Republican opponent was running for his seventh term, unopposed by any Democrat, and was Speaker of the House. I issued six press releases and delivered four speeches (or it may have been the other way around, I can never remember), two of them on the radio. I spent $44, $36 of which was for campaign brochures produced by the '78 Colorado Party, which I didn't want and never used. So you could say my effective campaign expenses amounted to $8. (Just think what would've happened if I'd spent $16 ...)

On the basis of advice that we were given at the time by "older wiser heads," I did everything wrong. I never wore a tie (unlike this morning; I'm wearing this to remind you that Rush Limbaugh only *thinks* he's the most dangerous man in America); I wore an old leather sports jacket and my shirt open at the collar. While the rest of that year's repertory company wore nondescript blue suits and mumbled their extemporaneous way through three-minute allotments at the League of Women Voters or the Association of University Women, I gave a humorous *prepared* speech consisting mostly of projected grocery prices in a society unburdened by taxes or economic regulation. I made a calculated habit of putting my *worst foot forward*, always starting with the Libertarian position on guns whenever I was speaking with liberal groups, and with our position on drugs when I was speaking with conservatives.

For those genuinely interested, I'll go into my reasons for having done that, for the method behind the madness, another time. Just now, let me tell you the results:

(1) I was the only candidate that year who made an eyebrow rise, who got a groan, a moan, a boo, a cheer, a hiss, a chuckle, or a belly-laugh, some of them even in the right places, from his audiences;

(2) a Republican running for county commissioner confessed to me that he'd been afraid to utter the words "private property" before I entered the race — he won and only recently retired from many years of uttering them where it really counts;

(3) local officials of both major parties quietly took me aside, asked me to "give up this Libertarian nonsense," and be

their party's candidate next time;

(4) I won 10 times the percentage of the vote ever taken by any Colorado Libertarian in a two-, three-, or 23-way race, a record that stood afterward for many years;

(5) the '78 Colorado Party spent most of those many years inventing alibis to account for my accomplishment without giving up any of the cherished — totally ineffective but cherished — methods that my campaign had discredited;

(6) having conducted my experiment and seen the results dismissed as unesthetic and inconvenient, I never ran for office again, but left the LP for 13 years to pursue more productive things — including writing those 18 novels that, employing exactly the same methods I developed during my '78 electoral campaign, have brought thousands of people into the Libertarian movement.

They call me every week.

They write me.

I hear from them.

******

However, having predicted the invention of the digital watch, anti-abortion violence, the collapse of the Soviet Empire, the defeat of Bush, and the role of a third party in that defeat, I've come back to the LP now because of something I deeply regret having predicted correctly, in *Concert and Cosmos*, the novel that was canceled for political incorrectness. And that is the spectacle of America functioning as a last bastion, not of private capitalism as many of us expected that it might, but of *Marxism*, which, having failed everywhere else, still reigns supreme in American academia, mass media, Congress, and the current administration.

America faces terrible danger and the LP — unprecedented

opportunity. I've offered my credentials here as a writer and political observer, but my best credential is that I know more about the issues I'm about to discuss than anybody else, in or out of the LP, because I have dealt with them longer and in greater detail.

I call your attention now to *three facts* with a potential to alter the course of American, and therefore human, history. The first is that the LP has never won a million votes in a presidential election. Our first presidential candidate John Hospers ran in 1972 and got a few thousand votes. In terms like these, the only terms that count, we have never been a successful party, climbing slowly in our totals, maxing out at around 900,000 in 1980 with the Clark campaign, which had no less than five million bucks to throw around, and doing progressively less well ever since.

There are reasons for this.

Rather than creating its own unique style and structure consistent with the content of its ideas, the LP tried to imitate others and strove for some vague appearance of respectability.

This was a mistake.

The LP failed to differentiate itself from conservative Republicans — except by imitating liberal Democrats in the Clark campaign.

This was another mistake.

And the LP never decided who its customers are — and that was the worst mistake of all.

It is wrong, it is infantile, to petulantly shake our little fists at the two-party system or the networks or their current beneficiaries and blame them for our failures. In 1992 Ross Perot proved once again, as Norman Thomas and half a dozen others did before him, that a third party can indeed alter the course of American, and therefore human, history without electing anyone to office, simply through a fear on the part of the established parties that somebody from a third party might actually get elected. This phenomenon, Comrade Libertarians, is called "competition," and we're supposed to be the experts on it.

It's true that Perot had a couple of things going for him — like three and a half gigabucks and the "general unfocused anger of the populace," as Ted Koppel puts it. His disadvantages were: All the money in the world won't buy you *content*; and he didn't dare try to *focus* that anger (he doesn't dare today), because the instant he does he will lose supporters at one end of the conventional spectrum or the other. In short (nothing personal, Ross), he can't make policy because he can't afford to differentiate himself along any lines other than his own shriveled little personality.

On the other hand, differentiation will be *our* salvation and stock-in-trade. In the future, we will present ourselves, as we are uniquely entitled to do, not just as the purveyors of the wildest political ideas around (as true as that is, and as much as it may appeal to us on occasion), nor as respectably empty clones in sincere blue suits, but as the *only legitimate heirs to the Founding Fathers*.

The first step to achieving that kind of differentiation is "preaching to the choir" (as my wife points out, they're the only ones who show up in church reliably), gathering every precious sorely needed individual who already agrees with us. We haven't ever tried to do that. Instead, we have sent out mixed signals, alienating real individualists with one unprincipled ill-advised attempt after another to court uncertain allies at both ends of the spectrum, trying to please too wide an audience, too many people at a time. The result is our increasingly poor showing at the polls, and a feeling that whatever votes we do get may have no more meaning than chimpanzees pulling our lever at random.

The next step is to decide who our customers really are —

or who our real customers are. And what that amounts to is selecting an ideologically amenable group that suffers more from government excesses than any other (or is about to), suffers less from any illusion that a major party will help them, and has nothing to lose by switching to a third party — to us — and, within principle, to go after them with all our heart and all our soul and all our might.

Which brings us to the *second fact* with a potential to alter the course of American, and therefore human, history: The Republican Party has been trying, at least since 1988, to "broaden its appeal" by "moving toward the center," a process that consists of dumping traditional constituencies that Republican leadership perceives as "marginal" in terms of social acceptability or political correctness. Foremost among those marginal constituencies are gun owners.

Consider the following ...

Sarah and Jim Brady, those mavens of victim disarmament (and by the way, don't say "gun control" any more, say "victim disarmament") — Sarah and Jim are *Republicans*.

Sarah still calls herself a "conservative."

John Chaffee, the senator from Rhode Island who introduced a bill last year to confiscate every pistol and revolver in the United States of America, is a *Republican*.

George F. Will, columnist, theorist, and *Republican*, demanded repeal of the Second Amendment months before Michael Gartner, the "ultraliberal former president of NBC news." Please remember that, the next time you see an NRA commercial.

William Bennett, former *Republican* Secretary of Education & Drug Czar (pardon me, that's "*War* on Drugs Czar") calls for banning "assault weapons" — and I guess this is the place to tell you, if you don't know, that these "assault weapons" bills are invariably written to include the .25 automatic in your mom's purse, the .45 your dad brought home from Korea, the .22 rifle you learned to shoot with, and the shotgun over your mantelpiece. But their real goal is to outlaw that precise class of weapons most useful in controlling government.

Pete Wilson, *Republican* governor of California, cheerfully allowed that state's Roberti-Roos "assault weapon" law to pass when he could have vetoed it — and he's by no means any worse than his predecessor, *Republican* George Dukmejian.

Speaking of Republican Georges, *Republican* George Bush began his first campaign whimpering about small revolvers, and later betrayed the Second Amendment with an edict against imported "assault weapons." It should never be forgotten that the Waco massacre was *rehearsed* during *Republican* George's administration.

Republicans of the New Jersey Senate refused to repeal that state's ban on semiautomatic "assault weapons." *Republicans* of the U.S. Senate Judiciary Committee and later the entire U.S. Senate approved the appointment of *Jackboot Janet* Reno despite her publicly stated wish to confiscate every private weapon in America.

William F. Buckley, *Republican* novelist, syndicated columnist, host of "Firing Line," and editor of *National Review*, is said to have endorsed the Brady Bill.

Jack Kemp, the Great White Hope of *Republican* conservatism demanded, on a recent CBS "Face the Nation," a universal ban on semiautomatic "assault weapons."

And even Rush Limbaugh, "the most *Republican* man in America," although he pays occasional lip service to the Second Amendment, is good friends with Jack Kemp and an outright toady to Bill Bennett. Rush was a towering mountain of *Jello* all through the Waco siege.

Those examples are just off the top of my head and careful research will expose many more. But to get this picture hanging straight on the wall, Comrade Libertarians, during the time when the dump-the-marginals strategy was being cooked up, *Republican* Chairman Lee Atwater, who is, I'm happy to report, finally a *good* politician, stated that Republicans could afford to ignore gun people, who would vote Republican no matter what, because where else were they gonna go?

I propose to hold a seance and tell him!

The *third fact* with a potential to alter the course of American, and therefore human, history is this: As a direct result of the Republicans' feeble-minded self-destructive "strategy" of moving to the center by dumping marginal constituencies, Republican George *lost* in 1992 by a number of votes smaller than that of the "marginal" number of single-issue gun-owners. Let me repeat that — it doesn't seem to have ... I seem to have phrased it wrong: The number of single-issue gun voters is *greater* than the number of votes George Bush lost by.

******

Okay, to recapitulate:

● Libertarians have never won a million votes;

● Republicans are dumping voters they consider unfashionable;

● Republican George lost the election by fewer votes than the number he dumped.

The next question is, what can we do with these facts?

Can we use them in some way to change the course of American, and therefore human, history?

There are 65 million gun people in America. Twenty million of them report that they have occasional political feelings on the subject. Five million of them are single-issue voters. Only half of them are represented by the National Rifle Association, owing to hideous blunders and failures of courage on its part, which make the LP's blunders and failures resemble tactical genius.

Let me give you an example, okay? They needed desperately to get the word out — they wanted new members and so forth. At enormous expense, they got themselves an uplink, got themselves a satellite channel — and *encrypted* it.

Gun people are an angry desperate folk to whom we can appeal without any loss of integrity as long as we make it clear — and I always do — that the price of our support is the practice on their part of tolerance for those they despise. We can get between five and twenty million votes in the next general election simply by *asking* for them. But until now, we have not asked in the right way.

Which is where *differentiation* comes in.

In 1996, the LP can make as influential a showing as Perot did in 1992 if we keep our heads, remember who our real customers are, stick to our guns — and theirs — whether it's fashionable or not, and *differentiate* ourselves. We can't afford to compromise on even the slightest detail. A willingness to accept anything less than total victory *generates* the very self-destructive psychology from which Republicans and the NRA chronically suffer and which, I might add, got us into this mess in the first place. A Libertarian refusal to sell our principles out is the one thing — *the one and* only *thing* — that differentiates us from all the others in this arena. It is the reason, in the end, that gun people will come to trust us when others have proven untrustworthy.

The case against Democrats is self-evident; no effort is required to differentiate ourselves here. The hard work is differentiating ourselves from Republicans, and what we're up against is a long-held reputation they have — which they fail increasingly to deserve — for legislative friendliness to gun people. And there is the more serious matter of the NRA's slavish attitude toward Republicans and its suicidal unwillingness to make endorsements on any rational basis whatsoever.

What we have to fight with, in addition to our unique determination to operate strictly from principle, is (A) increasing liberal pressure on gun people, (B) widespread angry disappointment with the NRA among its own membership, and (C) that growing list of Republican betrayals (the morons hand us more ammunition every day) that offer the makings of countless inexpensive advertisements — in *Guns & Ammo, Women & Guns, The American Rifleman,* and so forth — advertisements that will yield five to twenty million votes, *if they're done correctly.*

******

Long ago at an LP regional conference, held in this city I think, I heard Ralph Raico give a talk that touched on the differences between Libertarians, liberals, and conservatives. Ralph asked us to imagine an archetypal "little old man in a raincoat," whose only human contact and pleasure in life is a dirty movie, a dirty magazine, an occasional moment with a prostitute. Ralph pointed out that a conservative's first instinctive reaction to this kind of abject misery is a desire to *add* to it, to take even those meager pleasures away, because, in the innermost recesses of their souls (and this is what differentiates *them* from Libertarians), conservatives are *mean.*

Now, if you call yourself a conservative and you *don't* feel this way, it's likely that you've misidentified yourself somewhere along the line or are in imminent danger of becoming one of *us.* If you believe that Ralph was wrong, just think about Pat Buchanan, or better yet, read his autobiography: Conservatives are ever on the lookout for new people to hurt and new excuses for hurting them. Nothing tickles them more than hearing that somebody's just been gassed or fried up at the Big House. I report this without rancor, as a fact of reality that we have, for better or worse, to deal with (I mean that sort of generically). In fact, it's this basic meanness that, projected onto others, gives rise to many of their uniquely conservative policies. (I've often said that conservatives tend to think all individuals are just a little bit *evil*, whereas liberals tend to think all individuals are just a little bit *stupid*. Guess it's a matter of projection on the part of the liberals, too — but I digress.)

There is a sci-fi cliche (and "sci-fi," by the way, is not the same thing as "SF"), splendidly beaten to death by Don Adams of *Get Smart*, that goes to the effect: "If only he'd used his genius for good, instead of evil." My plan, Comrade Libertarians, is to use conservative *meanness* for good instead of evil.

Here it comes, I think:

I used to believe the LP was in such bad shape because, having failed to hurt our enemies, it was only human to turn and hurt each other. Unlike other parties, Libertarians were, theoretically, less interested in gaining power, either personal or collective, than in achieving certain results. Unfortunately, these results always tended to be couched in excessively abstract terms, such as "creating a free society," and were therefore rather difficult to pursue, let alone achieve. It's very well to argue over doctrinal details; I've done it myself and I won't apologize. It made us the unique entity we are, the Party of Principle. It's well to say that we want a free society, but it's too general.

Whereas it's bad to focus on elections for their own sake until you're willing to lie, cheat, or steal to get votes. That tendency, along with the endless factional backbiting and nitpicking that occur whenever small-minded people struggle over minuscule amounts of power, was the reason I got out of the party 13 years ago, and, as you can see from its obvious lack of results, it didn't work anyway.

And that was only one of my *lesser* objections to it.

Now, I think that the problem all along might simply have been *lack of an achievable mission.* I also believe that our enemies have finally handed us one that will put us on the map in an unprecedented way, while making life a little more livable for each of us, every day, from now on. It's something that almost all of us can agree to and it'll give most of us something useful to do, which will minimize the internecine gouging that has all but destroyed us.

This is where "using meanness for good instead of evil" comes in. Remember how conservatives are always looking for new people to hurt and new excuses to hurt them? Well, let's *give* them somebody to hurt. From now on, don't just say the LP will do this or the LP will do that. Why should anybody listen to that? Why should they believe us? People *do* listen to questions, however, and they *will* believe the answers they supply for themselves. So whenever you get a chance — or better yet, whenever you *make* one — it might be well to begin something like this:

"Will the *Republicans* promise to veto all future victim-disarmament legislation?"

Sort of a standard, predictable, opening gambit.

Then how about: "Will the *Republicans* promise to repeal, nullify, or otherwise dispose of [I like that phrase, "otherwise dispose of"] every victim disarmament law — not one of which is constitutional — presently on the books?

"Will the *Republicans* promise to decriminalize the act of self-defense, so that it no longer costs, on average, your entire life savings to defend yourself from the state, once you've successfully defended yourself from a freelance criminal?

"Will the *Republicans* promise to arrest any senator, congressman, state legislator, county commissioner, or city councilman who introduces, sponsors, or votes for victim-disarmament legislation, and throw him in jail where he belongs?

"Will the *Republicans* promise to do the same with sheriffs, chiefs of police, mayors, governors, and *presidents* who enforce these unconstitutional laws?"

And at last, now you can ask: "Then why the hell are you still voting for *Republicans*? And why are you still waiting for the NRA to help, when the Libertarian Party, with its perfectly unbroken record of uncompromising commitment to the Second Amendment, can do more than merely *promise* — if you'll simply give us the *power* to do all of these things, by giving us your *vote*?"

And now you can say: "The Libertarian Party is grimly determined to put Jackboot Janet Reno, Howard Metzenbaum, and every one of their gun-grabbing criminal co-conspirators behind bars where they belong — if not today, then tomorrow, if not tomorrow, then next year, and if not next year, then five years from now, or ten years from now, or twenty — because if it's good enough for Simon Wiesenthal, it's good enough for us.

"There can be no statute of limitations on crimes against the Bill of Rights!"

But wait, there's more:

"If Metzenbaum should have the bad manners to croak before we can get to him, then we'll dig him up, wherever he may be, and replant him in a prison graveyard. And once we're done with Howie, and with repealing, nullifying, or otherwise disposing of every victim-disarmament law in America, we'll go on to Canada, to Japan, and to England and take *their* victim-disarmament laws away from them, because we're sick and tired of being beaten over the head with them — and because we have friends in Canada, Japan, and England who have rights."

Now, does that sound mean enough for you, Comrade Libertarians? Think we can get a few million single-issue voters to go for it? Think something like that may just alter the course of American, and therefore human, history? And isn't it better than getting only 900,000 votes?

Or 400,000?

Or 200,000?

And the broader result?

Well, to begin with, it shouldn't be too awkward to widen our agenda from uncompromising enforcement of the Second Amendment to equally uncompromising enforcement of all the rest. To put it another way, let me suggest that, quote, "Putting the civility back into civilization through the most stringent enforcement possible of the highest law of the land, the Bill of Rights," unquote, is better delineated, more achievable, and of more suitably limited scope than anything we've ever tried before.

I repeat: "*Putting the civility back into civilization through the most stringent enforcement possible of the highest law of the land, the Bill of Rights.*"

It also *recreates* the LP as the hard-headed no-nonsense party of Law and Order.

Or, we could just say: "Stringent enforcement of the Bill of Rights."

Or, we could say, as often and as publicly as we can: "*Bill of Rights enforcement.*"

(You can almost hear Jack Webb say that.)

"*Bill of Rights enforcement.*"

From now on, whenever I'm asked, "Bill of Rights enforcement" is *the* mission statement of the Libertarian Party. Since the Bill of Rights defines American political life, and is the centerpiece of our common heritage (it is, after all, the only thing that keeps us from being the world's largest banana republic), this simple mission is much likelier to be shared by other voters and clearly understood — even by the mass media — than anything we've ever offered before.

Bill of Rights enforcement.

Norman Thomas never got elected to anything, dear Comrade Libertarians, but the Democrats, mortally afraid that he would, adopted more and more of his platform until he didn't have to. We Libertarians can *force* the Republicans and the NRA to begin co-opting *our* platform, too. And I, for one, would be perfectly happy if that happened, because all I want out of this is a free society!

In the end we can expect one of two outcomes: first, a coup like Norman Thomas pulled off, the Republicans forced to straighten up and fly right — in effect *becoming* the LP the same way the Democrats had to *become* the Socialist Party — or second (and I suppose we could all regard this as the worst case), Libertarians becoming a political power in their own right, and more importantly, *on their own terms*, beginning with a paltry few million votes that the Republicans were planning to throw away, anyway.

******

Non-Libertarians always complain that we never explain (and probably have no concept of) how to get "there" from "here."

Well, I'll *tell* you how to get there from here.

Hell, I've been telling you for the last 15 years.

Never let a local gun show go by (hundreds are listed every weekend in the *Shotgun News*) without a table offering Libertarian literature and conversation.

Never let a local gun shop go without a friendly monthly visit, and lots of literature.

Never let a demand for more victim disarmament go unanswered on radio, TV, or in the newspaper.

Never let your answers be compromising or timid.

Always offer more (and for those of you who're taking notes, this is the part you're supposed to write down), always offer more, within principle, than the competition can bring itself to offer. You will note, here, that I have just redefined the word "radical": Always offer more, within principle, than the competition can bring itself to offer. When the NRA offers so-called automatic concealed-carry permits — which are a big thing right now — Libertarians must offer "Vermont Carry": no concealed carry law of any kind, whatever.

Stop being a hypocrite.

Stop thinking about it.

Stop talking about it.

If you don't already have one, it's time to get a gun and learn to shoot.

NOW!

And then teach somebody else. For preference, somebody in academia or the media. In and of themselves (and there's no way for a non-gun-owner to know this, but it's like sex, or having a baby, or something like that) gun use and gun ownership are astonishingly contagious and persuasive — in and of themselves — and far more effective than any hundred campaigns or candidates.

Above all, if for some reason you can't do any of these things, *for the love of liberty, don't deprive those of us who* can *of the tools we need to do the job!*

If I were an undercover federal agent — or being paid by the Republican National Committee — I couldn't think of a more agreeably suicidal notion to urge on Libertarians than to eliminate the Non-Aggression Pledge and water down the platform. If we tolerate this bastardization of our principles, we will lose the differentiation that is our only real political asset, and destroy the time-proven method for reaching prospective voters that works best on conservatives: reminding them (A) "There ain't no such thing as a free lunch," an idea they already endorse, (B) that even liberty isn't free, then adding, (C) that the cost this time isn't monetary, but ethical; if gun people wish to preserve their Second Amendment rights, they must, in return, tolerate and defend the rights that other people (such as gays or recreational drug users) cherish.

This point cannot be overemphasized: Gun people have suffered enough at the hands of pabulum-peddling politicos to recognize disingenuous "marketing" tactics the instant they smell them. Gun people will not buy anything any "Committee for a Libertarian Majority" has to sell. The only way to convince them that the LP is for real is to have the guts to tell them things they don't want to hear — in the same breath they're told they never have to worry about losing their guns again.

The *Real* Libertarian Party (think about it: "The *Real* Ghostbusters," "The *Real* Libertarian Party") is intellectually and ethically *tough* on its prospective members, in order to win their respect. *To mean something, it must cost something to join us.* Libertarians from a liberal background seem incapable of grasping this, and one-time conservatives fail inexplicably to apply the methods and standards to hypothetical others that attracted them to the LP in the first place.

Think about it. Did you join the party because you were told what you wanted to hear — or what you needed to know? If we proceed with the foam-rubber agenda being pushed on us by these Nerf Libertarians — these low-fat, low-sugar, low-sodium, low-cholesterol Libertarians and their flavor-free, substance-free, courage-free, intelligence-free notions — we will forever remain the merest shadow of the other two parties, tiny and insignificant, just as we are today.

What the hell ever happened to "Take big bites," as Lazarus Long advised us, and, "Anything worth doing is worth overdoing"?

Who are these people, anyway?

If they proclaim to the micromultitudes that Libertarians don't really oppose all taxes (because, oh dear, that would be *soooo* immoderate) and I say in an article read by half a million people that we oppose all taxation on *principle*, what are they gonna do?

If they eliminate the Non-Aggression pledge, leaving *someone else* to issue conspicuous enameled pins that will create two classes of Libertarian — those who can be trusted by the public and those who cannot — what are they gonna do?

If they dilute the platform, leaving *someone else* to distribute an even more radical model platform that will attract more real individualists than they can ever equal by trying to fool tree-hugging ecofascists into believing that their ideas are in any way compatible with ours, what the hell are they gonna do?

I'll tell you. They're gonna slink back to the so-called major party where they belong and where they feel more comfortable. Don't worry, they'll be back on our bandwagon next year, or in five years, telling everyone who'll listen that this "radical integrity thing" was their idea all along. In the meantime, we can use all the freedom-loving almost-Libertarians we can get among the Republicans. They may, in fact, prove crucial in our overall long-term strategy.

******

In summary, then (and I'm sure we're all greatly relieved to hear those words): my 32-years' experience inform me that the best way, probably the only way, for our tiny insignificant party ever to see its principles applied in the real world within our lifetime is to *differentiate* ourselves from all others by taking up the *unpopular* cause of a *persecuted* people, promising not just to *end* the persecution, but to *punish* and *humiliate* the persecutors promptly and energetically — in the process, forcing an established party to adopt *our* goals or levering *ourselves* to power. As our snowball begins to grow, even the media, those craven poltroons, will shift, with the help of a growing number of young Libertarians among them, and the era of Libertarianism will have finally begun.

That's what I mean by "Lever Action" — starting with nothing but our ideas, to become the dominant institution of the 21st century. As a lever must be rigid and a fulcrum solid, so the integrity of our ideas — the lever — and our pledge — the fulcrum — must be unbending and immovable.

It took me decades of self-defense consulting to realize that it isn't the power of a weapon that counts so much as the will to use it. A .22 in the hands of a grimly determined 98-pound woman is more effective than a .44 in the hands of an irresolute man.

The same is true of a political party.

Republican George had the most powerful political party in the world and look where it got him.

We have the least powerful, but it can be anything we have the will to make it.

The 21st century can be anything we have the will to make it.

And so can we, Comrade Libertarians, be anything we have the will to become.

Thank you.

Hillary Behind Bars

Presented to the Colorado Libertarian Party State Convention
April 29 - May 1, 1994

☙ ☙ ☙ ☙ ☙

All of us remember, if we're old enough, or if we watch Nickelodeon on a regular basis, a young TV situation comedy character, already dishonest and cynical at an early age, who would lie, cheat, steal, or suck up disgustingly to the principal character's mother and father — "What a lovely dress you're wearing, Mrs. Cleaver!" — in order to get whatever it was he wanted.

Now we all know that the actor who *played* that character grew up and became something else — a California highway patrolman, someone told me — but the character, Eddie Haskell, grew up and became Bill Clinton. Which is how we find ourselves living in a "Haskellocracy" and the reason we need to find our way back out again.

My purpose this evening is to suggest how we're going to do that.

Ladies and gentlemen, in September of last year, when I delivered what I sometimes refer to as my "default keynote address" to the Libertarian Party National Convention in Salt Lake City, Utah, I tried to make my remarks the distilled essence of thirty-two years of careful thought and hard experience in the movement.

What I said then, in the light of what had happened just that summer, thanks to that cigar-smoking old maid on PCP, Janet Reno, in Waco, Texas, was that for the foreseeable future, the Libertarian Party could do worse — much worse — given the direction of events and the temper of the times, than to emphasize political issues related to the Second Amendment — to the individual right to own and carry weapons — even at the expense of all other issues combined.

I pointed out that another well-known old maid, George Bush, had lost the 1992 election — exactly as I had predicted he would at the very height of his Gulf War popularity — by a number of votes smaller than the number of single-issue Second Amendment voters he and his party had chosen to betray on several occasions. I proposed that we Libertarians pursue those single-issue voters aggressively, by the relatively simple expedient of embracing a sufficiently principled and progressive Second Amendment position, and do with them *to* the Republicans what Socialist Norman Thomas did to the Democrats in 1928: Scare them into co-opting our position and maybe even some of our principles.

Without delivering the same speech here, I then defined "a sufficiently principled and progressive Second Amendment position" by proclaiming that we Libertarians should: (A) "outbid" the Republican Party, which is in the process of crumpling the Second Amendment up and pitching it in the dumpster of history, along with the rest of the Bill of Rights; and (B) "outbid" the National Rifle Association, whose principal distinguishing characteristic, since 1934, has been a palpitatingly spineless compulsion to surrender in the face of enemies like Diane Feinstein, Janet Reno, Hillary Clinton — or even Shirley Temple.

I said we can accomplish this by promising single-issue voters *not* just to resist all proposed and pending gun-control legislation — which I referred to as "victim-disarmament" laws — *not* just to repeal or nullify every one of the twenty-thousand victim-disarmament laws already on the nation's books at every level of government, *but* by promising to arrest, indict, try, convict, and imprison every city councilman, every county commissioner, every state legislator, every congressman, and every senator — past or present — who ever helped to write those victim-disarmament laws into those books, along with every police chief, every sheriff, every governor, and yes, every president — not to mention first ladies and attorneys general — who ever enforced them.

Most of us have understood for a long time that by denying individuals' unencumbered exercise of their inherent human right to own and carry weapons, people like Hillary and Janet are morally responsible for atrocities like the Long Island Railway shootings. Now we'll hold them *legally* responsible, as well. Never forget that we are the good guys, we of the American productive class, and they, the parasitic politicians and bureaucrats, Hillary and Janet, are the bad guys. They are the criminals. It is against the law — the highest law of the land — to enact or enforce statutes or ordinances mandating victim disarmament, or for that matter any other breach of the Constitution.

Along the way I observed that this tactic, offering to jail politicians, will work because those it addresses most directly tend to place punishing their enemies ahead of anything else they might achieve through the political process, and that in this instance, we could go along with that, and remain solidly within principle.

But for us, I concluded, we Libertarians who are "higher-minded" and *not* so vindictive, having acquired the support of those single-issue voters, could go on to generalize the tactic into an overall strategy both principled and pragmatic. The Bill of Rights, I reminded my audience, is a *law* — the highest law of the land — and it needs to be *enforced*. For the foreseeable future then, "Bill of Rights *Enforcement*" should become the *Mission Statement* of the Libertarian Party.

Now there's a *trick* here that knowledgeable Libertarians should be onto already: If you look at the Tenth Amendment to the Constitution, which reads, "The powers not delegated to the *United* States by the Constitution, nor prohibited by it to the States, are reserved to the States respectively, or to the people," or if you look at the Ninth Amendment, which reads, "The enumeration in the Constitution, of certain rights, shall not be construed to deny or disparage others retained by the people," you'll discover at least three fascinating things.

First, that even the Federalists, the very *worst* of the Founding Fathers from a standpoint of decentralized authority and individual freedom — even Alexander Hamilton and John Jay and James Madison, the villains of my books — were rabid Libertarians, compared to any political point of view today except our own.

I said "*at least* three fascinating things," because these Amendments also demonstrate (parenthetically in the present context) that the gentlemen Federalists and their colleagues and contemporaries understood what very few, including Supreme Court nominees, appear to understand today: that the document, the Constitution, is *not* the source of rights — they would have sneered at an idiot notion like that — but merely an acknowledgement of them for political purposes.

These Amendments are also all the evidence anyone needs that the Framers clearly understood the essentially *negative* character of political rights — "Ask not what your country can do for you, ask in what ways it's going to leave you the hell alone" — although I've often wished they'd been savvy or prescient enough to drive that point home by calling the first ten Amendments the "Bill of Limitations" (on government power) rather than the "Bill of Rights."

Second, to return to my original line of argument, that the unmistakable character of the *worst* of the Founding Fathers, Hamilton, Jay, and Madison, demonstrates that it is we Libertarians — not liberals and not conservatives — who are the only legitimate heirs to the intellectual and political legacy they established.

And third, that if these two Amendments alone, the Ninth and the Tenth, are stringently and energetically enforced, we will *have* the Libertarian society that we've all been working toward for so long, and that anything else we hope to accomplish along those lines will amount to little more than "fine tuning."

"For the foreseeable future, 'Bill of Rights *Enforcement*' should become the *Mission Statement* of the Libertarian Party." Let me tell you, *that* turned out to be a message more powerful than the medium that carried it. Before I knew it, at least partly as a result of my speech in Salt Lake City, I was being asked to talk everywhere. Publications of both a Libertarian and non-Libertarian character wanted me to write for them. My latest novel *Pallas* was selling better than anything I'd ever written. Four of my earlier works were suddenly about to be reprinted. My publisher and largest bookseller were purchasing radio spots to promote my work. In fact, I was offered my own radio show.

And I was asked again and again, by an astonishingly wide variety of individuals, not *if* but *when* I was going to run for a particular political office.

There are even those who claim — among them, a freelance columnist now working on a story about it for the *Wall Street Journal* — that my speech has already changed the course of history, since the delegates and leaders of one state Libertarian Party who heard it went home and initiated a referendum on concealed-weapons carry that was promptly co-opted into law by Republicans in the legislature.

Now, while all of this good stuff was going on, I was beginning to worry just a little bit. Here I'd spent the last fifteen years trying to motivate people, both Libertarian and non-Libertarian alike, to create a Libertarian society, and the appropriate method, I'd always believed, was what Ayn Rand called "concretization": persuading people, Libertarian and non-Libertarian alike, to envision that Libertarian society as vividly and in as much detail as possible. That technique had worked quite well in my 1978 campaign for the state house of representatives. The same technique had made my first novel, *The Probability Broach*, a "cult classic" among Libertarians and their fellow travelers, and that, in turn, had brought thousands of individuals into the Libertarian movement.

My problem was that the prospect of a political party willing to punish and humiliate their enemies was not only motivating conservatives in a new way — that, after all, was the whole reason I'd thought the idea up in the first place — but its effect on my "higher-minded" fellow Libertarians appeared to be an entire order of magnitude greater than anything I'd ever tried on them before.

I had a long talk with a friend of mine, that member of our movement who has risen higher in the newspaper business than any other individual. I asked him, are we Libertarians really as *mean*, deep down inside, as conservatives? In a movement already full of anarcho-hyphen-this and minarcho-hypen-that, had I created a *new* hyphenation: fascisto-hyphen-libertarianism? The sonofabitch *laughed* at me.

Then I recalled the light of new hope I'd seen dawning in the eyes of my comrades when I talked with them about jailing politicians and bureaucrats who abuse the Bill of Rights, and I recalled the tone of voice they used when they talked with me, and I knew they weren't such a bad lot, after all. They were responding the same way people had when Jack Kennedy said we were going to the Moon. They weren't moved as much by the thing itself as by what it implied; they didn't care much about the Moon, but they had a good idea what being able to reach it meant, for the American economy, for American technology, for American morale.

Let's take a few moments to examine *exactly* what my proposed new strategy means. ...

Ladies and gentlemen, we are living today in a period of what I call *"deplorably solved problems."* Poverty and unemployment are a "deplorably solved problem": All that's required is to eliminate the taxes and regulations with which government burdens America's productive machinery and within an amazingly short time everyone in the country will be wealthy by today's standards. The trouble is that politicians like Hillary don't want the problem solved, because that would leave them without anyone to "help," and bureaucrats like Janet don't like the solution, because it leaves them without a job.

Likewise, drugs are a "deplorably solved problem": All that's required is to repeal the unconscionable and unconstitutional laws that turn a nickel's worth of plant squeezings into a hundred dollars' worth of anti-music, crack babies, turf wars, and devastated inner cities. The trouble is that precisely the same artificially multiplied profits that feed the street gangs and the overseas drug lords also fund the drug czars and whole branches of government, and, as with poverty, none of those who profit from it want to see the problem solved.

So we come at last to violent crime, which is another "deplorably solved problem." The theory of an armed society that I expressed seventeen years ago in my first novel is no longer merely a theory: In Florida, where violent crime has plummeted forty percent since it became easy to carry a concealed weapon, and in Vermont, which was recently declared the safest state to live in because it was always easy to carry a concealed weapon, the theory of an armed society has been experimentally scientifically proven beyond the palest shadow of a doubt.

Violent crime is a solved problem: The solution is Bill of

Rights enforcement.

I recall a time, back in the '60s, when politicians would crow and strut and struggle to claim credit for a statistically meaningless fluctuation in the crime rate of only four percent. To them, to almost anybody living at the time, an unmistakable drop of forty percent would have appeared impossibly Utopian. Yet today, when America has seen it happen (and more to the point, has seen what *caused* it to happen), what it all means to politicians like Hillary and bureaucrats like Janet is not the arrival of the Millennium, but an unmitigated catastrophe: evidence that their crowing doesn't make the sun rise; and the threat of a proportional reduction in their *budgets* of forty percent.

Violent crime is a solved problem: The solution is Bill of Rights enforcement.

And increasingly, it's clear that rather than learning something useful from what's happening around them, rather than learning to live with crime as a solved problem and going on from there, politicians and bureaucrats are willing to enlist the aid of the hopelessly putrescently corrupt mass media to lie and distort the truth in order to deprive Americans of yet another peace dividend.

Violent crime is a solved problem: The solution is Bill of Rights enforcement.

Don't talk to me — don't let anyone talk to you — about "vigilantism"; what America has *now* is vigilantism. What it has now is the Ku Klux Kops: dimwitted thugs in obsessive black nylon, running around inflicting one perverted brutality after another on innocent people at the behest of senile transvestites in long dresses — what my wife calls "the Grand Dragons of the Supreme Court." By contrast, what we Libertarians advocate is Law and Order: abject government compliance with the Bill of Rights — the highest law of the land — decent productive men and women of the Constitutional community joyfully taking up the burden of their own physical security, along with that of their children.

Violent crime is a solved problem: The solution is Bill of Rights enforcement.

We *know* the solution to violent crime, and the only thing that keeps that solution from going to work right here, right now, for each and every one of us, is Republican Senator Hank Brown, and those like him, who have apparently discarded whatever it was they once believed in. There are no words in the English language adequate to express the contempt that all decent individuals must feel toward those like Senator Brown, who would rather go on seeing people die in the streets than to relinquish the control he fondly imagines he has over their lives.

Violent crime is a solved problem: The solution is Bill of Rights enforcement.

The first ten Amendments to the Constitution are the exclusive property of the American people they were written to protect; *not* of the mass media, the so-called "fourth branch of government," who believe there's only one Amendment, the First, and that it only applies to them, *not* of the executive branch, *not* of the legislative branch, certainly *not* of the judicial branch of the very institution that they were written to protect the American people *from*.

The Supreme Court has been a particularly wretched custodian of the Bill of Rights, because of the inherent conflict of interest involved in their unconstitutional monopoly on the interpretation of it, and the fact that they haven't got a clue, and never had, regarding what the Bill of Rights is all about.

Twenty years ago, the Libertarian Party national platform committees of which I was a member called for outright abolition of the Federal Bureau of Investigation and the Central Intelligence Agency, on the grounds, among other things, that the Framers of the Constitution never intended America to have a national police force. Naturally, the few outside the party who paid attention to that particular plank thought we Libertarians were crazy, but as usual, they were wrong and we were right. It is now time, in the light of the murders at Ruby Ridge and Waco, for the Libertarian Party to lead other political parties in calling for — in demanding — the disarming of all federal agencies. This time, the public will listen, and from now on, if there's something these agencies want that can be obtained by the legitimate application of force, let them consult local law enforcement. If that had been the case last summer, all those people — men, women, and little children — would be alive today.

The one and only thing left that can save the American republic from the Democratic Party — which is the polite euphemism we customarily employ when we really mean "the socialists" — is the Libertarian Party. Likewise, the Libertarian Party is the only thing that can save the American republic from Republicans — which, increasingly, is a euphemism we employ when we really mean "fascists."

Case in point: Denver radio host and columnist Ken Hamblin pleads with his listeners not to let the issue of gun ownership and self-defense become the "property" of Libertarians, because the Libertarian Party will never amount to anything, since none of its candidates has ever gotten more than five percent, and in any case, Libertarians are all nut cases who refuse to stop at stop signs.

The reason Hamblin gives for his assessment of our collective sanity — that we oppose child labor laws — betrays not only an embarrassing ignorance on his part of economics and history and an astonishing inability to jettison the left-wing baggage he arrived on the pro-freedom scene with so recently, but that he has rendered himself, quite as deliberately as any "egg-sucking dog liberal" or darktown gang-banger, incapable of further learning in this area, because the facts would only disrupt his low-resolution picture of the world.

My guess is that Hamblin has been commiserating with his Republican pals in the legislature, whimpering about the pressure Libertarians are putting on them to do the right thing, in the right way, about gun ownership and self-defense. Of course, that's our job, as a third party out of power, and from his injured tone, it appears that we're succeeding at it. In the long run, if the Republicans continue to fail to perform, they'll be out and Libertarians will be in — but never mind all that. I also suspect that his recent very unbecoming hysteria over the Second Amendment rally on the Capitol steps was really about four hundred dollars he had demanded to speak for a few minutes, which the Libertarian rally organizers politely — and wisely — forbore to pay him.

If Hamblin would occasionally stop talking and *listen* for a change — neither of which seems to be in his job description or his character — he would learn that the issues of gun ownership and self-defense have never belonged to anybody *but* Libertarians, who kept it alive all by themselves for more than twenty years (starting when only nut cases were interested in it, long before trendy neo-conservatives like Hamblin decided to stick a delicate toe in), while time after time, the NRA dullwittedly fumbled the ball and the Republicans treacherously sold us out. When I started my first novel, back in 1977, I was the only writer on the entire planet — aside from one other self-designated Libertarian, Robert A. Heinlein — to advocate a universally armed populace.

But Hamblin won't listen; he'd rather suck up to the boys in blue and to Republican politicians, overlooking the fact that, if Martin Luther King had followed his advice in the 1950s — to avoid an independent effort, stick with major parties, champion only "respectable" notions regardless of the truth — there would still be two sets of public bathrooms and drinking fountains everywhere.

Hamblin has come about as far, intellectually, as anyone can reasonably expect a human being to travel in a single lifetime. To give him his due, he managed the great leap from liberalism to neo-conservativism, but by his own admission, he's an "old guy" and he doesn't appear to have another leap, great or otherwise, left in him. In many respects he remains a liberal and still "thinks" with some internal organ other than his brain. Like Rush Limbaugh, if he used both halves of his brain he'd be a Libertarian by now, and he knows it, and it hurts.

To David Segal, who organized the rally that so deeply offended Hamblin and his sensitive listeners, I say that the only thing more satisfying than being praised for your success is being denounced for it; you may be uncertain as to the sincerity of the former, but never of the latter. Robert LeFevre used to say that what we have in this country is a choice between left-wing socialists and right-wing socialists. More and more today it appears that Bob was wrong. What we have is a choice between right-wing and left-wing *fascists*.

My advice to Dave and to other Colorado Libertarians is that we waste not another moment on Ken Hamblin. He's just another fascist, right-wing or left-wing, whose *punitarian* answer to everything is to put more people in jail. He's no black Rush Limbaugh as he claims, he's just a black Newt Gingrich. And, as such, he's made himself a part of the problem, not a part of the solution.

We have no time left to spend in a futile attempt to persuade those who willfully misunderstand everything we have to say. For the most part, hearts and minds on the other side are closed for good. Spend your time and energy gathering up those who already agree with us, or who already have a reason to travel with us, and we will not only win over the formerly recalcitrant and attract new individuals willing and eager to be of real help, we will achieve victory.

Be warned that at the moment, many of our conservative fellow travelers are all but useless to us — and to themselves. They can't see that the legislative fever-pitch at which things are preceding in Washington represents desperation on the part of the Marxist trash in the White House, who know full well that this is the last chance in the world they're ever going to get to run things.

Our conservative fellow travelers would rather swap paranoid delusions with one another about United Nations forces riding invisible helicopters from Mars than roll their sleeves up and do some real work. They'd rather whine like what P.J. O'Rourke calls "bedwetting liberals"; they'd rather wring their hands and bemoan their fate than plan and execute a counterstrike in this culture-war they talk about incessantly. All it seems they can do lately is whimper about the horrible things Hillary and Janet have done to us already; the horrible things Hillary and Janet are doing to us now; and the horrible things Hillary and Janet are about to do to us — instead of concentrating on doing it back!

Perhaps we can begin the therapy they need to get them out of this funk by teaching them that the words "conservative" and "Republican" are fully separable.

Don't waste too much effort trying to explain Libertarian positions to them on issues like abortion or the War on Drugs — and *never* make excuses or apologies.

We're right and they're wrong.

Instead, tell your increasingly angry and disenfranchised conservative friends that we're not asking them to *marry* us.

We're not asking them to have our baby.

Lever Action

We're not asking them to agree with us on each and every issue.

We're not asking them to *become* Libertarians.

We're not even asking them to join the Libertarian Party.

We're asking them to hire us to do a job — by consistently voting for Libertarian candidates — a job no other party seems willing to do: Enforce the Bill of Rights.

The fact is, our own longtime customary practice of blindly persuading individuals to join the Libertarian Party — or of persuading individuals to join the Libertarian Party blindly — without fully understanding exactly what Libertarianism and the Libertarian Party are all about must be brought to an immediate halt. On at least two occasions — the Ed Clark campaign and the Ron Paul campaign — it has come *that* close to destroying us as an institution and we must now begin to repair the damage by emphasizing "service to clients" — that is, keeping promises to voters — rather than membership in a club, and by educating each and every newcomer in what it really means to be a Libertarian.

If you want to do something and you're not up to public speaking or electoral politics, then help create a permanent system of education internal to the Libertarian Party.

******

It's important to act now. Come 1996, the Republicans — who've gotten it right precisely once in thirty-five years and couldn't locate their own overly developed posteriors with both hands and a city block full of Klieg lights — will trundle out the same menagerie of drooling retards and moral cripples they've inflicted on us, and on themselves, for so long, complacent in the false belief that Hillary will have performed so badly by then that Bill will be a pushover.

Or is it the other way around?

In any case the Republicans may offer us William Bennett, the most soft-spoken and thoroughly evil figure in contemporary politics, who consciously, deliberately, rejected Libertarianism and makes Darth Vader seem like Barney the dinosaur.

They may offer us Robert Dole. What is it about Bob Dole that always makes me want to reach for a garland of garlic, a crucifix, a mallet, and a sharpened wooden stake? Has anybody ever seen Bob Dole's reflection in a mirror?

They may offer us Jack Kemp, who was so determined to reverse the years of liberal excesses and abuses within the federal Department of Housing and Urban Development, to take everything done by his Democratic predecessors and turn it around, that he forgot that HUD turned around and *spelled* in reverse is "DUH."

They may offer us Dick Cheney, whose only virtue is that he isn't quite as blandly stupid as all the others.

They may offer us Dan Quayle, whose only virtue is that he isn't quite as blandly stupid as Dick Cheney.

It all depends on the polling data.

Libertarians have principles; they don't *do* polling. *Republicans* do polling, which is why they're running away from the Second Amendment and the entire Bill of Rights as fast as their nasty little legs can carry them, instead of leading the nation back to the basic civilities afforded by the Constitution.

One great problem Libertarians suffer is that we are often secretly — or not so secretly — more willing to see Republicans elected than Democrats. There are understandable reasons for this — philosophical, psychological, and historic — but it has to stop, for equally cogent reasons both principled and pragmatic.

As an example, it should be clear now that what seemed to be a tactical victory for Libertarians in Georgia two years ago was really a strategic loss. When Paul Coverdell, Republican candidate for the United States Senate, was forced into a run-off with his Democratic opponent, Wyche Fowler — thanks to the presence of a strong Libertarian candidate — the Libertarian should never have endorsed the Republican. It may have altered the course of history, but it gained us nothing — certainly not the gratitude of Republicans who helped bury the truth afterward — not at the time it happened, nor afterward in crucial votes like the Clinton budget, the Brady Bill, or the Feinstein amendment.

Perhaps it would help if I listed a few anti-gun, and therefore anti-Bill of Rights, Republicans for you — people who've recently made statements or cast votes against the Second Amendment: late party chairman Lee Atwater, William Bennett, Sarah and Jim Brady, William F. Buckley, George Bush, Senator John Chaffee, William Colby of the Nixon-era CIA, New York Mayor Rudolph Giuliani, Texas Senator Kay Bailey Hutchison, former cabinet secretary Jack Kemp, Republicans of the New Jersey Senate, Republicans of the U.S. Senate Judiciary Committee, Republicans of the U.S. Senate in general, Richard M. Nixon, Edwin O. Welles, also of the Nixon-era CIA, columnist George F. Will, California governor Pete Wilson, and New Jersey governor Christine Todd Whitman.

Only by repeatedly preventing the election of Republicans like these can we Libertarians make our case for Bill of Rights enforcement; and anyway it's better to elect the socialist scum you know than risk another betrayal of the Constitution at the increasingly vile and duplicitous hands of the Republican Party.

As Paul Atreides reminds us, "The power to destroy a thing is the power to control a thing." Presently we Libertarians will be able, and in each and every case must prove willing, to assure the victory of a liberal Democrat, no matter how repulsive, over a Republican, in every single election until the Republican Party begins to straighten up and fly right — or becomes as extinct as the dodo.

Tell your Republican friends that if they truly wish to reform their "Grand Old Party," they must be willing to punish it. Tell them that we Libertarians are offering our services as a bludgeon — or a rattan cane, if you prefer. Tell them, in a phrase they understand, that if they spare the rod, they'll spoil the child. Tell them, in a phrase they at least claim to understand, that they must be willing to *destroy* the Republican Party in order to save it.

Tell them they must *get right with the Bill of Rights*. Don't temporize, don't euphemize, don't let them rationalize any longer. Tell them to *be real — and be redeemed*. Ask them whatever happened to whatever it was they once believed in.

I am a Life Member of the National Rifle Association, but not a happy one. To that organization and its leaders, I would say, don't bargain for us any more in Congress or the nation's legislatures; don't write legislation you imagine isn't quite as bad as whatever the bad guys have in mind; don't wheel and deal for us. You're not up to it; every time you try it, you wind up getting shafted. You wind up getting *us* shafted. *We* wind up getting shafted. Try sticking to a principle; try sticking to the highest law of the land, the Bill of Rights. Try being, for the first time since 1934, what the liberal media say you are: unbending, determined, indomitable, obdurate, persistent, resolute, stubborn, tenacious, uncompromising. And if you don't know what any of those words mean — past performance implies that you don't — try looking them up. In the meantime, don't bargain for us any more. Don't do us any more favors.

To the nation's politicians and bureaucrats, to the Pat Sullivans, the Dottie Whams, the Regis Groffs, the Tom Nortons, the Wellington Webbs, the Roy Romers, the Hank Browns, the Patricia Schroeders, the Bill Bennetts, the Jack

Lever Action

Kemps, the Janet Renos, the Hillary Clintons, and to everyone else like them across America, I advise them to get out their almanacs or encyclopedias right now, blow off the dust, and bone up on the Bill of Rights. From this moment forward they're being watched by millions of eyes, and they have vastly more at stake, here, than simple re-election. Early in the 21st century, they may find themselves serving time in prison for something they've *already* done — or failed to do.

Let Hillary and Janet do the worrying, about the horrible things we're about to do to them!

"The laying of a Country desolate with Fire and Sword, declaring war against natural rights of all Mankind, and extirpating the Defenders thereof from the Face of the Earth, is the concern of every Man whom nature hath given the Power of feeling. ..." So said our philosophical ancestor, Thomas Paine, in *Common Sense*.

One way or another, America is going to wind up with a political party that will *enforce* the Bill of Rights — just as soon as the Republicans decide whether they or we Libertarians will put Hillary and Janet and all their little friends behind bars, not for Whitewater capers, not even for Vincent Foster, but for "crimes against the Constitution."

Whenever you begin to feel discouraged, I want you to imagine an old lady twenty years from now, tall, stoop-shouldered, wearing thick glasses and a dikey haircut, shuffling along with a canvas bag hung over her shoulder, one of those sticks in her hand with a nail in one end, picking up bits of paper trash as part of her hundred thousand hours of public service, cleaning up America's shooting ranges.

Party on, Janet!

And party on, Hillary. America — or at least Joe-Bob Briggs — loves movies about "Bimbos Behind Bars."

Let's see how they like the real thing!

Libertarian Second Amendment Caucus Statement of Principles

ᏣᏯ ᏣᏯ ᏣᏯ ᏣᏯ ᏣᏯ

The Libertarian Second Amendment Caucus opposes all proposed and pending victim-disarmament laws — commonly but improperly known as "gun control" — and, given the political power, will:

1) repeal more than 20,000 victim-disarmament laws already on the books (none of which is Constitutional or consistent with individual or human rights) and abolish all agencies, at every level of government, responsible for enforcing them;

2) decriminalize concealed-weapons carry and the act of self-defense;

3) pardon and provide restitution to anyone ever harmed or even inconvenienced by victim-disarmament laws;

4) arrest, convict, fine, and imprison any public official who ever enacted or enforced victim-disarmament laws; and

5) where a violation of individual or Constitutional rights has resulted in a fatality, impose the maximum penalty on all such public officials.

Libertarian Second Amendment Caucus General Resolution

ᏣᏯ ᏣᏯ ᏣᏯ ᏣᏯ ᏣᏯ

WHEREAS the right to self-defense is neither socially conditional nor politically collective, but inherent in the basic nature of each and every individual human being, and implies an unlimited right to obtain, own, and carry weapons of any kind, and

WHEREAS the individual right to self-defense can neither be denied nor granted by kings or constitutions, by legislative or judicial acts, nor is it subject to regulation or to the democratic process, and

WHEREAS the individual right to self-defense includes the right to self-defense against the state — all power exercised by the state being derived from individual rights and being therefore inferior to them,

BE IT RESOLVED that the individual right to self-defense necessitates repeal or nullification of any law:

● requiring licensure or registration of weapons, weapons owners, weapons makers, weapons dealers, or gunsmiths;

● taxing ownership or transfer of weapons, weapons accessories, weapons parts, or ammunition;

● denying free choice of manufacture, price, acquisition, method of carry, concealment or concealability, caliber, power or form of ammunition, configuration, social accepitbility, quality, safety, or security of storage, ammunition capacity, operating mode or rate of fire;

● regulating local, interstate, or international transport or transfer of any weapon or associated item;

● restricting gas, electric, jointed, or edged weapons, impact-resistant clothing, or any other protective device; or

● permitting the state or its employees to retain, sell, or destroy weapons taken from individuals.

BE IT FURTHER RESOLVED that government agencies charged with enforcing such laws be abolished, their records destroyed, that any individual ever arrested, indicted, or convicted under such laws receive unconditional release and restitution to all previous rights and property — and that the past and present employees of these agencies (rather than the taxpayers) be responsible for this restitution, and

BE IT FURTHER RESOLVED that any elected or appointed public official who advocates, introduces, sponsors, or votes for such laws — or has done so in the past — be removed from office as the 14th Amendment provides and prosecuted under felony statutes for violating his or her oath to uphold and defend the Constitution, as well as violating the natural, fundamental, and inalienable human, individual, civil, and Constitutional rights of the people of the United States of America.

The Twenty-Ninth Amendment
ᏟᎧᏟᎧᏟᎧᏟᎧᏟᎧ

Given the known hostility of the current administration to the Bill of Rights — especially the Second Amendment — the priority American forces are assigning to the house-to-house disarmament of Haitian civilians, and the feeble excuses offered for it in the media, it should be clear by now that this operation, like the one in Somalia, is designed to train our troops to do the same thing here in the States. If so, it is important to circulate the following as widely as possible as a warning to those in power of the dangers of abusing it.

SECTION I: It is forbidden under any circumstances for any American military or police force to deny — or to be ordered to deny — any American the free exercise of any right protected by the first ten amendments to the United States Constitution.

SECTION II: In the absence of a formal declaration of

war, it is likewise forbidden for any American military or police force to deny — or to be ordered to deny — foreign nationals in their own territories the free exercise of any right protected by the first ten Amendments to the United States Constitution.

SECTION III: No claim of emergency, nor the age or condition of any person, is sufficient grounds for violating or evading the provisions or intentions of this Amendment.

SECTION IV: Any elected or appointed official at any level of government who violates or evades the provisions or intentions of this Amendment is subject to imprisonment and fine for each violation; should a death occur as a result of said violation, the official in question shall be subject to the death penalty.

Tea in a Whole New Bag
ᴄᴅ ᴄᴅ ᴄᴅ ᴄᴅ ᴄᴅ

More and more it seems that nothing can bring this country's politicos and bureaucrats back under control (to the extent they ever were) as the Founding Fathers intended. Bureaucrats are more anonymous and unreachable every year, and no matter how incensed we get — or how many of us get that way — politicians reelect themselves like clockwork.

Though it's all the rage among those concerned with such matters, I've never been satisfied that term limitation won't achieve the opposite of what's intended, removing a final curb on runaway do-goodery and social experimentation. With respect to recent passage of what's supposed to be the 28th Amendment, the most naive American today knows more than

James Madison did of the way politicians fix things to suit themselves. They'll override ratification, agree to vote raises for their successors, or simply make their mercenary move early in their terms, in the comforting knowledge that voters will have forgotten what they did by Election Day.

It should be clear now that the imposition of Bill Clinton on the productive class — by 43% of the electorate — has only made things worse. In an age where half the average person's income already goes to taxes of one kind or another and the other half for goods and services with prices doubled by taxation and doubled again by regulation — and where bureaucrats represent a greater threat to life, liberty, and property than politicians — what's needed is something more certain than term limitation and harder to get around than Madison's schedule for congressional pay hikes.

Allow me to introduce the "Taxpayers' Equity Amendment":

1. No elected or appointed official at any level of government may receive more in total salary, benefits, and expenses during his term of office — or for five years afterward — than his average productive-sector constituent; individuals, and employees of companies, deriving more than 10% of their revenue from government will be excluded for purposes of calculating the average.

2. Those subject to the Taxpayers' Equity Amendment will be required to participate in the Social Security system for as long as it continues to exist; all outside income (from a business, inheritance, investments, a spouse's wealth, speaking fees — to name only a few examples) will be "invested in America" by being placed in randomly selected savings and loan institutions until the five-year period expires.

3. Those subject to the Taxpayers' Equity Amendment will be required to file weekly income/expenditure forms for scru-

tiny by the IRS, the media, and the public; telephone hotlines and lavish rewards for "whistle-blowers" will be provided; all salary and benefits of officials under suspicion of having violated the Taxpayers' Equity Amendment will be suspended pending the results of any investigation.

4. Violations of the Taxpayers' Equity Amendment will result in summary removal of that official, loss of salary, benefits, expenses — along with all deposited monies — and no fewer than 25 years in that federal maximum-security prison currently deemed most violent; introducing, sponsoring, or voting for legislation meant to evade the Taxpayers' Equity Amendment, or to falsify the statistical base on which calculations are made, will be treated as violations.

The primary goals of the Taxpayers' Equity Amendment are:

(A) to punish politicians and bureaucrats for past, present, and future crimes against the lives, liberties, and property of "We the People of the United States";

(B) to make sure their fortunes rise and fall with ours — so they're forced to scrape along day by day like the rest of us, one paycheck away from bankruptcy; and

(C) to give them something better to do with their time than to continually threaten, at our expense, our fundamental rights and well-being.

It'll also save taxpayers around $300 billion a year.

The Taxpayers' Equity Amendment can begin working now, before it ever passes into law (even if it never does), if it's circulated widely via computer bulletin board networks and other means, appears frequently in magazine and newspaper letter columns, and if it's sent to all your favorite office holders.

Have fun ...

My Three Tax Programs
ഗ ഗ ഗ ഗ ഗ

From time to time America suffers what boils down to doubly artificial — and completely unnecessary — "shortages" of petroleum. The story that usually makes it to the headlines is of naughty OPEC reducing production in order to get higher per-barrel prices.

Less publicized is a dismal truth that there's plenty of petroleum right here in the USA — hundreds of years of "proven reserves." This isn't counting natural gas — there's another 2,000 years' worth of that. Nor does it count oil shale, which contrary to popular belief is not impossible to extract, just a little more expensive.

The truth is dismal because environmentalists have politicians by their tiny little *cojones*, despite the fact that policies they push — aromatics to replace lead, catalytic converters, and MTBE all come to mind — do worse damage to the planet and its inhabitants, human and otherwise, than what they replaced. Even the idiot liberal Democrat governor who preceded the idiot liberal Republican governor currently slopping at the public trough in my state had enough sense to oppose political tinkering with the chemistry of gasoline until he was overruled by an idiot liberal Republican legislature.

As usual, when gas prices take a hike, there's talk of lifting the burden on "working families" by reducing federal excise taxes that add a thick percentage to the price paid at the pump. (Industry estimates that completely untaxed gas would cost 68 cents a gallon.) That's all it ever amounts to, of course — talk. Democrats, the theft-and-mass-murder party, don't even bother talking any more, while Republicans, the we-can-rob-and-kill-you-cheaper party, are too cowardly and stupid to do anything about it even when they're in the majority.

At the moment, they can't even bring themselves to cut gas taxes a measly 4.3 cents, while real people ask why not do away with gas taxes altogether, at least for the duration. The money isn't being invested in any special dedicated fund — any more than Social Security money is. It's being poured into the gaping maw of a general fund where highways compete with the War on Drugs and funding for the BATF.

I'm often asked what I'd do about taxes if I were president. Keeping in mind a general policy I'll save for the end of this article, two things need to be done right away.

The first, which I'll call Program One, would bring relief to all of us, not just "working families." It's also a test of the motives of apologists for the Welfare State. It would permanently remove all taxes, at every level of government, on the necessities of life: food, clothing, shelter, and transportation.

By "all taxes," I mean *all taxes*.

Farmers, for example, would be exempt from property tax on the land they work, and from taxes on equipment and supplies. They'd pay no income tax because it would just be passed on (no way to avoid it, even if they wanted to) to consumers. Transportation, processing, and sales of food would likewise be exempt. How could a program be kinder, gentler, or more humane? Yet I guarantee Democrats and Republicans will scream like stuck pigs at the very thought.

They'll scream louder when nothing that you wear, head to toe, can be taxed at any level of production. And when nothing about your home can be taxed, from the steel and lumber in its frame and the glass and gypsum in its walls to the asphalt or tile on its roof.

The same policy would apply to production, distribution, sale, and possession of all the nation's private rolling stock: cars, trucks, planes, trains, boats, and ships. No more drivers' licenses, no more license tags — in short, no more police-state tracking numbers. Of course, it would be illegal to tax lubricants and fuels.

Program Two: It's widely recognized that "the power to tax is the power to destroy." Therefore, in the interest of preserving the Bill of Rights, anything mentioned in the first ten Amendments to the Constitution — any object or activity protected by the highest law of the land — will be tax exempt.

We already exempt religions from taxation, although the hoops they jump through to obtain recognition from the government defeat the very purpose of the First Amendment. It's inconsistent not to exempt speech, as well; many states won't permit the sale of newspapers to be taxed for that very reason, although the policy doesn't go far enough.

The Smith Administration would go further. And unlike Program One, under which the necessities of life would be detaxed, there's room for a president, having sworn to uphold and defend the Constitution, to act unilaterally. Since taxes can be (have been) used to chill or destroy the free exercise of liberties guaranteed by the Bill of Rights, it makes sense to nullify those taxes.

No act of self-expression would be taxable. No pen or pencil, no sheet of paper, no typewriter or word processor, no computer, radio, telephone, or television could be taxed, from factory to user. Nor any canvas, clay, paint, or block of marble. Telephone and Internet service would be tax-free. Those who live by self-expression — writers, painters, sculptors, programmers — would pay no income tax: not preferential treatment, simple obedience to the First Amendment.

Likewise, I'd eliminate all taxes on weapons, ammunition, and accessories, starting with an 11% excise tax crammed down our throats by the NRA. There'd be no further punitive taxes on items — like machineguns and short shotguns — the government doesn't approve of. To make sure this ban stayed in place, I'd make it a felony for anyone to record the serial number of a weapon that belongs to someone else, and perhaps even require the removal of serial numbers once they'd served their legitimate purpose during factory production.

The other eight amendments would be protected exactly the same way. Nothing to do with the security of your home and possessions or your defense of them or yourself in a court of law would be taxable.

No real libertarian — and not many real conservatives — will ask how I plan to "pay" for all this tax hatcheting. Fact is, we suffer at least 100 times as much government as we need (conceding we need any) at every level: city, county, state, and federal. If I enforce the law, eliminating agencies and programs not permitted by the Ninth and Tenth Amendments and by Article I, Section 8, of the Constitution, there will be less government to pay for. How much less depends on who you listen to. Walter Williams estimates two-thirds, I say 95%. Read the pertinent documents and see what you think.

It'll be fun finding out.

Someone's bound to ask how I hope to get these programs through in the current political climate. If I were president, it would hardly be in the current political climate, would it? Also, these programs are designed to appeal to touchy-feely prejudices: How can we *possibly* permit children's clothes and baby food to be taxed? Finally, nothing can ever be accomplished if someone doesn't break the ice by being the first to talk about it publicly. That's what I'm doing here.

Make no mistake: All taxes are evil. When you take somebody else's property and they don't want to give it to you, there's only one word for it, no matter how many others voted to do it or what kind of funny hat or silly uniform you wear.

That word is *theft.*

Until recently, historically, hardly anybody paid taxes. What little taxation there was was in the form of tariffs, or an income tax that only applied to the top 5% (which isn't right, either; I'm simply discussing history here). Taxes were virtually invisible. But they are not invisible any longer, and our culture is much the worse for it. What example does it give children — has it given children for the last 75 years — to run a civilization on theft?

Which brings us to Program Three, an everyday struggle in which I pledge to rid civilization *forever* of the very concept of taxation. Let such starved and withered future governments as we allow to exist try funding themselves with bake sales and telethons.

It works for Jerry's kids.

My China Policy
cʒ cʒ cʒ cʒ cʒ

Every other day, all the online news services I read are full of China rattling its ideologically rusty *ken* at America, usually over control of the island nation of Taiwan.

Recently, having failed to intimidate Taiwanese voters out of choosing a candidate — from a new party, the first time since the little nation's birth in 1949 — sworn to declare full independence from the mainland, they've begun mustering huge numbers of troops on the coast and making threatening 100-fighter flyovers.

China claims Taiwan as a lost province, sort of the way Ethiopia "belonged" to Italy. Leaders and people of Taiwan are those — or the descendants of those — who escaped Mao's butchery back in the 1940s. Taiwan's repressive government is nothing worth defending (the new electee promises changes), but for a long time the U.S. government backed it to the hilt. My earliest political memories are of China railing at America over Taiwan.

Well, *practically* my earliest memories. I also recall a Korean War in which China (and Russia, to a degree unrealized by most people) found a way to get someone else, the poor dumb North Koreans, to fight their battles for them. That war has never ended officially.

Not surprisingly, China represents new hope for Western Cold Warriors, lonely and afraid in a world that got remade despite their best — or worst — efforts to the contrary. Here they were, never having to stand down from the power, prestige, and plenty of World War II, playing with thousands of trillions of bucks, running roughshod over the unalienable individual, civil, Constitutional, and human rights of everybody on the planet — when the damned Russians had the bad manners to wimp out!

Now they'll tell you they won the Cold War, citing this or that policy or program, trying to make heroes of themselves. But the Soviet Empire was doomed — as I said in my novel *The Nagasaki Vector* almost a decade before it happened — to collapse of its own weight. If the Cold Warriors had really had their way, that collapse would never have happened. After all, they subsidized and supported the poor lame Soviets for seven decades. Who wants to lose a cushy job?

Now, having only their phony War on Drugs, right-wing militias that look statesmanlike compared to the current administration, and the cardboard specter of international terrorism to fall back on, the Cold Warriors, desperate to retain their hold on this culture, are trying to pump life back into their second-string foe. Why else did Clinton hand nuclear secrets and guided missile technology to them?

Campaign contributions are the insignificant tip of the iceberg. Rush Limbaugh won't tell you that, any more than Dan Rather would. They're both part of the dirtiest racket in history. Washington *needs* a credible enemy to keep from forking over the Peace Dividend it's owed us for 10 years.

Let there be no misunderstanding: The Chinese government is evil and violent. Almost as evil and violent as a government that confined, tortured, poison-gassed, machinegunned, and incinerated 82 helpless innocent individuals — 22 of them harmless beautiful little children — in their own church, in broad daylight, on national TV, put its pitiable handful of surviving victims on trial for having defended themselves, and once they were duly acquitted of any wrongdoing, threw them in prison anyway for 40 years.

Nor is it just Clinton. Bush 1.0 barely spanked the hands of China's leaders over Tien Anmen Square because that's how all leaders of the modern Management State wish to govern: Zero Tolerance for individual liberty. It's the treatment we can expect whether Algore or Bush 2.0 is elected in November — policywise, they're identical peas in a New World Order pod.

But certain inconvenient facts get in the way of turning China into the next boogeyman to scare taxpayers with. Even Algore and 2.0 want to sell things to a billion customers — hard to do if you're reliving the Cold War. For their part, China's aging leaders want the fruits of economic freedom and the progress it engenders — but without allowing people anything resembling political liberty. They should get along well with the current crop of Republicans; they want exactly the same thing. The basic model for both is Franco's Spain.

Another inconvenient fact is that (with rare exceptions like Tibet) for many centuries, China — even Red China — has not been particularly expansionistic. They've always had peculiar ideas about other countries, none of which have ever seemed quite real to them, center of the universe that they see themselves to be. A Chinese emperor once sent a huge fleet around the world, not to intimidate and conquer, but to give presents away and tell everybody what a swell guy he was.

Somebody told me a story that illustrates the Chinese ambivalence toward conquest. Annam — the place we call Vietnam — was always a pain for China. Emperors fervently believed they owned the place, but their tax collectors (and their armies) kept coming back in body bags. Finally, one general returned to the imperial capital to report that he had conquered Annam. The emperor promptly had him beheaded. History showed it was impossible to conquer Annam, so he must be a liar. And if he wasn't, he was too dangerous to have around.

China today lies in the unsteady grip of frightened old men in the unenviable position of having outlived the ideas that guided them all their lives and justified every atrocity they ever visited upon their fellow beings. What they desperately fear — besides losing power — is communication: between their people and the West; between their people and each other. They fear the shortwave, the modem, and the fax the way Schumer and Feinstein fear high-capacity semiautomatics in the hands of their constituents. For them, the sight of a replica of the Statue of Liberty — a direct product of the communication they fear — being carried through the heart of their domain must have sent waves of terror through their ancient arthritic bones.

Those who think they own us have yet to figure out what's more beneficial — to them: trade or war. That "war is the health of the state" is a fact well-known to leaders on both sides. At present, China's empty threats are meant more to impress their own than us — that the worst enemies of China's government are China's people is another well-known fact — but it's worrisome to deal with a handful of geriatric bastards who know they won't have to live with the consequences of plunging their nation into total war.

What's more worrisome is that U.S. leaders are as frightened and desperate. Having been impeached, the president (whose murderous foreign policy is now understood as a way to cover up his domestic behavior) is about to be disbarred. There's talk of criminal charges once he's out of office. Waco is in the news again. The vice president stands exposed as corrupt. The GOP frontrunner has abandoned his traditional constituency to fulfill his obligation to the Brotherhood of the Bell, advancing the agenda of corporate statism.

Meanwhile, grassroots resistance against the police state America has become gets more effective every day. Dozens of vile plots have been destroyed by shining the harsh light of the Internet on them. To obsolete leaders frantic to hang onto the lives and property of others at any cost, the prospect of war — of the dictatorial excesses it permits — is bound to be increasingly attractive.

On the other hand, ethical leaders of an ethical nation — the kind of nation ours was supposed to be — dedicated to self-defense, not foreign adventure, require no outside threat to retain power. Unafraid of a rising tide of individualism in the world, they'd have no trouble taking advantage of it, to deal effectively with China.

China's leaders may not be expansionistic, but they might slag Taiwan, which they believe belongs to them, to make a point. My plan is meant to prevent that. Next time China threatens to rain nuclear missiles on our West Coast cities — as they've been doing every day now for months — I'd offer to shower them with presents, just like their imperial treasure fleet did long ago.

My China policy would operate at multiple deterrent levels. First, just the news that what I'm about to describe is being given serious consideration at the uppermost levels of government should be enough to make Chinese leaders hesitate.

If that doesn't work, the next step is to let contracts out and actually manufacture the "weapons" (patience, now), sending samples to the leaders of China for them to evaluate. No fear, here, of giving secrets away. The technology is already well understood by everybody, and has been, practically since the turn of the last century. The next step is to refit B52 strategic bombers to deliver the "weapons."

From vastly higher than antiaircraft rockets reach, the next step is to drop the "weapons": hundreds of millions of tiny flesh-colored plastic radios, made to fit the human ear, in plastic packages that let them flutter safely to the ground. The radios themselves will be light and sturdy. No need for a tuner, a crystal will suffice; the audience will only be listening to one station. The radios will run for a year on a hearing-aid battery, forever on a photocell, receiving broadcasts 24 hours a day, seven days a week, from satellites. I'm told it's harder to jam signals coming down from space than those broadcast from the surface of the planet.

And what broadcasts they'll be! Thomas Paine and Thomas Jefferson — in Mandarin and another half-dozen "major" Chinese languages — Leonard Reed, Peter McWilliams, Thomas Szasz, dramatized works of Ayn Rand and Robert Heinlein, informing the listener over and over that his life and all the products of his life are his property and no one else's. Maybe there'll even be room for a Suprynowicz or Smith.

The plan will be bankrolled by selling commercial time (a billion listeners are attractive to any sponsor), but only to companies that, unlike Smith and Wesson, haven't betrayed the Bill of Rights (and the customers who've kept them in business for more than a century), but instead have sworn to uphold and defend it. The Chinese government, of course, will make it a capital offense to be caught with such a radio. We'll retaliate by threatening to escalate from the enlightened self-interest of Rand to the ruthless egoism of Stirner.

It was socialist Arthur Clarke who showed us the way, in a short story that predicted communications satellites (and entitled him, he believes absurdly, to part of the profits). At appropriate times there'll be programs for children, at others, programs for adults, apolitical entertainment meant to keep the radio listeners listening: *Winnie the Pooh*, *Story of O*, real freedom of the airwaves.

Sooner or later, China's leaders will have to back off, and we can begin negotiating them out of everything they think they own. Either that or they may face an uprising fomented by our sudden refusal to broadcast the last chapter of an Agatha Christie novel. All's fair, as they say, especially against a government that twisted our elections to impose William Jefferson Blythe Clinton on us.

Don't look for him to undertake this program. It's clear by now he's a traitor who belongs heart and soul (as little of those as he possesses) to the Chinese Communists (the only masters he could run to after the Soviets folded). What remains is to examine the rest of this country's leaders in Congress, the Senate, and elsewhere, to see if they don't serve the same masters.

Meanwhile, if my China policy works, we may have to think about dropping millions of tiny little radios on America.

Or maybe tiny little color TVs.

Operation Safe Streets
ᑕᕓ ᑕᕓ ᑕᕓ ᑕᕓ ᑕᕓ

Fellow Libertarians:

I've just received our national committee's mailing to LP members on "Operation Safe Streets," an attempt to raise money internally by promising to try to persuade disaffected Republican gun owners to vote Libertarian. The "program" outlined in this mailing (they failed to send their proposal in its entirety for review) superficially resembles policies I recommended in my address to the national convention in Salt Lake City last September.

But this mailing, more than anything else, impresses me as a putty-pale, wimpified replica of the National Rifle Association's hypocritical "Operation Crime-Strike," and typifies the timidity and ineptitude that have kept the LP tiny and insignificant throughout its 23-year history. The one fitting and effective message to the nation's gun owners at this moment is that "crime" has nothing to do with *rights*; that the LP opposes all proposed and pending victim-disarmament laws — commonly but improperly known as "gun control" — and, given the political power, will:

1) repeal more than 20,000 victim-disarmament laws already on the books (not one of which is Constitutional or consistent with individual or human rights) and abolish all agencies, at every level of government, responsible for enforcing them;

2) decriminalize the act of self-defense;

3) pardon and provide restitution to anyone ever inconvenienced in the slightest by victim-disarmament laws;

4) arrest, convict, fine, and imprison any public official who ever enacted or enforced victim-disarmament laws; and

5) where such a violation of individual or Constitutional rights has resulted in a fatality, impose the maximum penalty on all such public officials.

Anything less than the above, stated any less strongly than above, will have no effect except to convince this nation's gun-owners that Libertarians are the same sort of cowards, four-flushers, and idiots as those who run the other two political parties.

Sincerely, L. Neil Smith,
Founder, Libertarian Second Amendment Caucus

A Desperate Suspension of Disbelief
ઝ ઝ ઝ ઝ ઝ

Given the choice between a mass-murdering clown and a tired old political whore, America has chosen the mass-murdering clown. While the 1996 election doesn't come as any surprise — nobody was ever able to convince *me* that the country would be better off in Brady Bill Bob Dole's hands than in Waco Willie Clinton's — it does continue a process of disillusionment in my fellow human beings that began about the time of the Libertarian Party nomination of Harry Browne.

Harry, as you must know by now, didn't attract enough voters to populate Wyoming.

The Morning After, I was describing to a favorite aunt my ... let's call it "spiritual distress" over the deliberate choice my countrymen had made to keep a bloody-handed baby-burner in the White House. In defense of American voters, my aunt asked, "Given the corrupt collusive nature of the media, how could people *know* what Clinton did at Waco?" Afterward, my wife Cathy asked, "How could they *not* know?" Both questions (and recalling how Philadelphia re-elected the evil mayor who authorized the infamous MOVE bombing) made me think.

I'm not sure who it was (Edgar Allan Poe, maybe) who called the essential element in absorbing a work of fiction "a willing suspension of disbelief." Although the reader knows that what he's reading is untrue, with the help of a skillful enough author, he can pretend otherwise for the sake of amusement or enlightenment.

It strikes me that this is like welfare-state politics, where people may know that what they vote for will have, at worst, a negative effect, and at the best, none at all. Yet they wish to believe otherwise, and with the help of a skillful enough politician, they can achieve a "*desperate* suspension of disbelief."

This certainly explains a lot, concerning people and events. For example, the frustrating way that, although it's known the minimum wage causes minority unemployment, it keeps getting raised. Or that, although it's been *proved* that gun control accomplishes nothing but harm, people want to believe it will stop crime. It's a hell of a lot easier than doing what would *really* stop it.

Politicians, academics, and the media are the worst, because they mostly constitute the bottom of the national barrel, so hopelessly and deliberately self-befuddled that they've become incapable of doing anything genuine for a living.

Which explains the way *they* vote.

Civilization is a mess, only one or two calamities from violent collapse. The formula for fixing it is simple: enforce the highest law of the land, the Bill of Rights. Free people have incentives to maintain civilization. Slaves don't.

As long as Americans go on being allowed to make essentially meaningless choices between essentially identical candidates, they'll go on believing that they're free. Pro-freedom candidates who want to win must first teach voters that they're *not* free, and that's no task for any gradualist, moderate, or "pragmatist."

(As for those who know they're not free, they need to learn you can't get what you want by voting for something else. Gun owners may finally learn this lesson the hard way as they see how many Republican congressmen vote for Brady II.)

What complicates the matter is that, at some level, Americans *know* the truth of their political and economic serfdom, but they're hell-bent in their determination to maintain the self-delusion that they're free. It makes them desperate to believe that anyone who runs afoul of the government (say, Randy Weaver or David Koresh) *deserves* whatever happens to him. They *have* to believe this, and they bitterly resent anyone who makes it more difficult for them.

The secondary formula we may derive from all this isn't as simple as Bill of Rights enforcement, and no matter how you slice it, it's going to be a lot of work. But the only proper strategy for Libertarians and Constitutionalists is:

(1) pound the voting public *incessantly* with one poignant and horrific story after another of the violent abusive manner in which government *hurts* people;

(2) emphasize the completely unsuspecting *innocence* of the government's victims;

(3) never fail to point out how such travesties are *inevitable*, and will get worse and worse, as long as certain fundamental principles are neglected; and

(4) finish up, *not* simply with the demand for Bill of Rights enforcement (or some other reform we believe desirable) that this was all leading up to, but

(5) a warm colorful *picture* of what everyday life will be like for the listener under the much-improved circumstances we're asking him to help bring about.

This formula must be used relentlessly. Its undeniable effectiveness is predictable from the success with which socialists employ their own formula of tear-filled anecdotery to get their political way — as contrasted with our customary appeals to reason, principle, and law. Ours differs in that we want to smarten people up, not dumb them down, and therefore, we eventually bring them back around to exercising their rational faculties. We also provide them — and this is my specialty — a concrete vision of the reward that awaits them.

That's what we *must* do.

Here's what we must *not*.

From this moment of electoral ignominy on, I refuse to entertain another word regarding the advisability of gradualism, moderation, or "pragmatism." Their emphasis among the highest levels of the Libertarian political movement now appears to have been driven, all along, by the basest of ulterior motives, anyway: a desire for unearned wealth.

Even the densest and most cowardly among our tiny and insignificant number must understand, from the campaign disaster most recently behind us, and many others that preceded it, that these approaches — which were self-evidently specious to begin with — have been discredited once and for all, thoroughly and beyond question. Nor will I argue seriously with anyone who holds the contrary.

Instead, I'm going to go on following the course I set forth on 19 years ago, when I pursued the five-step formula above, to write *The Probability Broach*.

A Lesson in Practical Politics
ᖰᖰ ᖰᖰ ᖰᖰ ᖰᖰ ᖰᖰ

I have never claimed that Libertarians can win national elections at this point in history.

If they could, we wouldn't be *in* this mess, now, would we? If Libertarians could win elections, a 12-year-old could walk into any hardware emporium in the land, slap his cash down on the counter, and walk out with a brand new Thompson submachinegun, no papers signed, no questions asked, like the Founding Fathers intended. If Libertarians could win elections, there'd be no taxes of any kind, nor any economic regulations, and we'd all be effectively eight times as rich as we are now.

But that isn't really the point, is it? What Libertarians *have* demonstrated is that we can keep *others* from winning elections. We can take away that 5% a candidate needs to defeat his opponent, and let the other guy win. And if you don't think *that's* a threat politicians will take seriously, you've been living in a cave since 1912, when Bullmoose Teddy Roosevelt stole the presidential election from Republican William Howard Taft — as punishment for abandoning certain principles Roosevelt believed in — and delivered it to the Democrat, Woodrow Wilson.

Please note that I'm not asking anybody to like us, I'm not asking anybody to kiss us on the lips, and I'm certainly not asking anybody to have our baby. Hell, I'm not even asking anybody to vote for us at the climactic electoral moment. All I'm asking, very simply, is that you tell *politicians* you're going to vote for us (if it helps, you can think of it as lying to *them* for a change), and keep telling them that, until they give us what we want.

Lever Action

You might want to start with the 42 House Republicans with skulls full of anchovy paste who voted against lifting Clinton's illegal rifle and magazine ban.

Just as an experiment.

But set all of that aside for just a moment. Suppose the worst happened. Suppose you got into that voting booth and discovered, for whatever reason, that you just couldn't resist flipping the lever or punching the hole beside the name of the only candidate for that position who has explicitly sworn to repeal every gun law — make that, "victim-disarmament law" — that was ever passed.

Suppose you — gasp! — voted Libertarian! Afterward, of course, your friends would say that you'd wasted your vote. But only because they're ignorant of history and, on top of that, can't count. They don't know about Socialist Norman Thomas, principal architect of today's welfare state, who got a million votes (2%) back in 1928 and threw a scare into the Democrats they *still* haven't recovered from. They don't know about the Dixiecrats, or about George Wallace, or Eugene McCarthy, none of whom was ever elected President, but who changed the course of history, simply by running.

They even seem to have forgotten Ross Perot, who was able to help Clinton defeat Bush only — repeat — only because Bush, as a matter of the usual suicidally idiotic Republican National Committee policy, deliberately insulted this country's hard-core one-issue gun voters. If we'd learned that lesson when it was offered to us (or the if RNC had), I wouldn't have to be writing this now.

Look at it this way. Say the Libertarian gets 5% in some election and the other two guys split the remaining 95% between them, averaging 47.5% apiece. The Libertarian may have been a Second Amendment advocate like me, which means that the Democrat won. Or he may have emphasized legalizing drugs, in which case his 5% made a Republican victory possible. (I know exactly what you're gonna say — making this thing work right is a *lot* like backing up a tractor-trailer.) In either case, it was the Libertarian who made the difference and determined the outcome of the election, which is more than you can say for the other two guys, no matter *how* many votes they got.

And get this: Libertarians — uniquely — can *choose* which candidate will win, through a process of political "cross-dressing." People know me as a gun guy. They've never heard me make the case for ending drug prohibition; it's not my specialty, but I can do a pretty fair job of it, and have. Throw in the famous (or infamous) Libertarian tolerance for a wide range of lifestyle choices and our abhorrence for censorship of any kind, and I can take my 5% out of any Democrat's hide as easily as I can any Republican's.

If I want to.

But only if Republicans give me a good reason (Brady Bill Bob Dole is *not* a good reason), or even better, they take my conservative vote away from me by being stronger than I am on the Second Amendment, on taxation, on regulation, on hard money — or maybe just by keeping their damned promises!

In any event, to return to our example, you tell *me* which numbers actually decided the election, their 47.5%, or my measly 5%? Now, divide the 47.5% that *didn't* determine the outcome by the 5% that *did*, and you'll see that, in terms of having a real say about what happens, voting for a Libertarian is more than *nine and a half times* as effective as voting for a Republican or Democrat. It seems to me that the surest way to *waste* your vote is by delivering it, undeserved, to either of the traditional parties.

Would it really be so awful if Libertarians turned out to be responsible — at least in part — for repeal of the Clinton rifle and magazine ban or the Brady Bill? They're going to be, regardless of how anybody feels about it. We're *never* going to go away. So the sooner people get used to it, the sooner they'll begin feeling good about it. If it's only a matter of time, why not start now, and get it over with, the same way I learned to eat my green beans when I was a kid?

Or would you really prefer that these stupid unconstitutional laws stay on the books, rather than have to acknowledge someday that there might be something to some of these Libertarians, after all, if not to Libertarianism itself?

Would it really be that painful?

To repeat, I have never claimed that Libertarians can win national elections, only that we can keep *others* from winning them. Think of it as the one service we can reliably offer to America's gun owners. We're all fools if we fail to make whatever use of it we can.

The Return of the Creature
◁◈▷ ◁◈▷ ◁◈▷ ◁◈▷ ◁◈▷

Well, the hiatus is over at last, and I'm in the middle, just now, of the oddly difficult transition from creating long works of fiction to writing short works of what I sincerely wish wasn't nonfiction. I think some word is in order concerning what I've been up to.

In mid-October of the next-to-last year of the 20th century, I more or less dropped out of cyberspace and politics to attend to the higher priority of feeding my family and saving my career by finishing a book by the time specified in the contract. I completed *The American Zone* front to back, on December 5, my daughter's birthday.

In some ways, my return to my profession was a tremendous release, almost a vacation. Besides *The American Zone*, I attended to many other projects. I wrote two books in 1999, the other one being *The Mitzvah*, with Aaron Zelman, founder and director of Jews for the Preservation of Firearms Ownership. I prepared *Forge of the Elder*s, my poor, truncated, two-book Warner trilogy, for republication this April as a single volume by Baen Books. I took steps to revive the seven-book series — heptalogy as I call it — that begins with *BrightSuit MacBear* and *Taflak Lysandra*.

At the urging of my stalwart agent/attorney Tom "Hobbyt" Creasing, I started *The Steamcoach Pillagers*, a North American Confederate *western* I've wanted to write for 20 years. I adapted "TimePeeper," a movie treatment I've had kicking around almost as long, into a long story (cartoonist Rex May wants to call it a "novelito") that you'll see in print next year. Rex and I continued the work of five years (so far) on our outrageous collaboration, *Texas ueber Alles*.

A speech I gave to a Colorado State University physics class will turn into both an epic novel and a non-fiction book about asteroids. And I struggled some more with a novel I don't even want to name yet, but that is both a labor of love and a work of great hope for me and my family.

Before I knew it, Christmas was upon us, an imperative never to be denied in any house occupied by a 10-year-old. Despite the fact that we're not religious and we observe it as a cultural holiday, it's a busy season, thanks to *Winter Wishes*, the annual ice show at our local rink. My daughter had a pivotal part. Dressed from head to toe in golden sequins, she was the first skater out onto the ice, under bright lights, to open five performances of *The Wizard of Oz*.

Then came the bleakest dumbest New Year's I can remember. For the sake of my resume as an SF writer and futurist, I'm happy that, months in advance of the biggest non-event since Comet Kahoutek, I got it into public print that Y2K would come to *nada*. Less predictable was what people — the governmental subspecies in particular — might try. Night skies leading up to January 1 seemed especially full of military aircraft and, as always, there were 10 times as many cops on the street as there ought to be in any free country.

My little family watched TV in the security of our living room and took a peek at Drudge and other sites every couple of hours. I knew there'd be no technical problem, but kept my 12-gauge within reach beside my best battle rifle — and my most competent autopistol on my hip — the whole evening. I imagine many of you spent New Year's the same way. As soon as 2000 came to New Zealand without any ill effects, I felt vindicated in my prediction and we all relaxed and enjoyed our copy of *Strange Days*.

So here we are, now, in the last year of what I disagree with the Cato Institute and call the *worst* century in human history. True, we got Marconi, the Wright Brothers, the Internet, and Sarah Michelle Gellar. We also got World War I, World War II, and World War II Versions 1.0, 2.0, 3.0, ad nauseum — call it 150 million steaming corpses — plus more than 100 million more, murdered by their own governments in acts *separate* from war. In all, more than a quarter of a *billion* men, women, and helpless, harmless, little kids (the current population of the US) obliterated by something worse than anything it ever claimed to protect us from, a disease masquerading as its own cure.

But once again, I've digressed. Something people-related about Y2K that *was* predictable was the reaction, afterward, by the doomsayers, snake-oil salesmen, survival pimps, and their idiot customers. Not one I'm aware of apologized to a world that hadn't needed their brand of crap or confessed they'd been mistaken (at best) or had cruelly exploited a sad, dying, once-great nation already terrorized and sucked dry by the baby-butchers of Waco.

Some are *still* saying that we ain't seen nothing yet (they must have a lot of bean-curd jerky and military-surplus tampons left in their basements to palm off on some sucker). The majority are simply pretending the whole thing never happened, that they moved out to the frog-boonies for the fresh air and bought that yellow Honda generator for the aerobic exercise of yanking its cord. Nobody — with the noble and solitary exception of one good and valued comrade who knows who he is — has even written to acknowlege that I was right.

In many ways, that situation reminds me of the political campaign I launched last July 4th. As you may recall, I promised then that if a million individuals publicly endorsed my candidacy — along with the platform of Bill of Rights enforcement that was my only reason for undertaking it — I'd run for President as an independent. Allow me to repeat that: I said I'd run for President as an independent on the condition that a million people endorsed the idea.

Now the funny thing about that — like the vanishing Y2K alarmists — is that somehow, people heard and remembered the promise, but forgot the condition, which remains unfulfilled to this day. People expected me to start acting like a candidate, which I most decidedly am not and never will be unless a million people ask me to be.

And what did they expect of me as a candidate? They'd liked me well enough when it appeared I'd be different from other candidates. When I turned out actually to *be* different, that was something else.

They wanted me to go to conventions when I'd said I'd run as an independent if I ran at all. They wanted me to travel when I'd said I'd confine my efforts to the Internet and other electronic media.

They wanted me to pretend to be things I'm not — or stop being the things that I've been all my life — in order to get on TV. They wanted me to "tone down my rhetoric" — they *always* want me to "tone down my rhetoric" — when what they'd claimed they'd liked about me before was that I was honest, principled, and above all, plainspoken.

One old friend even called to beg me to go easy on the LP, as he was one of a group trying to win me that party's nomination. I was well into book mode by then, or I'd have asked him how I could accede to his request and remain the person he wanted to see nominated.

They wanted me to "clean up my act." They didn't like it that I was photographed in my favorite red T-shirt at the end of one of the hottest days on record in Fort Collins. They said I looked drunk when I was hot and tired and simply waiting for a table in a restaurant and hadn't even had my goddamned margarita yet. In effect, they said I shouldn't look like a 53-year-old white guy. They ordained that no candidate could wear a beard as scraggly as they thought mine was.

They even pretended to confusion when I said I wasn't seeking the LP nomination, but wouldn't turn it down if it were offered.

When this sort of nonsense happened for the hundredth time, I asked myself (in the words of P.J. O'Rourke) what the fucking fuck it had to do with Bill of Rights enforcement. The answer is *nothing*, proof positive that the American political process trivializes everybody and everything. The fact that I have a 10-year-old daughter and two cats is probably more important than what I stand for. What was most dismaying was that I was getting it from libertarians.

Meanwhile, thanks to the break I had to take to work for a

living, a plethora of embarrassing glitches on our Web sites, and the fact that everybody has an idea that's just a little bit better (if all the energy expended trying to get me the LP nomination had been spent, instead, gathering endorsements, I'd be President of the Philippines today), the endorsements failed to amount to more than a trickle. We're in the process of sorting them out, but if I have as many as 2,500, I'll probably faint dead away.

What does this mean?

Well, it means that Captain Bringdown (who also knows who he is) — a middle-aged adolescent who made one Great Leap in his lifetime and spent the next three decades doing pathetic Renfield impressions for entities unfit to lick his shower thongs, while sneering at anybody who continued trying to accomplish something real, the renowned pragmatician who handed the LP over to the sleazy con-gang who now run it for personal profit, the shriveled spirit whose response to my announcement last year was a sophomoric e-note predicting I'd never get as many as 10,000 endorsements — it means that Captain Bringdown gets to snigger at those of us still foolish enough to believe we might win a free country within our lifetimes.

Personally, I find that humiliating and intolerable, but it's out of my hands. To reiterate, I'm not a candidate, I'm just an individual whose friends have so far failed to convince him to run.

With my absolute non-candidacy clearly understood, permit me to observe that there isn't a single specimen running for President with any party this year who's fit to be a restroom attendant for the worst of America's Founding Fathers. It's time that we stopped marvelling over that, or even being disgusted by it, and actually did something about it, instead. I've done what little one man can to offer folks a chance, but disappointingly few have taken advantage of it.

Unfortunately, I don't know how to quit and probably wouldn't if I did. I don't necessarily regard this as a positive trait.

Over the next few weeks and months, I'll keep my original offer open. We'll fix the glitches and count the endorsements. I'll write regular columns on the issues of the day. At the same time, recalling what it was like to get back to what I was meant to do, I'll keep writing books. I'll also be taking my non-campaign in a slightly different direction now and again, suggesting what life will be like as a consequence of stringent enforcement of the Bill of Rights.

For the past 50 years, for example, there has been a cheap simple way to eliminate air pollution with infrastructure already in place, without taking anyone's property away or violating anyone's rights.

I know how to get ordinary people into space to stay — performing an ultimate humanitarian act along the way — not only at no involuntary expense to anyone, but at a profit unimaginably immense.

Make no mistake: Mine is the only political effort that has a chance at achieving an effect. If a million people demand enforcement of the Bill of Rights, it will change everything. No Republican, no Democrat, none of the current crop of minor candidates can make that promise truthfully, especially whoever gets the LP nod. Now that I've exposed the weakness of last cycle's candidate by beating his brains out in opinion polls both online and off, they're ready to switch to a dweeb who wants the party to stop talking about ending the War on Drugs. How much more bankrupt can the LP get?

Doubtless there will still be those who want to offer advice on the way my hair is cut. For them I have one question: Would you rather live as we do now — continue the futility that has marred the last 30 years — or create a nation where the Bill of Rights is enforced?

If it's the latter, help me — or get the hell out of my way.

Rally Me Not on the Lone Prairie
ର ର ର ର ର

A couple of years ago I delivered, at a rally of few hundred of my closest comrades, a well-written and impassioned speech from the steps of the Denver Capitol into a 40-mile-per-hour hurricane and a total absence of radio microphones or TV cameras. Since then, more people have read that speech on our local computer bulletin-board system than were aware of it the day it was given.

Since then, as well, I've refrained from participating in any more political rallies, although I love making speeches, especially about the Second Amendment and individual liberty, and most observers, I'm confident, will agree that I do a reasonably decent job of it. Before now, I've never really given my friends much of an answer when they asked me why I don't do rallies any more. Before now, I simply followed my instinct and didn't analyze it very much beyond that, because there were (and are) so many other things that must be done if we're to advance the individual right to own and carry weapons, and individual rights in general.

In one sense, it's a simple matter of profit and loss, or of cost-effectiveness. A rally subjects our side to certain risks without offering very much, if anything at all, in the way of potential gains. One idiot, or one agent provocateur, with one shot from a starter pistol could turn a peaceable assembly for a redress of grievances into what the round-heeled media would be certain to portray that evening (and for weeks afterward) as a riot of skinheads.

What's more, we now live in a bizarre political era in which many on our side are prepared to believe that the government itself engineered the explosion in Oklahoma City — and it's increasingly hard to find an argument sufficient to reason them out of it. And yet it doesn't seem to have occurred to anybody that a vastly less corrupt city administration, or one dirty gendarme with a scoped bolt-action rifle, could kill two birds with one stone by assassinating some especially effective leader and then seeing that the blame was laid on one of our own in the same way that fans of celebrities are said sometimes to injure or kill the very object of their adoration.

And for a while yet, my friends, though I believe things are starting to look up a trifle, it ain't gonna get any better out there.

Sometimes — often — it's worth it to court danger in a good cause. But what do we get for the risks I've described and many others I haven't thought of? We get dementedly twisted coverage by the media — if we get any coverage at all — pictures of the kind of unshaven paranoid who wanders the streets raving at the voices that torment him, wrapped in the American flag and wearing a propellor beanie. If our folks are packed shoulder-to-shoulder for hundreds of yards, we get long shots of empty parking lots and sound bites of our least articulate and craziest-sounding speaker.

I've seen all of this happen and much much more.

And so, my friends, have you.

I also deeply detest the politically prudent — and at the same time philosophically contradictory — necessity of attending such affairs unarmed. If nothing else, it serves to illustrate the way we're playing in the enemy's ballpark, with his ball and bat, by his rules, based on his fundamentally collectivist assumptions.

A rally is a show of numbers, a demonstration of potential force, a brutal straightforward statement that, hey, there are a lot more of us than there are of you, and if you don't quietly go along with whatever the hell we want, we'll just beat you up and kill you. Like it or not, that's the basic premise democracy is built on.

But our struggle isn't about numbers. If it were, we'd have lost it long long ago. It's about being *right*. Likewise, it isn't about democracy. It isn't about the will of the majority. It's an essentially anti-democratic struggle to retain and expand certain individual liberties (and perhaps the very concept of individual liberty itself) as embodied in a document — the Bill of Rights — written specifically to preserve those liberties from the will of any majority determined to diminish or eradicate them.

Whether only six people show up at a Second Amendment rally, or sixty, or six hundred, or even six thousand doesn't matter. It has nothing to do with the intelligence, truth, or justice of our cause. We'll never bring the numbers to our rallies that attend the most simple-minded grunt-and-sweat at the local stadium. And that alone should tell us something about the real importance of numbers.

We are just beginning to learn that we are at our best when the intelligence, truth, and justice of our cause is unobscured by irrelevancies like how many there are of us or how pretty we are. After a long dark night of humiliating defeats at the hands of demagogues and their media accessories, we now see a faint and as yet faraway glow of a coming dawn and victory. When it is in our hands, we'll owe it to radio and cybernetic communications. Wherever our ideas are free to go head-to-head, uncensored and on their own merit against their authoritarian antitheses, we always win.

In the end, I don't suppose I'm saying don't hold rallies. I don't suppose you'd listen if I did. I'm saying don't be amazed when you don't find me there. Last night I stayed up writing an enjoyably humiliating letter to a newspaper editor, reminding him that journalists once took the side of the people in this country against the government. Later today I'll post that letter on the Internet.

I feel another one just like it coming on.

I'm also writing a speech to be delivered later this year (indoors) in *our* ballpark, with *our* ball and bat, under *our* rules.

That's what I'm good at and that's what I'll do.

And you can *count* on that.

Tactical Reflections
❧❧❧❧❧

These observations, written in three or four "collections" over several years, derive from my 30-odd years (and odd years they've been) of experience as a libertarian activist, as well as from my personal struggle against gun control — properly termed, "victim disarmament" — which has lasted almost as long.

I write novels for a living and never thought of myself as an aphorist. The first collection of these ideas seemed to congeal out of thin air shortly after I read a biography of Admiral Lord Nelson as part of my research for *Henry Martyn*.

The second, I dedicated to my good friend and "spiritual advisor," Ernest Hancock of Phoenix, Arizona, in the confident belief that, if more of us were like Ernie, America would be a better, freer — and, admittedly, noisier — country.

******

Always attack in *perpendicular* fashion, from an unconventional and unexpected (but relevant) direction. The enemy will be unprepared; you can strike him with your full strength, while he finds nothing to attack effectively.

All religions are equally vile. What the Aztecs did with people's hearts, Judaeo-Christianity does with their minds.

America's historic misfortune is that her people have never been quite equal to the ideals upon which she was established.

Any point of view that fails to assume — and to accept — that males and females will inevitably perceive one another as "sex objects" is simply deranged.

As much as "sunshine soldiers" or "summer patriots," beware an ally — more common than you know — whose fear of the uncertainties of success moves him to surrender at the very moment of victory.

The average media personality rises to his level of incompetence simply by getting up every morning.

Believe what you like about "wasting your vote," but nothing will ever alter a fundamental assumption on the part of Democrats and Republicans — and the vast bureaucracy they've created together — that even the slightest manifestation of individuality (let alone individualism) is a threat that must be dealt with.

Better the "Me" generation than the "Duh" generation.

Beware of geeks bearing GIFs.

Beware those — in New York, Hollywood, and generally in life — who would make you a "star" because you're fresh and original, then spend the rest of your career trying to make you into a carbon copy of everybody else.

165

Lever Action

Choose your allies carefully: It's highly unlikely that you'll ever be held morally, legally, or historically accountable for the actions of your enemies.

Choose your *enemies* carefully: You'll probably be known much better and far longer for who *they* were, than for anything else you ever managed to accomplish.

Conservatives are accustomed to being called fascists and are well-prepared to defend themselves on that ground. Liberals are used to being called socialists. Those labels can be *switched*, however, and remain valid and instructive. It also catches them completely unprepared.

"Credible deniability" is probably more highly esteemed for the degree of psychological relief it offers its users, than for any political immunity it affords them.

Do not be deceived by the mere *appearance* of purpose. A string with one free end will often tie itself in a knot in a high wind. That's no reason to go looking for a Great Knotmaker.

Don't be disheartened by opinion polls or the outcome of elections. History has *never* been made by the majority and it never will be.

Euro-American welfare statism's preoccupation with "the halt and the lame" isn't an iota healthier than the obsession of ancient Egypt's priest-kings with death.

Ever notice how those who believe in animal rights generally don't believe in human rights?

Ever notice that the "Golden Age" of television was when sponsors had the strongest control over program content?

The fact that nobody asks you to sing is *not* an indication that you should sing louder. This sounds obvious until it's applied to matters like mass transportation. There are virtually *no* private mass-transit companies. This does not represent the failure of the market to provide a needed service, it represents the failure of an unneeded service to *go away*!

The function of government is to provide you with *service*; the function of the media is to supply the Vaseline.

Give the other guy an Angstrom unit, and it'll be reported that you gave him a parsec.

Go straight to the heart of the enemy's *greatest strength*. Break that and you break him. You can always mop up the flanks and stragglers later, and they may even surrender, saving you a lot of effort.

Great men don't "move to the center" — great men *move* the center!

The great secret of life lies in choosing the right woman. It's a *mother's* job to tell you not to play with fire. Marry the girl who tells you, "Go ahead."

Hell hath no fury like the well-nursed resentments of a younger sibling.

Hey, Hollywood, what's this throwing-the-gun-down-in-horror nonsense? When you see that you've driven a nail, do you throw away the hammer?

I was surprised to discover that children have to be taught to tell the truth. Lying, as a path of least resistance, is easier and comes more naturally. Children also have to be taught that life is more important than television.

If the backside pockets of your jeans are your "hip" pockets, does that make the ones in front your "un-hip" pockets? Then why is it that it's the ones in back that are *square*?

If there were a generic one-word expression for one "whose fear of the uncertainties of success moves him to surrender at the very moment of victory," it would be "Republican."

If you can avoid it, never play on the other guy's field, by the other guy's rules, or with the other guy's ball. He didn't design *his* system to give *you* the advantage. Remember that organisms defending their own territory are twice as effective as an intruding attacker.

Lever Action

If you lose, go down *fighting*. It costs nothing extra, and now and again ...

If you're not a little bit uncomfortable with your position, it isn't radical enough. How can you be *too* principled? Take the most extreme position you can — you're claiming territory you won't have to fight for later, mostly against your "allies."

In real life, a Smith & Wesson beats four aces, and Charles Darwin beats Bishop Berkeley.

In this world we live in, there are good ideas and there are bad ideas; those who can't tell the difference conduct opinion polls.

It has been my experience of life — my conservative fellow travelers to one side — that girls who don't believe in premarital sex usually don't believe in sex *after* the wedding, either.

It is moral weakness, rather than villainy, that accounts for most of the evil in the universe — and feeble-hearted allies, far rather than your most powerful enemies, who are likeliest to do you an injury you cannot recover from.

It is not the purpose of education to produce good citizens, but to help children become successful human beings. The former is properly identified as "indoctrination" and, when undertaken at the taxpayers' expense, should be illegal.

It is unlikely that your opponent thinks of himself as the bad guy. Of course, he may be wrong ...

Just what "life" is being defended here? I seriously doubt whether 99.99% of the anti-abortionists who wave their gory photo-placards around at demonstrations could tell a human fetus from that of a rabbit or a rat.

Know, down to the last cell in your body, that the *other guy* started it. He's the one who put things in an ethical context where considerations like decency and mercy have no referent. The less pity moves you now, the sooner you can go back to being a nice guy.

Know, otherhandwise, that the easiest most humiliating path to defeat is thinking that to beat the enemy you must be *like* him. Avoid the temptation to set your values aside "for the duration." What's the point of fighting if you give up what you're fighting for? If remaining consistent with your values leads to defeat, you chose the wrong values to begin with.

Know when to give up a lost cause. Anyone who needs to be *persuaded* to be free doesn't deserve to be.

The late 20th century Left fawns obsessively over animals, because an animal has no intellect, is incapable of challenging their discredited ideas, and can't say, "Leave me the hell alone and get a life, geek!"

Let the *other guy* offer compromises. Think of them as rungs on a ladder. Keep your own goals fixed firmly in your mind and make sure you never move any direction but upward. That's how the other side got where they are. It works.

Lies can be custom-tailored; truth comes straight off the rack — one size fits all. (This gem by my wife, Cathy L.Z. Smith.)

"Little" people, finding themselves in a position to say "No," *will*.

Manned spaceflight versus robotics? Let's see ... on your wedding night, would *you* be satisfied to send in a remote, and receive telemetered progress reports?

"Manx" is the noise a cat makes when you cut its tail off.

Many of life's tragedies — and comedies — arise from a misconception women suffer from: that sex is optional.

Money, first and foremost, is a medium of communication, conveying the information we call "price." Government control of the money supply is censorship, a violation of the First Amendment. Inflation is a lie.

The more fundamental position is the highest ground, allowing the most "perpendicular" attack. If he argues politics, argue ethics — things seldom go beyond this stage. If he argues ethics, argue epistemology (look it up). If he argues epistemology, argue metaphysics. If he argues metaphysics, you're up against Darth Vader and you're in trouble. Switch back to politics and accuse him of being out of touch with everyday reality. Or ask him if he's stopped beating his wife.

The most dangerous and successful conspiracies take place in public, in plain sight, under the clear bright light of day — usually with TV cameras focused on them.

Never aim at *anything* but total achievement of your goal: the utter capitulation of the enemy. Every effort involves inertia and mechanical losses, so adopting any lesser objective means partial defeat. Total victory means you don't have to fight the same fight again tomorrow.

Never look down your nose at the popular culture or self-righteously shun contact with it. How can you hope to *change* something you know nothing about?

Never soft-pedal the truth. It's seldom self-evident and almost *never* sells itself, because there's less sales resistance to a glib and comforting lie.

No process, event, or situation has ever improved under media scrutiny.

One of the sadder facts of human existence is that power will get you through times of no brains better than brains will get you through times of no power.

Once you've taken a public stand you know is right, never back down; anything less than a rock-hard stance will allow your enemies to nibble you to death.

The only way to beat the government is to *become* the government.

Over two centuries, American democracy has acquired something analogous to an immune system to protect it from the merest threat of wisdom, intelligence, honor, decency, individuality, or courage. Anyone entering the system who exhibits any of those undesirable attributes sooner or later finds himself broken and cast aside — if he is fortunate — or assimilated.

People who fear confrontation and avoid it at any cost will be eaten alive by their own children.

The people who worry most about "controlling their appetites" are the very people who least need to. And the people who need to most never do.

"The perfect is the enemy of the good," you say? I say that if nobody ever insisted on the perfect, there'd never *be* any good.

Politicians, bureaucrats, and cops all see the Constitution in about the same light in which your great-grandmother saw the Sears-Roebuck catalog: a fine useful thing to have around — although its principal application may be somewhat different than its authors intended.

"Question Authority"? To hell with that — hang it up by its thumbs, cut off its toes, and let it drip dry!

Remain the judge of your own actions. Never surrender that position by default. When the enemy screams "Foul!" the loudest, you know you're doing him the most damage. Those who *help* him scream are also the enemy.

Sarah Brady is no lady — and Diane Feinstein is no Einstein.

Second thoughts, failures of confidence, nervous last-minute course-changes are all detours and recipes for defeat. The time to think is *before* the battle — if possible, before the *war* — not in the heat of it.

She never said a word during labor, but four and a half years later, as we stood in my daughter's bedroom, hip-deep in toys and trying to clean the place up, my wife glared at me and said, "You did this to me, you sonofabitch!"

The shortest path to victory is a *straight line*. He who remains most consistent wins.

The simple-minded credo of the dirt-worshipper goes, "Four legs good, two legs bad." Otherhandwise, "Two wheels good, four wheels bad." The abysmal self-hatred thus revealed sends the imagination reeling in shock, disgust, and pity.

Tell me what *you* think, not what you think other people think. If you voted in terms of what *you're* ready for, instead of what you've convinced yourself others are ready for, we'd have had Constitutional government, a Libertarian society, and eradicated socialism half a century ago.

Sometimes stereotypes are 180 degrees off course and common sense isn't worth the paper it wasn't written on. For example, see who goes on longer having a good time and who, by contrast, is the first to get tight-lipped with indignant outrage: an individual secure and unbending in his principles or a compromise-prone "moderate."

Stereotypes can be a would-be objective observer's undoing: In terms of surface area alone, for example, is it human males or females who *shave*?

There are two kinds of people in the world: those who say, "There are two kinds of people in the world," and those who do not.

There is no *away*? Then where are Bill and Hillary going to go? Those who lead through authority have rivals on whom they must expend as much energy and attention as they do on their enemies. Those who lead by example have *enemies*, but no rivals.

Those who sell their liberty for security are understandable, if pitiable, creatures. Those who sell the liberty of *others* for wealth, power, or even a moment's respite deserve only the end of a rope.

To be human is to live by means of the artifacts that humans devise. To build a home, and scorn a weapon, is hypocrisy. It's also a good way to lose the home.

Truth is a valuable commodity that you don't automatically owe to anyone. Remember, however, that lies are even more expensive — they're tiring and costly to maintain — and even a tiny one can utterly *destroy* you.

Try never to speak of your enemies by name. Any publicity is still publicity — and there are those for whom *your* disapproval constitutes a recommendation.

Understand from the minute the fight begins that you're going to take damage. Accept it. (You'll always suffer more from the idiots and cowards on your *own* side than from any enemy.) Keep your overall goal in mind above all. Those who swerve to avoid a few cuts and bruises defeat themselves.

There is indeed some justice in the universe. Simply say "I'm not a crook" enough times, and everybody will start believing that you are.

"Wake up, America," you demand? America doesn't *need* to "wake up" — by which, of course, you mean pay attention to whatever *you* think is important. If America weren't already awake, paying attention to what each individual thinks is important, your milk wouldn't have gotten delivered this morning and you wouldn't have any electricity this afternoon.

Want a clear indication of what the welfare state is really all about? Note that the barest necessities of life — food, clothing and shelter — are all *taxed*.

Washington, D.C: where they took a perfectly good swamp and turned it into a sewer.

Well-timed silence is an effective bargainer. Most people fear silence at a level below conscious analysis, and rush to fill the emptiness with *accommodation*. A difficult tactic to learn and use, but it works.

What *about* GATT and NAFTA? If an agreement is more than a paragraph long — and it's between two *governments* — then it *ain't* about free trade!

When you boil it down, all group behavior is about eating and all individual behavior is about sex.

Why is it so hard to understand that the reason the first ten Amendments — commonly known as the Bill of Rights — are trampled underfoot by politicos and bureaucrats is that the Founding Fathers failed to provide a suitably harsh penalty for it?

Why is it virtuous that Indians used "every part of the buffalo" while meat companies that use every part of the cow or pig are "peddling garbage to children"?

The worst thing about Bill Clinton is that he's even given oral sex a bad name!

You cannot force me to agree with you. You can force me to *act* as though I agree with you — but then you'll have to watch your back. *All* the time.

You may never convince the other guy, but it's often worthwhile to keep arguing for the effect it has on bystanders, especially his *allies*.

III

THE SECOND AMENDMENT

Suppose You Were Fond of Books ...
ᥴᴕ ᥴᴕ ᥴᴕ ᥴᴕ ᥴᴕ

Suppose you were fond of books ...

You liked their leather bindings, their fancy endpapers, the way they speak to you of other times and places, the way they feel in your hand.

You even liked the way they smell.

Naturally, you were aware that books are dangerous. They give people ideas. Over the long sad course of history, they've resulted in the slaughter of millions — books like *Uncle Tom's Cabin*, *Das Kapital*, *Mein Kampf*, even the Bible — but you had too much intelligence, too much regard for the right of other people to read, write, *think* whatever they please, to blame the books themselves.

Now suppose somebody came along who agreed with you: Books are dangerous — and something oughta be done about it! Nothing you couldn't live with: Numbers could be stamped inside them, a different number, not just in each kind of book, each title or edition, but in each and every individual book.

"We can keep track of 'em better that way — it'll help get 'em back if they're stolen."

But wait. ... Isn't the right to freedom of expression, the right to create, exchange, and collect books — without a trace of government harassment — to read, write, and think whatever you please, supposed to be guaranteed by the First Amendment to the U.S. Constitution? No matter who thinks it's wrong? No matter how "sensible" their arguments may sound for taking that right away?

You tried to defend your rights, but nobody listened. You appealed to the media; they were even more dependent on the Bill of Rights than you were, and American journalism always gloried in its self-appointed role as watchdog over the rights of the individual. But the sad truth was that during its long self-congratulatory history, it was more like a cur caught bloody-muzzled time after time, savaging the flocks it had been trusted to protect.

You were alone. You insisted that books don't kill people, people kill people. They laughed and told you that people who read books kill people.

Time passed. ... Still they weren't satisfied. They wanted the serial numbers written down in record books. Then they wanted your name written down beside the numbers, along with your address, your driver's license number, your age, your race, your sex: "Cause we gotta know who's *reading* all these books!"

Soon they were demanding that bookstores be licensed. They forbade you to buy books by mail or in another state and required that your dealer report you if you bought more than one book in a five-day period. Then they forbade you to buy more than one book a month. They demanded that you wait five days, a week, three weeks before you could pick up a book you'd already paid for — at a store subject to unannounced warrantless inspections and punitive closure by heavily armed government agents. In Massachussetts and New Jersey, the mere possession of a book meant an automatic year in jail. At one point they offered to spend tax money to buy your books: "You've got too many. This is a purely voluntary measure — for the time being."

Now they want to confiscate any of your books they think are *too long*: "No honest citizen needs a book with *that* many pages!"

Your taxes will be spent to burn them, and somehow you have a feeling that it's just the beginning, that some dark midnight, no matter how peaceable or agreeable or law-abiding you are, you're going to hear that knock on your door. ...

Yes, books are dangerous. They start holy wars, revolutions, and make people dissatisfied with their lives.

But this is ridiculous!

Is it a nightmare? Another Gulag horror story? A blood-soaked page from the history of fascism? No, it's just the commonplace oppression people suffer every day when they feel about *guns* the way you feel about *books*.

Okay, maybe that feeling's hard to understand. But just try justifying your own love of books to, say, an Ayatollah Khomeini. The very requirement that you must, in violation of your basic human rights, will make you inarticulate with rage.

Gun owners laugh at the notion of human rights, because they have none.

Sure, guns *are* dangerous. Like books. Like books, the right to create, exchange, and collect them without a trace of government harassment is supposed to be guaranteed. No matter who thinks it's wrong. No matter how "sensible" their arguments may sound for taking your rights away.

So what makes you think your books are any safer than your neighbor's guns? Whether you like books or guns, the issue's the same: *When anybody's rights are threatened, everybody's rights are threatened.*

Ban a Gun — Go to Jail
 භ භ භ භ භ

The Constitution, without qualification, states that the individual right to own and carry weapons will not be infringed. Title 18, U.S. Code, Sections 241 and 242 ordains as a crime the violation of anybody's civil rights. Part of the Fourteenth Amendment requires removal of any politician who defies the Constitution, barring him (or her) from public office in perpetuity. And, of course, betraying one's oath of office is perjury, which is a felony.

By attempting to ban semiautomatic weapons (or weapons of any sort), city authorities in Dayton, Ohio, and Rochester, New York, have broken all these laws. It's possible that conspiracy and racketeering statutes apply to their illicit activities, as well.

We all know how slight the chances are that any of these miscreants will be prosecuted for having violated our natural, fundamental, inalienable human, civil, and Constitutional rights under the current political circumstances. So do they, or they wouldn't have broken the law. However, as students of history, we also know that political circumstances change — a fact they seem to have overlooked.

If they can't be prosecuted now, why not a year from now? If they can't be prosecuted a year from now, why not four years from now? And if they can't be prosecuted four years from now, why not twenty? Simon Wiesenthal never gave up on the Nazis. Why should we — who feel that the Bill of Rights is all that keeps America from becoming the world's biggest banana republic — ever give up on the Dayton or Rochester perpetrators, or on any public servant who introduces, sponsors, or votes for gun control?

Perhaps more to the point at the moment: Why should we have any more regard for any law they pass than they have for the highest law of the land supposedly governing us — and them — already?

Von Clausewitz, the eminent Prussian strategist, said you should always give the enemy a way out, so he won't fight like a trapped animal and be likelier to retreat. So what can these criminals in Dayton and Rochester do to avoid weeks, months, and possibly years of looking over their shoulders, waiting for the long arm of the highest law of the land to seize, humiliate, and punish them?

Three things: They must repeal the offending legislation; they must resign from office immediately afterward; and they must promise, publicly and in writing, never to seek or hold public office again.

Meanwhile, we can offer them a few words of advice: Don't listen to the torrent of lies spewed out by Sarah Brady and her fascist front-group. Don't let that pickle-faced harridan and her tent-revival meat-puppet get you into more trouble. Her First Amendment rights are unimpaired by any oath of office to uphold the Constitution and she's not going to jail when the reckoning comes due.

You are.

The Atrocity Engineers

*Delivered at a Libertarian Party Second Amendment Rally
on the Denver Capitol Steps, April 18, 1993*

Some years ago I watched a broadcast advertised as "news," in which a citizen was about to read a part of the Bill of Rights, the first ten amendments to the Constitution, to a gaggle of politicians holding illegal hearings with the intent of further suppressing the individual right to own and carry weapons.

These hearings were illegal, among other reasons, because the Colorado state constitution warns that the individual right to own and carry weapons isn't "to be called into question" — which, of course, was precisely the publicly expressed purpose of the hearings.

As we've all had occasion to learn the hard way, the mass media — television, radio, newspapers — never cover this issue with anything even remotely resembling fairness, accuracy, or, for that matter, intelligence, and this particular day was no exception. Before the citizen had even begun to read what the Supreme Law of the Land has to say regarding the individual right to own and carry weapons, some inane commentator's ill-informed and feeble-minded voice-over cut him off.

Now an educated and reflective individual, better aware of history and the world around him than the average mass-media reporter, understands perfectly well that the Second Amendment was drafted specifically to discourage authoritarian ambitions within the government. By now he also understands that the mass-media expression "assault weapon" is actually authoritarian code for precisely the sort of hardware that, given today's technology and circumstances, best meets that specification.

Thus an educated and reflective individual, better aware of history and the world around him than the average mass-media reporter, refuses to surrender his "assault weapon" — regardless of whatever legislation gets passed to intimidate him — because, for instance, he never wants to see his country taken over by militaristic thugs, as happened earlier this century in Germany.

"But that's ancient history," the mass media invariably simper (and to them, it is); "such events have nothing to do with now."

Very well then, an educated and reflective individual, better aware of history and the world around him than the average mass-media reporter, refuses to surrender his "assault weapon" because he never wants to see his whole town driven from their homes and marched to death on country roads, as happened not too long ago in Cambodia.

"But that was far away," the mass media invariably simper; "such events have nothing to do with real civilization."

Very well then, an educated and reflective individual, better aware of history and the world around him than the average mass-media reporter, refuses to surrender his "assault weapon" because he never wants to see his kids or his neighbors' kids dragged into the street to have their arms and legs broken by uniformed goons, as has often happened in Palestine under "civilized" Israeli occupation.

"But those are unique circumstances," the mass media invariably simper; "such events have nothing to do with America."

Very well then, an educated and reflective individual, better aware of history and the world around him than the average mass-media reporter, refuses to surrender his "assault weapon" because he never wants to see entire square blocks of his community bombed into ashes by police helicopters, as happened a while back in Philadelphia.

Furthermore, an educated and reflective individual, better aware of history and the world around him than the average mass-media reporter, refuses to surrender his "assault weapon" because he understands that politicians anywhere are capable of engineering such atrocities. Over sixty blood-soaked centuries they've demonstrated exactly what they're capable of, time and again.

Lever Action

Right down the line, from power-hungry federal "czars" to publicity-hungry county sheriffs, the atrocity engineers are completely out of control, justifying their latest crimes against the Bill of Rights with a phony "War on Drugs," which the mass media reporters — who aren't one bit more responsible than when William Randolph Hearst was at the helm — whipped up for them in the first place. The plain inconvenient truth is that a century ago, when today's illegal drugs were as easily and cheaply available as aspirin, there wasn't any "drug problem."

Not until the atrocity engineers created one.

Thus an educated and reflective individual, better aware of history and the world around him than the average mass-media reporter, refuses to surrender his "assault weapon" because he never wants to be murdered in his own home under a hailstorm of gunfire and grenades because the vice squad got the wrong address — or simply because he told a cop he wanted to be left alone.

It's happened more than once in Colorado.

It happened recently in Waco, Texas.

Somewhere in America it happens every day.

And now, with their uniformly slanted opinionizing over the "assault weapon" issue, the mass media have handed the atrocity engineers yet another opportunity — although they may not realize it yet, and by the time they do, it will be too late.

When the day comes that they're covering a story that the authorities don't want covered, and a tiny, palm-sized, .25 caliber "assault weapon" is conveniently "discovered" by a cop in some reporter's camera bag or glove compartment, I hope they'll remember that I warned them it would happen. I doubt they will. Neither their memory nor their attention spans seem to be that long.

The maintenance of civil order and social democracy is in our hands. It has been there all along. It was never anywhere else. In a nationwide study, Professor Don Kates at the St. Louis University School of Law found that the police succeed in wounding or driving off criminals only eighty-one percent as often as armed citizens do, and are fifteen percent more likely to be wounded or killed themselves. More than five times as many cops shoot an innocent individual in the process as civilians do.

Five times.

The maintenance of civil order and social democracy is in our hands. It has been there all along. It was never anywhere else. "We the people" were naive and lazy to believe that anything so important can safely be entrusted to "authorities" or "experts" through elections or through any other process. Self-defense, against individual criminals or criminals sanctioned by the state, can no more be delegated to somebody else than eating can, or sleeping, or any other bodily function.

History warns us that delegated responsibility becomes power.

And that power is inevitably abused.

The maintenance of civil order and social democracy is in our hands. It has been there all along. It was never anywhere else. If civil order and social democracy are ever to be restored to America, our emphasis now must be on enforcing the Bill of Rights.

On Bill of Rights enforcement.

We must take that power out of the hands that have abused it and break it down — break it down — into units so small that it can no longer be called "power," but simply "responsibility," which, unlike power, comes not from the barrel of a gun, but from the minds and hearts of the individuals behind it.

What About England?
ᴄᴐᴄᴐᴄᴐᴄᴐᴄᴐ

You've probably noticed how arguments about gun control invariably have a way of getting around to England. Just when you've scored big with, "It's better to have a gun and not need it, than need a gun and not have it," some squib-loaded liberal will pop up with, "Oh yeah? Well, what about England?"

What about England, anyway? True enough, it's long been an embarrassment to advocates of firearms rights, a millstone, an albatross, an out-of-work brother-in-law around our necks. No getting around it, England has extremely strict gun control — seven years in Slam City for an unlicensed "offensive weapon" (meaning anything worth defending yourself with) — and very little violent crime.

Which ain't the way it's supposed to work, right? "When guns are outlawed, only outlaws will have guns." Shucks — not even the outlaws (except for an occasional IRA member) have guns in the blissfully peaceful Socialist Kingdom on the North Sea.

But comparisons between cultures can be tricky. England's strict laws and low crime rate don't necessarily have any more to do with one another than America's (relatively) light restrictions and high crime rate, or Switzerland's armed-to-the-teeth attitude and virtually non-existent crime. Things — nations, customs, people — are more complicated than that.

What's more, the complex truth is on our side. The purpose of this article is to prove that to you, so you can prove it to others. Last November, when Massachusetts voters pulled an important brick from the foundation of gun control's Big Lie, the myth that "The People Want Gun Control" was shattered. Shattering myths about England will remove another brick. One by one, as the bricks vanish, the Big Lie will crumble, and once again our firearms rights will be secure.

In an article titled "Libertarianism: The Gun Owners' Unseen Ally" that I wrote for *Guns* magazine in July, 1976, I showed how many academics and intellectuals — philosophers, sociologists — not only actively support firearms rights, but that the subject-matter of their respective disciplines gives us ammunition as well. Never was this more true than in the case of England, gun control and crime.

A life-long student of English psychology and culture, I grew up in the most antiquatedly British part of Canada. As my interest in guns increased, so did my puzzlement over the seeming paradox of English gun laws and crime rates. In 1975, I married a lady who had lived in England for 12 years, shared my interests, and finally bullied me into investigating in person — ironically enough, in the bicentennial summer of '76.

To understand the English, concentrate on a couple of important truths about history and sociology — and unlearn one common misconception: that the English are in any significant way like Americans. It just ain't so.

In the first place, fundamental differences in the way each of us looks at things drove us apart considerably more than two centuries ago — the Revolution was simply a Farewell Address.

The English are afflicted with a basically European awe and respect for authority. They are helplessly incapable of understanding why we colonials chopped down the King's pine trees, killed his deer and tarred-and-feathered his tax collectors.

Since Independence, we have gone increasingly separate ways. Today, despite a common historical origin and language — superficialities that obscure vastly more important dissimilarities — there are more points in common between the English and the Japanese than there are between the English and ourselves.

For example, consider the difference between political democracy (the system in both the U.K. and the U.S.) and social democracy (truly practiced nowhere but the United States of America).

We are accustomed to the idea that anybody can become rich, famous, important (or poor, unknown, or insignificant), purely by his own efforts and some luck. There are occasional injustices, and we often feel that young Horatio Alger might have a tougher time making it today, yet he still can, if he has enough grit.

In England, class is the name of the game, and Horatio doesn't stand an anchovy's chance of getting to the upper crust. It's almost impossible for Americans to understand the full meaning (and inescapable doom) of the English class system.

In England, your family, your location, the financial status you were born into, but most important of all, your accent put you in a place where you'll remain for the rest of your life, no matter how hard you work, how smart you are — even (or especially) how much money you make.

You can't change your fate. England is too small, her institutions too narrow, her memories too long. Your background follows you everywhere. People often deny this is true today, then disprove their denial with a casual, unconscious remark. The system, like its twin brother in India, endures despite reformers, educators, the government.

A person's social status can be measured — his life ruined forever — by the amount of shirt cuff he lets stick out beyond his jacket sleeve. I am not exaggerating or kidding; it is literally, horribly, true.

If an individual were to devise cheap simple solutions to all of England's many social and economic problems, no matter how sensible or workable they were, no one would give him a moment's notice — if he expressed himself in a lower-class accent. If America's motto is "Build a better mousetrap," England's must be "I knows me place."

What does all this have to do with crime and gun control? A hell of a lot, and here are some for-instances: Traditionally, servants — the lowest class of all — are responsible for the upkeep of their masters' homes. (See PBS TV's "Upstairs, Downstairs" for a highly accurate picture.) This includes cleaning, cooking, maintenance — and security! Policemen — public servants — are also almost exclusively lower-class. Here it comes: No right-thinking high-born English gentleman could possibly think of trusting a servant with a weapon.

When the rulers of England were foreigners — Norman French — they dared not allow a conquered people to go armed, for fear of being skewered on a clothyard shaft by one of their own slaves. A wise robber-baron keeps his subject — from whom his wealth is extorted at swordpoint — defenseless.

The Welfare State bureaucrats presently bleeding England dry must unconsciously have similar fears, for they take similar precautions. The situation is made for them: The upper class depends on the lower class for security, the lower class depends on the police, and the police, naked as they are, depend on the Majesty of the Law. The notion of self-defense is beyond the understanding of the English people.

To show how far this has gone, an upper-class girl I know, the niece of a former Prime Minister, told me her father could never consider contaminating one of his $5,000 shotguns on anyone as vulgar as a burglar!

As amazingly warped as that may seem, it is nothing remarkable for the British. It did help this poor confused colonial to believe something else he was told: In England, criminals themselves are largely lower-class, and since no one wants to be considered a peasant, very few people commit crimes! Hard to believe, unless you understand the brutal power of the class system.

But there is a more basic reason for Britain's crimelessness. Criminologists (honest ones, not scapegoaters who blame everything on handguns) recognized long ago that a high crime rate is a sort of back-handed compliment to any society, a testimony to its vigorous good health.

When there is freedom to choose the kind of life you want to lead — and lots of different lifestyles to choose among — a certain percentage of individuals will choose crime. But when a rigid class-bound society limits individual choice, there is less opportunity to be a criminal — or anything else — and, therefore, less crime.

Crime is a sort of tax we pay on individual liberty. There will always be those who use their freedom to damage others, but worse, there will always be some jackass around to suggest that we combat crime by limiting individual liberty. The wisdom and virtue of a society can be measured by how little that jackass is listened to.

In America, a person can be whatever he strives for, tycoon or criminal (or both!). In England, you are what you are until they put you into the ground. You are born — and that's all, brother — a Cockney or a Mountbatten-Windsor, a peasant or a Lord.

Fascist and Communist countries are relatively crime free because their governments crush individual choice. England has even less crime: The force of custom is a hundred times stronger than the force of law. Is a low crime rate worth the terrible price England pays? Would you like to be chained forever, right where you began, with no chance of bettering yourself — just to reduce crime? Would you impose a similar decision on your children?

The "enlightened" liberals you argue with are answering "Yes!" — their demands to regulate firearms are really demands to regulate human lives. Prohibitionists don't trust anyone (including themselves) to make decisions; they want everything frozen, fixed, predictable. "A place for everything — and everyone in his place."

It's a kind of motion sickness: Anti-gunners, anti-hunters, anti-technologists, anti-capitalists rail against progress and growth. They desire to impose their frightened static view of the world on everyone else — by force, if necessary. Theirs is a medieval — feudal — outlook; they mistrust and despise the healthy dynamic world of individual choice and human action.

And they have won in England.

Ordinarily, good old individual cussedness could be expected to screw up the planners and manipulators now and then. But England suffers even today from a culture-wide state of shock. World War I, the overnight loss of her "invincible" world empire, has frozen her customs and institutions (including her Welfare State mentality) at about 1914. The English secretly wish the last sixty-five years hadn't really happened.

England lost one third of her male population in that war — the country still feels as though it were run to suit someone's prissy maiden aunt. Everyone wears his galoshes, carries his umbrella like a good little boy, and the sweet grandmotherly State provides food, clothing, shelter, medicine, entertainment. The people are so happy they can hardly stand it — until they go carve somebody up with a meat-axe. England may not have much crime, but when it happens, it's spectacular as all get-out.

English crime is increasing. At least half the cops (according to police journals I was shown) want to start gun-toting, and I know a place right in the middle of London where, "offensive weapons" or not, you can discreetly purchase, from a salesman who is the stereotype of the suave and supercilious English butler, a wicked swordcane or a lethal umbrella. I've a pet theory that they might have something to do with London's lack of muggers and other pests; any professional hardcase is going to think twice about taking on people who carry, rain or shine, a handy and effective club.

Maybe folks are getting fed up with living in a country run by little old ladies of both sexes. I don't know. I do know that, in London's frustrating maze of streets and alleys, I passed through plenty of neighborhoods snatching reflexively at my left armpit for two pounds of iron I'd regretfully left in a cabinet 5,000 miles away. And I'm not talking about the really rough places where Jack the Ripper and Professor Moriarty purportedly used to hang out.

Furthermore, England's got a couple of types of crime not reported in the statistics our liberal friends are always waving at us. First, there's the Irish Republican Army, murdering people and blowing things up — another topic I disagreed about with the Prime Minister's niece. I said they're a bunch of cowardly punks who wouldn't last two weeks in Montana. She was aghast at such Yankee barbarism, and with Oriental resignation, schooled me in the proper attitude: Let the IRA kill as many people as they want — they'll get tired and go away when they see the English spirit can't be broken. She's dead right, of course: that was already accomplished half a century ago.

Parenthetically, the British people — like our own liberals, ever on the lookout for a scapegoat — hold us responsible for the IRA. Seems we greedy capitalist types ship the nasties all their arms and ammo. Unfortunately, this is a little hard to square with the police displays of captured IRA hardware I saw on the BBC — every one of them a Czech AK-47.

Another kind of "hidden" British crime is the Welfare State itself, a tax system that can rip off productive people — and has — for the sake of the non-productive, in excess of 100%! That's big-time crime, in my book, and has brought the English economy — and morale — to their knees.

England's rigid class system and rapacious government have left the people with an Asian fatalism. The country's going down the tubes and everyone knows it, is resigned to it, from the defeated free-enterpriser to the enterprising burglar. There's no hope in England because there's no opportunity. For the same reason, there's no crime.

Forget guns. They don't figure in the picture at all.

Nipponese, Ted!
ભ ભ ભ ભ ભ

I take second place to nobody in my admiration of things Japanese. Like nearly everyone I know, I own a Japanese car and the bulk of my household electronics were crafted in the Land of the Rising Sun regardless of what it says on the cabinet. I believe that Japan's standards of quality control (instilled, ironically, by American mentors after World War II) should be everybody's standards. I favor free international trade, without a hint of regulation or restriction, and the utterances of its Japan-bashing opponents often make me feel ashamed of my own country.

That said — and it needs saying — it's time to strangle in its cradle a particularly vile notion, being pushed on us now by the minions of Ted Turner, that the Japanese have anything to teach us about civilized conduct, violence, or the ownership of weapons.

At issue is the sad case of a Louisiana man who mistook a

costumed non-English-speaker on his doorstep, a Japanese student looking for a Halloween party, for an intruder, and shot him to death. CNN and the Japanese talking heads were giving it plenty of play before the trial, but when the shooter was acquitted, they flew into a frenzy of America-bashing that made Joseph Biden's gibbering diatribes on Japanese trade practices sound lucid by comparison.

In Japan, we're endlessly informed, guns have been forbidden since the 1500s. And there's good reason for Turner's sudden interest in Japanese culture. England, the traditional gun-control utopia, is falling apart. The general disintegration of what was once the greatest civilization in history (back when Dr. Watson was free to slip a .455 caliber "life preserver" into his greatcoat pocket) is tragedy enough. What's even more tragic — and stupid — is the perfect correlation between its increasingly and gratuitously stricter gun laws and a skyrocketing rate of violent crime that our media never quite get around to telling us about.

Another thing they won't tell us about is the history of Japanese gun control. Following their "discovery" by the Portuguese in 1542, the Japanese took to firearms rather enthusiastically, and today, scholars still debate exactly what made medieval Japan return, en masse, to pointy sweat-powered weapons and "give up the gun." Some idiots believe it was a Noble Experiment, akin to the development of American democracy. But are you aware of what a technically upgraded peasantry usually does to expensively armored aristocrats whose ancestors have invested whole lifetimes learning to wield cumbersome inefficient weapons for no other purpose than to "protect" those peasants out of everything they've got?

Self-appointed bigwigs anywhere always have a vested interest in disarming their potential victims. Japan's noble gangsters (of which Hideyoshi Toyotomi was the boss in 1592) were a bit quicker on the uptake — and a whole lot fast-and-fancier-talking — than the Tammany in control of medieval Europe. Japanese peasants let themselves be conned and threatened out of their guns by the Al Capone of their culture, condemning themselves to centuries of bullying by thuggish Samurai, one savage dictatorship following another, and a state-sanctioned race hatred and class prejudice that today constitute Japan's greatest problem. Finally, they let themselves be herded by fascists into a disastrous war that ended in the obliteration of Hiroshima and Nagasaki.

Am I actually claiming that *gun control* is the ultimate reason that two great and beautiful cities were incinerated by American atomic bombs?

You bet I am.

Our media don't talk very much about contemporary Japanese crime, either, but I'll give you a clue: Without victim disarmament laws, today's Japanese might not be dependent on machinegun-toting Yakuza (for which read, "Japanese Mafiosi") for patrolling the Ginza and making it the only safe street in Tokyo after dark.

America's gun laws, too — 20,000-plus of them — are historically rooted in race hatred and class prejudice. When you don't like someone, however evil or irrational your reason, the last thing you want him to have is a gun. In the 19th century, Italians, Chinese, the Irish, and above all *blacks* had somehow to be disarmed, or society's overlords (who had plenty of guns themselves) wouldn't feel safe. Today, Turner, his wife, and other liberal advocates of victim disarmament are notorious for owning guns themselves, but "deeply concerned" with keeping them out of the "wrong hands" — meaning those of the productive class.

Yet the Second Amendment was written so that Americans might never be dominated by the breed of criminals who

ruled classical Japan, and, for the most part, it's worked. And
when Japanese tourists arrive, the first thing many of them do
is go out to a target range to rent one of the repulsive imple-
ments that make America so detestable. And when evening
shadows fall, or they're just out of ammunition, they're happy,
exhausted, and not too terribly anxious to return to a land where
such marvelous toys are prohibited.

Maybe they'll learn about gun ownership the same way
they learned about quality control. I suspect that's what Turner
and his Japanese symbiotes are *really* afraid of.

So shut up, Ted, you mealy mouthed, gun-toting hypocrite. America may be "the only country in the world that allows such easy access to weapons," as your henchbeings are
so fond of pointing out; it's also "the only country in the world"
that enjoys formal separation of church and state (and thus
avoids violent religious conflict) — not to mention an unfettered media on which you've grown obscenely rich. It's "the
only country in the world" in lots of ways, and nobody's going
to let you turn it into a replica of disintegrating England, socialist Europe, or medieval Japan.

Shut up, Jane, the same to you.

Shut up, CNN and Headline News.

And with all respect, shut up, Japan.

You don't know what you're talking about.

Twelve Tips for Safer Schools
ᏆᏆᏆᏆᏆ

When I awoke the other day, the "morning guys" on
Denver's KOA radio, tight-lipped and quivering with outrage

because the U.S. Senate had declined (however temporarily) to bugger the Second Amendment — and still sucking hard on the Littleton shootings weeks after they'd happened — were asking their listeners for ideas on "improving school security."

Here, more or less at random — and overlooking the rather obvious question: if the security of schools was really improved, then what would these eaters-of-the-dead do for a living? — are a few ideas of mine. ...

First, give up trying to find any reason that crazed mass-killers do what they do. I know that'll leave thousands of hours of empty air time, but they're crazed mass-killers, after all, and they *have* no reason. What's more, just as you don't any get cleaner by wading through a sewer, you won't get any saner by exploring the minds of the insane.

Stop jumping at shadows. Although the first ten Amendments are an evil incantation to the average school board member or administrator, there's no exercise of free speech, for example, that poses any real threat to anybody anywhere — except, of course, to advocates and apologists for the police state, which thrives on lies and suppressed truth. Try to stand up for principle (NEA members note the spelling — I'm not talking about the keeper who ties your shoes and wipes the drool off your chin). The Bill of Rights is not a laundry list of authorized privileges, but a law that places absolute limits on what government may do. To ask whether it applies only to adults, or to kids as well, is to miss the whole point, regardless of what the Supreme Court (themselves the drooling product of the public-school system) may claim.

Beg someone with a brain to help you. If you're polite enough, maybe they'll tell you that there's nothing about a school uniform that prevents the use of pipe bombs or high-capacity semiautomatic weapons. Don't ask former drug czar and intellectual thugboy William Bennett about this; he needs to beg someone with a brain to help *him*.

Recognize the real threat. Compulsory, tax-supported, government-regulated educational facilities have not only been made into prisons, they're what liability lawyers call an "attractive nuisance." Mass shootings simply don't happen at private or parochial schools. (Which means, of course, that they don't happen to the children of public-school teachers!) And they *can't* happen to children who are home schooled.

Do something that works. Require all public-school teachers to become proficient with weapons and to carry them concealed at all times. (This might also improve discipline at certain "tough" inner-city schools.) If teachers refuse — or, what's more likely, prove hopelessly incompetent — then let them seek employment opportunities where they really belonged to begin with anyway, in the fast-food industry.

Do something else that works. Require all students to take a course each year in the safe and *effective* use of firearms. You'll be astonished at the degree of maturity and responsibility this will engender, and schools will no longer be soft targets. In the future, mass murderers will just have to do their killing at courthouses and airports.

Stop advocating cultural genocide. Children of the "gun culture" — despite the lying bigoted stereotypes created by mass media and government — seldom get into trouble, are remarkably self-directed and self-reliant (the real reason government and mass media want them controlled), and almost always grow up to make something decent and worthwhile of themselves. The same cannot be said of the children of liberals.

Ignore the media. The morons who pollute the airwaves on TV and radio every day know absolutely *nothing* of history, human nature, or the law. That's the reason they were hired in the first place. Their "expertise" lies elsewhere, entirely in the areas of station politics and hairspray usage. All they have to sell is a pathological fear of everything. All they have to share with you is their abysmal ignorance and their blind, churning, mindless hatred of anyone who can think for himself.

Ignore politicians. They're almost as bad as the media. I'm not the first person to observe that America would be vastly better off in the hands of any 600 individuals randomly chosen from any telephone diectory in the country (with the possible exception of Little Rock, Arkansas) than with the creatures leaving slime tracks in the halls of Congress.

In particular, pay no attention to Bill Clinton. The feral boys at Columbine High only killed 15 innocent helpless people. Bill and his boys killed 82 people at Waco — 22 of them innocent helpless little children. He's killed countless thousands in the Balkans with his bully bombers, and (speaking of bombers) there's mounting evidence that Timothy McVeigh had exactly as much to do with the explosion in Oklahoma City as Lee Harvey Oswald did with the assassination of Jack Kennedy.

Last, but far from least, don't fight fire with fascism. The one and only thing that makes America the most peaceful, productive, and progressive civilization in history is the freedom enshrined in — but not granted by — the Bill of Rights. Lose that, and you'll turn this country into exactly the kind of violent, impoverished, and backward Third World cesspool that Clinton, McCain, Gore, Chaffee, Feinstein, Warner, Schumer, Allard, Lautenberg, Frank, and Campbell really want to rule.

Kids and Guns at School
అ∽ అ∽ అ∽ అ∽ అ∽

Somebody had to be the first to say it — and I was, 16 years ago, when I wrote my first novel, *The Probability Broach*.

In that book, an American policeman is suddenly plunged into an alternate world where dropping a weapon in your pocket every morning is as ordinary and unremarkable as doing the same thing with a wallet, and even children carry guns.

Of course, what I meant, writing that part of the book, was that children *especially* carry guns. They're little, not very strong, and they need guns more than big people do.

In the wonderful world of *The Probability Broach*, there weren't any public schools, and not only were administrators — that is, the owners and operators — of various private school systems not disturbed at the prospect of their little charges toting magnum semiautos to class, they offered courses to improve the kids' proficiency with them, just as their parents deemed proper.

The customer, after all, is always right.

Look: In our world, in the 19th century and well into the 20th, kids and guns went together like ham and eggs. Boys could be seen everywhere, every day, wandering the countryside with .22 rifles dangling from their grubby little fingers. True, times have changed, but only to the extent that it should now be something better than a .22 (the likeliest game being bigger and meaner than the squirrels, rabbits, and rats of an earlier era), and little girls should carry guns, as well.

Should anyone argue that these rifles and their owners belonged to a rural period of history, rather than the urbanized America of today, I'll concede, and add that this seems like an argument in favor of handguns.

The only thing wrong with kids bringing guns to school is that the wrong kids bring them, for the wrong reasons. Moreover, the solution isn't metal detectors in doorways, locker searches and seizures that make it tough to teach the Fourth and Fifth Amendments, or the mandatory expulsions for a year that even Rush Limbaugh advocates; it's simply rearranging things so the right kids bring guns to school for the right reasons.

Self-defense.

Everybody's basic human right.

I know that all liberals, the majority of conservatives, and even many libertarians are going to have trouble with this concept — once they awaken from the apoplectic coma it sends them reeling into — though it wouldn't have troubled science fiction author Robert A. Heinlein (who turned out to be right about so many other things, as well) even 30-odd years ago, when he wrote *Red Planet*, a novel that concerns itself with this very subject. The same people — liberals, conservatives, even many libertarians — often have trouble with an even simpler idea: Freedom works.

Any time, any place.

Consider: In Orlando, Florida, as we know by now, a massive increase in the number of rapes was halted and reversed by the expedient of offering classes in firearms-handling to several thousand women over one long hot summer (see Paxton Quigley's *Armed and Female* for details even I had never heard before).

We also know, in general, that wherever ordinary people exercise the Constitutional right to arm themselves, crimes of confrontation diminish, whereas exactly the reverse is true wherever that right is narrowed or suppressed.

So I ask, why not take that valuable lesson to school where it belongs? Why continue to maintain the public-school system as a sort of holiday camp away from reality, if reality is what we're interested in conveying to our children?

Unlike liberals, conservatives, and many libertarians, I don't believe the Bill of Rights begins to apply to an individual only when he or she reaches some arbitrary age of legal majority. In my experience, adults have just as much difficulty exercising their rights intelligently as children do. In fact, children seem to understand rules — such as, "No one has a right to *initiate* force against another human being for any reason" — better than those who have simply grown bigger and older without getting wiser.

As long as public schools exist, they should be required by law to offer mandatory courses in safe and effective gun-handling. It's a historic fact that hoodlums, for the most part, lack the self-discipline to shoot well. So, over the course of time, they'll be out-classed — and out-shot — by kids capable of learning the shootist's craft, and the problem will be solved.

Forever.

Or until people forget the lesson and have to learn the hard way all over again.

I do have lingering doubts about the schools' ability to teach anything — let alone safe and effective gun-handling — to anybody, and the real answer is to abolish public schools altogether.

But that's another story.

Murder by Gun Control
∽∾ ∽∾ ∽∾ ∽∾ ∽∾

Why is everybody being so damned polite?

No sane individual living in the last days of the 20th century would knowingly welcome Nazis, the KGB, the Khmer Rouge, the ATF, or the FBI into their homes. We've learned too much from what happened to Jews in Germany, Kulaks in Russia, "landlords" in China, everybody in Cambodia, and victims of state terrorism at Ruby Ridge and Waco.

But let the Jackbooted Thugs' Ladies' Auxiliary slap on makeup and broomstick skirts, let them prattle in squeaky little girl voices and breathe their vegetarian breath all over us, and for some reason we think we have to ask them in and offer them chamomile tea.

Well, to hell with that. I used to give a lecture at the local university that began like this: "Until this morning you could plead ignorance for positions you take or fail to take on the moral and political issues of the day. When you leave this classroom an hour from now, having heard the facts I'm about to present, it'll either be as a brand new libertarian or as a fully self-aware fascist monster."

Today I say the same to politicians, bureaucrats, trigger-happy cops, Handgun Control, Inc., Colorado Governor Bill Owens, and those so miserably lacking in originality that they had to plagiarize Louis Farrakan (of all people) and launch a "Million Moms March." Also, anybody else who thinks it's morally acceptable to use the hired guns of government to take everybody else's guns away.

Gun control may have felt like a nice, warm, fuzzy idea to its advocates back in the 1960s. Today, however, owing to a great deal of serious legal and historical scholarship — and a series of horrifying but highly educational events — anyone who wishes to violate the fundamental covenant on which this nation is based, by attempting to outlaw personal weapons, has to get past three extremely inconvenient but absolutely incontrovertible facts.

(1) Every year, in this nation of more than a quarter billion individuals, a few thousand (three-quarters of them suicides) are killed with firearms, while *millions* of Americans successfully use personal weapons to save themselves and others from injury or death. Guns save many many times more lives than they take.

(2) In every jurisdiction that has made it even microscopically easier for individuals to carry weapons, violent crime rates have plummeted by double-digit percentages. Vermont, where no permission of any kind is required to carry a gun, is named in many respectable surveys as the safest state to live in.

(3) More telling and urgent, every episode of genocidal mass murder in history has been preceded by a period of intense disarming of the civil population, usually with "public safety" or "national security" as an excuse. According to Amnesty International — hardly a gang of right-wing crazies — in the 20th century alone (in events entirely separate from war), governments have slaughtered more than a hundred million people, usually their own citizens.

The U.S. is far from immune. Look up "Operation Keelhaul."

Clearly, if those millions had been armed, they couldn't have been murdered by their own governments. And if the governments hadn't known where all the weapons were and who possessed them, the people couldn't have been disarmed. It follows, then, that no amount of gun control — especially "soft" measures like registering guns or gun owners — is reasonable or safe. Those who tremble at the idea of personal weapons — "hoplophobes" is the diagnostic term — are fond of saying that guns are made for only one purpose. Well, gun control serves only one purpose, too — the incapacitation and extermination of whole peoples.

That's why we call it by its right name: "victim disarmament."

If you think it can't happen here, ask Donald Scott (look him up, too). Ask Vicky and Sammy Weaver. Ask 82 innocent men, women, and children (two dozen beautiful, harmless, helpless little children) from the Seventh Day Adventist church at Mount Carmel near Waco, Texas. Oops, you *can't* ask them, can you? Because they're all *dead* — murdered in cold blood by government terrorists who have yet to be brought to justice.

Let's ask some questions that everybody on my side's been too polite — too damned polite — to ask before.

What kind of mind would sacrifice millions for the sake of a few thousand, especially when it's been demonstrated beyond a shadow of a doubt that victim disarmament can't save even those thousands?

What kind of mind wants a return to mean streets and ever-soaring crime rates?

What kind of mind collaborates with agents of mass murder and genocide?

Make no mistake: You victim disarmament types are sick sick people, in the words of T.D. Melrose, who'd rather see a woman raped in an alley and strangled with her own pantyhose than see her with a gun in her hand.

You're people, down deep in your blackened shriveled souls, who wait like vultures, secretly delighted whenever atrocities like the Columbine shootings occur — atrocities whose only significance to you is their usefulness in advancing your political agenda. Dancing in the blood of innocents, just like the lying, thieving, murdering rapist you've sent to the

Lever Action

White House twice in a row.

You're people who, like German voters in the 1930s, have empowered and unleashed on your decent and unsuspecting neighbors the most evil and violent terrorist bureaucracy in American history.

You're people, in short, who must be stupid, insane, or evil to continue arguing — in the face of indisputable facts and irrefutable logic — that others must be forced into a state of helplessness and victimized by individual criminals or the state.

Stupid, insane, or evil.

You are morally responsible for what happened at Waco. It was undertaken (bad choice of words, probably) by your favorite agency, the Bureau of Alcohol, Tobacco and Firearms, at your behest, in your name, in pursuance of the policies you've always advocated. The blood of those babies, of their mommies and daddies, is on your head. You did it. You killed them as surely as if it were your hands at the controls of those tanks.

Stupid, insane, or evil.

Harsh words, but what's the point in being polite to advocates of mass murder and genocide? Those are the alernatives: stupid, insane, or evil. Smart people, sane people, good people know, in the words of Robert A. Heinlein, that "An armed society is a polite society."

If you were interested in saving lives — even one life — you'd join me in demanding that the Bill of Rights be stringently enforced, that the 25,000 gun laws on the books (each and every one illegal, each and every one responsible for the injury or death of countless individuals) be repealed, nullified, or otherwise disposed of.

Immediately.

For the children.

You'd agree that, as long as we permit the public-school system to continue to exist, it has an obligation to instruct children, starting in kindergarten, in the safe and effective use of firearms.

Allow me to repeat that: "safe and effective use."

Emphasis on "effective."

Now don't go all soft and skooshy on me. I can see the razor wire and bayonets behind your New Age gobbledygook. I can hear the tramp, tramp, tramp as you goose-step to the Horst Wessel Song. I can smell the first faint traces of gas seeping from your chambers of death.

Let's make it clear for the dimmest bulbs among you: The kids at Columbine High didn't die from too many guns, they died from too few. I'm not suggesting that the teachers should have carried guns — not as franchised agents of the state. They should have carried guns as ordinary individuals, exercising a sacred right, and in performance of a solemn duty to protect the young lives that were placed — very foolishly, as it turned out — in their hands.

What's more, those young lives needed weapons, too. Instead, they were forbidden the means of self-defense — even, in effect, the *knowledge* of self-defense — and like millions of victims before them, their numbers were added to the ongoing Gun Control Holocaust.

And you killed them.

Stupid, insane, or evil.

You killed them all.

How many more helpless individuals will have to die for you — be sacrificed on the altar of your nice, warm, fuzzy idea — before you see what you've done? Don Kates, Gary Kleck, Sandford Levinson, John Lott, all were card-carrying liberal college professors who somehow forced themselves to look at the facts instead of the lint in their bellybuttons. All (and others) have reached the conclusion that the Second Amendment says exactly what we "gun nuts" always claimed it did, and that society is better off if its members have personal weapons handy. "More Guns, Less Crime" is how Lott puts it.

"Million Moms March," indeed. When you came to my town of 100,000, all you could attract was four deluded idiots. There were *16 times* that number out in the parking lot, picketing your meeting!

Measly Minuscule March.

Stupid, insane, or evil. Those are the choices. Be honest. Call yourselves "Mush Minded Morons" if you decide that stupid is the least intolerable of the options available. If you choose insane, how about "Mentally Mangled Messes"? If you want to go straight to evil, "Mass-Murdering Monsters." They're alliterative as hell, and truthful.

Stupid, insane, or evil. Like it or not, after today, those three words are going to start hanging around your necks like the fabled rotting albatross until, no matter where you go, no matter what you try to say, the first association your presence calls up in people's minds will be "mass-murdering genocides."

Stupid, insane, or evil.

Or all of the above.

Your choice.

Armies of Chaos
ᘓ ᘓ ᘓ ᘓ ᘓ

Before anyone proposes more gun control, he or she should know about a simple deadly weapon four times as powerful as Dirty Harry's legendary .44 Magnum — and at least twice as concealable — that *can't* be controlled.

This simple deadly weapon can be made by anyone —

even a child — with unpowered hand tools in an hour's time using $5 worth of materials, most of which are available around the house anyway. In traditional form it's reusable an unlimited number of times, and modern plastics have rendered its disposable version electronically undetectable. You can clear a room with such a weapon (more of a hand-held directional grenade than a gun — sort of a recycleable Claymore mine) and it's just one of hundreds of similar time-proven designs.

Complete instructions for building this simple deadly weapon could be given in half the space I'm using here and not require a single illustration. Or it could be done as a line-drawing and not require a word. Either way, the results would Xerox splendidly and reduce, for effortless distribution, to the size of a 3X5 index card.

No, I'm not making this up.

Self-styled liberal academics and politicians generally suffer an ancient Greek prejudice against the manual trades and often fail to comprehend what it means, with respect to banning weapons, that we're a nation of basement lathe-operators. Americans unknowingly tend to follow Mohammed's precept that, whatever a person's station in life, he or she should also do something manual, if only to stay grounded in reality. And if there's any lingering doubt about the ease of basic weapons-craft, ask the Israelis who, early in their nation's history, turned out submachineguns little more complicated than what I'm discussing here, in automotive garages lacking even a lathe.

Civilized restraint precludes my describing the weapon in any greater detail here. Many gun enthusiasts will know by now exactly what I refer to, anyway. It's in everyday use in much of the Third World, especially where governments foolishly believe that they've outlawed weapons. But that, of course, is impossible — unless the same governments want to try repealing the last 1,000 years of civil engineering.

Lever Action

Now suppose somebody went ahead and wrote out those easy-to-follow instructions, made that line drawing, or simply Xeroxed it from any of 100 sources already in print. Suppose the plans for a reusable undetectable weapon four times as powerful as a .44 Magnum and twice as concealable began circulating on every junior high school campus in America. Or suppose they were simply sent to the media, which can never resist giving viewers step-by-step directions for committing a crime — even as they bemoan the terribleness of it all.

So what, you say. So this: Within hours, every self-styled liberal academic and politician extant would begin to weep, wail, and whimper (the only thing they're really good at) and before the media-amplified screaming was over — but after the legislature had met — we'd find that the rights protected by the First Amendment (not created or granted, mind you, only recognized and guaranteed) are no more secure than those supposedly protected by the Second. Free expression would be trampled under without another thought or a moment's hesitation by the same jackals, vultures, and hyenas currently leading the stampede to outlaw weapons — using exactly the same excuses.

When Xerox machines are outlawed, only outlaws will have Xerox machines.

Human rights are indivisible because there's really only one — the right to remain unmolested by the government or by anybody else. Those who threaten one right threaten them all — and aren't really "liberals" by any definition of the word. Suppressing the human right to own and carry weapons is a step toward suppressing the human right to read, write, and think. Ask Canadians, for whom censorship is a fact of daily life, and for whom certain "assault" books (many of them published by Paladin Press) are on the "hafta-smuggle-it-in" list.

The same thing can and will happen here. Haven't we had

ample warning in the way self-styled liberals, assisted by the corrupt media, suppress their opposition on these and other issues? Or in their willingness to present lies as truth while the truth is called a lie? Or in the fact that elected officials who advocate gun-control — which is a felony — are still at large instead of behind bars where they belong? The very existence of a gun-control lobby gives the lie to any claim they make to liberalism. The word "liberal" itself is false advertising, and the question arises: Why do we go on applying it when the word "fascist" is so much more appropriate?

A popular bumper sticker proclaims that "Gun Control is People Control." More to the point, and far more sinister, gun control is *mind* control. The relationship only begins with ludicrous attempts by self-styled liberals to convince a population protected by the Second Amendment that the Bill of Rights doesn't mean what it says. Weapons consist of more than machined steel or wood, cast aluminum or plastic. As John M. Browning or Sam Colt would tell you, their second-most vital component is an idea. (The first, for better or worse, is the will to use them.) Without that idea behind it, all the steel, wood, aluminum, and plastic in the world doesn't make a weapon.

Those who would outlaw weapons must first outlaw the knowledge of weapons.

And those who would outlaw the knowledge of weapons must outlaw knowledge itself.

Similarly, civilization consists of more than just impressive public buildings and a battery of arbitrary rules. Its continued existence depends absolutely on the day-to-day good will of each and every individual. History (especially recent Soviet history) proves that this good will depends on how well individual rights are respected. Alienate the individual, lose his good will, and you lose civilization itself.

Think I exaggerate? Take another look at Beirut, Los Angeles, or the World Trade Center.

Every day we learn again how dependent we've been all along on individual self-restraint. Self-styled liberals label this lesson "terrorism," because it makes them feel better and helps them to forget until tomorrow. But it doesn't matter what they call it. In sufficient numbers, disaffected individuals become armies of chaos, reducing whole civilizations to archaeological rubble.

And, as with most violence in our culture, it is self-styled liberals who will make it happen here.

On Concealed Carry and the NRA
ଔ ଔ ଔ ଔ ଔ

Many individuals have asked me where I stand on the issue of concealed-carry permits — and whether the Libertarian Second Amendment Caucus, which I founded several years ago, is likely to join in political coalitions with other organizations that concern themselves with Second Amendment issues.

I've put off writing about these matters before now, because it isn't easy, knowing that you're likely to alienate good friends and allies by insisting that they face hard truths. But the press of current events — the increasingly obvious reluctance of the new Republican majority in Congress to make good on their promises to the gun owners who elected them, along with an insane eagerness on the part of nominally pro-gun organizations like the National Rifle Association to accept utter defeat on the eve of total victory — make it impossible to put it off any longer.

As Robert A. Heinlein once observed, "The human race

divides politically into those who want people to be controlled and those who have no such desire." To take it a step further, there are natural-born Tories in life, who only feel comfortable when they're groveling to some kind of authority, and there are individuals who won't grovel, no matter what it costs them.

This nation, America, was created by the latter sort, while the former ran away to Canada where, for the next eleven generations or so, they could comfortably grovel to kings, queens, and socialist bureaucrats. And just as some Canadians have since learned better than their Tory predecessors — we'll be hearing more and more from them in the near future — many descendants of those first Americans have become the very thing their ancestors fought so hard against.

Those who beg permission from the government to exercise a right they already possess are not free men and women. They're Tories; they're grovelers. They'd beg permission from the government to breathe, if they were told it was required of them. If they were told it was required of them, they'd beg permission from the government, even to grovel.

A license — government permission — to carry a concealed weapon is nothing but the latest kind of gun control, the latest kind of groveling. There's no way to euphemize it; there's no way to excuse it. It isn't necessary: Nobody needs the government's permission to carry a weapon, concealed or otherwise. And it's illegal under the Second Amendment to the United States Constitution for government, at any level, to require it. That's right, it's illegal; and it's a primary goal of the Libertarian Second Amendment Caucus to jail those in government, elected or otherwise, who obstruct the Bill of Rights in any way.

It's also dangerous: It converts a fundamental human right into a privilege that the government may see fit to deny to anyone, for any reason, at any time it wishes. How anyone could be aware of history for the last hundred years — especially the last fifty — and not acknowledge this basic truth is beyond understanding.

From their public words and actions, it's clear that those who presently control the National Rifle Association — I don't mean the duly elected Board of Directors — are Tories and grovelers, no matter what they claim to the contrary. Just listen to what they say if you doubt it, or read their literature. Half of it is devoted to demonstrating to their masters in the government just what excellent Tories and grovelers they are. Notice, too, the way that some of them claim lately to be "tough" — but how they invariably reserve their toughness for individuals ostensibly on their own side who happen to disagree with them, rather than for real enemies of individual liberty and the Second Amendment.

Now those who presently control the National Rifle Association want uniform laws from state to state regulating the way Americans will be allowed to carry weapons. To get them, once again they're "wheeling and dealing" in Congress — with my rights as the stake — a fool's game they always lose because they're such embarrassingly clumsy amateurs, playing against the pros. Instead, they should simply demand the immediate fulfillment of Republican promises to repeal unconstitutional gun laws, which could never have been passed without the cheerful assistance of the likes of "Brady Bill Bob" Dole and Newt "Suspend the Bill of Rights" Gingrich.

As one who's fought the battle of the Second Amendment for more than 30 years — all the while watching in unbelieving disgust as the National Rifle Association bargained away my rights through bad tactics, worse strategy, an utter lack of moral principle, and an overpowering urge to grovel to authority — I challenge those who presently control the National Rifle Association to deny or affirm a principle put forward by the Libertarian Second Amendment Caucus as the Atlanta Declaration:

Every man, woman, and responsible child has an unalienable individual, civil, Constitutional, and human right to obtain, own, and carry, openly or concealed, any weapon — rifle, shotgun, handgun, machinegun, anything — any time, any place, without asking anyone's permission.

If those who presently control the National Rifle Association cannot affirm this principle, then they are enemies of individual liberty who should resign immediately and leave the field forever to those Americans who can manage to remember what their country and its Constitution are all about.

If, on the other hand, they affirm it — and publicly abandon their advocacy of anything less than stringent and uncompromising enforcement of the Bill of Rights (along with their disgraceful eagerness to accept excuses and "clever" strategies from Republicans instead of decisive and effective action) — I'll be happy to advise the many friends of the Libertarian Second Amendment Caucus to join with the National Rifle Association in a coalition to advance the cause of individual liberty.

Screen, Scran, Screwn
෬෬෬෬෬

I've made no secret of the fact that I oppose this trendy rush toward a universal concealed-carry permit system.

It's a strategic error in the good old-fashioned style of the National Rifle Association (not to mention an exceedingly dangerous precedent) to let government, at whatever level, issue you a license to do something that's *already* the natural, fundamental, inalienable human, individual, civil, and Constitutional right of every man, woman, and responsible child: to obtain, own, and carry, openly or concealed, any weapon — handgun, shotgun, rifle, machinegun — any time, anywhere, without asking anyone's permission.

There, I said it and I feel better.

Having been often accused of negativity in the past, however, I do feel obliged to suggest an alternative that will accomplish the same objective with none of the terrible political side-effects, and at the same time take into account something few of us have addressed: the individual right *not* to keep and bear arms.

Let's face facts: What we seek is legal immunity for something many of us have been doing anyway, acting on a belief that, "It's better to be tried by twelve than carried by six." But what of those — and there are lots of them, possibly even more than there are of us — who actually believe (for whatever reason) that it's better to be carried by six? What about those who've been wandering around *unarmed* without official sanction and have no such immunity to look forward to?

In short, what of the plight of the *gunless*?

Now I can hear you out there saying, "But there *is* no right *not* to own and carry weapons — show me in the Constitution where it says there is!" And I have to admit, you've got me. But I can't see anything wrong with making it a *privilege*.

Like driving.

The sensible thing, it seems to me, is to assume that everyone is armed. (Cops would certainly live longer if they did and be a lot more polite in the bargain.) After all, the wording and intention of the Second Amendment is plain, even though the rights it guarantees have a history of being viciously and illegally suppressed. However, if an individual can show sufficient reason why he *shouldn't* own and carry weapons, who are we, in all humanity, to stop him — provided certain common-sense precautions are taken for the good of society as a whole.

Is he mentally or morally handicapped, given to uncontrollable episodes of pacifism or a demented belief that he has a right to initiate force against others or to delegate it to someone else? Does he suffer a paranoid fantasy that groups exist as something other than an aggregate of the individuals who comprise them — and even have rights in and of themselves? I'd say that qualifies him. For fifty bucks — oh, hell, make it a hundred fifty — he can have *my* permission for two years *not* to own and carry weapons, and put in for renewals by mail.

Visa, MasterCard, or American Express cheerfully accepted.

Can he show sufficient need? Does he feel an urge (say, when somebody says he'd like to be alone, goes into his own house, and locks the door) to cordon off the building, surround it with sinister windowless vans and fat men dressed in fetishistic black, and remonstrate with him over a bullhorn, while getting ready to fill the place with bullet holes and burn it to the ground? *Bingo!* Another permit *not* to own and carry weapons — no further questions asked.

Burglars, muggers, rapists, and politicians, of course, will always be given priority, and we can even provide something like food stamps for those who can't afford to buy official permission to disregard the highest law of the land.

Now don't tell me this law is unenforceable; we all know better. For instance, we can start using metal detectors properly: when it *doesn't* go beep and the subject can't produce appropriate paperwork, he'll be cavity-searched right there in public to find out what he's carrying *instead* of a gun. We can take Judge Abner Mikva's advice, offered long ago, and install such devices in every doorway, rather than just in airports and courtrooms, to insure compliance. The Fourth Amendment protects people from unreasonable searches for *something* — it doesn't say anything about searching them for nothing!

Come to think of it, I wonder if dogs can be trained to sniff out the *absence* of a weapon. ...

Given the past performance of the government in this area, many of America's non-gun owners may be a trifle suspicious at first. After all, a single pen-stroke by a treacherous legislature could easily alter the phrase, " ... the sheriff *must* issue a permit not to own and carry weapons ... " to " ... the sheriff *may* issue a permit not to own and carry weapons ... " and we all know where that leads. It could instantly undo all our good intentions and hard work.

We'll simply have to assure them all that we have absolutely *nothing* like that in mind.

Not just now, anyway.

They should trust us.

The way we (who ought to know by now that the past participle of "screen" — as in "background check" — always turns out to be "screwn") have learned to trust them.

We Don't Need No Stinkin' Bodges
⊂❂ ⊂❂ ⊂❂ ⊂❂ ⊂❂

My earliest memory of the National Rifle Association is of their grim resistance to the idea of licensing gun owners and registering guns. Even at the tender age of 11, I found it a commendable stand I supported — and still do — with every fiber of my being. This was in happier days before our enemies got organized, bumper stickers hadn't been invented, and the wittiest slogan we would have printed on them was, "Register Communists, Not Guns."

More than 30 years have passed; what we find instead of grim resistance today is a morally enfeebled NRA not just advocating, but demanding, the licensing of owners and the registration of guns. They call it "concealed carry permits," and "easing restrictions." What they don't say is that the restrictions were illegal to begin with, the only way to deal with them is jury nullification or repeal, and any other approach to the problem is fraudulent. Lobbying for licensed carry, they've become America's largest, best-bankrolled, gun-control organization.

One state permits no such restrictions on the right to carry weapons — Vermont — named by a national civic organization as the safest state in America to live in. Some of our fellow travelers even profess to agree with me that our objective should be "Vermont Carry," but claim the way to achieve it is gradually, "one step at a time."

The first step is to pass a clone of the licensed carry law that reduced crime in Florida 20 to 40 percent over 10 or 15 years. Such laws, usually written by politicos ignorant of, or indifferent to, the Bill of Rights, generally call for a birth certificate or photo ID, fingerprinting, background check, approval of your personality by local cops, the serial number of your gun (you may register another for an additional fee), and some classroom study of weapons handling or the idiotically sacrificial laws governing self-defense, before, at last, you're permitted to exercise the unalienable individual, civil, Constitutional, and human right of every man, woman, and responsible child to obtain, own, and carry, openly or concealed, any weapon, rifle, shotgun, handgun, machinegun, anything, any time, any place, without asking anyone's permission.

One group pushing hard for licensed carry is dealers and certified instructors who will provide the required training. In some states, they charge as much as $250 (in addition to the license fee itself) for something rather like the Vatican "indulgences" — pardoning sins for cash — that sparked the Reformation. Such "entrepreneurs" are maggots, feeding off the rotting carcass of the Second Amendment, the same collaborationist vermin who begged the BATF to put their small competitors — so-called "basement dealers" — out of business.

Once you've jumped through the hoops, being added to the list of those with permits — a public record that can't be withheld from the media — makes you a target for thieves. Our enemies will want the list to plan attempts at confiscation; I'm told that gun grabbers have tried this already in Florida, a state where, if teachers learn that your kid comes from a gun-owning home, his record is flagged as a member of a dysfunctional family. And, of course, being *refused* a permit is probable cause for the cops to shake you down any time they like.

"Our" argument, I guess, is that, seeing what a success such a law can be, legislators will be anxious to compound that success by taking the next step, and then the next, making it easier and easier to carry concealed until the final restrictions are eliminated and we're all toting Vermont-style. The problem with this is that it won't happen. Rather than a flight of stairs, we're building a wall between us and our rights.

Say the law works; crime falls 30%. After a decade, we go back to the legislature and argue that, since the carry law is such a success, it's time to *repeal* it? This is not a useful argument. And in light of the fact that the last thing they'll want is to stir up the fury they endured to get the law passed in the first place (for which we now appear ungrateful), the politest thing they'll say is, if it ain't broke, don't fix it. When somebody brings up the Second Amendment, they'll ask, why didn't you mention that when you begged us to turn an inalienable right into a government-granted privilege?

Nobody with political experience — or a minimal regard for the truth — can tell me this isn't what will happen. It's what always happens when you trade long-term values for short-term expedience, a "stupid lobbyist trick" our side seems really good at. If licensed carry becomes the rule across America, rather than "easing restrictions" we'll have planted 50 Sullivan Acts to bloom on the grave of the liberty. We'll have stopped being a nation of humans standing on two feet; we'll have become a pack of collared dogs.

We'll have become Europeans.

Sometimes I wish I could feel differently about this issue. I've lost friends over it, and been involved in screaming arguments in my own home with former allies so pathetically eager to "get right" with the law they can't be made to see how they're throwing away their rights — and mine — with both hands. But just as I resent the arrogant presumption of any politician who makes himself part of the process of suppressing my rights — then doling them back out to me, piecemeal and damaged beyond recognition — I resent even more the bovine gullibility of so-called gun-rights activists not simply willing, but pants-wettingly eager, to accept such heel-on-the-neck treatment, on the argument that it's their own heel on their necks.

I wonder how they'll feel about lawsuits and restraining orders to stop this rape of the Bill of Rights. As my wife Cathy puts it so eloquently, if you beg for permission to do something it's already your right to do, you deserve to be told, "No."

Am I the NRA?
ငော ငော ငော ငော ငော

This coming August I'll have been a Life member of the National Rifle Association for 22 years. If you're not a member yourself, it may surprise you to learn that, by the standards of that organization, born just after the War between the States, this isn't particularly long. I know people who've been in the NRA twice as long as I have, and one or two who've been members three times that number of years.

It is long enough, however, to make me wonder, as one does upon occasion in any long-term relationship, whether, knowing everything I know today, after 22 years, I'd do it again. Lately, the answer seems to be — and I'm sure the NRA will be devastated to learn this — that I'd have to think about it.

Knowing everything I know today, I'd want assurances this time that the NRA is willing and able to perform the task that brought me to it. I'd been in Junior NRA as a Scout, but the course of my life had taken me away from shooting (it seems hard to believe now) until just before that surrealistic year of 1968 when, as a newly fledged handgun owner (we'd had an incident in the neighborhood), I recall sitting in front of the TV watching the assassination of Bobby Kennedy, knowing the proclivity of liberals to blame everyone but the perpetrator, and thinking, "Boy, we're gonna get it now."

And so we did.

And so I joined the NRA, although it took me five more years to get the cash together for Life membership. Since then, we've lost one fight after another until today, the infringements we deal with — on an unalienable individual, civil, Constitutional, and human right that was supposed to be absolutely guaranteed — are beyond anything most members of the NRA

22 years ago would have believed.

I was one of a few who saw the ugly future ahead, even then. Four years after I became a Life member, I wrote my first science fiction novel, full of dire predictions. I also wrote letters, not just to politicians, but to editors of gun magazines, even to the NRA's top banana, the guy who looked so much like Nikita Khrushchev, urging them to stop fighting the Battle of the Second Amendment as a holding action, a tactic we have seen was bound for inevitable defeat, and adopt an offensive strategy.

Those editors (with a remarkable exception whose good judgment I'll repay by *not* associating his name with mine) laughed me off as an alarmist. I never heard from the bald guy at the NRA. And why should I? Who was I? Just some nobody, worried over what was about to happen to his unalienable individual, civil, Constitutional, and human rights. For that matter, who am I today? Just a 22-year Life member wondering whether he'd do it all over again, remember?

As I say, I'd want assurances this time, sort of a prenuptial agreement, before I slipped the metaphorical ring on my trigger finger. My 22 years of experience have taught me a few things — a dozen of them, roughly — about defending the Second Amendment. For the life of me, I don't understand why they haven't taught the same things to the NRA.

First, I'd want the NRA not to write any more legislation. It's said the NRA leadership wrote the Gun Control Act of 1968 (before my time, if you'll recall). I know they wrote the Maryland Handgun Ban because they were afraid that something worse was in the works. Fear seems to be their principal motivation, not anger or determination. Invariably, it steers them toward a submissive repulsive "strategy" of doing the enemy's work before he can do it himself.

Second, I'd want the NRA not to trade away any more

rights it "thinks" are less important for those it "thinks" are more so. The leadership would find, if they ever asked, that their membership often disagrees with them. The "cop-killer" bullet fiasco comes to mind, where we got trivial reforms in a devil's bargain — letting them make some bullets illegal — which serves our enemies so well today that one particularly repellent and evil senator has based the sunset of his career on it.

Third, I'd want the NRA to stop supporting government activities irrelevant, even harmful, to the Second Amendment. Increasingly, gun owners see that the War on Drugs, to name an example, was meant from the outset as a calculated assault on the Bill of Rights, especially on the Second Amendment. It must end if there's to be anything left of the Constitution in the 21st century. That isn't the NRA's job, and it should butt out of the debate. Its "Operation Crimestrike," celebrating patently illegal incursions against individual rights, is nothing more than a sustained humiliating grovel — like having to watch another kind of civil-rights advocacy crawl up on the verandah and whine, "See, Massah, what a good boy Ah is?"

Fourth, in the same context, I'd want the NRA to disconnect all future discussion of the Second Amendment from the totally unrelated topic of crime. My rights have nothing whatever to do with anything anybody else does, right or wrong. If the crime rate were only one-tenth that of today, my rights would be unaffected. Likewise, if the rate were ten times what it is, it would have nothing whatever to do with my individual right to own and carry weapons.

Fifth, I'd want the NRA to reject all future argument about the "sporting use" of weapons — why look like an imbecile, pushing the AK-47 as a deer rifle, when it meets the Founding Fathers' *actual* criteria so elegantly? — in favor of frank and frequent public reference to the original Constitutional purpose for an armed citizenry, which is to intimidate the government.

Sixth — and this may be the most important point I'll make, so pay attention — I'd want the NRA to adopt as its principal and publicly acknowledged objective the repeal or nullification of every weapons law, at every level of government in America. The Second Amendment is explicit about this and requires no esoteric legal interpretation. Check the dictionary meaning of "infringe" if you doubt my word.

Seventh, in support of that objective, I'd want the NRA to print ads, half a page in every issue of all its periodicals, reminding members of the duty and power of an American jury to nullify any law it believes unjust or unconstitutional. Alcohol prohibition died this way. Gun prohibition could, as well. All it takes is eight-and-a-third-percent of the population, one twelfth, to carry it off.

Eighth, I'd want the NRA to establish programs to educate the police in their absolute obligation (given the Nuremburg trials after World War II) to enforce only those statutes — and obey only those commands — that are lawful, i.e., Constitutional. For many decades, the NRA has spent a lot of resources in what can only be described as sucking up disgustingly to the military and the cops; it's past time we got something out of it. (I'm an ex-reservist, my brother's a deputy, and we both grew up in the Air Force, so don't give me a hard time — this is the truth, and we all know it.)

Ninth, I'd want the NRA to give up the self-defeating notion that you can keep guns *out* of the hands of the "wrong" folks, while simultaneously and miraculously keeping them *in* the hands of the "right" folks. Each of us is somebody else's badguy. In the last century, laws were passed to keep guns from Italians and the Irish. Earlier this century it was blacks and now it's those who believe in the Bill of Rights. Get it straight: The latter could never have happened if the former hadn't been possible. No more background checks, NRA, no more prior restraint. History, ancient and recent, clearly shows that if the badguys have guns, the only way to handle it is to make sure as many goodguys have guns as possible.

Tenth, while we're on the subject of prior restraint, I'd want the NRA to abandon its strategically idiotic enthusiasm for government-controlled concealed carry — illegal under the Second Amendment — in favor of uncontrolled and legal "Vermont Carry." If it won't, I guarantee that in years to come, someone will say: The NRA wants your name on this piece of paper *before* you'll be allowed to exercise your unalienable individual, Constitutional, civil, and human rights. The NRA wants your age, address, phone, sex, race, social security number, photograph, and fingerprints as a cost of doing what the Framers meant you to do without all that. In short, it wants to impose the very system of gun and owner registration we've been fighting more than 60 years!

Huey Long, virtual dictator of Louisiana in the 1930s when Mussolini was making the trains run on time, was asked by the press, "Will we ever have fascism in America?" "Yes," Long replied with a grin, "but we'll call it *anti*fascism." I can guarantee that someone will say all of this, because if nobody else does, I will. And to the advocates of licensed carry, I say now: Don't you realize how pathetic you look, lying there with your *own* foot on your neck?

Eleventh, I'd want the NRA to make endorsements based on a candidate's respect for the Second Amendment, regardless of his affiliation or its estimate of his chances. It's suicidal — if only because it denies us leverage we'd otherwise possess over the Republicans — to say a third-party candidate can't win, and on that self-fulfilling basis, withhold endorsement that could give him, and us, a victory. If "NRA" stands for "National Republican Association," let it be said plainly and stop what amounts to a consumer fraud. If not, then if a candidate is unwilling to be photographed for public consumption firing a machinegun, a semiautomatic rifle with a long curved magazine, or a pistol with a fat two-column grip, he can't be trusted whatever his affiliation, and shouldn't be endorsed.

Twelfth, I'd want the NRA to reduce its Board of Directors to no more than 20, so they can lead instead of turning things over to a tiny often misguided elite. One director I know told me the NRA is in trouble precisely because its huge unwieldy board flounders helplessly, leaving policy in the hands of a "troika" with its own agenda. It's time for that to end.

In general, I'd give the NRA the same advice I give everybody else. Never let anybody keep you from enjoying your rights to the fullest, not for a day, not for a minute. Never let anybody stand in your way. Never accept even the most reasonable-sounding excuse for why you can't have everything you deserve. Never accept compromise.

Worse than thieves, murderers, or cannibals, those who offer compromise slow you and sap your vitality while pretending to be your friends. They are not your friends. Compromisers are the enemies of all humanity, the enemies of life itself. Compromisers are the enemies of everything important, sacred, and true.

So, would I join the NRA all over again, after 22 years, knowing everything I know today?

I guess I'm still thinking about it.

Give me a reason, NRA.

How Much Do You Want
to Keep Your Guns?
ᬞ ᬞ ᬞ ᬞ ᬞ

Would you agree to permit adults to buy, sell, read, write, make, listen to, or watch whatever books, magazines, records, tapes, or movies they want, no matter how pornographic — *if they agreed to let you keep your guns?*

Would you agree to tolerate Buddhists, Moslems, Taoists, Scientologists, Satanists, atheists — *if they agreed to let you keep your guns?*

Would you agree to let women control their own reproductive process and have abortions (at their own expense) — *if they agreed to let you keep your guns?*

Would you agree to allow people their own sexual preference, homosexual, bisexual, heterosexual — *if they agreed to let you keep your guns?*

Would you agree to halt the "War on Drugs," to leave others alone, even to ruin their lives with alcohol, nicotine, heroin, cocaine, marijuana, LSD, or any other substance — *if they agreed to let you keep your guns?*

Would you agree to respect the rights of anyone, no matter their race or national origin — *if they agreed to let you keep your guns?*

******

No sane human being would sacrifice the rights he personally considers precious just for the sake of imposing his own tastes or opinions on others. Yet often it seems each of us disapproves of, and wants to outlaw, some one little thing that somebody else cares about or wants.

226

Little things add up: With more than two hundred million of us, split into thousands of pressure groups, all working at the same time for one kind of Prohibition or another, it's no wonder government controls ratchet tighter around our lives every day. Until now, it's been a one-way process, with everyone on every side winding up the loser — except, of course, for politicians, bureaucrats, and lawyers.

But we can work together to reverse that process by making a commitment to respect and defend each other's rights, no matter how much each of us may personally disapprove of any particular exercise of those rights. That doesn't mean you have to do anything bizarre or perverse yourself. I'm married, straight, a daddy, and don't use drugs (I'm literally an Eagle Scout); I don't even drink. But I don't give a damn what my allies do with their own lives, as long as they want to be free and can help me stay that way, too.

The one limit is an obligation never to *initiate* force against another person — since that's how we began losing our rights in the first place.

Would this change the way we're accustomed to thinking about freedom? No, it would make our thinking consistent, put teeth into the Bill of Rights, and limit the power of politicians, bureaucrats, lawyers — and Prohibitionists — to control the way we live.

Which means that every man, woman, and responsible child in this country would be free once again to obtain, own, and carry, openly or concealed, any weapon — rifle, shotgun, handgun, machinegun, *anything* — they feel is desirable for sport *or* self-defense, any time, any place they want, without asking anyone's permission.

The other side's counting on us to remain divided, intolerant. That's how they got us where they want us to begin with.

I intend to keep my guns — and the rest of my rights, as well.
How about you?

Clinton's Crimes Are Hitler's Crimes
cↄ cↄ cↄ cↄ cↄ

Forty-nine years ago, I first raised my hand to my heart
and pledged allegiance to the flag of the United States of
America and to the republic for which it stood, one nation,
indivisible, with liberty and justice for all.

A year or two later, First Amendment be damned, God got
edited into it, an event I should have seen as a dire warning; it
wasn't long afterward that I began a lifetime of learning that
everything the pledge represents is a sick twisted lie.

Think I exaggerate?

Then explain Waco.

It would never occur to most Americans (or it won't until
it's too late) that for the past eight years, they've been casting
ballots in a series of referenda on the Holocaust. In the 1930s
and 1940s, Hitler rounded up social and political undesirables
— homosexuals, Gypsies, Jews — and imprisoned them in
camps to be worked to death, cruelly experimented on by sa-
distic butchers pretending to be scientists, killed by diseases of
overcrowding, fatigue, and malnutrition that people hadn't died
in Europe from for centuries, gassed to death and the valuable
gold removed from their mouths — even the commercially
salable hair from their heads — before their murdered mutilated remains could be incinerated to anonymous ashes in ov-
ens that will be infamous for 1,000 years.

That's what we're all voting on, each November: whether

we think the Holocaust was commendable or not. Because, historically and morally, there isn't a speck of difference between what happened then in Germany and what Bill Clinton ordered done in 1993 to another group of social and political undesirables, at Mount Carmel, outside of Waco, Texas.

Then, as now, most people approve the current regime's acts of mass murder, pretend they didn't know what was going on, and keep silent from a well-founded fear that the same could happen to them or from an even more contemptible fear of being embarrassed if they make a fuss. After all, anybody who'd speak up for that "Wacko from Waco" David Koresh must be a religious, right-wing, racist, neofascist gun nut, right?

Then as now, the national media — consisting largely of failed personalities who crave power, but (due to severe emotional handicaps) are unable to do more than enjoy its exercise vicariously — echo the government's lies while helping it bury incriminating evidence. Why, those Davidians believed differently than others do and, even more horrifyingly, they *acted* on those beliefs. Besides, they had *almost* as many weapons in their home, per capita, as the average Texas family!

Almost.

Meanwhile, the Clinton Administration, like all leftist regimes, floats serenely upon the ocean of blood it's spilled in order to take and keep power. Of course, compared with the 200,000 murders in East Timor that we now know Clinton shares culpability for, Waco may seem like small potatoes to a collectivist like he is, with no regard for the unique irreplaceable value of a single individual.

Yet this is more than merely a matter of right versus left, conservative versus liberal, Republican versus Democrat. This is a matter that transcends ordinary politics, a matter of right and wrong and, ultimately, of crime and punishment.

For years, now — seven of them, to be precise, plus 51

days — I've wondered incessantly, to myself and others, why Bill Clinton isn't in jail, instead of smiling down upon the election prospects of his "vice perpetrator." Why aren't Janet Reno and the other orcs who did Clinton's evil bidding during the Mount Carmel affair making the same lame, revealing, gratifyingly futile excuses that Adolf Eichmann made, from inside a glass box exactly like the one he spent his final public days in?

What I wonder most of all is why Bob Dole never denounced his opponent for the mass murderer he is. Could it have something to do, by any chance, with the embarrassing fact that what happened to the Branch Davidians was conceived, approved, planned, and rehearsed during the *Republican* Bush Senior Administration? And why hasn't Bush Junior brought it up — it happened in the state he governs.

Come on, Republicans, I know you read what I write; that's one reason I write it. Let's hear why your guy isn't saying the one thing that could get him elected and shut down forever the despicable party that refused to rescue German Jews when it was given a chance, and sent Japanese-Americans to concentration camps in the 1940s. Is it because, despite your prattle about respect for the law, you have as little genuine regard for the highest law of the land — the Bill of Rights — as Clinton does? As Gore does? Or is it simply that you want to retain the power to commit exactly the same kind of atrocity yourselves?

Regardless of who wins or loses the next election, it's going to present me with a serious personal problem. I know what Clinton's guilty of. And so does everybody else. I know that Gore stands for exactly the same things.

How can I go on offering friendship, doing business, even being *civil* with anyone I know voted for this evil gang? I'm not talking about the first time around in 1992. Anybody can make a mistake, I suppose. To my eternal chagrin, the first time I voted it was for Richard Nixon. But anybody who voted for Clinton in 1996 or for Gore this year is approving what happened at Waco after the fact. They're rubberstamping it, ratifying it, becoming Clinton's accessory to mass murder.

The deaths of 82 innocent people — 22 of them children — are on their conscience.

And any presidential campaign that doesn't scream its outrage over Waco from the housetops is much worse than an accessory. It's a bloody-handed co-conspirator.

This November as you step into that booth, do the *human* thing, the thing that separates us from animals: Learn from the experience of others. Remember the hardest lesson history ever taught our species. Remember the millions Hitler slaughtered and the dozens Clinton's only started with. Try to imagine what it must feel like to be confined, terrorized, gassed, and burned to death — what it must feel like to be a German Jew or a Branch Davidian.

Remember that — for the sake of this nation's future, as well as for the future of our own children — there can be only one political issue of any importance.

Remember Waco.

On the first Tueday in November, remember Waco.

Diana DeGette Wants You Dead
ও ও ও ও ও

It may come as a surprise to many to learn that I didn't kill John F. Kennedy in November of 1963. I have an alibi and witnesses — well, one witness, anyway. At the time, I was hundreds of miles away from Dallas' Dealy Plaza, in my last-period junior biology class at Choctawhatchee High School near Fort Walton Beach in Okaloosa County, Florida. My witness is my high school girlfriend, with whom I am still more or less in touch via the Internet.

Likewise, I did not kill Robert F. Kennedy or Martin Luther King, although I was convicted by the media and punished by the Democratic Party for both murders. So were you, despite the fact that there are questions still to be answered about the deaths of King and Bobby, and nobody has a clue who killed Jack. The '68 Gun Control Act got hung around our necks like a rotting albatross where it remains today with other dead fowl, such as the "cop-killer-bullet ban," the "ugly-gun-and-maga-zines-that-look-like-penises ban," and the Brady Bill, brought to us by the great guys and gals at the RNC, "Brady Bill Bob" Dole, Proprietor.

Every one of America's 70 million gun owners has been treated, over the past 35 years, as if he or she personally peered through the cross-haired glass of that Mannlicher-Carcano (or the Mauser that apparently really did the job) and squeezed the trigger. Over the past 35 years, every one of us has been made to feel more and more like a criminal, skulking along inside the dusty darkness of society's wainscotting, for nothing more than the act of exercising and defending our natural right — the right of every man, woman, and child — to obtain, own, and carry weapons.

We all know the facts. Several million times a year, people successfully defend their lives, their property, and their rights using guns. Most of the time, it isn't even necessary to fire them. I've displayed a weapon in this way three times in my life and didn't pull the trigger, although I wouldn't hesitate to do so.

At the same time — stripping away morally and legally justified shootings, as well as suicides (the exercise of another basic human right no matter what a prosecutor-stacked jury says) — a few thousand times a year people are killed by other people using guns.

The majority of my readers will see the point immediately, but so-called liberals have trouble thinking clearly, so I'll explain it as best I can. Look at the numbers (documentation on request): several *million* lives saved; a few *thousand* lives lost. Until now, maybe you were ignorant, and maybe that's even an excuse. But from this moment, we'll all know exactly what you are. If you're willing to pass a law that sacrifices several million lives to a few thousand, you're either insane or a fascist monster.

If you support any form of gun control — let's call it what it really is, *victim disarmament* — you're insane or you're a monster.

Maybe both.

I've had it to here with so-called liberals sticking their fingers in their ears and chanting, "I'm not listening to Gary Kleck! I'm not listening to John Lott!" The Littleton murders could easily have been prevented — by adhering to the letter of the highest law of the land — and it's the fault of these thumb-sucking, bedwetting, infantile evaders of objective reality that they weren't.

But there's another point that most of us in the freedom movement don't seem to have considered. Leaders of the other side — the slavery movement — know the facts, too. Parasitic vermin like Sarah Brady, Bill Clinton, Charles Schumer, Diane Feinstein, Chris Dodd, Barney Frank, Frank Lautenberg, Carolyn McCarthy, and Diana DeGette command legions of flunkies — you pay their salaries — to catalog those facts so they can be twisted to serve the slavers' agenda.

Allow me to repeat: Victim disarmers know the truth, too. They can't *not* know the truth. But why would they pass laws sacrificing millions of lives on the shopworn and thoroughly discredited claim that it might save a few thousand?

Brady, Clinton, Schumer, Feinstein, Dodd, Frank, Lautenberg, McCarthy, and DeGette all know the truth. But they promote a murderous lie. Are they stupid? As much fun as it would be to believe it, they wouldn't be where they are — their drinking straws deep in the carotid arteries of the productive class — if they were stupid.

No, it's *we* who've been stupid.

Ever look at what *else* these creatures vote for?

Would even one of them vote against raising taxes to 100 percent and putting every American on welfare? Would any one object to America's streets being policed by blue-bereted UN thugs? Would any one resist a campaign to outlaw private freestanding homes and force everyone into Utopian "arcologies"? Would any one oppose making owning an automobile — except for their own limousines — or refusing to use mass transit a crime? Would any one speak out against forcible implantation of transponders under our skin so we can all be traced and tracked constantly? Would any one of them resign over the passage of a law declaring our children to be government property?

Why do I have to ask these questions? Do you have an instant's doubt? I know what they are. You know what they are. They know what they are. They're the aspiring slave-holders of the 21st century.

At this moment, more Americans own guns than at any other time in history; crime has begun falling at an unprecedented rate. Brady, Clinton, Schumer, Feinstein, Dodd, Frank, Lautenberg, McCarthy, and DeGette would like you to believe it's their gun laws and other wholesale violations of the Bill of Rights that caused this drop in crime, but we know better — and so do they. Everything they brag about has been tried before — there were 20,000 gun laws already in place when Clinton took office — and it's all failed utterly.

What's different this time? For liberals who didn't get it, check the previous paragraph: More Americans own guns than at any other time in history and as John Lott tells us, "More Guns, Less Crime."

Brady, Clinton, Schumer, Feinstein, Dodd, Frank, Lautenberg, McCarthy, and DeGette don't want less crime. Less crime means less need for government, fewer excuses to violate our rights and steal the fruits of our labor. Worse, people capable of defending themselves against criminals are capable of defending themselves against government. Very hard on the slavers' agenda.

What do Brady, Clinton, Schumer, Feinstein, Dodd, Frank, Lautenberg, McCarthy, and DeGette want? Gun owners are the largest and most easily identifiable group of self-sufficient individuals. Self-sufficient individuals threaten their slavers' aspirations. Self-sufficient individuals must be eliminated and the best way is to sacrifice millions of them, claiming it will save thousands.

What do would-be slave-holders want? Clinton, Schumer, Feinstein, Dodd, Frank, Lautenberg, McCarthy, and DeGette want you dead.

They want you dead.

They want you dead.

Lever Action

Whodunit? Wellington Webb!
ᙍ ᙍ ᙍ ᙍ ᙍ

Unless you've been in a sensory deprivation tank for the last 48 hours, you know that a couple of evil young creatures entered the Columbine High School Tuesday morning in Littleton — a town where my daughter skates competitively every year — and murdered something on the order of twenty-five of their fellow human beings, wounding many more.

A number of things need to be said about this event. The first is, don't emulate the media morons by wringing your hands and asking why it happened. There *is* no "why." This was a psychotic crime for which, by definition, there can be no comprehensible motive. Notice that I'm *not* saying the killers weren't responsible. Psychotics talk themselves into their psychoses with a staggering dedication and persistence.

Equally obvious is the fact that if even two or three of the targeted students had been carrying competent weapons of their own, this never would have happened — it would probably never have begun in the first place. These vermin were counting on their victims to be helpless, and helpless they were — made that way by politicians who have plenty of reasons of their own for wanting their constituents helpless.

What? Am I suggesting that *kids* carry guns? Sure. I wouldn't trust public-school teachers to tie children's shoes, let alone defend them.

I'm also invariably suspicious when spree-killers like these are found oh-so-conveniently dead at the end of their spectacular display, unable to comment articulately on their heinous crime or to inform us who put them up to it. I'm even more suspicious when what they do — like bringing guns to school — has been the specific object of endless weeks, months,

236

or years of harping from leftist politicians and the round-heeled, hairsprayed, fear-mongering airheads in the mass media.

I'm even more suspicious when the photogenic bloodletting occurs at the very moment that the legislature is enthusiastically debating "liberalizing" gun laws — an appropriate choice of phrase meaning that they're preparing to graciously permit us to beg them for their official permission to exercise our basic human and Constitutional rights. Following a background check, of course, along with a hearty fingerprinting, a rousing urine test, a robust rectal examination, and a $200 or $300 fine for daring to believe we're still Americans.

I'm most suspicious of all when a President best known for taking sexual advantage of his semi-retarded employees, raping women on two continents, stealing everything that wasn't nailed down from the Arkansas Attorney General's office to 1600 Pennsylvania Avenue, selling his nation's military secrets for campaign contributions, leaving a trail of dead bodies behind him, bombing thousands to death overseas to punish us for questioning his authority, murdering 82 men, women, and children in broad daylight, on national TV, then putting the survivors on trial and when they're acquitted, pressuring a corrupt federal judge into sending them to jail anyway ... where was I?

Right — when a President rushes onto the nation's airwaves with a statement that sounds like it was prepared hours before the shootings, trying to turn a local travesty, one that glaringly demonstrates the utter failure of his policies, into justification for ... who knows what?

It's just too good. Rich kids (stir up the old class envy, there!) with black trenchcoats (too expensive — shoulda been a dress code) practicing a lifestyle the media call "Gothic" (can't have that, now — everybody oughta *look* the same so they'll all *act* the same), listening to rock 'n' roll (didn't we warn you about that in the '50s?), and communicating on the Internet (that tool of the Devil!) take their guns (hey, wait a minute, didn't we outlaw guns for kids?) and their homemade bombs (no! stop! this isn't going where we wanted it to go at all!). ... Paragraph cancelled due to lack of politically correct conclusion.

One thing is beyond dispute. Every one of these deaths is the moral — and will someday be the *legal* — responsibility of Denver mayor Wellington Webb. Every drop of blood in the Littleton shootings is dripping from his hands, as it drips from the hands of every pundit and politico who spent the last few decades doing everything possible to render every adult within his jurisdiction — let alone every kid — harmless and helpless.

This is the moral cripple who has his thugs steal your car if they find a gun or knife in it. Every syllable Webb spoke in his most recent attempt to suppress the Second Amendment ("Denver knows how to make laws for Denver!") came straight from the copybooks of George Wallace and Lester Maddox, with the modern equivalent of Bull Conner to do the enforcing. Every word was karmically transformed into a hollowpoint bullet speeding straight at the heart of one of the poor children — defenseless at his demand — who died or was hurt in that school.

Those killers were acting in Webb's political behalf — just as they were at Ruby Ridge and Waco, for which he also bears full moral responsibility — because they were carrying his policies to their ultimate end. When people are disarmed, they're made easy prey for ordinary criminals — or for governments. This is what we saw at Waco; it is what we're seeing in Yugoslavia; it's what's happened in Littleton.

Right now, perfectly reasonable people are asking me if it's possible that events like this are *created* by politicians like

Webb and Clinton to prevent the loosening of gun laws or to stampede the passage of more stringent ones. I confess I've asked myself the same question more than once. There are just too many "coincidences" involved.

The best way for Wellington Webb to dispel suspicions like this before they come to be entertained by a wider group is to renounce his fetish for victim disarmament, stop murdering the children all around him, and leapfrog the cowardly, stupid, and dishonest Republicans in the Colorado legislature by loudly demanding repeal of every law that limits the individual right to own — and especially to carry — weapons.

Let's hear it for Vermont Carry, Mayor — or do you *like* being morally responsible for massacres like those at Ruby Ridge, Waco, and Littleton?

Listen to the Women
ဏ ဏ ဏ ဏ ဏ

A fellow I know offers what he thinks is instruction in self-defense for women. Among other things, he advises them to buy .22 caliber pistols because they're cheap to feed (which is true enough), easy to get proficient with (also true), and, in his opinion, perfectly adequate for killing or driving off a rapist, mugger, or burglar. The trouble is, his opinion and advice in this final connection are likely to get his students killed.

Another fellow I know had a teenage accident that taught him everything *we* need to know about the adequacy of .22 rimfire. His single-action revolver fell from a bunk bed and fired a cartridge that was (regrettably) under the hammer, putting a slug into his midsection — the part we all try to hit when we're practicing self-defense. He didn't even know that he'd been hit until he saw a tiny drop of blood forming in the area of his solar plexus. While his family was running around screaming, he called a doctor, got dressed, and waited for the ambulance.

Now this isn't just another entry in the Great Stopping-Power Debate, an endless mostly male ritual that never produces useful answers because it isn't really intended to. (It serves purposes of its own, which are perfectly respectable if you follow cultural anthropology.) For the moment, let's agree that, all other things being equal, big guns are more effective than little guns, and therefore it's reasonable to assume that an individual should learn to use the biggest weapon that he or she can handle comfortably, safely, and efficaciously.

Which brings us to the meat of the question — or rather to the muscle. You can't avoid the plain fact of anatomy and physiology that women possess only about half the upper-body strength of men. Yet all of the women I shoot with manifest a pragmatic interest in medium to large-bore centerfire weapons ranging from .38 Special to .45 Automatic. Some outshoot me on a regular basis; most can do it at one time or another. Not many lean toward .44 Magnum, .445 Supermag, or .45 Winchester Magnum, but that's a reflection of our physical differences — and it's also another male thing, a matter of ceremonial accoutrement.

My 98-pound wife shoots an NRA Hunter's Pistol with the same six-inch Smith & Wesson Model 610 that I do, a great big revolver with a full-length lug under a heavy barrel chambered for 10 millimeter automatic. For Falling Plates, she uses a Colt Series 70 Gold Cup .45 identical to mine. The first handgun she ever fired was a four-inch Ruger Security Six with full-powered .357 Magnum loads (at 25 yards she kept every shot on the paper) and her deer rifle is a model 1895

Marlin in .45/70. I can't shoot the damn thing; it makes my eyes water.

In practical circumstances, the same in which I rely on a three-inch Detonics .45, she prefers a tiny two-inch Smith & Wesson .38 Chief's Special, not because she's anyone's delicate little flower, but because, even minus the lethal hardware, her purse (that of a wife, mother, and working woman) is already heavy enough to qualify as field gear for Infantry Basic Training.

But what's the point of all this? Put very simply, I'm confident that we're going to win the Battle of the Second Amendment. I've been confident ever since JoAnne Hall's column started showing up in *Guns & Ammo,* and that confidence has been strengthened by the publication of Paxton Quigley's *Armed and Female,* by the advent of *Women & Guns* magazine, by Lenda R. Jackson's Patrick Henryesque speech from the Denver Capitol steps, and by Nancy Bittle's brilliant appearance on *Street Stories.*

But why should any of that make such a difference?

Well, in case you hadn't noticed, our species is divided into halves, each seeing the world in a slightly different way, providing humanity as a whole with perspective each would lack without the other.

Survivalwise, that's worked pretty well over the million or two years we've been around. My wife contends that men are strategically oriented and women are tactically oriented. For example, male gunfolk typically tend to focus on history, the Constitution, and the significance of the Second Amendment in maintaining individual liberty, social democracy, and Western civilization; female gunfolk tend to focus on protecting themselves from the mutants lurking around the edges of that civilization. Both priorities are correct; neither is complete without the other.

Lever Action

And yet there are still gunshops today where women feel unwelcome and whose proprietors, when they condescend to acknowledge women at all, invariably offer the "little lady" a .25 automatic to defend herself with. It seems that, just as there are useless, gutless, mindless females who protest that they could *never* shoot anybody, even to preserve their own worthless lives or those of their children, and just as there are cretinous cops (the same cops, in my experience, who get trounced by female competitors) who advise women not to arm themselves because some rapist, mugger, or burglar will only take their little gun away and hurt them with it, so there are still male gun people who don't understand that trying to fight this battle without female help is exactly like closing one eye in combat.

The point I'm making here is not feminist (that movement may be responsible for the remaining communication problems between the genders) but individualistic. Nor is it directed at a majority of male shooters, mostly younger ones, who have gotten the point, but at a minority of fossilized idiots who haven't.

It's the women among us who have finally gotten the media to listen to us after decades of bigotry and persecution. It's the women and their increasing willingness to provide for their own physical safety in a society gone berserk that are at the heart of the ongoing effort (of its concerns, if not of its politics) to make concealed carry of weapons legal. It's the women who will provide the final nudge we need to secure our individual rights, to end the insanity of victim disarmament, and to recreate a culture in which some value is placed on civility.

The least we can do is listen to them seriously and not treat them like retarded children when they try to help us by helping themselves. We owe them the courtesy, when they're learning the craft, of offering them the same advice we'd give any male beginner, then let them make their own minds up about what they really need.

They're going to do it anyway.

Taking the Mag Pledge
ᑫᑫᑫᑫᑫ

I'm sitting here at my kitchen table looking at three semi-auto pistol magazines manufactured by a company I happen to respect and admire.

I can't say the same thing for the magazines, however. Through no fault of the company in question, they've been rendered "politically correct," mutilated in a crude and unconstitutional attempt to limit their capacity to no more than 10 cartridges apiece. The sides of the rectangular steel tubing have been saw-cut laterally about an inch and a quarter from the floorplate, leaving only a deeply depressed dimple fore and aft that allows a modified follower and its spring to pass by, but not the additional cartridges these magazines were supposed to hold.

The result of this alteration (make that vandalism), performed at the illegal command of a government that has long since overstepped its Constitutional bounds, is a gun I don't wholly trust, dependent as it is on two tiny quarter-inch spans of sheet steel (already badly stressed by the process of making them into dimples) that could fail me the very next time I slap a magazine into the weapon, or when I shoot it (like most of my favorite guns, this one has substantial recoil), spewing unfired cartridges and magazine parts all over the neighborhood, leaving me a small expensive iron club to defend myself with.

This, of course, is *exactly* what the authors of Bill Clinton's illegal ban on "ugly" guns and magazines intended. They aren't at all interested in stopping violent crime; if they were, they'd be passing out handguns like this one (with decent magazines, mind you) on every city street corner in America. They're not interested in stopping accidents; if they were, they'd quit badgering that tired old whore, the NRA, and let her get on with doing the one thing she does right, teaching people — especially little children — to handle firearms safely. No, the authors of Bill Clinton's adequate magazine ban want me, and everybody like me, *dead* — the sooner the better — if not from calamitous mechanical failure, then from a 12-goblin street gang when all I've got is 10 rounds in the magazine and one more in the chamber. California's legislature — not one member of which would have lasted five minutes at the Nuremburg tribunals — has even tried to make it a crime to carry a spare magazine. They want us dead because we — and our guns — are nothing but a noisy unaesthetic obstacle in the way of their establishing the well-planned, *well-disciplined*, planetwide socialist Utopia that is the focus of all their wishes, hopes, and wet dreams.

And everybody else's nightmares.

It's worthwhile in this connection to recall that the current law was first advocated by that fine feathered fascist William Bennett, supported by the wimpy blubberings of George Bush, rammed through by the parliamentary chicanery of Brady Bill Bob Dole — and that Sarah Brady is a lifelong Republican. That's just the top of a long list of lying traitorous criminals like Texas senator Kay Bailey Hutchinson, Colorado senator Wayne Allard, New Jersey governor Christie Whitman, Pennsylvania senator Arlen Specter, and the spectre haunting Utah, Senator Orrin Hatch, the most evil figure in American politics. Now tell me again, who is it who's been wasting their vote all these years?

Unlike our former Republican allies, who reef their sails at the slightest indication of a change in the wind, no amount of argument, no compendium of facts, no detail of history or the law can swerve the socialists who call themselvs liberals from the course their moral and political ancestors plotted for them more than a century ago. (In the '60s, they were the morons who babbled incessantly about the Revolution; now they know it's their last shot before Alzheimer's sets in and all they can babble about is DentuCreme and Depends.) To them, human nature is plastic, something that can be squashed, kneaded, rolled out, and remolded to their liking — as long as it isn't fortified by inflexible materials like blued steel, and polished walnut, and the Constitution.

You can't change their minds; they haven't any.

The only way to stop them is to sink their little boat.

All these nautical metaphors remind me of an old song I rewrote lightly and had my characters relive in my novel *Henry Martyn*. The *Golden Vanity* was a merchant ship, all but harmless and pursuing its own business when it found itself being overtaken by a pirate. The situation looked hopeless until a little cabin boy volunteered — he'd been promised a pile of valuta and the captain's daughter — to swim over and drill holes in the enemy ship with his "little brace and auger."

The plan worked perfectly. The pirate vessel sank and the *Golden Vanity*'s crew and cargo were saved. Of course, the captain, being a major contributor to the Republican National Committee, rewarded the heroic cabin boy by refusing to pull him back aboard and letting him drown. But the point here is that one hand, one tool, or one idea can sometimes reverse the motion of what may seem like vastly greater entities.

That's why I'm calling now on firearms companies that do business in the U.S. and Canada to make a solemn public pledge that, once this evil stupid law is repealed, nullified, or otherwise set aside, they'll replace every one of the mangled feed devices they've been forced to sell, with full-capacity magazines, at no charge to their customers.

We're not talking about anything that will cost anybody much. The customer sends his mutant magazine in. He gets a new one back — it's probably the same follower, spring, and floorplate outfitted with a fresh tube — by return mail. The expense is nothing compared to the good will engendered, and can be written off as advertising, in any case. The important thing is to make the pledge right now, while it's politically incorrect to do so, not later when it's safe and therefore meaningless.

I know that the gun companies — with a handful of disgustingly conspicuous exceptions like Ruger, Smith & Wesson, Mossberg, and Colt — aren't responsible for this evil stupid law. And yet, in the post-Clintonian post-socialist era to come, there will be a new cast of characters on the firearms-manufacturing front. In the past, outfits like Ruger, Smith & Wesson, Mossberg, and Colt felt they could afford to stab their civilian customers in the back, because they had police and military sales to fall back on. In the future, federal and state governments under the control of Bill of Rights enforcement advocates won't do business with such companies. There may be laws forbidding transactions with corporations that aren't completely Bill of Rights compliant.

In this and any other part of the market you can point to, there have always been good companies, operated by intelligent principled individuals, and bad companies operated by dishonorable idiots. My intention is to drive a permanent wedge between the two. From this moment forward, gun companies will identify themselves publicly as being firmly on the side of their civilian customers and the Bill of Rights, or on the side of overreaching, insatiable, voracious, brutal statism.

More importantly, this will establish in the minds of friend and foe that there *is* a post-Clinton, post-socialist, post-gun-control era coming, that it can't be stopped, that it should be anticipated and planned for. The sooner we do that, the sooner that era will arrive.

So how about it, gun companies?

How about taking the mag pledge and telling us whose side you're on?

Smith & Wesson Must Die
ↂ ↂ ↂ ↂ ↂ

Over the past couple of weeks, a third of my e-mail has concerned a decision of the Smith & Wesson company to sign an "agreement" with the Clinton Administration — supposedly in order to avoid massive state lawsuits — to act as if the Second Amendment had never been written.

What began as a depressing event — foreshadowing, many feared, the end of private gun ownership — has suddenly turned into something else. Gun Owners of America announced what promises to be an effective boycott against S&W. One by one, other companies told the Clintonistas where to shove their "agreement." When everybody said the Austrians would geek, they didn't, and neither did the Belgians — although Ruger and Beretta are lying low — and distributors and dealers have started sending S&W products back to Springfield, where they came from.

Most recently, S&W's Chicago law firm has quit them.

Even Utah Senator Orrin Hatch — arguably the most evil individual in politics today — could see which way the wind was blowing and has introduced legislation in the Senate to forbid any further federal participation in lawsuits against gun companies. And a credible move is now underway in Congress to render the S&W "agreement" null and void.

It's sad to think that S&W, which predates the War Between the States, introduced the self-contained metallic cartridge, and in the 1980s gave us the wonderful "Ladysmith" program — encouraging women to learn to defend themselves by redesigning weapons specifically to fit the female hand — has sunk to the low, crawling, yellow-bellied pusillanimity that signing Clinton's "agreement" required. But the fact is, S&W never did make managerial decisions particularly well, whether it involved Second Amendment politics or merchandising of weapons.

Just in my lifetime, S&W has come up with bonnet-bees — or some focus panel has, or some overly blonde vice president's wife — so stultifyingly imbecilic that it's embarrassing even thinking about them. Back in the '60s, when they were owned by something called Bangor Punta (which always sounded to me like one of Tarzan's animal friends), they called publicly for handgun registration. This latest display of the white feather is hardly unprecedented. They've always been Second Amendment weaklings, likely due to their location in the only state carried by George McGovern, and the fact that — despite their actual sales numbers — they've always seen themselves primarily as a police outfitter.

Managerial decisions? If ever there was a "suicidal corporation," S&W is it. Their .41 Magnum Model 58 Military and Police — featured prominently in my first novel, *The Probability Broach* — is a slick, no-nonsense fighting instrument that, employing two cartridge power levels, can take a man down or stop a car with only a little added weight or bulk compared to the traditional (and woefully inadequate) police .38

Special. One of the finest combat revolvers ever conceived, S&W discontinued it, rather than producing it in stainless steel — and in .44 Magnum and .45 Colt — as anyone with any brains would have done.

Managerial decisions? In the 1990s S&W had somebody working for them who created what we all ended up calling the "gun-of-the-week" program, under which S&W came out with more innovative concepts over the short span of a year than they'd introduced in the 50 preceding years. Of course, the man responsible was run out of the ancient outfit with extreme prejudice and to this day they're ashamed to talk about him.

Managerial decisions? In my capacity as a competitive shooter and retired gunsmith, S&W's Model 610 was technologically and historically the best revolver ever produced anywhere by anyone. Naturally, after only a year or two of production and almost no attempt to promote it to gun buyers or any other part of the public, they discontinued its manufacture.

Managerial decisions? There are those who may disagree, but again, in my opinion as a competitor and a gunsmith, S&W never could make decent semiautomatic pistols, although they've wasted several fortunes trying to get it right — and failing every time. Their incompetence may even account, at least in part, for the remarkable longevity of Colt's 1911A1. Having shot (and repaired) many S&W autos and listened to the lamentations of their owners, I have never been moved to buy one.

S&W revolvers are something else altogether. Magnificent "engines of destruction" made legendary (most recently) by Clint Eastwood's "Dirty Harry," they occupy a different plane of existence. I love them all. My collection includes a .38, a .357 Magnum with an adjustable front sight, a 10mm auto (that's the M610 I mentioned above, a sixgun chambered for the 10mm autopistol cartridge — it also shoots .40 S&W),

a .41 Magnum, a .44 Magnum, and a .45 ACP that works the same as the 10mm. Once again, as a shooter and gunsmith, I agree they're a trifle antiquated, designwise, and fragile compared with Ruger's output. But nothing can match their eye-pleasing elegance and hand-pleasing grace.

I risk boring the non-gunners (and non-wheelgunners) among my readers, because I want them to understand fully — in technicolor and 3D — how painful it is for me to write the next few paragraphs. The proposed boycott of S&W and other measures are good as far as they go. I support them all wholeheartedly. However, they don't go nearly far enough.

Smith & Wesson must die.

I'm not saying that they don't go nearly far enough to satisfy our purely emotional desire for justice, retribution, even revenge. I'm saying that they don't go nearly far enough to guarantee our continued *survival*.

Smith & Wesson must die. Smith & Wesson must be amputated from the American social body like the gangrenous excrescence it has become and thrown out with the rest of the medical/political waste. Otherwise, the infection will spread.

Smith & Wesson must die.

Understand that it's going to take more than a boycott; S&W was prepared for that or they'd never have signed Clinton's "agreement." Being owned by an English holding company, it's more than likely that their "surrender" was a put-up job to begin with, a gift from Tony Blair, intended to give Clinton what he needs to destroy an entire industry — exactly as he's promised his comrades under international agreements he's made to eliminate every personally owned weapon in the world.

Smith & Wesson must die.

I've heard that the S&W CEO — in a manner foully reminiscent of the late Republican National Committee chairman

Lee Atwater — has been confiding to the media that his customers are "a little crazy just now, but they'll be back." What that tells me is that this time — unlike many similar moments over the past 50 years — we can't be satisfied to fend off the latest attack and survive with minimal losses.

This time it has to cost them something. Have no qualms about it. A corporation isn't private property — it's only an extension of the state. Yes, that's what I said. In applying to the state for special powers and immunities, a corporation becomes an *extension* of the state.

Smith & Wesson must die.

A boycott is not enough. Our goal must be to make life completely impossible for S&W — in exactly the same way anti-nuclear activists made life impossible for the nuclear-power industry in the 1960s and 1970s. We must interdict S&W's sales to government agencies at every level, starve the company, and kill it. For those who have the means, we must find judges who will issue injunctions against city, county, or state purchases — especially preferential purchases — of S&W products.

Smith & Wesson must die.

For those who don't, picketing public buildings is an alternative, as is attending the meetings of your local city council or county commission. Remind them that they've taken what's supposed to be a sacred oath to uphold and defend the Constitution. Tell them that, in choosing to do business with a foreign corporation savaging the Bill of Rights, they're violating both the letter and the spirit of that oath.

Smith & Wesson must die.

Get every one of your gunny friends to help. If you see an S&W auto or revolver in a cop's holster, don't bother him — in these post-Waco days he'll probably kill you if you do, and cook you, and eat you, and get a commendation for it — but find out if your city has a contract with S&W and demand that it be terminated immediately on the grounds (if all else fails) that the company falls short of Bill of Rights compliance.

Smith & Wesson must die.

Lawyers among us need to enjoin HUD and other government agencies prepared to reward S&W for its cowardly behavior. One of the goodies Clinton promised S&W (and anybody else who signs on) is preferential treatment in the purchase of weapons by the Department of Housing and Urban Development and similar agencies. (I was unaware that HUD is a major weapons buyer — that's something, in itself, that should be looked into.) I could be mistaken, but doesn't that sound illegal to you?

Whatever happened to competitive bidding?

Smith & Wesson must die.

Choke off S&W's sales for six months while the courts muddle the whole thing, and S&W will miraculously find the grounds they need to abrogate the deal. It's either that or be thrown onto the cliche heap of history. As New York's nasty attorney general can attest — he's the disappointed little creep whose cherished plans have backfired and who's now trying to argue that a boycott is a violation of antitrust laws — it was signed under extreme duress that he himself helped apply.

(This is the pocket Nazi who warned gun companies to comply with his demands or prepare to greet their bankruptcy attorneys at their door. What they need to tell him is that times change and regimes change with them. He *will* learn to obey the highest law of the land or prepare to greet federal marshals at his door with a big noisy collection of manacles, leg-irons, and belly-chains, and TV cameras to record the moment as they shove him into the Black Maria and haul him away.)

Smith & Wesson must die.

In the long run, this war will be won in the court of popular opinion. We've always known — and now, thanks to Gary Kleck and John Lott, we can prove — that guns and gun ownership save lives. Which means that anything or anybody who interferes with unencumbered ownership of and free access to guns endangers lives. In today's battle of sound bites and slogans, that translates as "S&W kills kids."

We need to talk publicly about S&W's "Kid Killer Kontrakt."

Smith & Wesson must die.

If you ever hope to live in a civilization where you can walk into a hardware store, put your cash on the counter, and walk out with the weapon of your choice — without ever having produced identification or signing even a single piece of paper — then Smith & Wesson must die.

Maybe once they're bankrupt, no more than a name, and in the hands of pro-gun Americans again, we can go back to buying their beautiful revolvers.

Smith & Wesson must die.

Right-Wing Socialism
ᑕᕼ ᑕᕼ ᑕᕼ ᑕᕼ ᑕᕼ

For most of its overly prolonged history, the late unlamented Soviet Empire had to rely on five percent of its farmland to produce eighty percent of the food its subjects subsisted on. What made that five percent so different? Well, it was the only agricultural land that the Dictatorship of the Proletariate allowed — under strict and complicated regulations — to be farmed by private individuals for a profit.

In these enlightened times, we chuckle smugly to ourselves

over a Marxist system of centrally planned destitution in which a "command economy" generated everything from bread to shoes. The bread tasted like the shoes and the shoes (all of them left ones) possessed the enduring properties of bread. Even certain elements of the American Left are beginning to contemplate eliminating state coercion in areas like the heavily collectivized industry of education. These days, "everybody knows" — except maybe Castro and the Communist Chinese — that everything the government touches immediately turns into something considerably less valuable than the proverbial agricultural byproduct.

Everybody, to all appearances, except that celebrated bastion of rugged individualism and unfettered free enterprise — the Republican Party.

Consider the following: For just about a century, we've relied on government-supplied *expertism* to protect our rights, property, and lives in America's cities. Over that same century, slowly in the beginning, but with frighteningly increasing velocity every decade, those cities have been getting deadlier to live in and easier to die in.

Every collectivist remedy imaginable (New York's 1917 Sullivan Act comes to mind) has been given a try — more prisons, harsher penalties, sterner judges, capital punishment, midnight basketball, *always* more restrictions on individual rights — and nothing ever produces changes greater than the random statistical noise associated with such phenomena (although that never stopped any administration from puffing itself up over a one percent fluctuation in the crime rate).

Until Florida.

In Florida, following events in Orlando that led up to easing the restrictions on concealed weapons (after 20 years of bitter fighting retreat on the part of *expertists* still stuck in the 19th century), one percent of the citizenry endured the unconstitutional hassles and personal insults involved in obtaining a carry permit, and violent crime (depending on who performs the calculation) plummeted 20 to 40 percent.

Now, of course, legislators in two-thirds of the states are trying to achieve the same result by the same means, at every turn with an hysterical emphasis on retaining rigid control over something the Bill of Rights (to which they've all sworn undying loyalty — but then, what good are the promises of politicians?) says will *not* be controlled: the unalienable individual, civil, Constitutional, and human right of every man, woman, and responsible child to obtain, own, and carry, openly or concealed, any weapon — rifle, shotgun, handgun, machinegun, *anything* — any time, any place, without asking anyone's permission.

In this respect, they resemble the former — and observe: *extinct* — Soviet planners who believed they were being progressive and openhanded whenever they generously consented to increase privatized farmland another percent under the latest glorious Five-Year Plan.

The truth is, they have no choice. American cities have become gangrenous abcesses on the fundament of what was once the most advanced civilization in history. We've gone from densely populated 19th century cities that didn't see a single rape or murder over the span of a decade to neighborhoods that can't make that claim for two nights running. Collectivist policies in force over the last century — foisted off on Americans by both parties — are directly to blame, and this has become embarrassingly obvious to everybody, even mass media.

Now they want us to clean their mess up — the mess they couldn't handle — while continuing to labor under exactly the kind of idiotic and illegal policies that created it. No matter that they often call themselves Republicans, they still demand an effect without a cause. They want a free lunch just like every other two-bit socialist on the planet.

Part of this is attributable to an honest (if appalling) state of ignorance tenderly passed on by universities and law schools from one generation unto the next. There's a story, for example, that a state attorney general was pondering, a couple of years ago, the question of at what age the Bill of Rights begins to apply to juveniles. (Sad to say, this represented an improvement: The overwhelming tendency has been to deny that its guarantees of protection apply to juveniles at all.)

Apparently nobody — in high school, college, or in law school — ever bothered to inform the future attorney general that the Bill of Rights, *per se*, doesn't apply at all to juveniles, and never will, even if they live to be 100. It doesn't apply to you or me. It only applies to *government*; it's irrelevant what anybody's age happens to be. The document is nothing more (and nothing less) than a list of things government can't do no matter what, and, as such, it's been misnamed. (It's worth pointing out that it doesn't call itself "Bill of Rights" in the Constitution.) It should be called the "Bill of Limitations."

But I digress.

The point is that, while Republicans claim they've carried off a revolution, they're peddling the same shopworn socialist goods as their left-wing Democratic counterparts, and there's no conceivable excuse.

Not after Florida.

Decency — and the Constitution — demand immediate repeal of Clinton's illegal semiautomatic and magazine bans and Republicans offer more prisons. Decency — and the Constitution — demand immediate repeal of the vile Brady Bill and Republicans offer more executions. Prisons and executions are a right-wing socialist substitute — no sorrier or sillier than midnight basketball — for the proper course of action, removing every remaining legal barrier to individual self-defense.

Decency — and the Constitution — demand immediate repeal of laws hindering the right to own and carry weapons and Republicans in state legislatures everwhere offer a tangle of strict and complicated regulations that would make a Soviet planner's latest glorious Five-Year Plan for agriculture appear progressive and openhanded by comparison.

So much for the revolution.

Why Did It Have to Be Guns?
ca ca ca ca ca

Over the past 30 years, I've been paid to write almost two million words, every one of which, sooner or later, came back to the issue of guns and gun ownership. Naturally, I've thought about the issue a lot, and it has *always* determined the way I vote.

People accuse me of being a single-issue writer, a single-issue thinker, and a single-issue voter, but it isn't true. What I've chosen, in a world where there's never enough time and energy, is to focus on the one political issue that most clearly and unmistakably demonstrates what any politician — or political philosophy — is made of, right down to the creamy liquid center.

Make no mistake: All politicians — even those ostensibly on the side of guns and gun ownership — hate the issue and anyone, like me, who insists on bringing it up. They hate it because it's an X-ray machine. It's a Vulcan mind-meld. It's the ultimate test to which any politician — or political philosophy — can be put.

If a politician isn't perfectly comfortable with the idea of his average constituent, any man, woman, or responsible child, walking into a hardware store and paying cash — for any rifle, shotgun, handgun, machinegun, *anything* — without producing ID or signing one scrap of paper, he isn't your *friend* no matter what he tells you.

If he isn't genuinely enthusiastic about his average constituent stuffing that weapon into a purse or pocket or tucking it under a coat and walking home without asking anybody's permission, he's a four-flusher, no matter what he claims.

What his attitude — toward your ownership and use of weapons — conveys is his real attitude about *you*. And if he doesn't trust you, then why in the name of John Moses Browning should you trust him?

If he doesn't want you to have the means of defending your life, do you want him in a position to control it?

If he makes excuses about obeying a law he's sworn to uphold and defend — the highest law of the land, the Bill of Rights — do you want to entrust him with *anything*?

If he ignores you, sneers at you, complains about you, or defames you, if he calls you names only he thinks are evil — like "Constitutionalist" — when you insist that he account for himself, hasn't he betrayed his oath, isn't he unfit to hold office, and doesn't he really belong in *jail*?

Sure, these are all leading questions. They're the questions that led me to the issue of guns and gun ownership as the clearest and most unmistakable demonstration of what any given politician — or political philosophy — is really made of.

He may lecture you about the dangerous weirdos out there who shouldn't have a gun — but what does that have to do with you? Why in the name of John Moses Browning should you be made to suffer for the misdeeds of others? Didn't you lay aside the infantile notion of group punishment when you left public school — or the military? Isn't it an essentially European notion, anyway — Prussian, maybe — and certainly not what America was supposed to be all about?

And if there are dangerous weirdos out there, does it make sense to deprive you of the means of protecting yourself from them? Forget about those other people, those dangerous weirdos; this is about *you*, and it has been, all along.

Try it yourself: If a politician won't trust you, why should you trust him? If he's a man — and you're not — what does his lack of trust tell you about his real attitude toward women? If "he" happens to be a *woman*, what makes her so perverse that she's eager to render her fellow women helpless on the mean and seedy streets her policies helped create? Should you believe her when she says she wants to help you by imposing some infantile group-health-care program on you at the point of the kind of gun she doesn't want you to have?

On the other hand — or the other party — should you believe anything politicians say who claim they stand for freedom, but drag their feet and make excuses about repealing limits on your right to own and carry weapons? What does this tell you about their real motives for ignoring voters and ramming through one infantile group trade agreement after another with other countries?

Makes voting simpler, doesn't it? You don't have to study every issue — health care, international trade, etc. All you have to do is use this X-ray machine, this Vulcan mind-meld, to get beyond their empty words and find out how politicians really feel. About you. And that, of course, is why they hate it.

And that's why I'm accused of being a single-issue writer, thinker, and voter.

But it isn't true, is it?

A Conspiracy Theory — Sort Of
❦ ❦ ❦ ❦ ❦

Boys and girls, it's Remarkable Coincidence Day at the Mickey Mouse Club!

Just as the political fluid they'd sucked out of the Columbine murders was running dry (and hadn't produced the legislative results desired by the creatures of the night dedicated to eviscerating the Second Amendment as a prelude to "reducing us under absolute despotism"), by the Remarkable Coincidence mentioned above, a loose screw in Atlanta obligingly filled his family and everybody else in sight full of holes (I know, he bludgeoned his family to death, but it's the thought that counts), providing the Darksiders with enough go-juice (eight quarts to the corpse) to get their anticonstitutional parade another block further down the road to serfdom.

For my part, I'm long past believing that any of this is mere happenstance, although I resisted the idea for as long as I could.

Look at the facts: We've all heard of steam engines, right? Well international victim disarmament — the gun-control industry — is a *blood engine*, consuming thousands of acre-feet of the stuff every year, helpless to advance its agenda a millimeter without plenty of formerly warm bodies to wring out like crimson-saturated sponges and drain into its insatiable maw. If enough victims fail to die, then how can international victim disarmament — the gun-control industry — hold its press conferences and photo opportunities decrying "violence in America" and demanding that the killing be stopped (by making it harder for those who *don't* kill other people to exercise their right to own and carry the only proven means of *preventing* the killing)?

If violent crime increases, then international victim disarmament — the gun-control industry — wins. If violent crime decreases, international victim disarmament — the gun-control industry — loses. You tell me: Will international victim disarmament — the gun-control industry — ever propose any measure that decreases violent crime?

(The same formula applies to the National Rifle Association: If victim disarmament is forever on the rise, then the NRA wins — using the perpetual menace of its sister organization, Handgun Control Inc., to frighten gun owners into pouring rivers of mazuma into their already overstuffed pockets. If victim disarmament is ever finally discredited, tossed on the ashheap of history where it belongs, then the NRA — and its six-figure executives — will be out of work.)

As a direct result, *more* innocents die, as they did at Luby's Cafeteria in Killeen, Texas, where victim-disarmament laws worked just as they're supposed to, failing to keep a murderer from his appointed rounds, but assuring the deaths of his victims who had law-abidingly left their guns in their cars. In Littleton, teachers and students, exercising their right to own and carry weapons, could have ended the killings at two: Klebold and Harris. Knowing this, Klebold and Harris might never have plotted to murder their fellow students.

It's this sort of thing that international victim disarmament — the gun-control industry — wishes to prevent at any cost.

They want your death.

They *need* your death.

There can be no question that international victim disarmament — the gun-control industry — *makes* those corpses, every helpless one. The only question remaining is whether it does so only indirectly, by suppressing your right to the machinery of self-defense, or by deliberately staging the incidents in which that killing — so very centrally important to their wishes, hopes, and plans — gets done.

As I say, I resisted the latter idea — that some or all of these marvelously photogenic killing sprees were planned and carried out to achieve political ends. Trouble is, as suspicious as I am of coincidence, I'm more suspicious of *convenience*.

How is it that the specific hobbyhorse that international victim disarmament — the gun-control industry — happens to be riding this week always manages to rock its way into schools, post offices, or other places where folks have been stripped of their right to self-defense, just in time to write the supremely desired conclusion in carmine exclamation points? If this week it's "Saturday Night Specials," then the designated dingbat kills a bunch of people with a snubby .38. If next week it's submachinegun lookalikes, he shows up with a KG or a Kel or whatever the hell they call them nowadays.

But I admit, I'm prejudiced, having been subjected to the bigotry, prejudice, harassment, persecution, outrageous lies, and 25,000 Jim Crow laws that international victim disarmament — the gun-control industry — have imposed on me and my fellow gun owners over the past half-century, most recently with the wholehearted enthusiastic support of the Republican Party and the National Rifle Association.

Being prejudiced — and fully as subject to wishing on a star as anyone else who's been involved with politics for a long time — let me tell you what I'd do about this situation if by some bizarre turn of events I found myself elected President of the United States.

First, I'd appoint what's termed a "blue-ribbon commission," made up of people whose integrity I trust, to investigate every shooting over the past few decades that was used to stampede passage of laws that violate our rights. In the majority where the killer had recently been under psychiatric "care," I'd want to know what "therapy" was involved and by whom it was administered. Special attention would be accorded those incidents in which the perpetrator tidily killed himself before he could be arrested and interrogated. Maybe we'd find out once and for all if there's a conspiracy.

Nor would this be a gaggle of nameless faces and faceless names, like the ones who decided that Lee Oswald found a way to shoot around corners in mid-air, or that David Koresch had it coming because they believed he'd found a way to molest children they hadn't thought of. If you're reading this, you might find your own face (and parts south) on such a commission, along with those of your friends and comrades.

More generally, there's a greater need for a similar set of blue-ribbon commissioners to investigate every item of legislation passed since about 1912 where an artificial panic was generated to push the bills through. The laws in question would be repealed, nullified, or otherwise set aside, and the people of this country would regain freedoms taken from them under false — or even real — pretenses.

Those responsible for taking those freedoms would be dealt with under due process of law. It's a bit late to punish the Sullivan who disarmed New York, but the vision of sending federal marshals to haul Diane Feinstein and Charles Schumer off the Senate floor in manacles, belly chains, and leg irons — putting new creases in their thousand dollar outfits — is one of the things that keep me going these days.

And ultimately (but not finally), a Libertarian president's best asset would be a Bill of Rights Compliance Commission, given the task of identifying which government activities meet the tests of the Ninth and Tenth Amendments and which don't, the latter to be terminated.

Opinions vary as to how much government that would leave. I think we should determine the answer empirically, don't you?

IV

REPUBLICRAT POLITICS

Prometheus Bound — and Gagged
ఴ ఴ ఴ ఴ ఴ

Consider, for just a moment if you will, all of the myriad things poor "liberals" have to be against these days, simply in order to retain their social credentials and remain "politically correct."

First and foremost, I suppose, comes smoking. Every bigoted gaggle of prune-faced prudes desperately needs some poor fool to pick on constantly and feel superior to — usually because they have so many things to feel inferior about, themselves. Eventually, if they are able to gain enough political power, they can beat him up and kill him.

For Hitler, it was Jews.

For fat Southern 1950s deputy sheriffs in mirrored sunglasses, it was blacks.

For their Volvo-driving wine-and-cheese gobbling equivalents today, it's those who enjoy tobacco. Never mind that nobody hurts anybody with tobacco but himself — that there's no scientifically respectable evidence that "secondhand smoke" hurts anybody. If these fascist geeks so much as glimpse somebody smoking a cigarette, downwind and five hundred yards away, they fall into a gasping stupor, and when they come out of it, they can be heard to demand in a lapse of self-control that smokers "go back to Virginia where they came from."

It's hard to choose, but I guess the private automobile and

the internal combustion engine usually occupy the next place on the list of "liberal" hate fetishes, although for some — apparently our soon-to-be ex-vice president among them — these items of 19th century technology take first place on the hit parade, despite the countless blessings of swift reliable transportation, personal self-sufficiency, and privacy — not to mention employment — they provide us with.

I really ought to stop trying to put these things in any kind of rational order; there's nothing rational about it. Let's just agree that another thing you hear lefties whimpering about all the time is the individual right to own and carry weapons — with a particular emphasis on firearms. Very few left-thinking folks have the moral courage to swim upstream on this one, even though the widespread ownership and use of guns has been proven — Florida is a fine example of the phenomenon — to dramatically reduce violent crime. And never mind that the mindless prohibition of such useful artifacts works an unfair, often deadly, hardship on women, the elderly, and minorities — while giving criminal gangs and individual brutes the upper hand.

Judging by their usual performance in the appropriately named "criminal justice system" — not to mention *West Side Story* — "liberals" have a certain fondness for criminal gangs and individual brutes, anyway.

Then there's the highly respectable two-million-year-old human practice of eating red meat — rare, medium, and well done. "Real food for real people." The worst way you can offend "liberals" in this area is by insisting on cooking it yourself over a shimmering charcoal grill in your own backyard — more guff about secondhand smoke, I presume.

And don't forget the sorry self-contradictory specimens who enjoy whining about the accumulation of garbage in America's precious and dwindling landfills — or was that wetlands? — but who demonstrate vociferously against doing the intelligent thing and incinerating it into a fine white ash.

Last, but certainly not least, is that ultimate of "liberal" bugaboos, nuclear power.

Now in case you missed it, what do all of these "horrors" have in common? Well, to begin with (consider this a hint), most people — although by no means all — have to *ignite* tobacco in order to enjoy it properly.

And modern personal weaponry employs smokeless gunpowder, consuming it as a *fuel* to propel bullets toward burglars, rapists, and freelance tax collectors in America's alleyways and municipal parks.

The key political word in the phrase "internal combustion engine" seems to be "combustion." Almost every one of the lame-brained substitutes "liberals" adore so well would eliminate the use of that foul four-letter word, "burn," which is also inextricably involved in eating meat (unless you're a lot braver than I am), cooking it indoors or outdoors, and properly disposing of the refuse afterwards.

And while nuclear power doesn't really *burn* anything, most of the feebs who oppose it think it does. It's especially interesting to note, in this connection, that during the late and largely unlamented 1960s — that period of greatest "liberal" hatred and distrust of *computers* — these now ubiquitous devices (I'm using one right now) were invariably portrayed as failing in a shower of sparks and curtains of black smoke. When it became clear, even to "liberals," that this doesn't happen, computers somehow miraculously became acceptable.

Clearly then, today's "liberalism" consists principally of a delayed emotional reaction to the discovery, somewhere around a hundred thousand years ago, of *fire*. The question that comes to mind — to my mind, anyway (although I will confess, to quote Tom Hanks in a much better role than *Forrest Gump*,

267

that they pay me to be this way) — is, "What the hell took them so long to find out about it?"

Fire good.

Fire good.

Fire good.

Put that way, over and over again, perhaps today's "liberals" will eventually get the message. Of course, once they do, they won't be "liberals" any more.

"Do It to Julia"
cs cs cs cs cs

I get it now.

Twenty-odd years ago, I remember being inspired by the sight and sound of William B. Ruger of Sturm, Ruger & Co., driving the current advocates of victim disarmament into disorderly retreat on national TV by the simple expedient of demanding — over and over again — to know the source of their statistics. It turned out that they'd made their numbers up — out of whole cloth or thin air, whichever metaphor you prefer — and good old Bill had caught them at it and finally outmaneuvered them into admitting it.

It is to be regretted deeply that the William B. Ruger we see today is a sadly different specimen. Having communicated with various members of Congress, suggesting that they outlaw any rifle or pistol magazine one round more capacious than any he happens to manufacture — "Do it to Julia!" is the way George Orwell described this syndrome in the novel *1984* — he now has his company enclose printed material with the firearms it sells, attempting to alibi the great disservice he did to the customers, past, present, and future, he has dishonored with his craven behavior.

I don't know what political party Bill Ruger considers himself to be a member of. But based on the nearly identical performance, recently, of somebody whose abject fealty I do know, I'm prepared to make a guess. Having treated the ears of America to his cowardly and cruel indifference with regard to the federal government's crimes at Waco, Texas, in the summer of 1993 (an indifference vastly exceeding Bill Ruger's magazine act for sheer self-serving pusillanimity), radio talk show host Rush Limbaugh is now enthusiastically denouncing the Oklahoma City bombers as "anarchists" — without any evidence or any knowledge of what the word "anarchist" means, except good old-fashioned Missouri knownothingism — and demanding that nobody hold him responsible in any way for that heinous act in Oklahoma or interfere in any respect with his Constitutional free speech rights in a misguided (or malevolently fraudulent) attempt to prevent more such incidents.

Fair enough.

To a point, I can sympathize with Rush. This administration — the most irredeemably evil in 20th century American history — murders people and then lies about it. With the wholehearted assistance of gentlemen-of-the-evening like Larry King, "Bill of Impeachment" Clinton and his crooked fascistic spouse are trying to use Oklahoma City as a bludgeon to render any further morally outraged talk about Waco or the Constitution not only politically incorrect, but thoroughly illegal. They have "anti-terrorist" legislation before the Congress at this very minute that will finish off the Bill of Rights for good. This worries Rush — who seems to be shaping up as a principal target of all this activity — as it should worry any American, especially those of us who earn our living through the exercise of our First Amendment rights.

Lever Action

On the other hand, where were Rush's worries about rights, First Amendment or otherwise, when the lives of the Branch Davidians and their children were being callously snuffed out for the "crime" of having defended themselves against BATF and FBI stormtroopers? Where were Rush's worries when government assassin Lon Horiuchi used a scoped high-powered rifle at Ruby Ridge to explode the skull of innocent unarmed Vicki Weaver? Were his worries tied — like the unused half of his brain that would otherwise transform him into a Libertarian — behind his back?

Now the final irony, as far as William B. Ruger is concerned, is that his squalid appeasement of the gun-grabbing Left has done him no good whatever. Instead, it has put the scent of blood in the water, and the political predators are after him much harder at the moment than they're after anybody else, because they can smell weakness. It's entirely his fault, and I have no sympathy for him.

And should it come to pass that Rush is one of those who fall victim to the dictatorial powers "Bill of Impeachment" Clinton and his crooked fascistic spouse want in order to stifle dissent in America, I'll have a tough time feeling sorry for him, either.

I'll be too busy trying to survive in a concentration camp that got built because the one individual who could have stopped it — with a single courageous word at the right moment in the summer of 1993 — played the bully's toadie instead (a role he no doubt learned sucking up to William Bennett), made fun of the government's latest victims rather than standing up for them, and waited to defend himself, and only himself, until 1995, when it was too late.

Feeding the Ducks

Robert Heinlein said that the smaller any unit of government happens to be, the harder it is to move. It's relatively easy to make enough fuss to alter the course of federal government, for example, but everybody "knows" you can't fight City Hall and that the most viciously dictatorial level of government is a local school board.

My daughter's home-schooled. And generally, I ignore my city government because I have far bigger fish to fry (or I'm taking the coward's way out; you may decide which for yourself). But because I'm willing to bet that one city government across this country is pretty much like another (they should all be given 24 hours to get out of town) and the trends they set have a regrettable tendency to spread upward and outward, I think it's appropriate to discuss them from time to time, so we'll all have an idea of what we're up against.

If it were only a matter of good old-fashioned Chicago-style graft, we could probably accept it philosophically. For example, say some city council somewhere passed a law that lawn-sprinkling systems (which our hypothetical city government urged us to install "because they save water") must now be inspected and a whopping fee collected for this "service." Never mind that the Earth got along perfectly well for the last four and a half billion years *without* the fee-collecting lawn-sprinkling-system inspectors who lobbied for this law. What we have here (and as usual, employing government as a truncheon) is sheer, primitive, plug-ugly *greed*, which I happen to define as an inordinate and potentially violent desire for unearned wealth.

But to make things worse, let's say that the same collection of droolers and mouth-breathers, unduly influenced by animal-rights fascists, passed a law ordaining that your five-year-old daughter and mine, upon pain of whatever it is city governments do to you (besides bore you to death between uncontrollable bouts of rolling on the floor laughing until the tears stream from your eyes) will henceforward, and in the face of more than a century of pleasantly civilized tradition, be forbidden to toss bits of stale bread, carefully saved up all week, to the ducks on the lake in City Park of a sunny Sunday afternoon.

This is the same bunch of frilly-dillies who proclaimed, after a wet early snowstorm recently brought down most of the tree limbs in northern Colorado, that you can't burn cottonwood (the only deciduous tree native to the area and the same species used for matchsticks) in your fireplace, because it smews aw icky (or baby-talk to that effect).

Let's get this straight, once and for all. Let me be the first in what I hereby declare as a new post-psychotic era of rationality and enlightenment to state that, despite decades of philosophically and scientifically unsupportable TV propaganda to the contrary, ducks, more or less like all animals, serve only three purposes.

First, they're for guys and their buddies in silly clothing to trudge out at some ridiculous hour of the morning and stand in freezing water with a bunch of smelly dogs and shoot. Believe me, I'm not knocking it, only describing it. I'm a hunter and shooter myself.

Second, in combination with other ingredients, they're for cooking, preferably by Chinese people, who in my opinion are the ones (rather than guys with smelly dogs, or their wives) who do it best.

Third, they're for the innocent and heart-warming delight of little children and their parents who enjoy feeding them in the park.

Now don't get me wrong, I *love* animals. I've owned dozens, and I eat as many as I can every day. But my experience is that those who argue in favor of *animal* rights generally don't believe in *human* rights, not in any sense intended by the Dead White European Males who founded this civilization.

The latter kind of rights is what that civilization's supposed to be all about. The former is a conceptual disease festering within the shriveled cortices of social and political parasites who, for reasons known best to them, abominate their own species almost as much as they abominate themselves. It's communicated, by such wretched creatures, to a vastly greater number simply too clueless to disbelieve it.

But since all animals are *property*, properly claimed or as yet unclaimed, and necessary to the survival, well-being, and amusement of their evolutionary superiors, it follows that animal-rights advocates are self-announced enemies of their own kind and should be *treated* as such. If everybody refrained from selling them food for about six months, some of them would get the point and come around and the rest would starve to death. In either case, the problem would be solved.

A great deal is made, and always has been, of Republicans versus Democrats or liberals versus conservatives, and some of it may even mean something. But these days, down here at the city level where we all have to live, everywhere you look, it's becoming a matter of the Lace-Panties Killjoy Party (the same pasty-pale troglodytes who also despise automobiles, guns, industry, smoking, and, as I've pointed out elsewhere, everything that's come along during the past 90,000 years as a result of the discovery of fire) versus the rest of us.

The question is, what are we gonna do about it?

Whatever we eventually decide, it's vitally important to remember that any government that can forbid your child to feed the ducks — and make you pay for unwanted and unneeded lawn-sprinkling-system inspections — can also murder 82 people in their own church in broad daylight while the whole world watches, and not only get away with it, but blame the surviving victims and put them in jail for 40 years.

After all, what's to stop them?

A Revolutionary Proposal
೧೨ ೧೨ ೧೨ ೧೨ ೧೨

In any undertaking, it's essential to call things by their correct names.

If you're in Denver, for example, and you want to go to Fort Collins and start to look it up on a map — but you decide, for some bizarre reason having to do with "political correctness" that you *have* to call it Colorado Springs — you're going to wind up going in exactly the wrong direction. Easy to see in matters geographical, I guess. Apparently somewhat harder when it comes to politics.

Consider the following, from my brand-new shiny CD-ROM *American Heritage Dictionary*:

LIBERAL. Not limited to or by established traditional, orthodox, or authoritarian attitudes, views, or dogmas; free from bigotry. b. Favoring proposals for reform, open to new ideas for progress, and tolerant of the ideas and behavior of others; broad-minded.

Now I ask you: Does this sound *anything* like the "liberals" we've all become acquainted with? Those who, according to neoconservative writer (or is he a neoliberal?) Ben Wattenberg, "live in fear of every known phenomenon"? Those who hate, loathe, and despise any technological result of the discovery of fire, 90,000 years ago? Those who've demonstrated that they're willing to do absolutely *anything* (including machinegun, poison gas, and incinerate 81 innocent individuals, 22 of them children) to silence those who disagree with them?

Or does it sound a lot more like the men and women who contribute to publications like *The Libertarian Enterprise*?

LIBERTARIAN. 1. One who believes in freedom of action and thought. 2. One who believes in free will.

The great Libertarian seminarist Robert LeFevre used to observe that, to any extent there's a "public sector" at all, then to that extent, you've got socialism. Accordingly, I propose to both the writers and the readers of *The Libertarian Enterprise* — and especially our conservative Constitutionalist fellow travelers who seem permanently behind the 8-ball where fighting their traditional enemies is concerned — a Noble Experiment in the interests of raising the level of American political discourse. Henceforth, when referring to a person or cause we used to call "liberal," let us substitute a much more accurate term, like "socialist," "fascist," or "dogwhistle," depending on the context.

SOCIALISM. A social system in which the means of producing and distributing goods are owned collectively and political power is exercised by the whole community.

Keeping in mind that this definition was almost certainly *written* by those I've proposed that we start calling socialists, it's probably advisable to examine it closely. In the first place, socialism is not "a social system," but an *economic* and *political* system rooted in the ethical notion (if you can stomach dignifying it with such a name) that rights are additive: that two individuals, or two million, somehow have *more* rights than a single individual.

That's hard to figure, since the only right any of us really has is to be left alone.

Second, please note that what they never seem to get around to telling you — until it's too late — is that the *ultimate* "means of producing and distributing goods" is the individual human being. Without that, all of the industrial machinery and all of the rippling wheatfields that such a phrase usually calls to mind are meaningless. What they're saying here in their own cute left-wingy way is that we as individuals are what ends up being "owned collectively."

Third — and a very interesting grab it represents, too — when "political power is exercised by the whole community," we don't call it "socialism," we call it "democracy." More cuteness. I haven't witnessed this sort of shuffle since Dr. Sun Yat Sen, the progenitor of Mao Tsu Tung, claimed, in an American money tour, merely to be a "democrat" instead of the Marxoid trash he really was.

FASCISM 1. A system of government marked by centralization of authority under a dictator, stringent socioeconomic controls, suppression of the opposition through terror and censorship, and typically a policy of belligerent nationalism and racism. b. A political philosophy or movement based on or advocating such a system of government. 2. Oppressive, dictatorial control.

Now this is a hell of a lot more like it. Adding a punitive $4,000 to the price of the average Japanese car qualifies as "belligerent nationalism," and I think we're all grown up enough to understand that "affirmative action" is left-wing code for "racism." "System of government" — check. "Centralization of authority" — check. "Dictator" — what would *you* call Lincoln, Wilson, either Roosevelt, Lyndon Johnson, or Waco Willie Clinton — intentions count for *something*, here. "Suppression of the opposition through terror and censorship" — we *were* speaking of Waco, weren't we? And who needs censors when the mass media line up to kneel down before you and ... acknowledge your authority?

DOG WHISTLE 1. A person whose asshole is so tight that when he farts, only dogs can hear it.

Okay, this one's mine, derived from *Strange Days*. Think of Henry Waxman and Charlie Schumer, Sarah Brady or Robert Reich, and no further comment is necessary.

So there you have it. And yes, I'm completely serious. Not only will we show "Socialist Party A," the Democrats, in an appropriate light (setting a journalistic trend that could change the course of American political history), but we'll also expose Socialist Party B, the Republicans, for what they really are, and have been, regrettably, since the Lincoln Administration. The reason they've never gotten the upper hand on their opponents is that: Due to the misnomer "liberal," they were never really fighting what they *thought* they were fighting; and because they didn't realize that they were socialists, too, they couldn't undertake to eradicate socialism without doing serious damage to themselves.

I'd say that publicizing such an unfortunate truth is a practical tactical objective.

Wouldn't you?

Your cooperation, while not mandatory, will be greatly appreciated.

Advice to Flat Taxers:
Go Jump Off the Edge
ఴ ఴ ఴ ఴ ఴ

Much is being made lately about reworking the tax system in general, and about a flat — or "single-rate" — tax in particular.

Popular thinking, among Republicanoid candidates and radio hosts, goes like this: A flat tax is "fairer" since everyone pays the same percentage of his income; and if we fiddle with it, allowing healthy up-front deductions, Democratic objections about it being "regressive" will dry up and blow away.

Trouble is, like most of what Republicans represent as "thinking," it's a crock of elephant dung.

We're left to wonder, for example, what's "fair" — or even "flat" — about somebody who makes $10,000 being expected to pay seventeen hundred (overlooking deductions and assuming a rate of 17%) and another, at $100,000, paying seventeen *thousand* because he works 10 times as hard — or effectively — as the first. Better take Limbaugh's advice: If the effect of taxation is to *discourage* the behavior being taxed (hence discriminatory rates on cigarettes and machineguns), let's eliminate poverty by taxing the *poor*.

None of the plans I've heard deal with the real evils of the system. Will corporate taxes be 17%, too? As a businessman, I'll go on being taxed *twice*, at a rate of 34%. Is *this* what "pro-business" Republicans consider in their tiny minds to be an economic stimulus?

How about the Western world's answer to the KGB? Keep in mind that even a national sales tax has to be *enforced* (the oppression is merely shifted to proprietors rather than householders) and that the government's style these days is to send

278

in flamethrowers and ask questions afterward.

How about it, Steve?

How about it, Rush?

How about it, Harry?

For the moment, let's table these "minor" (if unanswerable) objections, and consider something that, even with all this "thinking" going on, nobody seems to have *thought* of.

Over the past few decades, since Howard Jarvis tried to put the state of California in its place, folks have increasingly (if dimly) awakened to the deliciously seditious idea that they *can* fight City Hall and that they have something to say about their own destinies. The trend has been toward lower taxes, at least in terms of what people want, if not always in terms of what they get.

Bucking the trend every way possible, with the help of the round-heeled media and at the polls, politicians have enacted more and more Constitution-breaking measures like RICO, allowing their hired thugs to *steal* what they want, directly from individuals, to bankroll their continuing assault on the Bill of Rights — and amazingly, even when their victims are exonerated, to keep it. Highway Patrol goons stationed near my house flaunt an ill-gotten Firebird, which they've painted with their own gang colors.

SF author Larry Niven writes of a future where jaywalking is a capital offense, because convicts are a commodity in high demand as organ donors. But forget hijacked hearts and purloined pancreases: As long as Republicans and other professional idiots advocate such dangerously unimaginative plans to reduce what we're compelled to fork over, "law enforcement" will continue to grow more rapacious. This is only one proof that economic freedom ain't synonymous with political liberty, and a reason Republicans need reminding, forcefully and frequently, that the original "Contract with America" is the Bill of Rights. Until they stringently enforce *that*, they can bloody well forget everything else.

People often ask, "If you're so smart, what's *your* tax plan?" Until now, I've had to confess I didn't have one. Somehow it seemed inappropriate for a Libertarian to be thinking up better ways to steal from his fellow sapients. But now I may have come up with something I can run up the flagpole and people will salute — although with how many fingers remains to be seen.

How about the "Pay As You Like" Plan?

Under the PAYL Plan, we don't need to force anyone to pay, since, well, you don't *have* to force someone to pay what he *likes*, do you? And since what he pays isn't *necessarily* connected to his income, we don't need to force him to reveal anything about that, either. We can return to a polite era of economic privacy; the only time we'll display our tax receipts is when we're running for office and trying to convince people what swell guys we are. Since we don't need enforcement, we can — after putting all its employees, past and present, under a proctological microscope for the equivalent of war crimes — abolish the IRS.

But the best feature of the PAYL Plan (even better than abolishing the IRS) is that it will create a continuing referendum over how much government we really want. If Pattie Schroeder wants big government, let her contribute generously — of her own damn money — to that objective. If Reaganites want nuclear-powered submersible aircraft carriers, let the buggers cough up. Let 'em run bake-sales, clean out their garages, sell door-to-door cookies to buy what they've been forcing the rest of us to behave as if *we* wanted, too, all these centuries. We'll *see* how much we really want a BATF, a War on Drugs, farm subsidies, or food stamps, won't we, Boopsie?

Inevitably, some twit will observe that we already *use* the

PAYL Plan every day, deciding how many cans of beans to make, how many pairs of shoes, how many doodads for pierced nostrils. It's called the Market System and, as people around the world increasingly attest, it *works*. What I'm asking, I guess, is, if it works for "trivial" stuff like food, clothing, and shelter, why not for *important* stuff like studies of teenage video game addiction (remember when Pong threatened the Republic?) and photos of guys peeing on each other?

Because data from our referendum will be vital to national interests, let's include harsh penalties for officials (the few we have left) who fall back on harassment or threats to enhance their revenue, or who steal things like Firebirds. Hell, let's make it a *capital* offense. I'd be willing to pay *that* gas or electric bill, myself.

Hey, you gotta admit: A PAYL's better than a crock.

Bill Clinton's Reichstag Fire
○◇ ○◇ ○◇ ○◇ ○◇

How very convenient.

How very damned convenient.

A heinous act is committed in Oklahoma City — the bombing of a federal building in which many lives, including those of a dozen innocent children, are blasted away — and the spokesmen of both established political parties see nothing in it but another opportunity to nourish their insatiable desire for control over the lives of others at the irrational unnecessary expense of a sacred American tradition, more than two centuries old, of unfettered individual liberty.

The spectacularly popular Republican showman who frequently identifies himself on his national radio program as the "Doctor of Democracy" spends two days wallowing in orgiastic fantasies of collective punishment — a variety of socialism characteristic of Europe or Japan (where the light of the Constitution never shines) wholly alien to any place in America but the Army and the public schools. He pompously declares the moral equivalent of war and implies that it is time for Americans to sacrifice their time-honored and vital liberties for mere physical security.

Meanwhile, American history's most discredited president and his power-hungry wife get a second lease on their worthless and destructive political lives as, lower lip extended and trembling, he struts and pouts on national television like the comical transvestites in *The Rocky Horror Picture Show*, pretending to a strength of character and resolve he never possessed and never will.

Having done her level best to start a second Civil War, the Attorney General, a dangerously stupid and incompetent piece of work who has allegedly stated on more than one occasion that anyone is a potential criminal or terrorist whose opinions regarding life's most fundamental issues happen to differ from her own, is now free to assert without public opposition that she is vindicated.

Likewise, equally stupid and incompetent people in the national mass media, who have sucked up unceasingly during the 20th century to those in power and have lately made a habit of attempting to identify distinguished and respectable civil rights organizations such as the Libertarian Party and the National Rifle Association with hate-motivated groups like the skinheads and the Ku Klux Klan, continue to profit from the lies they shovel daily at the public.

Efforts in Congress — some of them apparently in earnest — to repeal more than four decades' worth of viciously unconstitutional legislation get sidetracked and, if the president and his cronies have their way, derailed altogether.

Outlaw government agencies responsible for one increasingly illegal murderously violent attack on innocent citizens after another receive a massive whitewashing by the whorish authority-bedazzled media, while local police who have taken to imitating those agencies renew their "license to kill."

Private talk and public forums on the Internet, previously immune to scrutiny, censorship, or control by the establishment media or the government, get closed down "for the duration" — for which anyone even faintly familiar with history reads "forever" — to the colossal relief of both major parties.

Americans who were beginning to regain control of their own political lives can now be lumped together with racists and perverts — and effectively silenced. The Bill of Rights, threatening for the past several years to make an unwanted resurgence in American political life, goes into the shredder, instead.

What a windfall.

What a damned convenient windfall.

It's exactly the kind of windfall enjoyed by Adolf Hitler's National Socialist German Workers' Party when the Reichstag, the seat of representative government in that country, burned down and the newly elected Nazi chancellor, blaming the fire on his political enemies, used it as an excuse to turn his country into a dictatorship. Historians are generally agreed that the Nazis themselves started the fire — whereas the pattern of the Democratic Party in America has been to wait around, like vultures on a cactus, until something horrible happens (the assassination of a presidential candidate, the shooting of a score of restaurant patrons) that they can make the best political use of.

Nevertheless, the effect is the same.

The simple politically inconvenient fact, however, is that terrorist incidents do not stem from any insufficiency of government, but invariably from too much of the stuff. This country's problems in the Middle East — very much on America's guilty conscience following the explosion in Oklahoma City — would not even exist if American politics were kept within American borders. Yes, that's what I said — and if this be isolationism, let us make the most of it!

If, as it presently appears, the Oklahoma tragedy relates, instead, to the infamous and tragically needless events of 1993 in Waco, Texas, then it is time to drastically reduce the role of government in American lives, as well, not to condone and expand the scope of the state terrorism that apparently provoked it.

There is only one way to accomplish that — and to prevent this bombing from being used as yet another excuse to terrorize and punish millions of Americans who had absolutely nothing to do with it — but there are many ways to begin.

First, all federal agencies must be disarmed, their employees forbidden to carry personal weapons on the job (or to wear masks or to affect military clothing) and their heavy weaponry and vehicles of war surrendered to the nearest units of a denationalized National Guard. These agencies must then be reduced to that number specifically authorized by the Constitution under the Ninth and Tenth Amendments. If a few remaining federal investigators wish something to be done that is both lawful and requires the use of force, they may apply to local law enforcement for assistance — and, more importantly, for consent.

Next, the "War on Drugs," a disastrous Republican error that, by design or otherwise, has provided most of the justification for government incursions on individual liberty in recent years — and has served only to enhance departmental appropriations, numbers of personnel, and the dictatorial power of bureaucrats and politicians (while enriching their nominal enemies, the so-called drug lords) — must come to an immediate screeching halt. It was never anything but a war on the Bill of Rights in any case. And any law — like RICO — that authorizes unconstitutional seizures of property must be repealed.

All foreign aid, defense assistance, and overseas military presence must end, and a drastic reduction in "diplomatic" activities undertaken, as well. Americans are not the "cops of the world" and every attempt to make them so merely adds to the likelihood of another disaster such as that we have just witnessed. Scholars mindful of the dismal political history of the 19th and 20th centuries once warned that the Vietnam War would lead to shrinkages of freedom at home, and they were right. We are witnessing the culmination of that process.

Stringent — make that, "draconian" — enforcement of the highest law of the land, the Bill of Rights, must become America's number-one political priority. The population that must be scrutinized all collect government paychecks.

These measures would constitute a good beginning. The question arises, how is it to be accomplished? Certainly not by relying on the Democratic or Republican Parties, which have long since betrayed all of their Constitutional responsibilities. Before the Oklahoma City bombing, the media were full of reports that Americans are hankering for a third party, although mention was seldom made of which party it might be or what they believe it should stand for.

America has had a third party for more than twenty years. Perhaps it's time to make use of it. Those who wish to see it achieve power and do the things listed above (and more) must work with those who only wish to continue living in a free country. If both groups — to give an illustrative example — were to begin putting bumperstickers on their cars that say,

"Next Time I'm Voting Libertarian," it wouldn't matter what all those bumpersticker *stickers* really intend. For some it would be the literal truth. For others — those who only want their own parties to straighten up and fly right — it would be a threat, one that could be conveyed in letters and phone calls, as well.

Try thinking of the Libertarian Party as a rolled-up newspaper, useful in making the Republican puppy (I've given up on the Democratic bitch) go where he's supposed to — not on that beautiful antique carpet we call the Constitution.

BAP! BAP! BAP!
BAD Bobby, BAD Newtie!
BAP! BAP! BAP!

Of course, to Janet Reno, such an exercise of free speech would be terrorism.

But then, so is the rest of the Bill of Rights.

Rumplestiltsclinton
∞ ∞ ∞ ∞ ∞

Historians over the coming years will be very interested to learn who was writing Bill Clinton's speeches for him in the days following the blast in Oklahoma City.

Perhaps Hillary is the likeliest culprit; stylistically at least, they bear a certain similarity to the temper tantrums to which she treated everyone when her national health-care schemes fell through. More than anything, since the moment Clinton first tried to use the Oklahoma City explosion as a bludgeon on his political enemies — and failed — his public pronouncements resemble the embittered maunderings of the psychotics you see stumbling along big-city streets.

It's vital to understand what really happened here. Acting as a kind of national psychic travel agent, with Oklahoma City as a one-way ticket, Clinton and his cronies planned a long, elaborate, collective, guilt trip for everyone — everyone — in the past couple of years who ever thwarted their socialist ambitions. However, with the absurd undignified exception of a handful of especially pusillanimous Republicans (Robert Dornan blackened his oath as a military officer and U.S. Congressman by declaring that he opposes the repeal of Clinton's blatantly illegal rifle and magazine ban, while Senator Orrin Hatch jumped on the occasion to weasel out of hearings on the Bureau of Alcohol, Tobacco and Firearms and the Federal Bureau of Investigation) — nobody came.

Hatch's lapse may prove the worst (if not the most disgusting) because, as the *Wall Street Journal* pointed out in a remarkable editorial just a few days into these particularly "interesting times," what the country needs most at the moment is justice, with regard not only to Oklahoma City, but to Waco, Ruby Ridge, and, others may add, less-well-publicized atrocities committed by the government (the name of Gordon Kahl comes to mind) over the last several decades.

Clinton thought that Oklahoma City would make it politically incorrect (or at least insensitive or unfashionable) to bring up Waco any more, and even that backfired on him. Thanks to his misguided and incompetent efforts, the national focus on Waco became tighter instead of more diffuse. People began asking themselves (and each other) why the lives of the children of federal bureaucrats should be any more precious than those of mere mortals. And by forcing the comparison, Clinton even managed to make Gordon Liddy look like a statesman.

Be that as it may, nothing is more pitiable than authority successfully defied. Even with the dubious help of flunkies like Leon Panetta and Janet Reno (who, more and more with

every passing day, seems to visualize herself, in her dull bovine way, sitting in a glass box like Adolf Eichmann, answering the world's angry questions about Waco), none of these
old-fashioned formerly reliable liberal tactics was working for
Clinton any more. Within just a few days, he was beginning to
wail and moan and stamp his feet exactly like Rumplestiltskin.

And with exactly the same political effect.

Which is to say, none.

Perhaps the most heartening historically important consequence of this ugly business will prove to be the long overdue
and potentially formidable alliance — in response to smugly
bipartisan threats posed to the Bill of Rights by pending "anti-
terrorist" legislation — between the American Civil Liberties
Union and the National Rifle Association. It will be equally
interesting to learn the position taken — especially on Waco
— by Amnesty International.

At the same time, it used to be observed of China that their
possession of nuclear weaponry was not quite the threat it appeared, because they lacked the missile know-how that went
along with it — in other words, they had no "delivery system."
Speaking politically — by which I mean, electorally — the
ACLU and the NRA have no such "delivery system," and neither does Amnesty International. But — however tiny and insignificant it may be at the moment — the Libertarian Party is
nothing but delivery system, and due to Waco, Oklahoma City,
and their aftermath, it may not stay tiny and insignificant much
longer.

The gibberings and ravings of William Jefferson Clinton,
while devoid of meaningful content, are nevertheless as mo-
mentous — simply because they're occurring — as the demo-
lition of the Berlin Wall. While nothing for America in the
21st century is likely to be the same, in terms of politics, as it is
now, thanks to Clinton (in an odd, perverse, backhanded way),

it will be light years closer to something the Founding Fathers would recognize than we happen to be at this moment — or have been, pretty much since the War between the States.

No, No, Kosovo! No, No, Kosovo!
ෆ ෆ ෆ ෆ ෆ

You know, it's damned hard to write about Bill Clinton.

(I was about to say "a guy like Bill Clinton" when I realized that the last guy even *remotely* like Bill Clinton had his elderly mother's belly cut open with a sword so he could see where he'd come from.)

It's also damned hard to shift from fiction, which I've been writing the past several months, to what we laughingly call reality. At least I believe it's reality — I think I'd hallucinate better than this.

But I digress.

I like to temper the outrage that seems to drive so much of my writing (it took the Littleton shootings — or rather the political vultures feeding off of them — to get me started doing columns again) with a little absurdity now and again, but Caligulito (as I've come to think of him) always seems to be just a little bit ahead of me in that department.

Take this business in the Balkans. Over the decades, to this baby boomer, Yugoslavia has meant Marshall Tito giving the finger to the Soviets, Montenegro as the birthplace of Nero Wolfe as well as the setting for one of his most interesting adventures, and finally, the most ridiculous automobile the world has seen since the three-wheeled Messerschmidt.

Like everybody else, I've been pretty unhappy that people

in the remnants of Tito's jackbooted stomping grounds haven't been able to get along with each other. I knew they'd been pretty artificially jammed together at the end of World War I, an arrangement almost Clintonian in its arrogant stupidity. I knew that they'd been held together by the brute force of an almost Clintonian police state until recently. I'd watched the way Czechoslovakia quite peaceably became Czecho and Slovakia and wished the Newgoslavians could do it, too.

But no.

Before you knew it, while the rest of the world was celebrating what looked like it was gonna be freedom by beheading countless thousands of statues of Lenin, the former people of that nation began beating up, raping, pillaging, and killing each other as if they'd fallen years behind schedule during the Tito regime and had to catch up.

It was ugly, it was stupid, and it was regrettable. But you know what? Never *once* did I imagine that it had anything to do with me. Or with you, for that matter. As a (now what's the right expression, here?) student of Ayn Rand, I've always rejected the bald unsupported assertion that I'm my brother's keeper. But even if I didn't, I think the brother that I'd most likely keep would live at least as close as Nebraska.

Or New Jersey.

But this was about Bill Clinton, wasn't it? Look what we have in the absurdity department: the infamous Vietnam era draft-dodger and self-described loather of all things military, conducting what's beginning to look like Johnson's late lamented war in Southeast Asia by dropping ordnance on the Serbians in quantities rivaling those dropped on Hanoi during the bad old days of Barry Sadler and Joanie Phoney — and at the same time imitating Nixon by secretly sending in ground troops while publicly proclaiming he has no intention of doing so.

Remind me to call up the Fort Collins Peace Center tomorrow and ask them where the hell they are with their protest songs and picket signs.

Now what are we to make of all this? Clearly, much of it can be attributed to the now-famous "wag-the-dog" phenomenon. If you keep an eye on Matt Drudge's wonderful Web site, you know that China, Inc.'s bagman Johnny Chung was never missing; he was just being hidden out in something like the witness-protection program and is now eagerly ready (bulletproof vest and all) to vocalize like the proverbial dinosaur descendent. Combine that with the steadily increasing number of allegations of rape against a pitiful excuse for a man whose greatest crime (in the view of this child of the '60s) is giving oral sex a bad name.

What does it add up to?

Kosovo.

I have a simpler (and sicker) explanation. Clinton, not very deep inside, is a cowardly pissant desperate to prove he's a *mensch* by throwing away other people's lives the same way liberals try to prove they're charitable (they're not, you know; they're the meanest tightest-fisted misers on the planet, and its worst racists, to boot) by spending other people's money. This whole thing is nothing more than a disgusting little prick trying to buddy up to his classmates in PE.

Of course, he's carried overcompensation to a level that can hardly be called sane. That's why my "exit strategy" for the Balkans (right after we crazy-glue Madeline Albright to Janet Reno and let them frighten each other to death) is to send the men in the white coats to 1600 Pennsylvania Avenue and let Algore take over for the rest of the term.

Stupid is better than crazy.

A Note to My Political Allies

I've been offline for several days, struggling to complete my current novel within the next few weeks, before my publisher sends somebody out to break my legs — "but never the typing fingers," they're always quick to add.

What little Internet traffic I've read leads me to see something I haven't seen before: that many of us, arguing about the values and goals we share — and the field upon which they must be fought for and won — don't seem to be speaking the same language. So I decided to steal a moment (don't tell my editor!) to try establishing some kind of common basis for future action. ...

I don't know what you think politics is. Too often we act as if the professionals we're dealing with on both sides are possessed of the same desire we are to be fair or logical or decent. They aren't. I've been around a long time, and I can number the exceptions on the fingers of one elbow. To understand the real nature of the political process, you must first strive to understand the nature of politicians themselves, creatures who are a lot like the not-quite-yet-evolved protein-string entities that swam the vile, stinking, organic soup of the Precambrian Era.

The Schumers, Waxmans, Clintons, and Schroeders we encounter in life (not to exclude the Doles, Armeys, Gingriches, and Gramms) simply slither from one affinity to any other, from any old attachment to any other, from any old bonding to any other, without anything resembling higher principles embedded in their primitive neural nets and ganglia. The Schumers, Waxmans, Clintons, and Schroeders are guided by nothing — absolutely nothing — but accidental chemistry of the moment.

The Schumers, Waxmans, Clintons, and Schroeders don't believe in anything, and always poke nervous fun at people who do. The Schumers, Waxmans, Clintons, and Schroeders don't stand up for anything, and are mortally afraid of anyone who does. The Schumers, Waxmans, Clintons, and Schroeders aren't motivated by anything except a churning acidic hatred of everything and everybody — especially themselves — and a compensatory psychopathology that leaves them with an unquenchable appetite for raw naked power.

You can't persuade Schumers, Waxmans, Clintons, and Schroeders of anything. The facts, or any appeal to what's legal or right, are insufficient to penetrate the stinking miasma of mental and emotional sickness that they carry with them and spread wherever they go. They want to run your life — they desperately *need* to run your life — and they aren't interested in anything that interferes with that.

Likewise, you can't bargain with Schumers, Waxmans, Clintons, and Schroeders. To make up for their fundamental inadequacy of character, they struggle, every day, to be able see themselves as far far above you. They have to, if only to keep from blowing their own brains out in self-disgust. (Which explains their hysterical advocacy of gun confiscation.) They see you as far far beneath them. And who, they ask themselves, feels obliged to keep promises of convenience made, say, to a garden slug?

It's extraordinarily difficult to dislodge Schumers, Waxmans, Clintons, and Schroeders through any conventional political effort: that process is the sewer they swim through, every day, and they know it vastly better than you ever will. What's more, any conventional politician you decide to rely on to defeat them is likely to turn out to be a whole lot more like them, the Schumers, Waxmans, Clintons, and Schroeders — and to share their vital interests and lack of genuine substance — than he is to be like you.

Another likely outcome is that your own people, in a mis-guided and always unproductive effort to become "pragmatic" and "practical," may begin imitating the Schumers, Waxmans, Clintons, and Schroeders, invariably by throwing out all of those pesky principles that have been "slowing us down" or "getting in our way," and with them, all of the reasons you started fighting to begin with. We're having problems like that in the Libertarian Party right now, with what I've called "Nerf Libertarians," and I don't know how it's going to turn out. You may end up hearing about "The *real* Libertarian Party™."

All I know is that I will never, never, *never* give up. I've been doing this for 34 years, and although I have no regrets for myself, I *don't* want my daughter having to battle like this all of *her* life, too. I'd much rather she did something real, something productive, something *human*, like digging up dinosaurs with a phaser or flying to the asteroids on photon sails, and never have to give politics another thought, perhaps because I've helped to make a world where it's *safe* never to give politics another thought.

But where was I? Oh, yeah: You can't put the Schumers, Waxmans, Clintons, and Schroeders away in a cell somewhere — yet.

All you *can* do is to rearrange life so the Schumers, Waxmans, Clintons, and Schroeders (not to exclude the Doles, Armeys, Gingriches, and Gramms) can't hurt anybody any more, basically because there isn't anything for anybody to vote on. After all, who has a moral right to vote on whether you smoke, own guns, drive a car, or *anything* having strictly to do with *your* life? In short, we need a politics-free America. A Schumer-Waxman-Clinton- and Schroeder-free America.

And that, more or less, is what political Libertarianism is all about, as far as I'm concerned, and what makes us different from Brand X and Brand Y.

Just thought you'd like to know.

Security
༺ ༻ ༺ ༻ ༺ ༻ ༺ ༻ ༺ ༻

I saw on television recently that they're planning to close the street in front of the White House — and call it a "pedestrian mall" — for fear that something like the Oklahoma City bombing might happen on Pennsylvania Avenue.

Fine. Most Americans don't know how tightly controlled Washington has already become, with sheaves of guided missiles poised to destroy a straying passenger airliner (or even good old Klaatu and Gort as they try to land their saucer on the White House lawn for a friendly interplanetary chat). This is a city where you're forced to obtain a police permit, not for a gun — guns are strictly forbidden and therefore in abundant supply — but for a camera tripod.

One of the basic truths everyone seems to be avoiding these days is that when our national leaders begin hiding behind guided missiles, body armor, "pedestrian malls," bulletproof glass, and tripod control, it's probably for a reason. If you make a career of stealing people's money and screwing with their lives, you're an idiot if you don't expect some of the more frangible among them — oops, did I let a Buckleyism slip, there? Just pretend I made a reference to those pots in our society most liable to crack under stress. Now where was I? Oh, yes ... the more frangible among them to begin screwing back.

Equally, you're a lunatic yourself if you believe, as Bill Clinton has repeatedly claimed since the disaster in Oklahoma

City, that you can dismiss it with the petulant accusation that anyone who rejects your "benevolence" is crazy.

At one time in the history of our technology, miners used to carry cages with canaries in them, deep into the mines, as a precaution against anoxia or poison gases. When the canaries, with their faster metabolisms, passed out, the miners knew it was time to get back topside in a hurry. Individuals like the Oklahoma City bomber are a civilization's canaries, indicating to everyone with half an eye to see (except, of course, for politicians and bureaucrats, society's chief generators of metaphorical gases) that something has gone dreadfully wrong.

Unlike politicians and bureaucrats, most Americans have a fair idea of what it is. They know that events like the Waco massacre and the Ruby Ridge murders are just the visible tip of an iceberg. Despite the most strenuous efforts at truth-suppression on the part of the mass media (who have sold out contemptibly to a government they were intended to continuously oppose), we've reached a kind of saturation level where everybody knows personally of some blatant violation of individual rights that somehow didn't make the evening news.

It may be "ancient history": the Hutterite boy in the first World War who, as a pacifist, submitted to conscription but would not wear the uniform. Chained up by the wrists from an overhead pipe in a flooded basement at Leavenworth, he died of pneumonia during a freezing Kansas winter. When his mother arrived to claim his body, she was informed that it had already been buried — in an Army uniform.

It may be something more recent: Mormons peacefully practicing plural marriage, according to their religious beliefs, whose homes were raided, whose families were herded together, sorted out, and photographed holding numbered cards, and who were illegally locked up by the government until they signed documents renouncing polygamy — instantly converting their children into bastards. This travesty happened in the 1950s. Yes, I said the *nineteen* fifties.

Clinton's protestations are, of course, ridiculous. It should be perfectly apparent, even to someone with only half a brain to think, that he and his wife are hell-bent on doing to the Bill of Rights what the Oklahoma City bomber did to the Murrah Building, or their Attorney General did to the Branch Davidians. They and their party have engaged in a relentless war against the very concept of individual rights for more than 60 years, and the only response ever heard above the level of a craven whisper from Republicans is that they, too, can strip Americans of their liberties — only they can do it cheaper than the Democrats.

Nothing since the November 1996 election indicates any real change in that symbiotic relationship. Today, the only free press in the world, the Internet, thunders with horror stories of house invasions, property seizures, kidnapings of children by witch doctors pretending to be protectors, false imprisonments and beatings, framings and murders of innocent civilians, none of them occurring in South Africa, Bosnia, or Haiti, but right here in America.

And one by one, as we see in Oklahoma City, canaries are beginning to keel over.

It's time for all of us "miners" to get topside in a hurry. "Topside" means a return to the basic operating principles that made this the most peaceful, prosperous, and progressive nation a sorry bloodsoaked world had ever seen. "Topside" means beginning to hold sacred once again 481 words that let each and every one of us know exactly where he or she stands, and that we may sleep peacefully at night without worrying that black-shirted goons may smash our doors in, tie us up, wreck our homes, steal our children, seize our savings and possessions, stomp our pets to death, and get away with it, Scot free.

Those 481 words are the first ten Amendments to the Constitution. The Bill of Rights. The highest law of the land. One or two of them may put you off a trifle, but you can bet your last dime that somebody else would love to repeal whichever one you happen to rely on most. So far, most of us have refrained from that kind of "mutual assured destruction" because, deep down, each of us understands that those 481 words are all that ever made America different from any monarchy or dictatorship, powerful or petty, on the planet. They are what must be enforced — stringently — if we are to be different once again.

Americans need to see the Bill of Rights enforced. They need to see commitment, a massive national undertaking comparable to that involved in sending astronauts to the moon or fighting World War II. They need to see several thousand politicians and bureaucrats hauled out of their offices in manacles and leg-irons, preferably by federal marshals, exactly the way "inside traders" were treated in the '80s, before this country can be entirely sane again.

One benefit to such an undertaking — that of rebuilding a free America — is that it would deprive the canaries of any legitimacy they might otherwise claim. Ironically, it would create conditions under which Clinton would be correct in observing that there is no justification or need to resort to violence out of a fear that the government is scheming to take your rights away. But it would deprive him and his own "Dark Forces" of their legitimacy, as well.

The alternative? Well, that would be going on the way we have been, wouldn't it? With the politicians and bureaucrats doing whatever the hell they want to us — and more and more of the canaries among us popping off — until all of America's streets are turned, first into pedestrian malls, and then into prison walls.

Stars and Bars
ఌ ఌ ఌ ఌ ఌ

I grew up in the Deep South — any deeper and I'd have been out swimming in the Gulf of Mexico. In the 1960s, going to junior high and high school, I hated what you might call "professional Southerners," with their rebel yells, their faded glory, their might-have-beens, their lame excuses, their poor white trash, and their goddamn Dixie cups. Spanish moss gave me a rash and Southern patriotism was often nothing more than an excuse for forced conformity and dullwitted bullying.

(What I didn't understand then was that in junior high and high school, *anything* is an excuse for forced conformity and dullwitted bullying.)

I disliked the Confederate flag and anyone who wore or displayed it. Shortly before his death, my own father gave me a leather belt embossed and painted with that flag and I have never worn it. I write an ongoing series of novels about *a* confederacy, the North American Confederacy, an alternate world that has no connection with and bears no resemblance to the Confederacy of Robert E. Lee and Jefferson Davis.

Over the years, my attitude changed a trifle as I learned more of the real War between the States, the reasons that people on both sides gave for fighting it, and especially the vicious power-hungry fascism and the perverse taste for mass murder that characterized the Lincoln Administration.

Still, I had no great liking for that flag. But now I'm beginning to reconsider even that, thanks to Mayor Wellington Webb of Denver. I would be extremely interested to hear what justification — under the Tenth Amendment to the United States Constitution — Wellywebb and his strange and corrupt administration have to offer for their bizarre and probably illegal behavior on the Capitol steps the other day in Denver.

You may have seen it on TV.

Just like every other large city in America, Denver has become a festering boil on the backside of an otherwise wonderful state to live in, a churning sinkhole of dirt, grime, crime, pollution, socialism, outright jackbooted thuggery, and welfare parasitism, lorded over by a comic-relief collection of latterday Mussolinoids whose antics and attitudes make the late Emperor Joshua Norton look like a serious statesman.

Travelers beware: This is the gang of slimy thieves who'll steal your car if the cops find a perfectly Constitutional gun or knife aboard.

"Liberal" Democrat Wellywebb — the very incarnation of one of those inflatable bopping-clown toys kids like to play with — is still stinging from a humiliating defeat at the polls some years ago, when the people of Colorado decided not to give special protected status to yet another minority (in this case, homosexuals) and we got labeled, consequently, the "Hate State" by the round-heeled Eastern mass media. For some reason, even a bogus Supreme Court declaration that the vote was unconstitutional failed to ease his agonies and those of his hangers-on.

Aside: Do my views on this subject make me "homophobic"? Hardly. I'd oppose special protected — and, I might add, *undemocratic* — legal status for middle-aged Polish-American males, which is what I happen to be. Exactly as each and every one of us is personally different, we're all politically the same under the Bill of Rights. That's all we need, and that's the way it should be. Nothing else is necessary.

More recently, Wellywebb and his drooling hordes failed miserably to use the Columbine High School murders as a lever to promote English-style victim disarmament in Colorado, even though the tragedy was milked beyond decency or belief by the media and despite the best supporting efforts of our evil and stupid Republican governor Bill Owens.

I repeat, evil and stupid: Bill Owens.

It appears sometimes there's a limit to what forced conformity and dullwitted bullying can accomplish — even when it's undertaken by "liberals."

So what — in an election year — did that leave Rocky Mountain bedwetters to be conspicuously liberal about, in order to work off with the press what they imagine is Colorado's shameful public image? You guessed it: the Confederate flag. That hated and controversial rag that currently flies over the state Capitol of South Carolina. Wellywebb and his sniveling gaggle of political mouthbreathers held a highly publicized rally on the Colorado Capitol steps to denounce what they called a vile symbol of slavery, racism, and oppression — by showing the Stars and Bars in a form big enough to land Navy fighters on!

It looked *beautiful* on TV.

Speakers included the predictable collection of crooks, cretins, crazies, and commissars, including His Dishonor himself and Allegra "Happy" Haynes, who always manages to look like a museum exhibit labeled "Marxist Woman." They all called for an economic boycott of South Carolina — significantly — like the organized homosexual boycott of Colorado so costly to convention-related businesses in this state.

Or so we're told.

Let's get this straight once and for all, shall we? The War between the States had no more to do with black chattel slavery than the War of Jenkins' Ear. The very fact that Frederick Douglass and his fellow abolitionists had to work so hard trying to *make* it be about slavery — well after the shooting had already started — is more than enough evidence of that. Abraham Lincoln thought black people were subhuman.

Wellywebb and his ilk have already cut George Washington out of public-school history texts, and Thomas Edison, as well. They're working on Thomas Jefferson (although presently, he's sort of stuck sideways in their gullets). What's next after South Carolina's flag, the Gadsden flag with its rattlesnake and politically incorrect dire warning? The Pine Tree flag that was the first flag this nation ever flew?

Let's stop kidding one another, shall we? From their previous work, we know too well what sort of flag Wellywebb and his bunch would raise over the South Carolina Capitol. It would feature a hammer and sickle.

Or a swastika.

To them I say, leave the battered South's history the hell alone.

After all, it's all they have.

For my part, to honor this boycott of South Carolina, I'm going to see if they make anything in that state that I want and can purchase online. In the name of undermining and defeating Wellywebb's attempt at forced conformity and dullwitted bullying, I urge you to do the same.

It's the *Stupidity*, Stupid!
ℭ⊛ ℭ⊛ ℭ⊛ ℭ⊛ ℭ⊛

I've written fan letters to three authors in my life; Poul Anderson was the first. Back in the 1950s, Poul, one of my boyhood literary idols and a writer I've described as "proto-libertarian," wrote a short novel called *Brain Wave*.

The premise was unique. The Earth, it seems, had spent the last several zillion years passing though an interstellar damping field that, among other things, affected the rate or efficiency of nerve impulses. Now, by chance and all of a sudden, the planet had finally wandered out of said field, and all kinds of interesting things were happening to the human race and its closest relatives.

Ordinary people were becoming ethereal super-geniuses, while chimpanzees and gorillas were answering those little employment-training ads printed on matchbook covers. There was even some tantalizing something in there, if I recall correctly, concerning elephants, although it's been a long while since the last time I read the book, and when I looked, just now, I couldn't find it.

The viewpoint character is a retarded guy. When the super-smart invent a faster-than-light drive and blast off to the stars (watch out for those brain-dampening areas, now), he and others like him who are now "normal" inherit the Earth.

Belated congratulations, Poul, for a brilliant and prophetic concept, even if you did get it 180 degrees the wrong way around. How could you know, back in the '50s, that, rather than *exiting* what we might term a galactic "Stupid Zone," the Earth has just wandered into one. And what's more, I can *prove* it.

Consider Bill Clinton. It is a source of unending frustration to Rush Limbaugh and those like him that the most maggoty piece of political meat to slide across the counter in decades — and his wife, Polly Pot the Deathcamp Dolly — continue to fare so well with the polled Herefords who make up the American electorate. Nobody doubts that the guy's as crooked as Huey Long's hind leg, or that he's lucky not to have OD'd or expired of venereal disease ages ago. (Say, maybe *that's* why his medical records are such a big-time secret.)

Limbaugh's beef (if you'll pardon another high-protein reference) is that, with regard to Bozo and Evita, those left-wing Little Rock fascists, evidence doesn't matter any more. Produce all of the incriminating facts and figures you can, offer the voting public a stack of Arlo Guthrie's "8x10 glossies with circles and arrows and a paragraph on the back"; they will not look or listen. The horrible truth is, they won't even bother to make up rationalizations or excuses any more. Waco Willie can slaughter dozens of innocent individuals — many of them little kids — and get away Scot free (although having seen what they did to William Wallace in *Braveheart*, I've begun to wonder about that phrase).

Of course, it doesn't help that Limbaugh is too squeamish to talk about Ruby Ridge and Waco — he was pretty much on the administration's side where the Branch Davidians were concerned — or that it's taken him this long to get around to mentioning Mena. There's no great mystery here: His wonderful GOP was involved right up to its pachydermatous posterior in all three of those disgusting episodes, and might not look too good if he were to "shine the light of truth" their way. (Imagine Bob Dole railing against the BATF and FBI when, following the atrocities in Texas and Idaho, he helped to multiply their appropriations geometrically.) Too bad, because this is just the sort of thing — the *only* sort of thing — that could possibly give the Republicans a victory over the Democrats.

Or take Bob Dole. It is a source of endless frustration to Libertarians who specialize in Second Amendment issues that Dole can do *anything* to gun owners.

Anything.

He can insult them openly to curry favor with the liberals, choosing (A) as his running mate, a slithering right-wing socialist welfare bureaucrat who hysterically demanded an outright ban on semiautomatic weapons on national TV, and (B) as his convention keynote speaker yet another infamously anti-gunner Republican. He can proclaim that he not only *won't* repeal the hated and illegal Clinton rifle and magazine pro-scription and the Brady law (speaking of stupid, giving James Brady — the world's largest and heaviest ventriloquist's dummy — a Presidential Medal of Freedom for the many years he's spent helping his ventri ... I mean, his Pat Schroeder-lookalike wife emasculate the Bill of Rights, is like bestowing a posthumous God and Country Award on Madalyn Murray O'Hare), Dole actually says he'll *veto* any repeal bill that comes across his desk.

Nevertheless, just as the late RNC chairman Lee Atwater predicted — and just like battered spouses who lack the cour-age to escape — gun owners will make up reasonable sound-ing excuses to stay with Dole, anyway. The idea that they might have someone else to vote for, someone who will welcome their help by repealing every gun law in the country, appears beyond their ability even to conceive.

It's that Stupid Zone thing, you know? I think I can even pin down when it happened. The old GOP brain doesn't seem to work the way it used to back in 1980 when the Gipper, as President-elect, *almost* repealed Nixon's idiot War on Drugs. If Earth had wandered into a neural-damping field, it would certainly explain, as little else can, the inexpressable inepti-tude of the Dole-Kemp campaign.

Or maybe it's less like an episode of *Star Trek: The Next Generation* than that. Maybe it's just the dismal fact that 64 years of welfare-state socialism, and the near-century of pub-lic education that made them possible in the first place, have turned Republicans — exactly as they have everybody else, including most Libertarians, apparently — into mental and moral defectives.

Maybe welfare-state socialism *is* the Stupid Zone.

A Tale of Two Hoovers
ᑲ ᑲ ᑲ ᑲ ᑲ

Okay, what've we got here?

The other day, the Federal Communications Commission gave the Federal Bureau of Investigation "new authority to tap digital and wireless phones." Justice Department functionaries are reportedly delighted. Privacy advocates and local phone companies are "bitterly disappointed."

What's wrong with this picture?

Well, suppose I gave my good friend, the brilliant columnist Vin Suprynowicz, "new authority" to rummage around in the underwear drawer of our esteemed colleague (and equally brilliant columnist) Claire Wolfe? She might well ask us by what right he and I are depriving her of her most intimate privacy — just before she drops the hammer on a heavy-caliber sixgun, consigning both of us to Peeping Vin and Neil heaven.

Pretty clearly, that kind of authority simply isn't mine to give, not to Vin or to anybody else. And just as clearly — to me, anyway, and I suspect to you — that kind of authority isn't the FCC's to give, especially to those fine upstanding law-enforcement paragons who murdered 22 babies and 60 other innocents at Mount Carmel. The few idiots I know who would take Miss Hardyville 2000 to task for shooting Vin and me all voted for George McGovern and collect fat government checks.

So anyway, now they're going to listen in on our cell phones — as if they hadn't been already — right along with tapping our landlines, breaking our encryption, peeking in our windows, and rummaging through our garbage. (Mine contains several wet smelly pounds of used cat litter every week. When I get politically depressed, it's uplifting to remember that human beings can catch and die of several ugly feline diseases.)

The Federal Communications Commission is a prototypical horror story of incrementalism and "mission creep," created by Congress in 1934 during the administration of Roosevelt II, but having existed since the '20s in the form of a "Federal Radio Commission," jawboned to life by then-Secretary of Commerce (and later President) Herbert Hoover.

There had been a panic-button 1912 licensing law on the heels of the sinking of the Titanic. In 1917, the instant that the outbreak of World War I gave them something that looked like justification, the government shut down and seized the equipment of thousands of licensed amateur operators, citing what would later be called "national security."

Contrary to lies spread for decades by the left, Hoover was no champion of the market system, but a right-wing socialist who hated and feared what he viewed as the chaos (meaning freedom) in which the market operates. Using overlapping and conflicting frequency as an excuse (in fact, all those problems of mutual interference had already been worked out by the fledgling radio industry), and an unsupportable assertion that the "airwaves" are the property of the people (meaning the government) rather than of the inventors and entrepreneurs who had learned how to use them, Hoover seized authoritarian control of the medium.

And we wonder today whatever happened to the First Amendment.

Fighters for Internet freedom take note.

The Federal Bureau of Investigation sneaked into existence (there is no such word as "snuck," nor is "dove" the correct past tense of "dive" — ahhh, I feel much better) in almost exactly the same manner as the FCC, establishing America's first European-style secret-police organization and forcibly reminding us of the self-destructive stupidity of accepting even the most innocent-looking compromise with authority.

Lever Action

It all started in 1908, when Roosevelt I created something called the Bureau of Investigation to look into Idaho land schemes and "white slavery." The "BI" went into the next decade to conduct "slacker raids" against draft dodgers and wage war on political radicals and those with the temerity to compete with government-approved socialism. A nasty-minded little BI clerk with a sick penchant for prying into other people's private lives (apparently because he had none of his own) compiled 450,000 dossiers on individuals he suspected of being Communists.

That nasty little clerk was John Edgar Hoover, who rapidly rose to second bananahood, and finally to temporary directorship of the BI, which eventually became the *Federal* BI in 1927, with Hoover at the helm, investigating "enemy aliens," Communists, and other chronic over-users of the First, Fourth, Fifth, and Ninth Amendments. Even the most superficial reading of the friendliest biography of the Director will establish that there is no way known to science or theology to weigh a soul as small and shriveled as that of J. Edgar Hoover who, as one source pointed out, invented the process of taking "administrative action" to overcome tiresome Constitutional objections to the Bureau's activities.

What's being missed in all this hoohah — the most important (and ironic) point — is what we have here is one completely illegal and unconstitutional gang of criminals generously bestowing upon another completely illegal and unconstitutional gang of criminals a power to violate the rights of individuals that neither has — nor ever had — the legitimate authority to possess or exercise, let alone pass on to others.

Usually, we of the freedom movement are happy if we can just lean on agencies like these and make them stop whatever they're up to, a case in point being the so-called "Know Your Customer Policy" under which banks were supposed to spy on the people who (sort of) trust them, and report to the federales anything they think is unusual or suspect. This time, however, talking them out of it is not enough — as current attempts to revive some of Bill Clinton's nastier executive decrees demonstrate.

This time it has to *cost* them something, or they'll be right back with something even worse than what they've just gotten away with.

Just as no nation with a Second Amendment in its Constitution has any place for a Bureau of Alcohol, Tobacco and Firearms, no nation with a First Amendment has any place for a Federal Communications Commission. And because the security of this particular nation *is* its freedom, there's no place for an agency like the FBI, the sole purpose of which is to curtail that freedom in the name of national security.

Try this experiment now. Tell everyone you argue with on the Net, say it to radio talk-show hosts, even write it to your Congressthing: Under the Ninth and Tenth Amendments to the Constitution, the very existence of the FBI and FCC is illegal and they must be abolished at once. Go further and say that it's this recent collusion between the wielders of the national gag and the fabulous baby incinerators that got you thinking maybe it was time to bring them into Bill of Rights compliance.

Which in their case means non-existence.

One is the legacy of Herbert Hoover.

One is the legacy of J. Edgar Hoover.

And like all Hoovers, they both suck.

V

A RANT FOR ALL SEASONS

An Ant for All Seasons
∽ ∽ ∽ ∽ ∽

Ants scurry about their world at random in great numbers, leaving behind long sticky trails of pheromone, chemically commanding anyone and everyone, "*Do this! Do that! Go here! Go there! Eat! Sleep! Work! Fight! Die!*"

The pheromone trails build up, one upon another, lapping, overlapping, tracing, back-tracing, up, down, sideways, overlay on grimy overlay, imperative after foul imperative, until the whole ant-world lies cloyed and covered in tarry, reeking, imperious filth.

Men speak, and as the words die cleanly in the air between them, they think about the words and speak anew. The surrounding environment of will, of choice, and of motivation is unpolluted. Their decisions, agreements, judgments, options, alternatives, preferences remain inside them, inside their individual minds. They do not clutter and befoul the physical space in which they all must live.

Ants cannot live like Men and more importantly, Men cannot live like ants. Yet that's precisely what we've been trying to do. For two centuries, ten generations, we've endured ant-like accumulations of obsolete discredited commands, ordinances, statutes, and decrees building up beneath our feet, slowing us, binding us, gluing us down like so much gum lying gooey on a sidewalk at high noon.

Lever Action

Keeping us from being what we might have been.

Keeping us impoverished, hungry, and stultified.

Keeping us from the one true destiny of Men, the stars.

As we've been told so often — by those who wish to live like ants — it's time to clean up the environment. To decide that we are Men, not ants.

Twenty years ago, when I first began pondering this subject, there were *five million federal laws* (and ignorance, I'd remind you, of the law is no excuse). Who knows how many now? Who knows how many state, county, and city laws? Who knows what they cost us — besides our future.

The Founding Fathers never meant the nation's legislatures to become full-time pheromone-factories. There's evidence that they envisioned Congress and the state assemblies as places Men would meet — occasionally — to deal with some emergency. And even then they may have been wrong. They must have been wrong, or we wouldn't be suffering all this clutter, this legislative pollution today.

I propose a Moratorium, a final Law, an Amendment to the Constitution creating a 100-year prohibition on legislative activity of any kind within the borders of the United States of America, during which the only thing a legislature could do would be to *repeal* old laws, mop up all the pheromones, clean up the environment.

Those who wish to live like ants, and they are many, will fight it, shrieking that they won't know what to do without their little sticky overlapping trails (desperately afraid, too, that they'll no longer be able to tell others what to do) and won't know how to live.

Those who want to live like Men will champion it.

And in that Century of Sanity, they will reach the stars.

The American Lenin
ↂ ↂ ↂ ↂ ↂ

It's harder and harder these days to tell a liberal from a conservative — given the former category's increasingly blatant hostility toward the First Amendment and the latter's prissy new disdain for the Second Amendment — but it's still easy to tell a liberal from a libertarian.

Just ask about *either* amendment.

If what you get back is a spirited defense of the ideas of this country's Founding Fathers, what you've got is a libertarian. By shameful default, libertarians have become America's last and only reliable stewards of the Bill of Rights.

But if — and this usually seems a bit more difficult to most people — you'd like to know whether an individual is a libertarian or a conservative, ask about Abraham Lincoln.

Suppose a woman — with plenty of personal faults herself, let that be stipulated — desired to leave her husband, partly because he made a regular practice, in order to go out and get drunk, of stealing money she had earned herself by raising chickens or taking in laundry, and partly because he'd already demonstrated a proclivity for domestic violence the first time she'd complained about his stealing.

Now, when he stood in the doorway and beat her to a bloody pulp to keep her home, would we memorialize him as a hero? Or would we treat him like a dangerous lunatic who should be locked up, if for no other reason than for trying to maintain the appearance of a relationship where there wasn't a relationship any more? What value, we would ask, does he find in continuing to possess her in an involuntary association, when her heart and mind had left him long ago?

History tells us that Lincoln was a politically ambitious

313

lawyer who eagerly prostituted himself to Northern industrialists who were unwilling to pay world prices for their raw materials and who, rather than practice real capitalism, enlisted brute government force — "Sell to us at our price or pay a fine that'll put you out of business" — for dealing with uncooperative Southern suppliers. That's what an export tariff's all about. In support of this "noble principle," when Southerners demonstrated what amounted to no more than token resistance, Lincoln permitted an internal war to begin that butchered more Americans than all of this country's foreign wars — before or afterward — rolled into one.

Lincoln saw the introduction of total war on the American continent — indiscriminate mass slaughter and destruction without regard to age, gender, or combat status of the victims — and oversaw the systematic shelling and burning of entire cities for strategic and tactical purposes. For the same purposes, Lincoln declared, rather late in the war, that black slaves were now free in the South — where he had no effective jurisdiction — while declaring at the same time, somewhat more quietly but for the record nonetheless, that if maintaining slavery could have won his war for him, he'd have done that instead.

The fact is, Lincoln didn't abolish slavery at all. He *nationalized* it, imposing income taxation and military conscription upon what had been a free country before he took over — income taxation and military conscription to which newly "freed" blacks soon found themselves subjected right alongside newly enslaved whites. If the Civil War was truly fought against slavery — a dubious "politically correct" assertion with no historical evidence to back it up — then clearly, slavery won.

Lincoln brought secret police to America, along with the traditional midnight "knock on the door," illegally suspending the Bill of Rights and, like the Latin America dictators he anticipated, "disappearing" thousands in the North whose only crime was that they disagreed with him. To finance his crimes against humanity, Lincoln allowed the printing of worthless paper money in unprecedented volumes, ultimately plunging America into a long grim depression — in the South, it lasted half a century — he didn't have to live through himself.

In the end, Lincoln didn't unite this country — that can't be done by force. He divided it along lines of an unspeakably ugly hatred and resentment that continue to exist almost a century and a half after they were drawn. If Lincoln could have been put on trial in Nuremburg for war crimes, he'd have received the same sentence as the highest-ranking Nazis.

If real libertarians ran things, they'd melt all the Lincoln pennies, shred all the Lincoln fives, take a wrecking ball to the Lincoln Memorial, and consider erecting monuments to John Wilkes Booth. Libertarians know Lincoln as the worst president America has ever had to suffer, with Woodrow Wilson, Franklin Roosevelt, and Lyndon Johnson running a distant second, third, and fourth.

Conservatives, on the other hand, adore Lincoln, publicly admire his methods, and revere him as the best president America ever had. One wonders: Is this because they'd like to do, all over again, all of the things Lincoln did to the American people? Judging from their taste for executions as a substitute for individual self-defense, their penchant for putting people behind bars — more than any other country in the world, per capita, no matter how poorly it works to reduce crime — and the bitter distaste they display for Constitutional "technicalities," one is well-justified in wondering.

The troubling truth is that, more than anybody else's, Abraham Lincoln's career resembles and foreshadows that of V.I. Lenin, who, with somewhat better technology at his disposal, slaughtered millions of innocents — rather than mere hundreds of thousands — to enforce an impossibly stupid idea that, in the end, like forced association, was proven by history to be a resounding failure.

Abraham Lincoln was America's Lenin, and when America has finally absorbed that painful but illuminating truth, it will at last have begun to recover from the War Between the States.

When They Came for the Smokers ...
⋙ ⋙ ⋙ ⋙ ⋙

An acquaintance of mine calls himself a "political smoker." He doesn't smoke. He never has.

But told some time ago at a Los Angeles supper club that he and other members would henceforward be forbidden to smoke, his immediate reaction was to borrow a cigarette from somebody sitting nearby, stand, and light it up in protest. As he sees it, his interests, in terms of his individual and civil rights, run parallel with those of smokers who are being increasingly stripped of theirs.

I am a former smoker.

I quit cold some years ago, after suffering a heart attack. Even before that, I never claimed that smoking was good for anybody, just that I had always enjoyed doing it — and that a great many lies were being told about it by individuals and groups who had gone beyond non-smoking to become anti-smokers.

But I, too, remain a political smoker.

Exactly like many another do-gooder-targeted group, smokers today are well along in the process of losing their human rights — and more and more, it seems, their very humanity —

to social parasites who, as H.L. Mencken is reputed to have put it long ago, awaken in the middle of the night, sweat-drenched and trembling with the morbid fear that somewhere, someone might be happy. Until now, there hasn't been an effective way to crush these lice on the American body politic — and their bloodsucking symbionts in media and government — between the thumb of the Ninth Amendment and the forefinger of the First.

Until now.

Let me suggest a couple of ways to begin dealing with them. Of course, you're free to employ one or the other, or both, or go off and think something up yourself. ...

Although I smoked two packs of Marlboros a day for 30 years, I indulged in cigars and pipes, as well. One thing I still haven't been able to do is dispose of my collection of the latter. Some I inherited from my father and an uncle. They're pretty, they were chosen to express my personality — the same way you buy a hat — and they still smell *wonderful*. I keep an ancient favorite on my desktop to this day, and although I'll never again fill it with tobacco and light it, I still pick it up — it feels comfortingly familiar in my hand — fondle it, and hang it off my lower teeth for a contemplative moment or two.

Drug paraphernalia.

So far, my ancient favorite hasn't left the house since that summer night when I was rushed to the emergency room with unbearable pains in my chest and left arm. But I'm thinking of taking it on a field trip to the non-smoking section of a restaurant or two. I know what will happen, and so, if you think about it, do you.

There are non-smokers like me, and then there are anti-smokers.

The anti-smokers all around me will begin to fidget.

They'll mutter to themselves and each other.

Lever Action

They'll glare at me.

Because what they're all about — what they've *always* been all about — has absolutely nothing to do with the presence or absence of first- or second- or third-hand smoke and whether it harms anybody or not. That's only their excuse.

What it has to do with is the complete unsuitability, in their twisted minds, of simple human pleasure in the lives of everyone around them. This used to be the preoccupation of Puritanical religions. Today, most of the people of this bent have abandoned religion, but they haven't abandoned the demented ecstasy they experience by shouting "Thou shalt not!" at everyone in sight — and being able to back it up with the brute force of governmental edict.

If I'm especially lucky, they'll complain to the manager, who'll be forced to confront me and my empty tobaccoless pipe and ask me to put it back in my pocket or leave the restaurant. Either that or, at my suggestion, he'll go back to the nicotine Nazis at the next table and tell them where to put their complaints — not in their pockets, but where the sun never shines.

So. My first suggestion is that you become a political smoker. Go to the nearest drugstore and pick out an inexpensive pipe, a pipe that's never had tobacco in it, a pipe that likely never will, a pipe that strikes you as attractive or expresses some aspect of your personality. They make all kinds of pretty ones, not only briar, but gold, silver, inlaid, and enameled. Think of it as a fashion accessory or an item of jewelry. Don't worry that it serves no practical purpose. What practical purpose does an earring or a necktie serve?

Display it in your favorite restaurant, on the bus, at the theater, at a children's daycare center, while visiting a hospital. What your empty pipe will accomplish is to inform beleaguered smokers that they're not alone, as media and government would have them believe. It will inform Prohibitionists that their reign of terror is coming to a long-overdue end, that they're up against a civilized solidarity that maintains the human, Constitutional, and American right to go to hell in your own way.

There used to be a certain class of people — people of a certain color — who by longstanding evil custom were forbidden to sit anywhere on a bus but at the back. After a century or so of such nonsense, one of them courageously refused to abide by this evil custom, and she changed the course of American history forever.

On another occasion, another class of people — those who for reasons of their own enjoy nicotine in its many forms — were also limited to the back of the bus.

Today, even that has been taken away.

My second suggestion to you is that we call such people "niccers" — after their recreational drug of choice — as loudly and as often as we can, so that the average tobacco Prohibitionist — say, California Congressman Henry Waxman, as nasty a piece of work as I've ever seen in more than three decades of political observation — will realize precisely who and what he has become.

I'm a political niccer.

Are you one, too?

Antismokers: Get a Life!
ငာ ငာ ငာ ငာ ငာ

I've had a long thoughtful letter from someone who likes my writing (he mentions me in the same breath as Rand and Bob Wilson!) and is beginning to think that he may be a libertarian. Like many another beginner (yours truly, back in the '60s), however, he has a little sticking-point he can't get past, and he isn't being helped in his moral struggle by government or the popular culture. That isn't what government or the popular culture are for, after all. On the contrary.

What prompted him to write was my essay, "When They Came for the Smokers..." My fan — call him "Safety Orange" — disagrees with it, and goes on to tell me about a grandfather who died of emphysema seven years after he quit smoking, and a grandmother and great-grandmother who died of breast cancer. "All of them were chain smokers," Safety says, "and the only thing that gave my grandfather his last seven years of life (before the last 18 months of decay) was the fact that he went cold turkey after 50 years of a 2-3 pack a day habit. ... I myself get a headache from smoke. ... It causes ... an allergic reaction in my body. My sinuses, after extended exposure to secondhand smoke, seem to [become] impact[ed], and ... feel like there is a Jamaican steel drum band playing in my nasal passages." Later, he declares, "I am even affected by people smoking in a car in front of me while driving on roads or highways."

Safety, there was a time in this country when men used to compare their muscles (or something) and women used to compare their cooking. Now, in this "Age of Entitlement," the only basis on which we ever seem to compete with one another is the degree of our victimization. Anti-smokers all tell themselves stories exactly like yours. Every one has excuses to offer — to others and himself — for whatever dictatorial policy he advocates. The anti-smoker carefully constructs his excuses so he won't feel so bad about himself when he agrees with others of his ilk to have those he disapproves of beaten up and killed.

Trouble is, your excuses don't work with me anymore, nor with anyone who can read my writing. It isn't my obligation

— and never was — to make you comfortable or to sacrifice my life to your phobias. What's more, I've had enough of a plethora of self-appointees on radio and TV who insist on telling me, in the most intimate and personal detail, how I ought to be living, and then claiming that by intruding on me in this manner — violating my privacy and diminishing my sense of self-determinism — they're performing a "public service."

Take nicotine, bad old C10-H14-N2, since that seems to be the issue here. I'll even state the "worst case," by bringing up "the children" before you do. As it happens, I'm a *former* smoker, but if I still enjoyed smoking, and if by my example, I were teaching my child to smoke, that would be *my* business and nobody else's, no matter how abominable the nicotine Nazis might think it was. Otherwise, what would become of their *equal* right to bring their own kids up as mewling, puking, bedwetting, socialist crybaby dogwhistles just like them?

Everyone has a right to pass his culture on. My life is my culture and, in the final analysis, so is my death. It's my right and duty to teach my way — of life *and* death — to my child. Whether cigarette smoking is healthy or not is irrelevant, since my health, and that of my child, is my culture, too.

When the nicotine Nazis start including in their preachment the fact that tobacco smokers are many times less likely to get Alzheimer's, Parkinson's, or schizophrenia, I may start taking them seriously. When they admit that kids used to inhale tobacco smoke as therapy for asthma, that it worked, and that it's a common occurrence for people to stop smoking and *become* asthmatic, ditto. Until then, all they have to offer is propaganda. Oh yes, and brute force.

Look. You live on a planet that has tobacco smoke as an atmospheric constituent, just as it has petroleum byproducts, asbestos fibers, and ionizing radiation (mostly from coal-fired power plants). We know all too well what we'd have to give up to get rid of the latter pollutants: the Industrial Revolution and all of its benefits, unprecedented prosperity, and life expectancies *three and a half* times longer than those enjoyed by pre-industrial people.

What we give up to get rid of tobacco smoke is *freedom*. The problem with whimpering about allergies or the aroma of tobacco from the car in front of you is that, in a democracy, I can cancel out everything you say with an observation: I like the smell. I especially like to smell it coming from the car in front of me on the highway. I think there should be more of that kind of thing, right away. Maybe there should be government programs to *provide* it.

Seriously — and unlike most ex-smokers — I like being where folks are smoking. Not only does it smell good, I know (despite the fact that the Bush Administration tried to suppress this information) that I'm in 10 times less respiratory danger than I would be if I fried bacon in my home a couple times a week. And I'm in *100* times less danger than I would be if I still had my parrot.

My defunct, dead parrot.

The danger of secondhand smoke is a hoax. It may be obnoxious to you (we all differ in our likes and dislikes; yours just happen to be fashionable), but you can't do anything about it without damaging your own rights in the doing. I don't like perfume, especially the kind that smells like Black Flag, but I have to share an elevator with a woman wearing it. I don't like the smell of new-mown grass mixed with gasoline. I don't like the smell of gas mixed with MTBE. And there's no stench like a couple of hockey teams just coming off the ice.

You may be right, Safety, that you're not a Puritan. But you're *helping* Puritans by holding their coats. Assuming you're sincere, there's only one thing to do: Be a *mensch*. There aren't any "No Smoking" highways. Roll up your windows. Buy an air freshener. Turn on the air conditioner; crank it to "High." Hold your breath. Get noseplugs. Use antihistamines. Endeavor to persevere. Do otherwise, and you aid those who'll find other excuses to control *you*.

People smoke. They have since before Walter Raleigh "discovered" tobacco, and they'll go on doing it long after Henry Waxman has tired of whistling for this dog and gone shrilling after another. Get used to it. Learn to live with it.

After all, people learned to live with you.

And if you can't be a *mensch*, life offers plenty of real stuff to whine about.

The Smoking Goons
ᏳᏸᏳᏸᏳᏸᏳᏸᏳᏸ

Maybe I'm a soft touch.

Sometimes I get so embarrassed for my fellow human beings — some of them, anyway — that I can hardly bear the squirming discomfort of it.

The latest such *deluminati* (in a year seemingly populated to the scuppers with them) are members of a Florida jury who decided that the makers of cigarettes are responsible for half a million bucketheads who somehow managed to mess up their lives and health with tobacco products, despite warning labels on every package and 30 years of vile, incessant, anti-smoking propaganda on radio, TV, and jungle drums.

It's as if these companies had dispatched goon squads out across the country to sit on their prostrate victims' chests, screw cylinders of the Devil's weed into their unwilling mouths, whip out the Zippos, and hop up and down on their helpless torsos to get a good draft going — over and over again for half a century. That sort of thing produces entertaining "X Files" episodes (use big-headed little aliens instead of tobacco companies and force the poor abductees to do all of their inhaling through their navels), but it makes for crappy law and crappy ethics.

The fact is, the goons in this story don't work for Big Tobacco. But dozens of them — carefully preselected — filled that court room, took that witness stand, and sat in the jury box at that money-monkey trial.

It began with a huge crop of low, nasty, snivelling cretins, inclined from birth (and aided by a dozen years of public schooling) to whiningly credit their every moronic blunder in life to somebody else. Millions of individuals smoke. Many get sick. Some sickness has a statistical connection with smoking. But decent people realize that they were the ones who made all the decisions in that chain of events. They aren't out to steal obscene piles of loot from whatever prey the current trendy set of idiotic beliefs will let them transfer the blame to.

Then legions of slick, Gucci-footed, socialist lawyers too lazy to chase ambulances and ideologically sworn to obliterate individualism and capitalism — while raking in billions of dollars for themselves in the process — rounded up this passel of larcenous droolers to serve as plaintiffs in the coming gang-rape of logic and the rule of law.

Next, a gaggle of dolts even dumber than the mewling plaintiffs was laboriously selected to lend credibility to a predetermined series of events. By the process of *voir dire* (columnist Vin Suprynowicz reminds us that that's French for "jury tampering"), any potential juror who showed a spark of intelligence, independence, or knowledge of the Constitution was savagely ejected, leaving only those with no education, initiative, or brains, the meat-puppets up whose quivering posteriors the Jim Hensons of jurisprudence could shove controlling fists.

It's an irresistible combination: self-congratulatory political correctness, Everestine heaps of green. Attila the Hun himself would swoon.

But don't think ill of your fellow human beings, dear reader. Show trials with phony victims and hand-picked juries are nothing new. They worked in revolutionary France, they worked for Stalin — hell, they worked for Estes Kefauver. The one and only innovation is that the Armani-clad pillagers conducting these legal travesties will realize profits rivaling the gross national product of several small European countries. The Visigoths must be looking down (or up) in envy as these new barbarians suck the marrow from this civilization's shattered bones.

Look. Lots of companies manufacture products that can be credibly presented in the mass media as dangerous: guns, cars, liquor, butter, knives, candy, perhaps even perfume. Every one of them is a potential source of wealth waiting to be plundered. The strategy of the day is to start with those perceived to have what might be called a drug-war-style liability: Once you start consuming their product, you can't stop yourself. (Potato chip makers and peanut packagers beware.) If you can murder a street dealer because the fruit of your loins was too damned stupid to just say no, then why not liquidate an entire industry?

And if, by maneuvering your hand-picked goons to render a verdict utterly ridiculous on its face to everybody but the goonier goons in the mass media, you can damage beyond repair the very notion of an English-style jury vital to a free society in the process, so much the better.

I sometimes entertain an intuition — which I freely admit I can't substantiate as yet — that what we're really seeing is nothing more than a turf war between the old cigar-pipe-cigarette crowd and a new aggressive band of pharmaceutical patch-gum-pill interlopers. Tobacco companies versus drug companies, with the drug companies and their pet state attorneys-general wielding the upper hand, at least for the moment.

Americans *will* have their nicotine. The only question is, who will be allowed to sell it to them and in what form? In a world where consumers are compelled to needlessly spend billions on a new product because Freon has been defamed and outlawed at the behest of its own inventors and manufacturers (the patent ran out, you see), the idea that drug companies are driving the war on tobacco isn't completely crazy.

Whether I'm right or wrong about that, behind it all, socialists of the Hillarist persuasion still strive for a system — thoroughly discredited by history and economics (as if something like that ever made a difference) — where there's no competition, no "wasteful duplication of effort," and no product liability because everything is produced (incompetently, it's true) by a government monopoly that can't be sued because it has sovereign immunity. The only defense that stands between the *Khmer Pinque* and this loathsome wet-dream of theirs is the relatively new concept of Bill of Rights enforcement. The Hillarists must be made to learn that smoking is a Ninth Amendment right, as is the manufacture, distribution, and sale of tobacco products. Anyone who violates these rights, including state attorneys-general and tobacco liability lawyers, deserves to contemplate the nature of his wrongdoing from the inside of a concrete box, having first impoverished himself paying restitution to those he victimized.

If we don't see to this, and right away, our kids will all wind up with slave collars around their throats, swabbing out the Hillarists' ashtrays.

The Lies of Texas
ର ର ର ର ର

Okay, what have we learned?

For reasons still being kept secret, a federal agency already known — well enough to be examined and rebuked by several legislative committees over the years — for a longstanding violent disregard of the law invades the home of a man whose religious beliefs and personal habits they abominate, violating his rights under the First, Second, Fourth, Fifth, Ninth, and Fourteenth Amendments to the Constitution.

The man and his followers fight back, killing four of the outlaw agency's minions, wounding many more, and suffering their own losses in the process. The agency responds by cutting off his electricity, water, and especially his contact with the outside world. The agents are then free to say anything at all about him — in pronouncements that contradict one another daily as the agency finds itself locked in a bitter power struggle with another outfit eager to gain credit for "straightening out the mess" — and, more importantly, to script his side of the subsequent "negotiations" any way they please.

The impasse lasts almost two months — at the same time, ironically, four L.A. cops are being given a second trial for brutalizing a single individual, sparking one of the ugliest riots in history. Armored vehicles surround the house, already ringed with snipers using scoped high-powered rifles. Loudspeakers playing obnoxious records at the highest possible volume and searchlights deprive those in the house of sleep (in the aftermath, nobody in authority will mention the effect this technique, originated by North Korean Communists as a battle tactic, may have had on their judgment).

Finally — another irony — on the 50th anniversary of the

rising of the Warsaw Ghetto, some of the armor punches holes in the house and gas of some kind is injected. The house bursts into flame and is reduced to ashes in less than an hour. At least 80 lives, including those of more than a dozen children, are snuffed out.

Spokesmen for the outlaw agencies, the Attorney General, and the President all hold press conferences to articulate a common theme: *Blame the Victim.*

He had illegal weapons — as soon as they can be prepared in a secret government workshop and planted among the cinders being "examined" by the agency that created them. He was abusing children — the tapes will be stored with the data on the JFK assassination. He set the fire — our snipers saw him doing it. Film at 11 — in 3000 A.D. He shot his followers who tried to escape — or was that Jim Jones? Best of all, he's dead — he can't say a damn thing to embarrass us, any more than when his contact with the world was severed at the start of the whole travesty.

A leading national paper claims 93% of the American people believe that a man who resisted a savage attack on his home is somehow responsible for everything that resulted. But when did you ever know 93% of Americans to agree on anything — doesn't this sound more like the outcome of a Soviet election than an opinion poll?

Very well, what can we infer from the above? For starters, never forget that, although Democratic careers are on the line (and rightfully so) over this fiasco, by the outlaw agency's admission, it was planned and rehearsed by a Republican administration. Which may explain why Paul Harvey, who evidently used up all his courage and integrity changing his mind (at about the same time I did) about the war in Vietnam — has been acting as little more than a mouthpiece for a state that has no regard for the Bill of Rights.

More importantly, when Rush Limbaugh, who's been a quivering tower of Jello during the whole thing, takes essentially the same stance as Bill Clinton, it's time for fundamental changes, if not in the system, then at least within yourself.

On March 5, back at the beginning, Mary Gingell, national chair of the Libertarian Party, issued a press release condemning the outlaw agency and calling for its abolition. In fact, the LP has promised in its platform since 1977, for at least 23 years, to abolish both agencies involved in Waco. I'm proud to say I was there and helped to write that plank.

True, the LP is tiny and insignificant (although less so than in 1977 — ask the Democrats in Georgia if you doubt it). But, alone in a howling wilderness of fascists scrambling now to cover their behinds with phony polls and Big Lies, the LP is right about what happened in Waco. And if their advice had been followed in 1977, Waco never would have happened.

Think about it. And think about the fact that, if you've had enough of political parties more interested in collecting and holding power — at whatever cost to the Bill of Rights, let alone human life — than in defending and expanding individual liberty, maybe the change it's time for within yourself is to make the LP less tiny and insignificant by a single voice and a single vote.

Think about it.

Weird Science
c❧ c❧ c❧ c❧ c❧

Everyone knows how to tell when a politician is lying: His lips move. What may not be equally obvious is that there are politicians and then there are politicians — and that the phrase "political science" is subject to more than one interpretation.

Years ago, we heard how "scientists" were worried that a new Ice Age might be coming, and later on that "nuclear winter" — smoke and dust thrown into the atmosphere by full-scale international unpleasantness — was a possibility. Something like that may even have killed the dinosaurs.

What we didn't hear was that no actual data supported any of this, that real-world events (the burning of Kuwaiti oil fields) tended to discredit it, that mostly it was propaganda meant to weaken practices that made America the most successful culture in history, and that the dinosaurs may just as plausibly have died of something like the Plague when continents drifted together, exposing them to new germs. We miss a lot like this, unless we listen closely. Prince William Sound, site of the famous oil spill, and Mount St. Helens weren't supposed to recover from their respective disasters for at least 100 years. That turned out not to be true, although you'd never know it from watching network nightly news or CNN. It doesn't fit their agenda to inform us that the Earth is vast and resilient and that nature is rougher on herself than we could ever be.

But for once, the media aren't entirely to blame. As ignorant of science as they are of everything, they trust "scientists" to unscrew the inscrutable. The trouble is that today's "scientists" have agendas of their own.

Nobody in government, that wellspring of scientific wherewithal, is going to offer grants to an investigator who states truthfully that there is no respectable evidence for "global warming." The money and power for bureaucrats and politicians lie in mass transit, and they hate the automobile — blamed as a major cause of the mythical crisis — as a source of privacy and freedom they find intolerable.

The same appears true of "acid rain," a deliberate hoax cooked up by the Environmental Protection Agency (which hates private industrial capitalism almost as much as it does your car), foisted on real scientists through trickery that has depended on specialists in different fields not talking to each other much.

The list goes on, always with a common disreputable thread. "Ozone depletion," for which evidence is even more suspect and contradictory than for acid rain or global warming, is no more than a last desperate attempt to indict private capitalism in an era when state central planning and the command economy have failed and can only find this final withered leg to teeter on.

Decades of anti-nuclear alarmism, resting on foundations of myth and panic-mongering, have failed to erase the fact that nuclear power is the safest, cleanest, most efficient source of energy known to mankind — and more to the point, that the greater amount of energy there is available to any individual in society, the freer that individual — and his society — become.

Honest studies on the effects of individual gun ownership and self-defense on crime — conducted by investigators who began as ideological opponents to those concepts, but that show massive reductions in the latter to be the result of the former — have been suppressed, most recently by the California state government.

And what the media didn't say about recent EPA "discoveries" on the effect of "secondhand smoking" is that, although some harm to non-smokers may have been detected, it was less (by an order of one or two magnitudes) than that associated with frying bacon a couple times a week or keeping a pet bird. It's almost enough to make you wonder whether there was ever anything to the claim that smoking causes cancer.

And that, of course, is the real threat represented by politically correct science. The world is a dangerous place. It would be nice to know the hazards. I've never believed smoking to be a healthy practice, but given a lack of credibility on the part of today's science, how am I to decide what to do about it? Nicotine is highly addictive, to that much I can attest from experience. Yet the stress of quitting may be riskier than to continue. There isn't any way to tell, thanks to the corrupting influence of government money on the scientific establishment.

Two centuries ago, the Founding Fathers spared us certain agonies to which every other nation in the world has been subject at one time or another, by creating a legal barrier between politics and religion. Each time some short-sighted individual or group has tried to lower the barrier (most recently over the issue of abortion), blood — real human blood, hot and smoking in the street — has wound up being shed.

Real human blood is being shed over scientific issues, as people's lives are ruined through the loss, to agencies like the EPA, of livelihood or of property it may have taken a lifetime to accumulate, to diseases caused by toxins associated with burning fossil fuels for electrical power, to bans on things like cyclamates when they die from the effects of obesity.

What we need now, if we hope to survive as a civilization for two more centuries, is another barrier, a Constitutional separation of state and science — including medicine. Knowledge is valuable; real science won't languish for lack of funding. The money will simply come from contributors unwilling to pay for lies, and everyone will benefit.

When You Wish Upon a Star ...
ɔ❧ ɔ❧ ɔ❧ ɔ❧ ɔ❧

If I were to choose a motto for our age, it would be "Wishing Will Make It So." No matter how sweetly you dress it up or how many cartoon crickets warble it against a starry backdrop, it's no more than a crude unsatisfactory substitute for philosophy or science, best suited to the bad-tempered whims of a two-year-old. Push it too far — how much aviation fuel is really in that tank as opposed to what you want to be there? — and it can even get you killed.

What a person believes is his own business. If nothing else, that's part of the process of natural selection. Lives based on a judicious respect for reality tend to be more rewarding. Those who see clearly and think straight are likelier to reproduce and their offspring are likelier to prosper. Those who choose less rational paths will be replaced, statistically, by those who make better choices, and the human condition will gradually improve. You may think this is cruel, but it identifies a real phenomenon. It's the way the universe works — has worked for billions of years — whether you like it or not.

The idea that wishing will make it so is most deadly when it's applied as public policy. Then, it doesn't matter that you opted to use your head, not when your choices are made for you. You're forced to suffer just as if you'd made the mistakes, instead of some bureaucrat or politician.

The classic case is the Volstead Act. For a century before its passage, its advocates, who believed that drinking is a Bad Thing (which indeed it may be) and demanded a law to keep people from doing it, ignored complaints that they were making a mockery of individual rights. For a decade afterward, they ignored its secondary effects, which proved more damaging to society than the use of alcohol.

Prohibition is to blame for a lot that's wrong with America today. It was the beginning of a popular disregard for the law. Millions of ordinary people, who became criminals by fiat overnight, responded by drinking more than ever, many of them for the first time, simply to assert their rights. With the stroke of a pen, previously acceptable behavior was lumped together with acts that everyone agreed were wrong — like murder and kidnapping. Moral lines became hopelessly blurred and have tended to stay that way ever since.

Prohibition put many unsavory types in business — big business, as it turned out — who are still with us. In a way that could never have happened if the do-gooders hadn't meddled in their private affairs, decent people were suddenly exposed to criminal (and legal) violence, just as if they were criminals themselves. And although it wound up being partly repealed, Prohibition also set precedents for government meddling in every other aspect of individual life.

Bureaucrats and politicians failed to learn the folly of "wishing will make it so" from Prohibition. Those who scream loudest about youth gangs today are the same ones to whom the minimum wage, just another kind of Prohibition, is a sacred article of faith. Never mind that any job at a buck an hour beats no job at five. Never mind that minimum wage generates unemployment by punishing those who would otherwise hire young unskilled workers. Never mind that if these kids had any kind of job, they'd soon learn enough to get a better-paying one. Never mind that they might even be too busy to join a gang. Never mind that the minimum wage raises the cost of goods and services so that its victims have a harder time obtaining food, clothing, and shelter — in effect, that bureaucrats and politicians invented the "homeless." These nasty-tempered two-year-olds — excuse me, the bureaucrats and politicans —

demand fulfillment of their wishes no matter who gets hurt, simply so that they can bask in the glow of their own self-righteousness.

To the twisted mindset of Prohibitionism, facts about the individual right to own and carry weapons are similarly irrelevant. Never mind what the supreme law of the land ordains. Never mind that gun control renders peaceful and productive people — women, minorities, and the elderly in particular — helpless in the face of a criminal element that bureaucrats and politicians created, just as they did the homeless. Never mind that legislators who violate their oath of office by advocating gun control should be in prison. They're out to strip a nation of its weapons come hell or high water, and they're not going to let a little thing like a decent regard for objective reality, social justice, or the Bill of Rights interfere.

But before you feel too smug, examine your own mindset.

You could be guilty of the same self-righteous nonthinking.

The so-called "War on Drugs" is simply Prohibition dressed up for the '90s. It can't stop people from making, selling, or using drugs any more than the Volstead Act stopped them from making, selling, or using alcohol. It has succeeded in boosting the price of drugs from pennies a pound to hundreds of dollars an ounce. It's driven weak competition from the market and created not just a livelihood where there wasn't one before, but a monopoly for the most violent and ruthless among them — and, not incidentally, for millions of bureaucrats, politicians, and cops, both honest and corrupt. Worst of all, it's given bureaucrats and politicians another excuse, acceptable to the media and the public, to raise taxes exponentially and stamp "CANCELLED" across the Bill of Rights.

Especially the Second Amendment.

Never mind that what you do to your own body is your business or you haven't any rights at all. Never mind that the only way to protect kids from drugs is the long, hard, grownup task of bringing them up right. (Let's start by abolishing the public schools, which concentrate and distribute self-destructive behavior the way public hospitals concentrate and distribute disease.) Never mind that before the turn of the last century, drugs were freely available and nobody showed much interest in them. Never mind that there wasn't any drug problem until the bureaucrats and politicians created it.

There's far more to the fight for the Second Amendment than simply wishing that the badguys would go away. We hand them a club — in the form of a contradiction — every time we agree to any kind of Prohibition, and it's childish of us to expect them not to use it.

Wishing can't accomplish anything by itself.

We're going to keep losing our liberties — and not just to own and carry weapons — until we get our own logical and ethical ducks in a row.

Big Brother is Watching You — Again
ɔ⊳ ɔ⊳ ɔ⊳ ɔ⊳ ɔ⊳

It doesn't seem all that long ago that I wrote a column ("Stop the Nagging," *The Libertarian Enterprise*, Issue 12) arguing that those, like the Ad Council (whoever the hell they are), the American Cancer Society, the American Heart and Lung Association, et alia, who apparently have no lives of their own and feel compelled to live our lives for us, should be shut up for good.

What I complained about then was the way these unspeakably foul creatures shove their proboscises into the deepest, moistest, most minute and personal recesses of our individual existences — what we eat, what we drink, what we smoke, how we bathe, how we breathe, how much we sleep, how often we exercise, what we wear on our personal thingies when we do fun things with one another — including a whole lot of stuff that isn't *anybody's* business, not even a proctologist's.

And don't let get them *started* on guns. They seem to have forgotten (if they ever knew) that Freud said it was feebs like *them*, who hate and fear weapons (not folks like us who own and enjoy them), who have serious crotch-problems. If you harbor any doubt at all about ol' Ziggy's judgment, take a good hard look at any major advocate of victim disarmament — Sarah Brady will do quite nicely — and then ask yourself: "Has this person *ever* had an orgasm?"

I'm *particularly* weary of being told by these socialistic geeks how to raise my daughter. My daughter is only six and a half years old — and she can *read.*

But as usual, I digress.

How did all of this insanity begin?

Why did we ever let these creeps into our culture?

Why do we tolerate them today, even for a nanosecond?

For example, whenever California Congressthing Henry Waxman bugs Americans about their fondness for tobacco, why doesn't anybody ever turn the tables on him, officiously demanding to know what made him such a slimy disgusting twit, where he finds those baggy linty suits, why he has such a big fat butt, and whether he's ever gonna get around to clearcutting that old-growth forest of nose-hair? The same kind of intrusive personal stuff he's doing to everybody else.

I pointed out that if a neighbor, friend, or relative came into our homes and started nagging us about the same things, we'd blacken both their beady little eyes, dump the aquarium on them, and throw them out into the peony bushes.

337

This morning, on the radio, I received overwhelming confirmation that I'm right. What I heard went far beyond the absurd hysterical assertion by the chemotherapy lobby that any red-meat or alcohol consumption at all increases your risk of cancer significantly. We hear that sort of crap every day — last time, as I recall, it was *milk* posing a deadly danger to America — and the more these Chicken Little squawks are disproved by reality, the more bizarre they become.

No, on this occasion, it was a troop of dungheads calling themselves the American Society of Microbiology, peeing all over themselves because we nasty little boys and girls don't wash our nasty little hands after doing whatever nasty little things we *thought* were supposed to be private in our public bathrooms.

How do they know?

Because they've been *watching* us!

They say they asked us first, the usual "random, representative sample," but they didn't like the — deservedly short, loud, and rude — answer they got.

So now we're being watched in the bathroom. ... Before I go any further, I'd like to know *exactly* what distinguishes these pervos from Peeping Toms the campus cops arrest from time to time, peeking into the girls' dorm rooms. In any decent civilization, these sickie dickies would be rounded up, made to kneel in the barrow ditch beside the highway, and shot in the back of the head.

Years ago, I thought it would be just splendid if wristwatches simply had numbers on them instead of hands. (Stick with me here, I'm not really changing the subject.) I wrote a short story, "Grimm's Law," about it, but before I could get it published (it took me over a decade), the first digital wristwatches began appearing on the market. Remember those first red LED models, the ones you had to reach over and turn on?

If I were Arthur C. Clarke, I'd still be publicly sulking because the manufacturers won't pay me a royalty.

Later on, inspired by Shea and Wilson's classic trilogy *Illuminatus!*, I decided it might be a good idea to have some self-adhesive labels made, to be affixed *inside* the doors of public bathroom stalls wherever the opportunity presented itself. I even planned to mention them in an SF novel that, as it happened, I never got around to writing. The labels, intended to salubriously heighten the anti-authoritarian paranoia of whoever saw them, would have read: "For your safety and convenience, you are being monitored by television cameras."

And now reality has beaten me to the punch once again.

Next time you're in a public bathroom (or in your own, for that matter, the way things are going in this country), ask yourself whether the mirror over the sink mightn't be one of those tricky one-way windows psycho-vultures are so fond of. Robert Bork, the would-be Supreme Court justice who said he couldn't find anything in the Constitution guaranteeing a right to privacy, should be ecstatic.

We can't shoot these losers — yet. It would cause the neighbors to talk about us and there would go our privacy again. But somebody reading this will know how to find out where these anti-American antisocial microbiologists get their money and how to ... er, cut it off. If they're funded by corporations, a modicum of public pressure ought to do the trick. If they're tax parasites pursuing their filthy habits at our involuntary expense, it's time to raise hell.

I'm tired of being nagged and spied on, and I mean to do something about it.

How about you?

I Hate Breakfast
c⊗ c⊗ c⊗ c⊗ c⊗

I don't know about you, but it annoys the hell out of me that someone else gets to decide that I can't have a cheeseburger and fries before eleven in the morning.

I hate breakfast and always have. Confronting eggs before noon — fried, poached, or otherwise — makes me bilious. Pancakes and waffles are worse. The one thing bacon is good for is sticking between lettuce and tomatoes in a sandwich (slathered with Miracle Whip — mayonnaise isn't the same at all) you'd choose for that vastly more civilized meal, lunch. And to paraphrase *Apocalypse Now*, the smell of maple syrup in the morning reminds me of ... napalm.

In my youth, I never ate breakfast. I was a night-person forced to suffer government indoctrination at daybreak. Eating anything under such conditions induced nausea; I was content to wait for lunch. I still rise early to get Cathy off to work before resuming labor on the current novel. I'm also a Type II diabetic who takes pills that make it absolutely necessary that I eat something. Still, the only thing the pimpled dimbulbs out along the fast-food strip will sell me is exactly the kind of glop I've spent an entire lifetime avoiding.

For over a century, corporations like Kellogg, Post, and a dozen others have spent quintillions of advertising dollars in a horrifyingly successful attempt to persuade mothers that the cattle feed they manufacture is suitable to foist off on helpless children before they're wide awake enough to defend themselves.

It's enlightening to learn the history of these companies. Vegetarians today believe that consuming animal flesh spawns an urge to violence in the human psyche. (Keep in mind what

I said about vegetarians in *Pallas*: You are what you eat.) A century ago, the overriding preoccupation was sexuality, especially what was politely referred to way back then as "self-abuse." (This was later defined in the '60s as "doing your own thing.") Kellogg and others claimed that laying off sirloins and stuffing yourself with hormone-absorbing cereal products closely resembling wood shavings would somehow prevent impure thoughts.

(For a hilarious examination of this topic, *The Road to Wellville* is a movie demonstrating that the goofiest garbage our grandmothers thought up — mine got undressed in her bedroom closet, even when she was alone in the house — are not too goofy for the hairsprayed heads of TV to attempt to convince us of today. Guess it proves you can hide as many bees in a bouffant as in a bonnet.)

Cereal magnates of the late 19th and early 20th centuries believed a lot of other goofy things as well — in particular, in various trendy forms of socialism, which they gleefully advocated and subsidized in a variety of manners.

Which brings us at long last, I think, to some kind of point.

Today's captains of the fast-food industry are no more contented simply to make billions of bucks than their corn-flakey predecessors were. They gotta be socially conscious. They gotta fry up potatoes in some tasteless petroleum byproduct instead of delicious natural lard. What's worse, they gotta shovel mountains of mazuma over to those very social and political causes most grimly dedicated to reducing us — the ultimate source of all their largesse, already forced to pay for too much of this nonsense through taxation — under absolute despotism.

There are entire countries with gross national products smaller than the amounts the founders of McDonald's have bestowed upon Democratic Party grabbies who routinely confiscate half of my income, have spent half their lifetimes (and mine) trying to confiscate my means of self-defense, and who would even take away my right to choose my own doctor. They support criminals who want to kill me or make my life so miserable that I'll kill myself. Small wonder, then, that they also feel entitled to decide for me what I should eat for breakfast.

I suppose it's possible that the fast-food empires have never looked at things in quite this way before. (People say that a lot about what I write.) What's more, if they feel right about offering me a rubber egg on a pasteboard muffin instead of what I really want, why shouldn't I tell *them* what to do? And so, on the very remote chance that they may be interested in making up for their malfeasances, misfeasances, nonfeasances, upfeasances, downfeasances, sidefeasances, or whatever other feasances they may be guilty of, I have a few suggestions.

Remember that, as a corporation in the act of seeking special privileges and immunities unavailable to mere individuals, you've made yourself nothing, more or less, than a branch of the government. The Constitution (especially its first ten amendments) was written as an absolute limit on government activity. Be aware that there is an increasingly popular idea in this country today that corporations (as branches of government) should be limited in exactly the same way.

Ask your legal department what *that* would cost.

Back before Disney Corp. got taken over by the AntiWalt, the fine folks at Disney reminded us, now and again, of what this country's all about. Way back then, militias were politically correct; they did a nifty series on the Sons of Liberty. They did a swell mouse cartoon about the Revolution and the Declaration of Independence called *Ben and Me*. They did a great movie about an 18th century British tax resistor (and the Navigation Acts that sparked our own revolution) called *The Scarecrow*.

Forget *101 Dalmations*, forget *The Hunchback of Notre*

Dame, forget *The Lion King* and the sick sappy substitute for philosophy that permeates all of them. Forget animal rights — animals are for breakfast. Let's have a slick, appealing promotion based on the Bill of Rights. (And before you offer up all the usual suit-excuses, you'd better understand that we know that *you* know that it's only boring if you try to make it *safe*; I'm sure we'll agree wholeheartedly that the Second Amendment isn't safe — it wasn't *meant* to be — and the First Amendment is even dangerouser.) Relax, you don't have to do anything Republican. Hell, you can be even trendier than Left. You can be *Libertarian*.

Try repairing the civilization you've worked so hard and spent so much to wreck.

And while you're at it, fry me a goddamn cheeseburger!

Some Not-Quite-Random Thoughts on Americans and Their Cars
ɔ❧ ɔ❧ ɔ❧ ɔ❧ ɔ❧

The private automobile, and the exhilirating sense of freedom it engenders, is central to everything unique in the American character. Today, it's come under attack by a coalition of prohibitionists and Luddites.

Every day, tens of millions of Americans employ what amounts to the best mass-transit system in the world to travel from exactly where they are to exactly where they want to go at exactly any time they desire. No lugging their groceries or bulky packages to bus stops, train stations, or subway terminals in the heat, rain, cold, sleet, or snow. No unwanted or dangerous company. No undesirable noises or smells.

Lever Action

Half of this "best mass-transit system in the world" — streets, roads, and highways — is a monopoly of various governments. The automobile itself belongs to individuals. While automobiles themselves improve a little each year, and have done so since before the turn of the last century, the failures of the best mass-transit system in the world are on the "public" side. Problems attributed to the automobile — air pollution, traffic congestion, lack of parking space, and most accidents, injuries, fatalities — arise from an unwillingness on the part of bureaucrats and politicians simply to resign themselves to the reality of the automobile (they've only had a century, after all) and adapt.

There's a reason for this. Those who want to be bureaucrats and politicians despise the automobile because (among other things) it represents so many well-solved problems they can't claim credit for and exploit. Also, it affords its owner a mobility and privacy that it absolutely kills their shriveled souls not to be able to intrude upon.

Nor, in a political society dedicated to "life, liberty, and the pursuit of happiness," should the recreational benefits of the private automobile be neglected. The simple pleasure derived from owning and operating fine machinery is something that bureaucrats and politicians comprehend only dimly enough to loathe and want to eradicate, recently by using "safety" as an excuse to regulate the function and appearance of vehicles they actually dislike for reasons of cultural or class prejudice.

A friend of mine with plenty of political savvy holds that the main thrust of the last 10 years of environmentalism and regulations governing the ownership and use of automobiles is to force Americans out of the countryside — as the Brits did so brutally to the Scots — into cities where they can be controlled. The first time he said this, I had my doubts. The more I learn, the more sense it makes. While our children and our grandchildren broil in crowded stinking tenements, Algore's vile spawn will ride to hounds in what used to be our backyards.

What they dare not acknowledge is that ownership and use of an automobile is a right guaranteed by the the first ten amendments to the Constitution, commonly known as the Bill of Rights, specifically by the Ninth Amendment, which provides for "unenumerated rights," and by the Tenth Amendment, which limits government to only a tiny handful of functions.

Should a Ninth or Tenth Amendment right be enforced any less stringently or energetically than those rights protected, say, by the First and Second Amendments? Absolutely not. The automobile and its owner should be accorded exactly the same protection that the First Amendment extends to freedom of expression, religion, and assembly, and the Second Amendment is supposed to extend to firearms and their owners.

If the automobile and its owners deserve Constitutional protection, it follows that the *enemies* of the automobile and its owners — in Congress, in legislatures, on county commissions, on city councils, and in university administrations — deserve to feel the full weight of the highest law of the land descend on them whenever they threaten those rights that we commonly associate with the automobile and its owners.

Two classes of objects and activities must never be taxed, no matter what trumped-up excuse bureaucrats and politicians pull out of the air to justify it. Food, clothing, shelter, and transportation are basic necessities of life. Anything guaranteed by the Bill of Rights should be sacrosanct. No aspect of the ownership or use of an automobile should be taxable — and if that causes problems with financing the present bloated level of government, so what? Since when are Americans obliged to have more government than they're willing — voluntarily, without the least trace of coercion — to support?

To drive this concept home, government must leave car

design and fuel formulas to the private market system that made them possible in the first place. (All that any government knows how to do is break things and kill people, neither of which promotes automotive safety or progress.)

It means defunding light rail, empty bus companies, and other transportation confidence schemes across America, and deregulating taxis for those who don't use a car, and using the enormous savings that result to improve roads or reduce taxes. We must also search for private alternatives to our present backward, stagnant, public-highway technology.

It also means eliminating driver licensing (something far better handled by insurance companies, if it has to be handled at all), along with the nationwide tracking and identification system commonly known as "license plates." Both represent powers that were unwisely granted to the government in the first place, were widely abused almost from the beginning, and today have become tools of a rapidly growing police state.

The right to privacy must be fully restored with regard to the automobile and made equivalent to privacy in homes (something that needs some work, too, if we don't want to end up like the Japanese, who are subject to random searches any time the police feel like it). Roadblocks to enforce DUI or seatbelt laws — an excuse to search for drugs, guns, or other things the police don't approve of — must be forbidden.

Seizures and "civil forfeitures" without due process have become common since the War on Drugs was instigated. They must not only be forbidden, but restitution must be provided to the victims of previous forfeitures, along with severe punishment for those who carried them out.

The next time some bureaucrat or politician starts spouting off about subways, light rail, or some other multibillion-tax-dollar confidence scheme to empty our pockets and control our movements, step on his toes, grab him by his lapels,

and shout up his nostrils (it's the only known way to communicate with these vermin) that the American people already
have the best mass-transit system in the world — one that takes
them from exactly where they are to exactly where they want
to go at exactly any time they desire — and fully intend to
keep it.

Perhaps a new bumpersticker should be printed that proclaims, "They Can Have My Car Keys — When They Pry Them
From My Cold Dead Fingers!"

Sex, Drugs, and Voter Registration
ღ ღ ღ ღ ღ

Childhood isn't what it used to be — and neither is adulthood.

To justify its vicious, cloying, and illegal dominion over
our existence, today's American Security State makes the absurd claim that we're all children who can't be trusted, even to
own and operate our own lives. We're all too familiar with the
terrible ramifications this has for grownups. What it does to
kids may be even worse. They get shoved *down* a notch to
make room for us.

They get *infantilized*.

Not long ago, small boys freely roamed the countryside,
equipped with .22 rifles. If anyone thought anything about it, it
was with approval. They were becoming self-sufficient. This,
however, is a quality the American Security State desperately
desires to stamp out. Now, if they kiss a little girl their own
age, if they give her an aspirin, or if they're caught reading
books by Rush Limbaugh, they're subjected by the vile min-

ions of the American Security State's compulsory indoctrination system to national humiliation and public ostracism.

As a longtime veteran of the individual liberty movement, I don't believe that adults will ever regain their freedom (nor will they deserve to) without sharing it, by re-elevating children. Decades ago, in a sanguine Libertarian Party national-platform committee debate, I insisted that the fact that kids sometimes have trouble exercising their rights *wisely* in no way separates them from adults, who often experience exactly the same problem. I also said (and this applies to grownups and kids alike) that you can't expect people to learn individual responsibility by denying them every opportunity to exercise it.

Those who disagreed with me back then on the issue of kids' rights, who feared embarrassment by what they felt voters might perceive as too wild and crazy a position, often willfully misunderstood and misrepresented what I had to say. I never proposed (as it was sometimes ridiculously claimed) that two-year-olds be given guns without supervision, or that they be exposed to recreational drugs. And only because the American Security State hadn't yet created kiddie porn as a way to smear and destroy dissenters, that subject never came up.

My principal concern has always been for kids who find themselves trapped in the horrible chasm between puberty and majority, drifting in a limbo that's nothing but pure social *invention* (not to mention a damning indictment of the way this civilization elects to raise and educate its young). In a ritual dozens of centuries old, a 13-year-old Jewish boy declares, "Today I am a man!" Way back then, that meant he was prepared to assume the responsibilities of adulthood, in a culture not a whit less complicated and difficult than ours, including property ownership and marriage. Today it means *bupkis*, thanks to intervention by the American Security State, acting for interests that stand to gain immensely from the artificial, and hopelessly unhealthy, extension of childhood.

But the essential point — and experience as a parent has only driven it home deeper — is that you *can't* make any hard and fast rules regarding when the average kid is statistically ready to drive a car, join the Marines, or buy a pack of Marlboros. There's no such thing as the average kid and, as any good Austrian praxeologist knows — but even Libertarians tend to forget when formulating policy — statistics may *not* be properly applied to human beings.

So where does all this get us? Let's dispose of voting. In general, I'm against it: I want to reduce the number of things people vote on to *zero*. But as long as the repulsive antisocial habit continues, I *do* favor giving the franchise to anyone tall enough to pull the lever or strong enough to push that thingy through the punchcard. What harm could it do? Could kids possibly do a *worse* job than was accomplished by this nation's adults, the last first Tuesday in November?

What good would it do? I always thought a poster of an impossibly cute little girl in a voting booth, wearing saddle oxfords and lots of petticoats, stretching with all her might to reach a lever marked "Libertarian," would be an absolutely splendid graphic. It would catch the eye, stir the heart, fire the mind — more importantly, it would be an investment. Once they were 18, kids would remember that *we* were the ones who wanted to trust them with the vote.

As to the rest, rid yourself of a "license" mindset. Nobody ever offered me a permit to own and operate my own life at what *they* deemed was a proper age — I'd have torn it up and thrown it in their faces. I began exercising my rights by asserting them effectively. The process, which has nothing to do with what you find in child-development or sociology books, is piecemeal and essentially Darwinian in nature. My folks were strong people; it required character to face up to them. I drank alcohol when I decided I wanted to badly enough to withstand the inevitable confrontation. Similarly, I showed up with a cigarette burning between my fingers when I decided it was worth it. I acquired — and began carrying — my first gun under precisely the same circumstances.

All this came a bit later in life than that sort of thing usually happens today, but I'm not sure what argument that makes. In the foreign nation where I spent the better part of my boyhood, kids start smoking when they're seven or eight, and grow up to be perfectly fine, independent, decent individuals — or they don't — like anybody else. Sex was the tough one; I had to assert myself more than once before my folks resigned themselves to the fact that it's *my* life.

We recently adopted kittens from the same litter. At nine weeks, one's tall and gangly like a colt, the other still little and round, but just as bright and healthy. They're different, physically and behaviorally. They're individuals. Zoologists observe more differences between individual humans than exist between whole *species* of lower animals. With that undeniable reality in mind, who the bloody hell dares to make prescriptions that work for everyone?

When is a kid ready? For what? How should I know? Which kid are you talking about? The thing to do is put these decisions back where they belong, in the hands of kids and their parents. Because the one thing we can say for sure is that sometimes they'll be right, and sometimes they'll be wrong, and that's a better record than social-welfare bureaucrats — who seek to control individuals politically by threatening to steal their kids — can lay claim to.

The only policy conclusion I can justifiably reach right now (aside from giving kids the vote) is that Colorado should have passed that initiative restoring to parents the right to raise and educate their children. If they get it on the ballot again, I'll

actively campaign for it, because its worst consequence — the
occasional abuse or death of a child at its parents' hands — is
nothing compared to the current Hillarian effort to *nationalize*
our children.

Also, we must re-examine the idea of "majority," in favor
of recognizing individuality.

For now, because I'm her daddy and it's my job, if anyone
offers my little girl sex or drugs, they'll die horribly. Years
from now, when I try to go on extending this protection to her
under circumstances she feels inappropriate (which, loving her,
I almost certainly will), she'll tell me to go to hell, do exactly
as she likes, and maybe we won't speak to each other for a
little while.

And she'll either be right or wrong.

But she'll be *free*.

The Most Thoroughly "Sanitized" City in America

Well, the American mass media finally got what they
wanted.

After weeks of begging, whining, screaming, and *pleading* — exactly the same way B'rer Rabbit begged, whined,
screamed, and pleaded not to be thrown into the briar patch —
the American mass media finally got their Olympic tragedy.
Somebody set off a pipe bomb at a concert in Atlanta's Centennial Park.

And nobody will remember to mention that when it happened, Atlanta was the most thoroughly "sanitized" city in

America, in the world, maybe even in world history.

Now the media can lick their lips bravely and pretend not to be perfectly delighted to be reporting on a phenomenon that they can all understand and identify with much better — brutal murderous destruction for its own sake — than what they were stuck with before: endless hard work, dedication, sense of purpose, courage, and raw talent of a kind they're totally incapable of comprehending.

And nobody will remember to mention that when it happened, Atlanta was the most thoroughly "sanitized" city in America, in the world, maybe even in world history.

Now all those lucky old dogs way back in '72 in Munich will have nothing on them, anymore. They can set years of jealousy aside and focus their itty bitty intellects on the thorny difficulties of distorting the inconvenient fact of a pipe bombing into something they can blame on gun owners and the Internet.

And nobody will remember to mention that when it happened, Atlanta was the most thoroughly "sanitized" city in America, in the world, maybe even in world history.

They will, of course, not lack for help from the government. That's what government is for, after all. Waco Willie Clinton and his baby-murdering stormtroopers will be there, in Washington, in Atlanta, and above all, on national TV, taking "serious measures" to transform the Land of the Formerly Free into something resembling Berlin at the very height of the Thousand Year Reich. (Republicans will argue forcefully that they can do it cheaper.) But this time, in true Olympic spirit and consistent with the American tradition of equality, regardless of race, creed, or color, we'll *all* get to be the Jews.

 And nobody will remember to mention that when it happened, Atlanta was the most thoroughly "sanitized" city in America, in the world, maybe even in world history.

What a windfall!

What a coincidence!

Were Clinton's *actual* numbers beginning to fall off a little? Was Bob Dole, Republican poster-boy for *rigor mortis*, beginning to catch up with him? Did Bill need another crisis to manage, the way he managed the Reichstag — I mean, the Oklahoma City bombing? Or am I simply failing to see the Big Picture?

Here the Cold War up and rudely took the coward's way out without giving anybody decent notice, leaving our leftover World War II fascist government (not to mention adoring hordes of tame journalists) with nothing to justify its existence, when all of a sudden — "for no particular reason" as Forrest Gump (or was it Al Gore) put it — the whole world went conveniently crazy and had to be put back sternly in its place. At the expense of the trillions upon trillions of dollars we all foolishly thought we were going to get back as our "peace dividend." At the expense of a few decades of progress uninterrupted by the mindless regimentation and destruction of war. At the expense of the tattered remnants of the liberties our Founding Fathers proudly bequeathed to us.

But hey, who's counting?

There can be no doubt that these are dangerous times. They've carefully been *made* dangerous by our "protectors." Thanks to no fewer than seven generations of voracious blunderers in government, virtually everyone in the world now hates America badly enough to kill Americans anonymously, by the hundreds.

Thanks to the relentless obliteration of the Bill of Rights by the same voracious blunderers, enough *Americans* now hate America to do exactly the same thing. Thanks to the voracious blunderers who manage elections, these people have been completely shut out of a political system that might provide a safe outlet. And thanks to the voracious blunderers in public education, they're no more able than Clinton to distinguish between the nation and its government.

Maybe no one in the round-heeled American mass media will *ever* remember to mention that when this happened, Atlanta was the most thoroughly "sanitized" city in America, in the world, maybe even in world history. There's certainly nothing in it for them, not even pocket change for hairspray. But the fact that it *did* happen, under those circumstances, proves that America can never be made safer by piling on *more* voracious blunderers or by giving them more power.

In case you haven't noticed, the more we do that, the worse things always get.

No, America can only be made safer by making it more free.

Patching the Patches
ᄋᕰ ᄋᕰ ᄋᕰ ᄋᕰ ᄋᕰ

By now you've heard of children and petite women being injured or killed by the airbags safety "experts" fought for 30 years to impose on the American public. Leave it to Gordon Liddy to describe what happens, saying the rapidly deploying bags, designed to hit large males in the chest, propel their smaller victims' heads like soccer balls straight back into the trunk at 200 miles per hour.

Yet nobody suggests repealing the laws compelling automobile manufacturers to use airbags. Just don't put your children in the front seat. Install switches to defeat airbags when little people sit in their lethal vicinity. Build "smart" airbags (as a substitute for smart politicians). And the all-around socialist favorite: Command manufacturers to slap big red warning labels on visors and dashboards.

Remember the flap, 20 years ago, over sleepwear? Kids were "deliberately exposed to carcinogenic chemicals" by heartless pajama capitalists. Socialist politicians, spraying saliva gobbets in their gibbering hysteria, organized a lynching until it was pointed out that manufacturers had been forced earlier, by the same politicians, to soak sleepwear with the gunk in question in order to retard flames. Whereupon, mysteriously, the whole affair dissolved without a whimper.

Which brings to mind Love Canal: homes, malls, churches, schoolyards, and what would later be known as soccer moms, built on an industrial dump capable of mutating every yard-ape within klicks into Ninja Turtles. Angry peasants grabbed pitchforks and torches to converge *en masse* on company headquarters (the situation being only slightly complicated by the fact that said company had gone out of business decades earlier) demanding justice or something like it.

We don't hear about Love Canal any more; the only role private enterprise played in that mess was a vain attempt to stop construction of the subdivision in the first place. Thanks to *Reason* magazine, we learned it was the Army that destroyed the land, later sold to a chemical company and subsequently *stolen* (the term is "Eminent Domain") by a school board that sold it to a developer. Company officials begged the board — in writing — never to let anyone build homes or schools on the land. Their warnings were filed away until *Reason* dug them out.

When I got interested in guns, media and left-wing politicians had just created a straw-man they labeled "Saturday Night Specials": cheap imported revolvers in small calibers. Impecunious blacks were equipping themselves in unprecedented numbers at a time when minority sections of America's largest cities were aflame. Not being original enough to generate a catch-phrase of their own, anti-gunners had revived a rude expression circulating a generation earlier, one that originally included a *second* N-word between "Night" and "Specials."

One result was 1968's Gun Control Act. Analysis of the victim-disarmament movement reveals that every gun law ever written meant to strip some racial or ethnic minority of the means of self-defense. New York's Sullivan Act was directed against Italians. California's semiauto ban was driven by terror of Asian gangs (created by drug prohibition and minimum-wage laws). The Brady Bill passed because too many women, in the view of politicians, were acquiring too many guns.

The technological result (as columnist Vin Suprynowicz reminds us) was an inner-city arms race. Banning cheap small-caliber revolvers created a vogue for the high-caliber, high-capacity, semi-automatic pistols legislators are now trying to outlaw (note that gangs only started carrying guns when switchblades were banned). If socialists had kept their ignorant mouths shut, homies would still be poking .22 caliber holes in each other (whenever their die-cast zinc popguns actually went off as the trigger got jerked); innocent kids wouldn't be catching stray nine millimeter slugs penetrating building walls and car doors.

Similarly, if you'll review gun publications of a decade ago, you'll find that nobody was interested in "assault rifles" (weapons chambered for medium-powered cartridges fed by high-capacity magazines) before right-wing socialist William Bennett, left-wing fascist Charles Schumer, and clueless mouthbreather George Bush began applying pressure to them. Airliner bombings didn't begin until passengers were searched for weapons. Militias didn't arise until Bill Clinton — threatening the Constitution they're meant to defend — made them necessary.

Are we safer since government forced gas companies to replace lead with carcinogenic additives? Are racial relations any better after two generations of forced integration and affirmative action? Were you aware that thalidomide doesn't cause birth defects, as the FDA still asserts, but simply prevents the perfectly natural, highly desirable, and spontaneous abortion of malformed fetuses?

As Robert LeFevre put it, "Government is a disease masquerading as its own cure." It's in the business of putting patches over non-existent punctures in the social fabric, and then, when the patches inevitably cause greater trouble than they were meant to repair, putting patches on the patches. At last count there were more than five million federal laws. And "ignorance of the law is no excuse." Multiply each of these ugly situations by five million and you'll begin to have an idea how we got into this mess. But how do we get out? I hesitate to propose another law, but a Constitutional amendment may be called for.

What we need is a moratorium (100 years would be a nice round figure) on legislation at any level of government. Five million federal laws certainly strikes me as *enough*. If weapons laws (for example) worked, wouldn't 20,000 of them have done the job already?

The single exception would be bills of *repeal*.

The same amendment would nullify Sovereign Immunity (and with it, Eminent Domain), which should have been junked along with other royal trappings during the Revolution, and exercise a Power of Congress to remove *everything* from the jurisdiction of a Supreme Court, which, of the three mythically separated branches of government, has been by far the worst custodian of the Bill of Rights.

Lever Action

Scalping Elmo
ᴄᴐ ᴄᴐ ᴄᴐ ᴄᴐ ᴄᴐ

They're scalping Elmo out there, and America (or at least the silliest of her most hysterical element) is outraged. You'd think they were plucking Big Bird!

I should explain, for the benefit of those who don't have a seven-year-old, that Elmo's a little red fuzzy character from "Sesame Street," and that a monsterquin manufactured in his likeness (called "Tickle Me Elmo") is everything this Christmas that the Cabbage Patch doll was in the '80s. News TV's hairsprayed heads (stimulated by the current Arnold Schwarzenegger comedy concerning mortal combat over a similarly popular plaything) are doing their absolute damnedest to incite riots in every toy section of every department and discount emporium in Clintondom.

Hey, it's their job.

Meanwhile, individuals with the foresight to have acquired a number of these *objects drat* are advertising them — in that vile seething cauldron of unregulated iniquity known as the Internet — at prices ranging to $200. (I don't know what they're "supposed" to cost — lucky me, my daughter's still into *Toy Story* — but it can't be much more than a double sawbuck.) And, for the first time *outside* the context of tickets to a theatrical or athletic event, I've begun hearing a perfectly commendable free-market practice (of rationing scarce commodities by a process of balancing supply and demand through *price*) being referred to as "scalping."

My, how sloppy media Marxists have gotten with their camouflage, since People's Heroic Soviet Chairperson and Mr. Clinton managed to get themselves rebeatified last November by fewer than half of those who bothered to vote. You begin to get an idea what the capital gains tax is *really* all about. Buying low and selling high — *all* buying low and selling high — is now by definition "scalping," to be punished, preferably by forcing all such antisocial miscreants to subsidize the Glorious Collective, through fines levied shortly after the crime or taxes payable upon excessive success.

Or maybe I'm just being mean-spirited, maligning the altruistic intentions of the moral cannibals who — oops, damn! There I go again — have all but destroyed this civilization in a relentless effort to control my life and yours. (There — I feel better.)

Maybe the moral measure of economic relationships is the "need" of the victims, er ... victimized by the unfair practice of selling stuff for more than you paid for it. Maybe that sort of activity is excusable *most* of the time (as long as you do it in the closet and scrub your hands afterward), but not when ... what? When folks need bread and flashlight batteries after a hurricane and hoard them unless merchants are left to ration them by exercising a natural right to put any frigging price on them they wish?

There I go again.

I confess that, despite its mindless political correctness, I watch "Home Improvement," because Tim Allen and Patricia Richardson make me laugh. (My daughter likes "Tool Time" and doesn't care to see all that other stuff.) One episode, however, never fails to make me mad: the one where Tim and Al, stuck with sitting through a local production of *Waiting for Godot*, try to unload a pair of hockey tickets and are arrested by Max Gail, last seen as Wojohowicz on "Barney Miller."

Let's get this straight: What's at stake here is a cold hard seat in a huge noisy structure (where you're not allowed to smoke) shoehorned full of cretins watching other cretins pushing a rubber English muffin around an arena that would be

Lever Action

better used as a Hunter's Pistol range. The team already has its money, having been happy to sell the ticket in the first place. The second buyer thought he wouldn't get into this splendiferous event and is ecstatic to pay several times face value not to miss it. The first buyer — able to dispose of his property any way he wishes — gets what he wants. Who the hell is being hurt here?

And didn't Walter Block already ask that?

The whole thing's sillier — if that's possible — when the commodity is a stuffed animal from a TV show (and network) that's supposed to be non-commercial and unconcerned with such vile capitalistic crassness.

Okay but, just to be fair, let's give it a final try before we toss this kind of "thinking" into the dumpster where it belongs. A principal objection to Elmo-scalping — judging by responses on a Web page dedicated to trafficking cruelly in fake furry flesh — is that it's unseemly to make a profit from little children at Christmastime.

Somebody call Mattel.

I'm sure you've noticed how, more and more, "for the children" is the excuse of preference for every fascistic atrocity — victim disarmament, drug prohibition, Internet censorship — professional dogwhistles like William Bennett and Charles Schumer desire to impose on a nation where the highest law of the land was *supposed* to be the Bill of Rights. I'm sick of hearing it. What I want for *my* child is a free society to live in when she grows up.

Moreover, I don't want her used as an excuse to beat up and kill people who refuse to become Bill and Charlie's slaves. Even at seven, she understands the issue better than the average voter. She doesn't want to be used as an excuse, either. More than anything, she looks forward, like her daddy and mommy did at her age, to growing up and controlling her own

360

life. You think I'm a hard case? Wait a dozen years. I'd hate to be anyone she finds standing in her way.

But to return to the point, and at the risk of repeating myself, if I buy Elmo, he's my property, to do with as I see fit. If I buy a hockey ticket — it isn't me, but an alien imposter; nevertheless — the principle is the same. It's *my* ticket, to use, sell, or run through a pencil sharpener and snort up my nose. The trouble with Bill and Charlie is that the only kind of property right *they* believe in is a right they imagine they have to own *us*.

Personally, I think Ayn Rand was onto something when she had the goodguys at the end of *Atlas Shrugged* admiring a new Constitutional Amendment: "Congress shall make no law abridging the freedom of production and trade ... "

Better yet, Alice, how about "Congress shall make no law"? Period.

A Culture of Harmlessness
ꕝ ꕝ ꕝ ꕝ ꕝ

The trial's over, but the memory will linger for a long time, due to a willful misunderstanding of its significance by the media, Left and Right.

Just so you'll know where I'm coming from, I have no idea whether O.J. Simpson is a killer, and because of that, I believe the jury arrived at the only verdict possible. Conservatives, handwringing over what they imagine to be a *recent* collapse of the justice system, want to forget that, in America, an individual must be presumed innocent by the state until its minions prove him guilty beyond any reasonable doubt. They pay lip service to the concept (if a conservative's a liberal who's been mugged, a liberal's a conservative who's been arrested), but their resentment of it is unmistakable.

Let's agree that although Simpson's defense attorneys may have been guilty of it in other connections, questioning evidence that might have been faked by a cop who hates blacks is *not* "playing the race card." If Mark Fuhrman were an environmentalist, framing Simpson because he refused to recycle, would his motive count or the character of his evidence? Would we complain that the defense was playing the "Earth card"?

Somewhere along the line, fascinated with their newfound liberty to say "nigger" (just as the Bobbitts freed them to say "penis"), TV hairsprayheads forgot that, in addition to uttering the N-word so many times it's expressable only in scientific notation, Fuhrman also told witnesses that he wouldn't hesitate to plant evidence to cinch an arrest. He claimed he *had* on more than one occasion. Of course, in a sense, that's irrelevant, since the jury never heard about it officially. But you can bet they heard it *unofficially* ("the jury will disregard" being a phrase in the same category as "the check is in the mail" and "trust me, I've had a vasectomy") and that it helped shape their decision.

Moreover, the body of evidence is not a menu. Nowhere more than in a court of law is it true that one rotten apple spoils the barrel. The prosecution cannot tell us, "This may be a lie, but this, here, is true, and, well, maybe this is a lie, too, but this is true." We wouldn't accept that from a sticky-faced five-year-old. Why should a jury accept it from a district attorney?

I could go on, asking if we really want juries to ignore broken chains of evidence custody, the incompetence of crime-scene and laboratory personnel, illegal police procedures, hallmarks of tampering, but I want to discuss broader issues: where the verdict came from; what it means for the future.

It's uncomfortable to put oneself in the place of Nicole Simpson or Ron Goldman, to imagine how they felt, what they thought, in their final moments. I've had moments when I was certain I was going to die, so in that sense, I can identify with them.

Yet in another sense, it's absurd. Unlike religion, magic, or liberalism, natural selection continues to operate whether you have faith in it or not. Callous as it may seem to declare it, the end Nicole Simpson and Ron Goldman came to was a result of deliberate decisions they made for themselves — with a little help from their friends.

To begin with, they lived in California where, as in New York, the penalty is worse for being prepared to defend ourselves than for being what we need to defend ourselves *from*. If either of them had carried a weapon that night, they'd be alive today. We might even know who *tried* to hurt them. If they and other Californians (not to mention all Americans) stopped tolerating laws (along with politicians and bureaucrats who pass and enforce them) requiring that we offer ourselves as human sacrifices, it's possible that the pattern of spousal abuse that prosecutors tried to use to prove that Simpson was a killer might never have begun. Awareness that one's prey may be armed is the most powerful deterrent known, short of an actual death sentence administered at the scene and moment of the crime at the hands of the intended victim.

By one method of analysis, then, it was Sarah Brady who killed Nicole Simpson and Ron Goldman, although they were probably willing accomplices, so eager to avoid the messy responsibility of defending themselves that, like most Californians, they rushed to believe her threadbare evil lies, and wound up dying for them. Good going, Sarah. Hope you sleep at night. Little wonder, over the past few years, that you've been making yourself scarcer and scarcer.

At the same time, I've surprised myself by feeling little or no sympathy for the parents of Ron Goldman and Nicole Simpson, who, like most white southern Californians, brought their children up in a culture of harmlessness, and therefore share responsibility for their deaths. They conscientiously raised their kids to be what Jeff Cooper calls "rabbit people" — human groceries — helpless (what purpose do rabbits serve, after all?) before whatever predator might casually choose to slay them. Revile me though you may for stating it that plainly, it doesn't alter the simple truth.

But there's more than one kind of predator. My mom was born in Los Angeles; my favorite aunt lived there for decades. Many of my friends live there today. Most Americans may not be aware that, at least since the 1920s, the LAPD has been infamous for its iniquitous brutality. All they recall are "Dragnet" and "Adam 12," propaganda meant to cover up corruption the way a cat covers up its messes in a litter box. Despite what we used to see on "Quincy," the city and county are fabled for crime-lab bungling, as anyone familiar with the Tate-LaBianca case can attest. It is this world-class incompetence that figures so highly in our haunting uncertainties over the deaths of Marilyn Monroe and Bobby Kennedy.

More to the point, Los Angeles is the site of the Symbionese Liberation Army fire, in which the erstwhile kidnappers of Patty Hearst were burned to death in a little frame house by the LAPD, using tear-gas cannisters known for their incendiary nature. Right off, this reminds us of something — in fact, it reminds us of *several* somethings. It reminds us of the murder of tax-resistor Gordon Kahl, trapped like an animal in another little frame house after a nationwide manhunt straight out of *Fahrenheit 451* and shot to pieces by jackbooted thugs who believe the IRS code takes precedence over the Bill of Rights.

It reminds us of a guy in Thornton, Colorado, who wanted

to be left alone and made the fatal mistake of saying so to a cop who put a call in to his buddies — the police forces of half a dozen neighboring municipalities — who beseiged his house, riddled it with bullets, then smashed in and shot him to death, claiming it was self-defense, until a coroner's report indicated that both the victim's wrists were broken by an earlier shooting and that he couldn't have lifted the gun the cops used as an excuse to *execute* him where he huddled in a closet. Local media said he was a nobody and the story wasn't worth following up.

It reminds us of the famous Philadelphia MOVE bombing, where, confronting an unpopular group conceded to have been disturbing the peace, police dropped explosives from a helicopter, destroying 60 houses, killing 11 people. Those disturbed by the Simpson verdict today didn't have much to say when the mayor who approved this atrocity was re-elected by the same majority the Bill of Rights was designed to protect us from.

Most of all, it reminds us of the vicious murders of Vicky and Sam Weaver at Ruby Ridge, and of the Waco Massacre, where abuse of power reached an ostentatious crescendo in the fiery deaths of more than 80 people under the directives of Bill Clinton, Janet Reno, and their henchmen who apparently still believe they're free to do anything they wish to the people whose rights they've falsely sworn to uphold and defend.

Now you're saying, "But that's irrelevant. What does it have to do with the murders of Nicole Simpson and Ron Goldman and whether her ex-husband is guilty?"

It has everything to do with them. Do you imagine that potential jurors never watch television? That they don't have memories? These murders occurred in (and the jury was drawn from) a nation in which officially approved savagery is becoming as commonplace today as it has been for centuries in South America.

Such outrages, and thousands more like them happening each day in America on a smaller scale, invariably occur at the hands of the very class who accused Simpson and were later shown to have lied about key elements of the case. Increasingly, we live in a culture dominated by what Karl Hess once called "The Lawless State" — a government more "anarchistic" than anyone out here who wants to see it altered or abolished. Its unrelenting monstrous criminality makes even the atrocities Simpson was accused of pale by comparison. One out-of-control individual blew up a whole federal building and killed 165 people in a demented attempt to even that kind of score. Letting one murderer go free may seem like small potatoes to jury members living in that context every day.

How long have philosophers warned us that autocratic, stupid, and gratuitous legislation — speed limits, gun control, alcohol and drug prohibition, confiscatory taxes, seizure decrees, environmental edicts, "health and safety" measures — nourish a people's contempt for law and order?

Very well then, in exactly what form did we expect that contempt to manifest itself? As right-wing talk show hosts have suggested, it's a matter of chickens coming home to roost. But these are of a different species than the radio guys suspect, and more ancient. In the light of no less than 14 unbroken decades of government violence and deceit (want me to list a few dozen more scandals and atrocities that have occurred since the War Between the States, or shall we skip it?), why should anyone, juryman or otherwise, believe anything attested to by any of the government's stooges?

To understand who's responsible for what's widely seen as an unjust verdict in California, look to the opposite coast. Ultimate moral responsiblilty lies with Bill Clinton, Janet Reno, Louis Freeh, Larry Potts, their triggerman Lon Horiuchi, *and that entire ilk*, whose treacherous, brutal, and illegal behavior serve as example and justification for the likes of Mark Fuhr-man.

Is there a cure? Certainly not any "Republican Revolu-tion," whose opening tragicomic act was to declare that evi-dence obtained illegally remains admissable as long as the po-lice claim to have gotten hold of it "in good faith."

I've no idea whether O.J. Simpson is a murderer and nei-ther do you. That's the problem: By now, we're *supposed* to. Whatever you think, whatever side you take, two things are true. First, a savage killer is free today to walk America's streets. Maybe it's O.J., maybe another person altogether; *somebody* wielded that knife. Second, *that* savage killer is no worse than those presently occupying the offices of President and Attor-ney General of the United States.

The cure? Try something that would never occur to Demo-crats or Republicans. *Enforce* the Bill of Rights as if it were exactly what it is: the highest law of the land. In due course, respect for American institutions of justice will increase, and with it, the likelihood that a murderer can be convicted by a jury whose members are sure of what their rights are and where they stand with their government.

In the end, the Simpson trial and verdict is not a matter of Right versus Left, or even of black versus white, but of *us* ver-sus *them*, "us" being the American productive class and "them" being what was once called the "new class" of police-state bureaucrats fastened on our necks like leeches. That being so, the Simpson verdict represents a positive result, restoration of a custom as old as the American Revolution itself:

We the People telling the cops to go to hell.

The Spider at the Center of the Web
ꞔꞔ ꞔꞔ ꞔꞔ ꞔꞔ ꞔꞔ

I saw David Rockefeller on TV the other day. He looked gratifyingly old. His brother Nelson, you'll recall, expired years ago while slaving over a hot secretary. It made me wonder how much time Ol' Dave has left, and more importantly, whether (e'er he shuffles off this mortal coil) he'll get religion and condescend to "Let My People Go."

Now, I'm aware that even Rush Limbaugh sneers at people who see Ol' Dave as the Spider at the Center of a Web of Conspiracy. Most times, I'm inclined to agree, though I confess that in my darker moments, I suspect this may be Rush's real purpose, the reason he's allowed by Powers that Be to prosper. Here's a guy who won't believe the FBI did anything wrong at Waco. He is, after all, a Phil Donahue employee.

You *didn't* know that?

What's more, with one exception I'll get to later, I've never been motivated by any purely economic argument for individual liberty. Compared with other aspects of what's been, for me, a life-long struggle, that bores me bug-silly. So do most of the individuals who appear obsessed by it. Even among those who call themselves Libertarians, two economists in the same room usually means a noisy disagreement.

Nonetheless, they reveal a basic truth that can't be denied, one at the heart of everything wrong with America. It's simple, really, depressingly simple, considering how long the scam's been operating. And it won't be the first time in history that a free people were gulled blind because they refused to believe that everyone isn't as basically decent as they are.

The recent Harry Browne campaign comes to mind.

But I digress.

You wanna be like Ol' Dave, buy a dozen congressmen and tell 'em, "Get out there and *spend*. I don't care how much you spend, even what you spend it *on* — that's another issue entirely — as long as you spend *more* than the IRS can rake in without starting a revolution. Then *I'll* come along and loan you enough money to make up the difference."

And collect the interest on that loan. I heard another guy on TV say that, at the moment, it takes the taxes of everybody west of the Mississippi just to pay that interest, and that before long, it'll take *everybody's* taxes and no payments will get made on the principal. He seemed upset that federal taxes now consume 20-odd percent of what we earn. I'm more concerned that, when you add state, county, municipal, and other governments, the percentage rises to more than 50.

The function of American socialism (and its leafy subsidiary, environmentalism) is to provide something to spend money *on*, filling the coffers of the very class socialists claim to despise. Marx must be spinning in his grave so fast he could be wired to generate electricity.

Even the "little people," all the "widows and orphans" who are held up as an excuse for trying to repair a system that should never have existed, even they expected, like most "victims" of a con game, to make out. When they elected Roosevelt, when they elected Kennedy, when they elected Johnson, they were cutting themselves a nice, thick, quivering, bloody slice of *us*. They were engaging, not just in cannibalism, but in its most repulsive form: They were eating their own young. Which is why I declared, in a Texas speech last summer — a speech I was bitterly criticized for making and one of the best I've ever given — "Screw Social Security. Let the bastards freeze in the dark."

Most individuals, political pundits and voters alike, never get past the question of what the money gets spent *on*. But that's a different game, played on a different level. Overarching it all is the corrupt matter of what we'll term "pseudocapitalism," and how for generations it has led us down what F.A. Hayek called "The Road to Serfdom." Clinton, Dole, and Perot serve exactly the same interest and it is that interest, rather than the government it owns and operates, that America's productive class find themselves the chattel property of.

Two or three generations ago, big-banking buckaroos like Ol' Dave used to be smarter. In the same way Romans saved themselves a lot of trouble by keeping their hands off local religion, our herders used to give their cattle — meaning us — *free range* to do what we wanted, as long as we worked hard to produce enough wealth to "service the debt."

Recently, senility and a degree of genetic depletion have set in, as they will with parasitic organisms. Ol' Dave has let his socialist front-men get out of control, penning the cattle too closely, making them dangerously discontent. Or maybe it's a matter of allowing his thin-blooded Ivy League-tutored offspring to embrace the phony-baloney ideology that was created for the same reason we put sand in a catbox.

The fact is, each of us pays half his income to one government or another, cutting his real wealth in half. Those we purchase goods and services from also pay half to government, except that they don't really pay — we do, through prices twice as high as they should be. Which cuts real wealth in half again, to a quarter of what it would be if everyone kept what they earn. It also costs to comply with idiot regulations. Dixy Lee Ray, in *Environmental Overkill,* estimated that it amounts to *another* halving, meaning that government sucks off *seven-eighths*; we're left to survive on one eighth of our productive capacity.

Let me say that again, so there'll be no mistaking it: Government consumes *seven-eighths* of everything we make or do;

we're left to survive on one-eighth of our productive capacity.

What I find fascinating is imagining (as I did in my book *The Probability Broach*) what it would be like to have *eight*-eighths of our wealth to play with and government was left to freeze in the dark, too. Similarly, if the debt was created in the first place, at the behest of those it's owed to, it should be repudiated, or personally paid by the congressional crooks who took it on themselves to incur it.

If you're not prepared to deprive them of their excuses, if you're not prepared to eradicate every evidence of socialism from America, including the bits of it you *like*, if you're not equally prepared to enforce the Bill of Rights — letter by letter — including the bits of it you *don't* like, then you're part of the problem you complain about.

VI

SCIENCE FICTION AND LESSER MEDIA

On a Clear Day You Can See Bulgaria —But Who Wants to Look?
ᴄᴈ ᴄᴈ ᴄᴈ ᴄᴈ ᴄᴈ

I've been a science fiction writer for 17 or 27 years, depending on how you look at it. During that time, it seems like there's always been some editor or agent on the phone, whining into my ear about how bad business is lately.

Of course, you have to accept some of this as a bargaining strategy on the part of editors — or excuses on the part of agents — for why writers should be happy to accept less money. That sort of thing's been going on since the first copper stylus got mashed into the first moist clay tablet. From an editor or an agent's point of view (and they are essentially the same, no matter what they claim to the contrary), writers should *always* be happy to accept less money.

But there's a particle of truth here, too: The same period has indeed been characterized by shrinking rack space for science fiction in grocery stores and drugstores, incongruously occupied by offerings with dragons, dwarves, enchanted swords, bazookas, and armored hovercraft on their covers. Where I differ with the editors and agents — to whom I've vainly attempted to communicate this point for virtually every one of those 17 or 27 years — is in my belief that science fiction is dying from self-inflicted injuries. Furthermore, I believe that I'm uniquely qualified to pontificate on this subject because in many respects, I'm the only writer in the whole wide world still writing the stuff.

Historically, science fiction has almost always been driven by some variety of Utopianism: stirring visions of the wonderful new universe that will "inevitably" result from practicing whatever it is the writer has to preach.

Almost always it has been some variety of socialism.

On rare occasions it has been *right-wing* socialism, a little-understood intellectual phenomenon in which the central idea is that the life, liberty, and property of the average individual should be sacrificed (or at least temporarily dragooned) for the sake of achieving certain collective goals — like constructing a base on the Moon, slaughtering pesky aliens, wiping out interplanetary drug pushers, or simply moving Antarctic icebergs to thirsty tropical consumers — goals such as those traditionally advocated by conservatives (or even outright fascists) ranging from E.E. "Doc" Smith to Dr. Jerry Pournelle.

But most often it was left-wing socialism, in which the central idea is that the life, liberty, and property of the individual should be sacrificed for the sake of achieving certain collective goals — like national healthcare or universal weapons confiscation — traditionally advocated by liberals or even outright communists. These unworthies have dominated science fiction since its inception, although 20 or 30 years ago they grudgingly made room for a few token right-wing socialists because the real goal of both camps (like the viewpoints of editors and agents) is essentially the same: sacrificing the life, liberty, and property of the individual for its own sake, *whatever* the excuse.

Sometimes I think the lefties moved over and made room for the righties because they became absolutely terrified of what *else* might be bearing down on them.

Me.

Well, not me, exactly, but somebody like me.

Only a lot worse.

Ayn Rand scared the living shit out of these people. An Evgeny Zamiatin or a Robert LeFevre or even an Ira Levin they could suppress or dismiss for one reason or another, which is why so few readers have ever heard of *We*, *Lift Her Up Tenderly*, or *This Perfect Day*. But little old Alice Rosenbaum was always right there in their nasty collectivist faces, her literary fists clenched, challenging their most fundamental assumptions in the very language (*skiffy*, the correct pronunciation of "sci-fi") that socialists of both stripes thought they had invented, stubbornly *refusing* to be dismissed or suppressed.

But what scared the lefties even more was the *actual* new universe that seemed to be resulting — inevitably, as it turned out — from the practice (by Joseph Stalin, Mao Tse Tung, Lyndon Baines Johnson, and Pol Pot, among others) of what they had been preaching since the time of H.G. Welles and Edward Bellamy.

It wasn't simply that the ideas of left-wing socialism weren't working, although that was certainly bad enough. Invariably, they seemed to culminate in the deaths — from causes ranging from starvation to firing-squad — of tens of millions of the proletarians they'd been intended to benefit in the first place. And even worse, under the stress-testing of harsh reality (this was before the Evil Empire collapsed in an unprecedented, although not exactly unpredictable, manner) they sometimes — often — mutated into right-wing socialism.

Which is how it came to be that all those lonely, toothless, quakey-voiced old-timers (of all ages) still eking out their existences in the philosophical badlands and political ghost-towns that Left-Wing Utopia has become — and even those lucky enough to be living in far greater luxury off the tailings of the statist mother-lode they once helped mine — have nothing but bad news for us now. They're mistaking the failure of their ideas for a failure of reality.

As a consequence, many of them have simply given up and become whining nihilists. Those who are more successful tell us tales today of interstellar super-states with the unquestioned power to quarantine whole sectors of the galaxy because, in their infinite wisdom, they've decided it would be bad for unsupervised individuals of differing species to meet and freely exchange ideas and articles of trade with one another. At the same time, they speak of local authorities with the technological ability to search individuals for concealed weapons or other contraband at a distance — a practice nobody in these stories ever resists or even complains about on humane or Constitutional grounds.

This kind of thing used to be a staple of *negative* Utopias like *1984* and *Brave New World*, furnishings for cautionary tales about a regrettable loss of liberty. Now it's taken for granted as inevitable, and probably even desirable, whatever other possibilities the future may present. The writers never seem to notice that nobody is listening — at least not to that part of the story.

So what happens to a community of timeworn left-wing Utopian writers who for decades have continued to insist on seeing a future that demonstrably — to anyone who isn't tenured, working for television, or living in Sri Lanka — doesn't work? Enter J.R.R. Tolkien, along with what seemed at the time like thousands of blatant imitators, sucked into the world-swallowing vacuum in the science fiction market created by the implosion of Marxoid idealism. Enter the dragons, the dwarves, and the enchanted swords. Bazookas and armored personnel carriers came later, and when they did, it seemed like a breath of fresh air.

And so, as irrationality and magic began to displace reason and science as the motivating epistemology, and as the genre began looking backward to feudalism and the Middle Ages (for all its socialism, science fiction *had* been a forward-looking literature of limitless perspectives), and as readers began to tire of narrowed horizons (not to mention the same old thing re-rewritten over and over), the rack space — "inevitably," once again — began to diminish.

It was the exceptions (and don't you hate it when this happens?) that proved the rule — and still do today. The books that kept the rack space open for all those parasitic and reactionary dragons, dwarves, enchanted swords, bazookas, and armored personnel carriers, the only books that didn't gradually decrease in number, were those with spaceships, aliens, and ringed planets still on their covers, those whose subtitles now always seemed to include the word "star," accompanied either by the word "wars" or the word "trek."

There is some truth in the idea that *Star Wars* succeeded partly by co-opting medievalism. And it's equally true that *Star Trek* and its progeny have remained as unabashedly old-fashionedly socialistic as *The Shape of Things to Come,* steadfastly (and this is an important secret of their success) refusing to acknowledge the utter demise of socialism in every other branch of the cosmos.

But both displayed a future (yes, I know, *Star Wars* claims to be set "a long time ago in a galaxy far far away," but who believes it?) featuring individualistic causes, violent adventures, and technology almost anyone could look forward to. Hence, their remarkable success in a period when science fiction generally lay dying, killed by the bankruptcy of its underlying ideas and a craven retreat from a future it knew it could no longer predict, create, or control.

But the question is, do we *really* want to grant to Lucasian neofeudal mysticism or to Roddenberrian military socialism a monopoly on the future by default? Lucas and Roddenberry did their jobs. They held the line for science fiction and preserved a remnant of that precious and dwindling rack space. But to put the question a different way, how do we go about *expanding* it again?

The one realistic answer will be a bitter pill for all the right-wing socialists, obsolete leftists, dwarfmongers, and bazookists to swallow. Science fiction died because its self-contradictory dreams died first. Its one hope is to usher in an alternative literature of a credible, yet fantastic, future worth believing in, worth working for, and therefore worth reading about.

That literature doesn't have to be created; it already exists. I'm proud to say that I had a hand in its creation over 15 years ago, along with a dozen other novelists of my approximate age and outlook. Even better, I know of at least a dozen more science fiction manuscripts by other, mostly younger writers with the same viewpoint as ours, languishing now for lack of proper editorial attention. I predict that if New York publishing doesn't make a place for them soon, they will make a place for themselves, and on their own terms.

I can't bring myself to believe that New York really wants that. The last time something like that happened, they got Rush Limbaugh. Do they actually want a *dozen* Limbaughs, with both halves of their brains fully operational (which automatically makes them libertarians rather than conservatives) occupying the intellectual void science fiction has made of itself?

It may already be too late; New York may no longer have a choice.

I hope so.

Merchants of Fear

Presented to the Boulder County Libertarian Party
February 20, 1994

☙ ☙ ☙ ☙ ☙

Whatever else Americans may disagree about, everybody agrees about the mass media.

We all know what we mean by the term "mass media" when we say it. What I mean by "mass media" is the aggregate of individuals involved at every level of production — especially in the "news" departments — of all television, virtually every newspaper, and most news magazines in America today. Like you, I have never been personally involved in any event that they managed to report correctly.

Socialist Nick Nolte makes a movie about the mass media and they're unhesitatingly portrayed as illiterate obnoxious slimeballs.

Middle-of-the-roader Burt Reynolds makes a movie about the mass media and they're unhesitatingly portrayed as illiterate obnoxious slimeballs.

Conservative Bruce Willis makes a movie about the mass media and they're unhesitatingly portrayed as illiterate obnoxious slimeballs.

Fascist Sylvester Stallone makes a movie about the mass media and they're unhesitatingly portrayed as illiterate obnoxious slimeballs.

Even libertarian John Milius makes a movie about the mass media and they're unhesitatingly portrayed as illiterate obnoxious slimeballs. This is not news to the illiterate obnoxious slime — I mean, to the mass media. They tell themselves — I've been there to hear them do it — that it's a sign they're doing their job right. They're so painstakingly accurate, so minutely unbiased, that nobody benefits unfairly and, as a natural consequence in this worst of all possible worlds, everybody hates them for it.

The trouble with this otherwise comforting theory is that they never entertain the simpler and therefore likelier explanation that everybody hates them because it's unmistakable to anybody regardless of his prejudices — especially anybody who's ever been one of their victims — how very badly they do their job.

The fact is that surveys, which media people openly admit to, show that fewer than twelve percent of their customers believe they're doing a good job, while the average profit margin in television is in the neighborhood of eighty percent.

And besides, they're illiterate obnoxious slimeballs.

I've often wondered why this might be so, but I've never doubted that it is. Even in the North American Confederacy, the libertarian Utopia from my first novel, *The Probability Broach* — a wonderful universe that I built by hand in which the goodguys won the Whiskey Rebellion of 1794, the government grew smaller and weaker from that moment forward, and, as a people, Americans never made another political mistake — even in this *best* of all possible worlds, I realized instinctively that the mass media would be illiterate obnoxious slimeballs.

As I put it, more or less, in *Forge of the Elders*, the infamous two-book trilogy I wrote for Warner Communications that turned out so politically incorrect they unilaterally canceled the third volume: American journalism has always gloried in its self-appointed role as *watchdog* over the dignity and liberty of the individual. But the sad truth is that during its long self-congratulatory history, it's been a lot more like a cur, caught bloody-muzzled time after time after time *savaging* the very flocks it has been trusted to protect.

I used to have a friend (the older I get, the more often I seem to find myself saying: "I used to have a friend") named Owen Lock, who was my first book editor at Random House. Owen, whenever I got upset because it seemed like certain people — say, the mass media — were colluding with various politicians to strip Americans of their fundamental rights, would tell me I should consider another simpler explanation. Over the years I've come to think of this as "Owen's Law" (because "Lock's Law" sounds like something you need to take shots for) and it goes like this: "Whenever it looks like a conspiracy, consider the possibility that it's only because they're stupid."

Owen's Law has served me well over the years — sometimes it's the only thing that's kept me sane — although I can't say the same for Owen himself. The ninth book I wrote for him, *Tom Paine Maru*, turned out so politically incorrect he unilaterally removed forty pages from it and that was the end of our association.

Nevertheless, I think there's something to this idea, with regard to the mass media, that "it's only because they're stupid." Have you ever known anyone connected with television, newspapers, or news magazines who had an IQ higher than the last professional who cut your hair or the average all-star wrestling fan?

Of course, it's always possible I'm being too harsh. Abysmal ignorance, although it really isn't the same thing at all, can often be mistaken for stupidity. The last professional who cut my hair, and practically any all-star wrestling fan, knows a *lot* more than the average individual in the mass media.

Mass-media people are a lot like public-school teachers in this respect. The time and energy public-school teachers might have wisely and profitably spent learning more about whatever it is they're supposed to be teaching — like reading, writing, and arithmetic — is wasted, instead, taking useless "education" courses.

Likewise, the time and energy the average person in the mass media might have wisely and profitably spent learning *anything* about history, economics, political philosophy — even logic — is wasted taking "journalism." As any real newsman could tell you — if there were any still alive — "journalism" is something you learn in the newsroom, at the hands of those who learned it before you.

Having considered both stupidity and ignorance as explanations for the repulsive state of the mass media today, however, I'm sorry to say that I find them both inadequate.

Nobody could possibly be *that* stupid.

Nobody could possibly be *that* ignorant.

Which brings us to the subject of corruption.

Corruption is not the same as conspiracy, you understand. Conspiracy is the act of conniving immorally or illegally with others to get your bread buttered. Corruption is simply knowing which side your bread is already buttered on.

A few years ago a conservative think-tank scholar named James Buchanan won himself a Nobel Prize by demonstrating that bureaucrats and politicians are inclined to use the power they've been given to pursue their own self-interest rather than the public trust. Why this is supposed to have been such an unprecedented or eye-opening observation I've never quite understood, but that's what happened.

However, Buchanan's thesis inspires us to consider just what constitutes the self-interest of people in the mass media. Maybe understanding that will help us understand them.

First and foremost, the interests of the mass media lie with tragedy or calamity of any kind — earthquakes, tornadoes, hurricanes, floods, volcanoes, avalanches, plagues. Intelligent, capable, and responsible men and women going to work every day to keep civilization running, feeding their families, and bringing their children up healthy and strong make lousy TV pictures or wire photographs.

This was true, in principle, even when the government consisted merely of the police, the courts, and the army. With the rise of the modern welfare establishment, the mass media have begun to imitate the superstate, inexorably swelling in magnitude and influence by feeding on death and disaster.

In short, mass-media people are the only creatures lower on the scale of evolution and fouler in their personal and public habits than the bureaucrats and politicians they report on. What they really want, deep down, is *power*, and — although occasionally they'll single out one crippled bureaucrat or smelly old politician the way hyenas cull the sick and wounded from a herd of wildebeests — they invariably suck up to those who already have what they want.

It's called "symbiosis."

People in the mass media tend more and more every day to look and act like elected and appointed officials. Remember that; it may be important later on.

They've long since given up the task of telling us what's happening in the world and become *merchants of fear* instead, preaching at us incessantly — for the sake of their corrupt collusive partnership with the bureaucrats and politicians — that the sky is about to fall on the backs of our unprotected necks, that we're all helplessly incompetent, and that our neighbors are criminally insane.

Intelligent, capable, and responsible men and women going to work every day to keep civilization running, feeding their families, and bringing their children up healthy and strong inevitably make lousy welfare-state politics, as well. Which explains why there's never really any good news, and why, if you watch television or read newspapers or magazines, life never seems to get any better.

Lever Action

At all costs, the merchants of fear and their political symbionts must avoid the *menace of solved problems,* which — exactly like the embarrassment of intelligent, capable, and responsible men and women going to work every day to keep civilization running, feeding their families, and bringing their children up healthy and strong — offer them nothing in the way of profit, politically or financially. They have to be careful, because there are solved problems everywhere they look.

Violent crime is a solved problem — all they have to do is repeal the laws that keep those intelligent, capable, and responsible men and women from arming themselves, and violent crime evaporates like dry ice on a hot summer day.

Poverty is a solved problem — all they have to do is abolish taxes and regulations that cripple those intelligent, capable, and responsible men and women and destroy their productive capacity, then stand back and watch the economy boom.

Health care is a solved problem — all they have to do is institute a Constitutional separation of medicine and state — no, let's make it *science* and state — and those intelligent, capable, and responsible men and women will make the price of health care plummet while the quality of health care soars.

Drugs are a solved problem — all they have to do is declare an end to the war on drugs (*U.S. Out of America!*), take the government-inflated profits out of the traffic, and watch the drug-war's walking wounded gradually transform themselves back into intelligent, capable, and responsible men and women. And by the way, Rush, wrong again: From the time the first prehuman, down from the trees on the Serengeti Plain, decided to eat leopard instead of being eaten, morality has never been defined in any way *except* by individual choice.

We all know it's true.

We also know that what I said before is true — that solved problems are a menace, offering no profit, politically or financially, to the merchants of fear or their political symbionts. Likewise, those intelligent, capable, and responsible men and women are a menace in and of themselves, offering the merchants of fear and their political symbionts neither clients nor victims. What *does* offer unlimited profit of both kinds is their daily calculated destruction of the Bill of Rights, so that society will continue to shake itself to pieces, generating plenty of gory colorful pictures for the cameras of the merchants of fear — and plenty of unrestricted power for their political symbionts.

Once again, it's called "symbiosis."

So, what can we do about it? I'm here tonight to offer three answers to that question, and you can pick whatever you like best and put it to use.

Here's answer number one:.

Everybody here will remember the way the state of Florida made it easier several years ago — despite all sorts of hysteria from the merchants of fear — for intelligent, capable, and responsible men and women to carry a concealed weapon for self-defense: Over a period when violent crime rose thirty percent in America, it fell ten percent in Florida, for an aggregate drop of forty percent.

It's an axiom among street-level law enforcement that you can't really eradicate crime, you can only *move* it. Some believe that using "The Club" gave rise to carjacking. Muggers in Florida began to pick on foreigners because they were afraid that their domestic victims might be armed.

Merchants of fear, desperate to discredit the principle of individual self-defense, treated these incidents, no more than a dozen in all, as if they were a crime wave (during the same period, several times that number of foreigners were mugged in New York City), while failing to report the real drop in Florida crime.

This politically selective reportage of Florida crime gave me an idea — why not do exactly the same thing to the merchants of fear? Over the past couple of decades, several organizations have been formed to monitor them — Accuracy in Media comes to mind — and yet the situation hasn't gotten any better.

What if a widespread group of individuals (there are National Rifle Association chapters in practically every county in America, after all, and Libertarian Party organizations in every state) began gathering local reports of misconduct by members of the mass media — everything from running a stop sign to murder — and issuing national press releases about them? What if statistical records were disseminated by a "media information clearing house" that treated the merchants of fear disproportionately and inappropriately — made them all appear to be criminals or potential criminals — just the way they treat us?

But wait, there's more.

Here's answer number two.

Some years ago, there was a series of debates on college campuses all over the country between arch-ultra-conservative G. Gordon Liddy, and semi-quasi-libertarian Timothy Leary. To my eternal regret, I never saw any of these debates and I don't know what points this pair of historic titans argued, but I understand they were a lot of fun, everybody involved made some money, and the debates themselves were completely phony — that Liddy and Leary, in fact, became fast friends who found less and less to disagree about as time went on.

It makes a great story, anyway.

I don't know whether the story is true or false, but thinking about it gave me an idea. Even before the recent elevation of Channel 9's assistant news director Butch Montoya to the position of Denver's manager of public safety, I was prepared to point out that individuals in the mass media see themselves as keepers of the public trust — at least they used to talk about that a lot — and that the corporations they work for, like all corporations, enjoy special powers and immunities by virtue of incorporation that raise them above the level of mere mortals like you and me and make them virtually an arm of the government.

"Virtually an arm of the government" — that ought to tell us something right there. Individuals who work for government customarily take a binding oath to "uphold and defend the Constitution against all enemies foreign and domestic." It's expected of them. In fact, they're compelled by the law to do so.

"Compelled by the law" — there's another phrase to conjure with, unless I'm greatly mistaken. If the merchants of fear were compelled by the law to take a binding oath to uphold and defend the Constitution against all enemies foreign and domestic, and if they were held to it stringently, if it were enforced, the American mass media — television, newspapers, and news magazines — would be completely unrecognizable within a week and no Democrat (and damn few Republicans) would ever be elected to office in this country again.

Now understand me when I say that, as libertarians, as members of the Libertarian Party, we would be morally and politically obligated to oppose such an idea, as an infringement of the First Amendment, but that it would be highly likely to find considerable support among our conservative fellow-travelers.

Like G. Gordon Liddy, to name a random example.

So thoroughly would we libertarians oppose such an idea — and I must say I'm surprised and shocked at myself for having thought of it — that it would probably be necessary to hold well-publicized debates, perhaps even on local-access cable television, in each of the fifty-two or -three states and territories in which libertarians are organized and on the ballot, and maybe even in the hundreds of cities and counties where there are Libertarian Parties, to wit:

"Resolved that all individuals involved at every level of production in the mass media be compelled by the law to take a binding oath, stringently enforced, to uphold and defend the Constitution against all enemies foreign and domestic."

Maybe we could even get William F. Buckley interested in sponsoring this revolutionary proposition as one of his "Firing Line" debates. Naturally, as Bill of Rights- and First Amendment-fearing citizens, we libertarians would take the negative. Our conservative fellow-travelers would take the affirmative.

Both sides would win.

The merchants of fear would lose.

But wait, there's *still* more.

Here's answer number three:

Our conservative fellow-travelers say that we're presently engaged in a "culture war" with the liberal Northeast, and I agree. The trouble is, you can't expect to win a snowball fight without snowballs; the other side has more ammunition — or greater respect for its ammunition supply — than ours does.

My novel *Pallas* is all about that culture war — in fact it's been called the *Uncle Tom's Cabin* of the Sagebrush Rebellion — and yet what I hear all too often from libertarians is that they don't read fiction. And what I hear all too often from our conservative fellow-travelers is that they don't read at all.

In order to fight a culture war, you gotta have culture. Believe me, history demonstrates that fiction inspires people to act in a way that non-fiction cannot. *Uncle Tom's Cabin* ended slavery in America; *Rocketship Galileo* put Americans on the Moon; *Atlas Shrugged* created the modern libertarian movement. Fiction tells truths that are more profound — or at least it tells the truth more profoundly than non-fiction. First thing to-morrow morning, call Laissez Faire and get their catalog. Buy as many of my books as possible — see, I know which side my bread is buttered on, too — and check out the works of a dozen other libertarian novelists in print.

Don't let our conservative fellow-travelers have a mo-nopoly on talk radio. If you want to do something simple, call the program director of every radio station you can receive, once a week for the next six months, and tell them they need to put a libertarian on the air. You may mention my name if you wish.

Politically, we are living through unprecedentedly terrible times — times when the government can murder a hundred people, a dozen of them children, in broad daylight on national television, and not only get away with it, but put the surviving victims on trial. But because of that, we are also living in times of tremendous opportunity. If libertarians — as a movement and as a culture — fail to take advantage of them, it will be nobody's fault but our own.

Thank you.

The Manchurian Lobbyist
ඬ ඬ ඬ ඬ ඬ

Gil Russell, Agent
The Meredith Scott Literary Agency
523 Third Avenue, New York, NY 10023

Dear Gil:

After writing 18 SF novels in 15 years, it's time for a

change. How about a thriller that'll keep you up and turning pages all night?

In the background, DoD has become no more than a welfare system for redundant engineers and foundering corporations. The military is only good for beating up on Third World losers, and can't tell an airliner from an enemy fighter-bomber. Against foes foreign and domestic, the only bulwark of America's unique historical institutions is an armed citizenry, growing restive under, and increasingly vocal about, an unbearable burden of taxes.

My first characters are left-politicos led by a senile, obsessive — but totally fictional — senator from Ohio and his colleague, a semi-convicted murderer from Massachussetts. They form a bipartisan cabal with the president, an ancient preppie bright enough to see that he's the Jimmy Carter of the GOP and determined to become its Lyndon Johnson if he has to destroy the republic in order to save it. They scheme to strip Americans of the hardware politicians always find so discouraging and turn people back into the loot-producing serfs Alexander Hamilton intended them to be.

They enlist the nation's top gun-control advocates, which look like any wine-and-cheese liberal pressure group. In fact, they're memberless fronts originally created by a Nixonian Odessa of ex-CIA types determined to drag Dick — or his political ideas — out of cryogenics where he stored himself two decades ago and prop him up in the Oval Office for one last hurrah. The spooks control the so-called mental-health industry, grim gulags where the light of the Constitution never shines and real-life mad scientists pump helpless captives full of memory-cauterizing voltage and identity-dissolving chemicals, producing customized high-tech zombies, sent home on disability payments to watch daytime TV and gobble Twinkies with inhuman patience until they're needed.

Now, periodically we get enough of the gore that electronic fear-merchants splash across our living-room carpets every night, or fed up with intrusive incessant nagging labeled "public-service messages." Some of us appear to have absorbed the fact that the Bill of Rights means what it says and that the state's latest moral substitute for war is being waged against freedom itself. It's then that one of these zombies gets a call with key words buried in it, "You have miles to go and promises to keep, Orville-Bob...," and takes up his saturdaynight-special or his evilassaultrifle (depending how he's been programmed), while the senators, spooks, and fear-merchants warm up the public-relations machinery.

The zombie finds a Campfire Girls convention and blows away as many photogenic victims as possible, then eats his front sight and yanks the trigger one more time. Psycho-vultures descend on the community and the media make a big deal of his history of mental illness without mentioning the 20,000 laws already on the books, which forbid him to own guns. Instead, they blame tens of millions of innocent gun owners (the killer isn't available for a post-bloodbath interview, but his neighbors all say he was very quiet), give 51% of their time to the front-groups that built the killer in the first place and 51% to the spineless, dull-witted, militantly moderate president and the senators from Ohio and Massachussetts who "spontaneously" produce a 1,500-page bill depriving us not only of guns, but of kitchen knives, keyrings, and fingernails.

Not one reporter asks why liberal Democrats are in bed with Nixon's CIA.

Anyone who tries to point out that this spectacular and convenient mass-Osterizing happened the very week the legislature began deliberating gun laws and that similar "coincidences" have occurred in three states over the last six months, is kept off the air at all costs. Maybe he'll get locked up and become the next trigger-zombie.

The new bill violates 153 Constitutional provisions and includes a death penalty for even thinking about Dan'l Boone's flintlock, but gets befuddled blessings from the president. TV keeps the pressure on: Lavishing thousands of praise-filled airhours on the "courageous" senators who wrote it, they simultaneously condemn it as too moderate, a sellout to the gun lobby.

Now for a plot-twist. The rich, powerful, multimillion-member group created to defend the principle of armed citizenry to the death (and take whatever heat ol' Prez won't accept as his part of the deal) inexplicably finds itself weak, poor, and inclined to compromise — although the media characterize it as unyielding. Its official spokesmen help by shaving their heads to enchance an already amazing resemblance to Nikita Khruschev. We don't find out until the next-to-last chapter that it's as stuffed with ex-Nixonites as the so-called liberal gun-control organizations.

I haven't figured out how the conspiracy gets exposed, but I gotta have a happy ending. Maybe, although they don't know it, the spooks were conditioned to kill themselves like zombies, to give the president credible deniability. The senators are convicted under a little-known statute for violating their oath of office and sent to a high-walled place with bars — where the regular tenants treat them the same way they've been treating Senate pages for years.

Maybe I should update it to include a president who really is a clone of Jimmy Carter and his wife, a reincarnation of Joan Crawford.

The media — this is where I'm having trouble. My first thought was, once the plot was exposed, they changed their ways when they realized that their First Amendment rights weren't any more secure than the Second Amendment rights of the gun owners they persecute. But I can hear you saying right now that no editor will go for that.

This is a novel, after all.

It has to be believable.

Getting Back at TV Propagandists
ço ço ço ço ço

As a novelist, I have a higher soapbox to stand on than most when it comes to talking back to the enemies of liberty. Yet it makes me just as mad when ABC, NBC, CBS, PBS, CNN, and NPR not only lie consistently and blatantly about the individual right to own and carry weapons, but insert their lies into programs billed as "news" and "entertainment."

It's been going on for decades. You know when a politician's lying — his mouth moves — but broadcasters lie with a twitch of an eyebrow or the slant of a shoulder. They load questions for the "man in the street" and get the public to lie for them. They even lie by making sure the badguy in a series episode has rifles and game trophies on his wall.

The most infuriating part is that you can't talk back. Broadcasters take advantage of the fact that any amateur, offered a chance to be on TV, is easily made to look foolish. Ask those who've tried: I give speeches where people laugh in all the right places and grown men weep. The one occasion I tried replying to a TV editorial, I looked like Archie Bunker. Most anti-gun propaganda can't be dealt with in this manner anyway, because the other side's too dishonest to present it as a straightforward editorial.

Since the Bill of Rights protects a broadcaster's freedom under the First Amendment to attack our freedom under the

Second, the next thought that occurs to the irate viewer is to get back at propagandists through their wallets, boycotting programs or their sponsors. I've never been impressed with the tactic. True, you deprive the enemy of income; you also deprive yourself of whatever he produces, maybe something you really need. Sometimes it's worth a sacrifice, sometimes it isn't, and individual opinions always differ.

The main problem is that for a boycott to be effective, you must persuade thousands, even millions, of others to go along — a lot of work and usually not very successful. No matter what this country's self-appointed political and religious leaders claim, self-sacrifice has never been what America is all about and it doesn't work as any kind of incentive. Robert Heinlein put it best when he said it's pointless to appeal to someone's "better nature." He may not have one. Better to appeal to his self-interest.

Which is where my thoughts had led me many times (and dumped me out at what seemed the end of the line) when one day I asked myself the *right question*: If boycotts don't work, what's the *opposite* of a boycott? Obviously, it isn't doing more business with the enemy. How about doing more business with whatever the enemy opposes?

Call it a *negative boycott*.

Since then, when I find myself subjected to anti-gun drivel disguised as "news" or "entertainment," I drop a quarter (or a dime, a nickel, or a penny) into a coffee can I keep beside the chair where I watch TV. Given the rate at which propaganda fills the air, it's no time at all before the can fills up. When enough accumulates, I don't give it to the NRA or any other organization whose policies I neither control nor necessarily approve. I spend it the best way I know, in the free marketplace of ideas — and hardware — acquiring another gun I wouldn't otherwise have bought.

Think about it: Another gun you wouldn't otherwise have bought.

Many benefits are generated this way with minimal effort and no pain. Appeal to the self-interest of enough gun owners, and hundreds of thousands — maybe even millions — of unforeseen gun purchases will occur. This will strengthen the firearms industry relative to the rest of the economy and even put some spine back into outfits that have taken the cowardly historically discredited route of appeasing an oppressor. It didn't work with Hitler; why does Bill Ruger think it'll work with Hitler's spiritual kin, Howard Metzenbaum?

Spotting anti-gun propaganda could make watching network TV interesting again — a minor miracle in itself — and might even develop into an educational game for the whole family. Kids would learn what the public schools never teach and desperately doesn't want them to know: ways to identify logical fallacies, fuzzy or missing verbs, and improperly weighted qualifiers in otherwise authoritative-sounding arguments about homelessness, urban street gangs, acid rain, ozone depletion, global warming, and the war on drugs.

The primary effect will be felt by our opponents as their own soapboxes slowly dissolve under their feet. Even now, each time the greatest sporting-goods sales team in America — Handgun Control Inc. — open their mouths about gun control or push for new legislation, thousands of individuals go out and buy guns of all descriptions "before it's too late." Some estimate that the last flurry of semiauto hysteria sold a quarter of a million such weapons in Colorado alone.

Until now, anti-gunners have encouraged the media to keep the public ignorant of this interesting inconvenient effect. But as word of millions of coffee cans filling up with coins — and suddenly being emptied — gets around, an inexorable certainty that anti-gun propaganda actually causes more guns to be bought will put a damper on broadcasters' enthusiasm to satu-rate the air with lies.

The best part (and most frustrating from the other side's point of view) is that nobody is in a position to think, speak, or act for you. It's your TV, your chair, your coffee can. In your home you're the only judge of what constitutes anti-gun pro-paganda. You decide how much to drop in the can. You're the ultimate beneficiary.

So let your local TV stations — and the networks — know what you're doing. And do it. Then trust in liberal guilt to do the rest.

The Medium is a Massage
ᑲ ᑲ ᑲ ᑲ ᑲ

Thirty years ago, a briefly popular but now nearly forgot-ten Canadian academic, Marshall McLuhan, made some ob-servations about human communications, some of which have outlived their creator.

For example, he was the one who coined the term "global village," although he never knew how cogent that idea would become following the advent of the Internet. He also origi-nated the concept of "linear" and "nonlinear" media — similar today to what we think of as serial and random-access sys-tems, applied to things like newspapers and books.

The most famous McLuhanism was that in modern com-munication, "the medium is the message," that what television communicates is, well, ... *television*. As near as I can make out, what he meant was that when we sit down to watch TV, that's *exactly* what we're doing. We're not sitting down to watch

Dan Rather (be still my stomach) or even *Buffy the Vampire Slayer* (be still my ... never mind), we're simply sitting down to watch *TV*, without much regard to the actual content.

In his day (I was young then, only starting on the long road to becoming a major social annoyance), I thought McLuhan was an overrated pseudo-intellectual. Looking back, there may have been a little to what he said. For example, one of the reasons this culture's in such a sorry state is that, instead of listening to talk radio to hear the *ideas* of Ken Hamblin, Gordon Liddy, Rush Limbaugh, Mike Reagan, and their guests, many listen to talk radio to hear talk radio, a sort of daily auditory wallpaper that enfolds and comforts them and validates their own ideas without challenging any of their prejudices.

Of course, liberals — make that "left-wing socialists" — already rely on this, dedicating every second of the media they control, TV and the movies, to advancing their evil and stupid agenda without disturbing what they imagine is their viewers' ideological slumber.

But it's vastly more interesting (in the Chinese sense) to watch the conservative — make that "right-wing socialist" — Rush Limbaugh apply the McLuhan principle. Each year his daily broadcasts have grown less challenging, more predictable, and ... I guess the only word is "soporific." Apparently, the Formerly Fat One sees his life's work as preventing an increasingly disgusted GOP rank and file from bolting a party that deserves it more than any other party has in history. (Yes, *including* the Commies when they signed their non-aggression pact with Hitler. The low, cowardly, crawling, yellowbellied, abject, obsequious, sniveling, pusillanimous surrender of Senate and House Republicans to Bill Clinton on every vital issue of the day is fully as reprehensible and disgusting.) What this requires is allowing his callers to discharge their anger safely, calming them down, and labeling those who won't be calmed down — perhaps because, unlike Rush, they still have something resembling integrity — "kooks."

Rush used to rub people the wrong way, and there was great value in that. But now he's just the national masseur. Unfortunately, that's not what got him where he is and it marks the beginning of the end for him as a shaper of America's political future. Perhaps he's even satisfied to sacrifice himself that way and retire.

But in the words of Patchett and Tarses, "I couldn't live like that."

Parallax

For Writers in the Round, March 16, 1990

☙ ☙ ☙ ☙ ☙

Ladies and gentlemen, I'm not a Toastmaster — I'm more of an Osterizer, actually — and I don't memorize my speeches, so you'll forgive the occasional reference I make to my notes. I promise you it won't be as painful as this handful of paper may indicate.

On the other hand, how did it turn out last time a dentist told you it won't hurt a bit?

Human beings have two eyes aimed in roughly the same direction, because each offers a slightly differing view of the world. The contrasting images they produce, superimposed in a portion of the brain called the thalamus, give us an "in-depth" picture of our environment, containing more information than would both viewpoints considered separately. We call such a picture "three dimensional," and the physical phenomenon which makes it possible is called "parallax."

For the same reason, we have two ears to tell us not just the direction noise comes from, but how far away the source is. Parallax informs us which way the train is coming from, where the woodwinds are relative to the brass, and who's the better guitar soloist in the Eagles' historic live performance of "Hotel California."

I often wonder if we don't have two nostrils to serve a similar purpose and whether we might have not only "smellivision" someday, but "smelleo," as well. Of course, that technical development was impeded in the 1950s by the popularity of TV westerns.

Notice that we don't argue about which viewpoint is "right." We accept the data from each of our eyes or ears or nostrils for whatever they're worth in building a mental image of what's going on around us. If we only had one eye apiece, one ear, or maybe even one nostril — a state I'm generally reduced to, thanks to my allergies — that mental image would be a great deal less informative, less enjoyable, and less useful in the individual struggle to survive.

It isn't simply individuals who struggle to survive, but entire species, and as a species we're equipped with mechanisms to take advantage of the phenomenon of parallax, as surely as we do with binocular vision, stereophonic hearing, and "smelleo." Over the past decade, for example, science has at last confirmed what we really knew all along — that men and women possess different neuroarchitecture and brain chemistry, which cause them to evaluate the evidence of their senses differently and arrive at different values and priorities.

This may not be "politically correct" thinking at the moment — more and more it appears to me that thinking itself is no longer politically correct — but it's scientifically verifiable, and it's extremely good news for all of us as a species.

Lever Action

Access to more than one point of view greatly increases the likelihood of correctly identifying the nature of reality and enhances the probability of survival. If a woman sees the world one way and a man sees it another, the resulting "three-dimensional" view — provided they can accept it and the mechanism that produced it — can be an endless wellspring of prosperity and delight.

We may never be precisely certain how male and female values and priorities differ, because individual human beings also vary from one another without respect to gender. Old people and young people, just to name a single example, exhibit differing views of the world, which produce differing values and priorities. But we don't need to understand them to accept that they exist and benefit from them.

As you might well anticipate, astronomers benefit from the phenomenon of parallax by taking pictures of the sky six months apart — that is, from opposite points along the Earth's orbit around the Sun — and comparing the images in various ways. It's like having a pair of binoculars 186 million miles wide.

We derive our broadest social parallax, our best three-dimensional image of human reality from the viewpoints, values, and priorities of differing cultures. If you're a productive-class American but you learn to see the world — even for a moment, at the most superficial level — the way it looks all the time to the Japanese or Moslems, then your life will be extended and enriched in more than spiritual or intellectual terms. To sell an icebox to an Eskimo or a manuscript to a New York editor, it helps to be able think like an Eskimo or an editor.

Naturally, not everything is culturally relative. Not every viewpoint is objectively valid. Civilizations have disintegrated and collapsed because their viewpoints, values, and priorities were dead wrong. For an individual observer, however, any viewpoint can be useful, and in the extreme instance, it's always worthwhile to peer out at the world for a while through the eyes of your enemy.

Also naturally, the whole process gets short-circuited if I force you to look at things the way I do, or even just to act as if you did. My father has always been angry that his high school stopped teaching German when World War II began — because it was "unpatriotic." He ended up as a prisoner of war in Germany, a situation in which being able to speak the enemy's language might have been advantageous.

All around the world today, closed societies — those societies that forcibly exclude divergent viewpoints, values, and priorities — are rapidly disintegrating and collapsing, while those societies that attempt to remain relatively open continue to prosper in direct proportion to how open they really are. Those relatively open societies of today, in turn, will find themselves vulnerable in the future, as even more open societies spring into existence — a process that I believe will dominate 21st century political life.

Which brings us to my real subject this afternoon, the field in which I've written seventeen and a half books so far, science fiction. It is the purpose of science fiction to grab hold of one of your eyes — metaphorically speaking, of course — and drag it *waaay* out to the side of your head in order to increase the available parallax — and therefore your own three-dimensional view of the universe — by several orders of magnitude. The basic difference between science fiction and horror is that horror does what I just described — literally.

As a medium-sized name in science fiction, I have addressed conventions across the country and lectured at grammar schools, high schools, and university classes. I've been interviewed on television and radio and by magazines and newspapers, which had temporarily run out of the little squibs that inform you that yak milk is pink and were desperate to close up the empty spaces between savings-and-loan advertisments with my equally valuable ideas and opinions. Whenever that happens, the interviewer or reporter's emphasis always seems to be on the idea that a science fiction writer's primary job is to predict the future.

Yes, I tell them, like many another science fiction writer, I have indeed successfuly predicted the future. But fortune-telling is not the most important facet of science fiction. Human behavior — which is what most attempted predictions will be about — is the result of billions of genetic permutations and combinations, multiplied times billions of differing life experiences, multiplied times billions of acts of free will. Look at any individual around you and you're considering the interaction of no fewer than one times ten to the twenty-seventh variables — which means that all human behavior is fundamentally unquantifiable and unpredictable.

It's this observation, by the way, and the resulting inevitable futility of central economic planning, which helped me to predict the collapse of the Soviet Empire.

The most important facet of science fiction is the parallax it strives to create. It's most helpful in this connection to understand that science fiction writers never predict *the* future, but only various possible futures — plural.

Sometimes we predict certain futures in the fond hope that having written about them will help make them come true. Certainly Neil Armstrong would never have walked on the Moon if it hadn't been for the literary advocacy of Robert A. Heinlein.

But self-fulfilling predictions, however satisfactory they may be when they eventually come to pass, hardly make for impressive fortune-telling. Sometimes we predict futures in the fervent hope that, by the very act of writing about them, they *won't* come true — "we" in this case being George Orwell and Aldous Huxley and Margaret Atwood, among others — and our success (which I suspect weather forecasters and government economists have noticed and are desperately trying to imitate) becomes measurable by how wrong we turn out to be.

In my own career — which in this respect is a bit like that of psychic Jean Dixon and other contributors to the *National Inquirer* — I find it most productive to predict the present or the past. My methods and objectives differ somewhat from Ms. Dixon's. I might predict a past in which Napoleon won the Battle of Waterloo, in order to see what kind of present that might have created. Personally, I'm grateful I wasn't born in France, because I can't speak French.

My purpose is to create parallax, to drag your mind's eye way out *here*, in order to let you see the world in greater depth than you might otherwise have done.

My first novel, *The Probability Broach*, is science fiction, but it revolves around the Whiskey Rebellion of 1794 because I felt in 1977 when I began writing it — exactly as I do today — that the American discussion of taxation was too narrow: Should we increase taxes one hundred percent or merely double them? I wanted people to see what America might have been like if taxation were against the law altogether. Apparently, I succeeded to some extent, because the book was published in 1979, has been out of print for many years, and I still get letters and phone calls every month from people whose minds I've managed to change on that issue and several others that the book considers.

How did I do that?

In the first place, by knowing what the hell I was talking about. There is a common view, especially prevalent in Hollywood, that science fiction is wild and crazy stuff, the purest fantasy, and that it doesn't have to make sense. That's one reason, I believe, that science fiction isn't read by more people.

The truth, of course, is that science fiction has to make *more* sense than other fiction, and not just because a technical error of the type or magnitude committed on every other page by Dick Francis or Stephen King will get Larry Niven or L. Neil Smith crucified at conventions by thousands of nitpicking fans.

It has to make more sense than other fiction not just because it's the last remaining genuine literature of ideas that can be found in Western civilization.

It has to make more sense than other fiction because science fiction writers do indeed make predictions — past, present, or future — that are often most difficult to believe when they're closest to the mark. Nobody believed me when I predicted that the Soviet Empire would fail long before the centennial of the Revolution. Science fiction writers therefore labor under a special obligation to convince their readers that these predictions, however unbelievable they may appear, rest solidly on valid observations of the real world.

Does any of this mean that you can't write science fiction if you aren't a scientist or an engineer?

Absolutely not.

"All" you have to be is an honest observer and a careful thinker.

True, you can write science fiction about hardware, like Charles Sheffield or James P. Hogan.

You can write science fiction about software, like Jerry Pournelle or Vernor Vinge.

But you can also write science fiction about "warmware" — meaning human beings — which requires even greater honesty and careful thought, like Zenna Henderson, whose stories of interstellar refugees from an exploding star stranded on Earth contain no science or engineering, as such, yet within their science fiction framework capture the essence of everything it means to be human.

It's true that I'm somewhat better versed in science and technology than the average individual, but that merely reflects my personal interests. My real expertise lies with history, psychology, and anthropology. And that's what you'll see in my books, along with the inevitable politics and economics — and always enough sex and violence to keep those *not* interested in history, psychology, anthropology, politics, or economics turning the pages. I'm happy to say that Robert A. Heinlein recommended my work to at least one aspiring writer on this basis alone.

The book I'm working on right now is about a boy growing up in a pioneer community on Pallas, the second largest asteroid in the Solar System. It's full of technical details about gravity, soil, and wildlife conservation, but it's also the most ambitious love story I've ever undertaken. My next book will concern whatever it is dead people dream about, but despite the topic, which makes it sound like a rather depressing fantasy, I guarantee that it'll make just as much sense as the book I'm writing now — and even have a happy ending!

So if you can remember that your principal objective is to create parallax, and that the farther out you choose take your readers, the more sense you're obligated to make along the way, then you can write science fiction, too.

And now I'll entertain some questions.

I don't promise to answer them, just entertain them ...

Lever Action

I'll Show You Mine
If You'll Show Me Yours —
A Challenge to the Canadian Mass Media
ಂ ಂ ಂ ಂ ಂ

For years I've been comparing the American mass media
to a trade that's only slightly older than professional gossip-
mongering, a trade that requires of its practitioners that they
sell themselves in the most intimate, base, and humiliating
manner to anyone who happens to have the wherewithal to
make the purchase.

I am not without my reasons for making this comparison.
The media will do anything — *anything* — to suck up to government authority. Oh, they may bring down an individual president here, an individual governor there. They may take aim at
this or that individual mayor or city councilman. The lower on
the totem pole of authority the individual happens to be, the
more savage they become. There's nothing they love more than
galloping after their victim in a pack and ripping the guts out
of some poor high school janitor or meter maid.

But I seem to be mixing my metaphors here, don't I?

On the other hand, these paragons of courage and integrity
have never seen a legislative or judicial violation of the Bill of
Rights they weren't willing to cheer hysterically — unless it
was *their* rights that they felt were being threatened. How could
they tell the difference? The rule of thumb is pretty simple,
really. To a member of the mass media, there's only one amendment to the Constitution — the First — and it only applies to
members of the mass media.

If anybody feels that I exaggerate, consider: Where is the
self-righteous soulful hue and cry to put Lon Horiuchi, the cold-
blooded sniper murderer of Vicky and Sammy Weaver, be-

hind bars, compared with the baying and howling that brought Nixon down for sending a few burglars to the Watergate? Why isn't Janet Reno in the same kind of glass box Adolf Eichmann sat in, for what she admits to having ordered done at Mount Carmel near Waco, Texas? Why didn't the so-called adversary press bring down the Philadelphia city government for the MOVE bombing? Where were they when RICO erased the Fourth and Fifth Amendments?

Lately, I've been reminded that there are significant differences between honest whoring and what we've learned to refer to delicately as "journalism." For one thing, after the workday is finally over, an honest whore can take a shower and douche, use a little mouthwash, and consider herself off duty. She may even get lucky, win the lottery or fall in love with Mr. Right, and leave "the life." A journalist remains what he is 24 hours a day, seven days a week. The thought of leaving "the life" invariably fills him with unutterable horror. And an *honest* journalist is an even rarer commodity than an honest politician.

Lately it appears (to nobody's great surprise) that Canadian journalism is an even sloppier-crotched doxy than its putrescently corrupt American sister. It seems that its toadyish practitioners are sycophantically determined to portray attendees at a Libertarian convention in British Columbia as racists and neo-fascists, for no reason better than that libertarians tend to preach self-sufficiency and customarily grant little or no legitimacy to round-heeled journalism's regular paying customer, established authority. Also, because "racist neo-fascist" is what you call folks you hate *this* year. Last year, I seem to recall it was "child molester." And two generations ago it was "communist."

Well, as one who has been similarly slimed by Canadian journalists — and kicked their slats out on the Internet on their own terms, until they laid off for a blessed while — I have a little challenge for our ink-stained brothers and sisters to the north. What do you say we compare 100,000 words' worth of editorials taken at random from "mainstream" Canadian newspapers and magazines with a similar amount of material from libertarian publications? Which do you suppose will contain the greater number of sexist, racist, elitist, or fascist ideas?

Be warned, however: We libertarians are considerably more fastidious than you are in these matters (which, after all, was the point of this essay). If, just as an example, you can't *prove* that affirmative action is a non-racist concept — on the grounds that it assumes that people of color can't compete in a free market and therefore must be "helped along" by the government at everybody else's involuntary expense — its advocacy is going to count against you.

If that sort of challenge doesn't appeal to you, then try this: Can any one of you go a single year — 365 days — without once advocating the use of *initiated* force against somebody, which is to say, beating him up and killing him for some pet political end? Hundreds of thousands of libertarians have been doing exactly that for *decades*. For all these years they've been doing more than thinking, more than talking, more than writing, they've been acting *ethically* — consistently, even when it wasn't easy — when you don't even know the meaning of the word. So tell me, just who is the real fascist, here?

The libertarians you mindlessly attack are better "liberals" than you are. They believe in free speech, in a free exchange of ideas, in freedom itself, when every day you demonstrate clearly that you don't. Look that word up in the dictionary — liberal — then hang your head in shame. But they're more than that, as well. They're something new, something never seen before on this poor, sorry, bloodsoaked planet, although we had a brief glimpse 220 years ago in the men who signed the Declaration that your ancestors scorned and ran away from.

These uncommonly kindly, unprecedentedly decent, intelligently gentle people — these libertarians — are the only hope our poor bloodsoaked planet has left.

If you dispute any of that, then there's my challenge, still hanging in the air between us. Compare our writings to yours. Compare our deeds to yours.

And if you're afraid to do that, then shut up.

Robert Heinlein Remembered

Take big bites. Anything worth doing is worth overdoing.
Robert A. Heinlein, *Time Enough for Love*

Imagine a lonely kid, undersized and overbright, living on an American air base overseas. Comic books taught him to read years before he started school and he'd tackle anything that fell open under his eyes. Anything about science or space travel leaped off the page as if printed in boldfaced italic. A neighbor's medical texts had such delightfully disgusting diseases you could practice having, and radio magazines ... in those days radios had vacuum-filled glass cylinders, see, and — radio?

You know, TV for blind people?

One day, sent to the library as punishment (so much, he grinned to himself, for the intelligence of authority), he ran across two books he hadn't seen before, *Red Planet* and *Tunnel in the Sky*. As would be the case years later with a certain little old Russian lady's name, he didn't know how to pronounce "Heinlein."

But the latter novel, he discovered, was about kids not much older than he was, slung across the galaxy as a graduation exercise to survive or die on a planet not even described to them beforehand. The protagonist's big sister, a tough Marine, gives him her favorite fighting knife to carry as a spare, a gift both practical and sentimental. (In time the reader would learn that Heinlein didn't see much difference between the two.) In the other book, even younger kids, on colonial Mars, rebel because the new headmaster at their company school confiscates the weapons they've always believed it their natural right to carry.

To the Air Force kid, this was powerful stuff that bent his head severely. He's writing this because it never got unbent. As a matter of fact, it got worse. But first he looked for more books by this guy Heinlein. What they were about, he found, besides science and space, was individual competence and the suicidal insanity of weighting it with political chains. What's more, each taught him something about the universe, the culture he lived in and, often, whether he liked it or not, himself.

Without knowing it, Heinlein became the advisor, confidant, sometimes the only friend of his childhood, setting standards against which the boy eventually came to measure all his adult conduct and achievement.

Over the past thirty years, I don't suppose a single day has gone by that I haven't thought about Robert A. Heinlein. The lessons I learned from him were endless, as they were bound to be, coming from a man of his pragmatic wisdom and a body of literature exceeding three million published words.

It's hard to recapitulate the second chance he offered my generation, given the abject failure of public schooling, since most of what he taught I've long since taken as self-evident. It certainly wasn't when I learned it; it was often painful and confusing. But it was needed. Twentieth century America's method of rearing its young fails to produce organisms fit for — or worthy of — survival.

If I cite different lessons at this moment than I might another time, if I discuss them in a different order than I received them, if I select different items than you might, that's one definition of art, isn't it? It's also a measure of the fact that, above all, Heinlein taught us to accept his wisdom without becoming followers. He taught us to become, and to remain, individuals.

The Green Hills of Earth formed my first coherent vision of the future, establishing the historical context for my own life, convincing me (as kids must be if they're to turn out civilized) that, just as millions of human beings preceded me in past ages, so millions more will follow in ages to come. At the same time, *Methuselah's Children* revealed to me that, yes, I do want to live forever, and that such a thing, given time and the stubborn application of reason, might just be possible.

Between Planets taught me that a kid never knows when the demands of adulthood will tap him on the shoulder. There are worse things that could happen. *Starman Jones* taught me that the adult world makes about as much sense as the average train wreck, and that it's the first duty of anyone who aspires to be a whole human being to start re-making the world the way he wants it. Toward that end, *Time for the Stars* showed me that the universe can be a bizarre hostile place, but that my feelings about that are irrelevant to dealing with it.

Citizen of the Galaxy showed me that it was possible — and important — to stand outside my own culture and try to examine it like an anthropologist or a visiting alien. "If This Goes On ..." from *Revolt in 2100* warned me that, in any culture, things are never what they appear at first glance. At the age of twelve, I was just as shocked as the viewpoint character to learn what was going on between the Prophet Incarnate's palace guards and his attendant Virgins.

Lever Action

Always listen to experts. They'll tell you what can't be done,
and why. Then do it.
Robert A. Heinlein, *"The Notebooks of Lazarus Long"*

Farnham's Freehold asserted that nobody — no race, religion, or ethnic group — has a monopoly on incompetence or cruelty, and *The Day After Tomorrow* argued back that a conclusion is never foregone, that the struggle is never over as long as one good man or woman is still alive. It also gave me a second lesson (my first was in *Double Star*) in how to cut up and dispose of a body, a skill I haven't needed yet, but you can never tell.

Beyond This Horizon proved to my satisfaction that "an armed society is a polite society," long before I had a firsthand chance to see it demonstrated over and over again in real life.

Glory Road taught me, as a novelist and a human being, that life goes on after they all live happily ever after. I've never believed love is all you need, or that it'll always find a way, but *The Door Into Summer* (along with *Double Star*, my favorite of Heinlein's books) brought me closer to changing my mind about that than any other book I've read. It also taught me that the most brilliant innovation is useless unless it rests on a foundation of necessity and familiarity.

Space Cadet represented another sort of graduation exercise for someone who was slated to become an individualist-anarchist. I often think about writing an entire essay dedicated to comparing it in detail with Arthur C. Clarke's superficially similar *Islands in the Sky*, in order to demonstrate metaphysical differences in worldview between the productive class and the parasitic over- and under-classes. In case I never get around to it, read both books — asking the question, "Who or what is responsible, in each instance, for whatever the protagonist achieves?"

412

In a sense, however, this is a futile exercise, not even scratching the surface of a lifetime's education. Other lessons I learned from Heinlein, I'll talk about another day. Let me dispose of the canard, as anyone could who actually reads his books (as opposed to whatever it is critics do), that he was a militarist, a racist, or a sexist.

Starship Troopers takes the most heat, which is peculiar, since the society it describes is founded by soldiers fed up with war, no conscription is permitted, the franchise won by military service (aggressively coeducational military service) doesn't apply until the service is over with, and the book's hero, like many Heinlein characters, is (unobtrusively) non-white.

Heinlein's alleged sexism amounts to this: He contemplated humanity as a product of billions of years of evolution by natural selection. Successful specimens were accomplished: heroic individualistic killer-apes, the most dangerous and relentless predators on the planet and, it remains to be hoped, in the galaxy. Half these dangerous relentless predators were women, whom his male characters valued and desired (incessantly, as what healthy male predator wouldn't?) as sexual partners.

But if that wasn't intolerable enough for the critics, these treacherous politically unfashionable females like sex themselves! (Usually with dangerous relentless male predators.) It appears he was married to such a woman. Because of what he taught me, so am I — another unpayable debt I owe him. And what more fascinating subject could a man find to write about?

Heinlein's real crime, of course, was the same as Ayn Rand's, and to a certain type with which the Libertarian movement seems particularly burdened, unforgivable. In a universe with few obvious signposts, he set standards that reason and experience suggested to him. It wasn't enough that he lived by them; he assessed others in terms of how well they succeeded — or failed — to measure up, calling things by their true names,

413

acting on their real nature, rather than anybody's wishes and fears. (It's most interesting to observe this in his fantasy novel *Waldo and Magic, Incorporated*.) This always angers and frightens those for whom an excuse is as good as a deed accomplished, for whom a well-chosen euphemism can affect the ethical quality of a deed.

> *Freedom begins when you tell Mrs. Grundy*
> *to go take a hike.*
> Robert A. Heinlein, *"The Notebooks of Lazarus Long"*

One crime, of course, leads to another, as surely as consuming mother's milk leads to heroin abuse. Heinlein's standard, like Rand's, was heroic. If I had a dime for every idiot who claims that real people aren't like that, that the heroes Rand and Heinlein wrote about don't exist, I wouldn't worry about publishers paying me on time. Not only do they exist, but Heinlein did a better job than Rand (who was occupied with other tasks) of teaching us to value the heroic in fiction, in real life, and — few lessons are as important — in enemies as well as friends.

Those who know Lazarus Long, Wyoming Knott, and Friday tend to like Han Solo, Marion Ravenwood, and Thomas Sullivan Magnum (an Oscar Gordon who, in a fictional universe less kind than Heinlein's, never found his Star). They have no trouble recognizing real heroes like Alvin York, H. Ross Perot (before he ran for president, when he was personally rescuing his employees from Iran), or Bernie Goetz, nor do they fail to appreciate, from a prudent ethical distance, heroic "villains" like Gordon Liddy and Oliver North. They know that what the Libertarian Party needs is a John Joseph Bonforte and what it always seems to get, in the end, is Nehemiah Scudder.

Some while back, in a local restaurant, my wife and I met an old couple from Carthage, Missouri, not far away mentally or geographically from Butler, where the papers say Heinlein was born. We happened to be the only four patrons in the room, and the old lady was up and examining photos of turn-of-the-century Fort Collins. Her sister, she explained, having looked us over and decided we were safe, had attended college here in Nineteen Ought-Something and wanted to know what had become of her alma mater.

I grew up in Fort Collins as much as my wandering Air Force life allowed, came back to college in 1964, and saw Old Main, subject of the restaurant's largest photo, erected in the 1870s as the first campus building, burn to the ground in that strange violent summer of 1968. I'd stood in the door of a bike shop across the street and felt the intolerable heat of it on my face. Telling the old lady about that started her off on the time her church burned down, what the firechief, the minister, and the insurance adjustor had said, the makeshifts they'd put up with before a new church was raised.

As old folks will, she rambled on about people I didn't know and didn't care about. I had my own preoccupations (I'd just heard that Heinlein had died) and had to exert every ounce of "mercy to the weak and patience with the stupid" his stories ever managed to exhort me to.

She didn't say anything unusually offensive (I admit that if I didn't feel bound by the Non-Aggression Principle, there wouldn't be a church left standing above its own ashes west of the Mississippi) and I even got an impression — something vague about a nephew who'd just re-enlisted in the Navy, another coincidence — that she'd pull off one of her arms and hand it to you if you were in need of it. But she reminded me of every tight-mouthed self-righteous Baptist I'd known in northern Florida where I went to high school; people who assumed, despite a basic ignorance of everything since Copernicus, that where they lived, how they thought and felt, what they were, was exactly where and how and what all human beings ought to live and think and feel and be, in Big G's image, Q.E.D. Anybody who differed, who valued the Bill of Rights, say, was a damnyankee liberal, affectatious, and perverse for the sheer pleasure of it.

I was dressed as I usually am, 14-inch boots, faded Levis, loud shirt with pearl snaps, wide belt with nickel-silver buckle embossed with longhorns and ponies. She made an assumption about my attitude toward life and events, that they didn't differ from those of a churchgoing Missouri sodbuster, which I usually enjoy demolishing. Wait until she found out I was an anarchist, an atheist, a connoisseur of pornography, a professional despoiler of American youth!

But for once something restrained me. I remained polite, didn't argue, listened through her whole dissertation, and suddenly understood how remarkably far Heinlein had propelled himself from this "American Gothic" mindset through a lifetime that, however long it had lasted, was far too short, for him and for me.

Centuries hence, when the difficult dangerous age we're living through is written of, what historians will say about the "Crazy Years" will resemble what was first written about them by a science fiction novelist decades before they began. The libertarian movement must go far to prove itself, but it may prove to be the one bright spot in an otherwise bleak era. The shadows of two powerful minds cast themselves over everything about that movement, whether we recognize it or not: the minds of Ayn Rand and Robert A. Heinlein.

What's astonishing isn't that Rand and Heinlein differed with one another, but that, coming from such different directions, they agreed so often. Neither of these giants was very

416

happy being called libertarian, yet the monument Rand left us can't be effaced, no matter how many pests pay pigeon respects to it. She gave Libertarianism a philosophical discipline to serve as its brain and backbone. What Heinlein gave it, no less vital if we're to effect the changes we aspire to, was heart and guts.

Both gifts were needed. As we've had occasion to observe, brain and backbone by themselves produce humorless puppets, wrenching without effect at their own strings. Equally, heart and guts, undisciplined, result in the directionless flailing we're used to seeing among conservatives. Perhaps the idea of Libertarianism, the unique concept of the Non-Aggression Principle, should have been enough, but with origins in this particular culture at this particular time, it was doomed to succumb, sooner or later, to cancerous factionalism among its proponents or a paralysis of liberaloid self-doubt.

Combined, however, the unique idea of Libertarianism, supplemented by suitable amounts of brain, heart, guts, and backbone, may just give us a ten-toe hold on the unstoppable wave of the future.

Serf's up!

> *Beat the plowshares back into swords.*
> *The other was a maiden aunt's dream.*
> Robert A. Heinlein, *The Puppet Masters*

Lever Action

Don Henley's Revenge
An Open Letter to America's Old Media
లు లు లు లు లు

A libertarian is a person who believes that no one has the right, under any circumstances, to *initiate* force against another human being, or to advocate or delegate its initiation. Those who act consistently with this principle are libertarians whether they realize it or not. Those who fail to act consistently with it are *not* libertarians, regardless of what they may claim.

I respect the fundamental right involved, but I've never cared much for militias. I'm an *individualist*. As anyone who knows me will attest, I don't play well in groups.

Recent media attempts, however — using events like Oklahoma City and BATF harassment of Georgia and Arizona militiamen — to tar libertarians with a brush of racist neofascism, have accomplished what the pleading of friends never could.

I know many individuals who've never smoked tobacco, yet consider themselves "political smokers" (defending the basic right to choose). I know flaming heterosexuals who consider themselves "politically gay." Thanks to the corruption of the round-heeled media, which have transformed themselves from government's adversary into an eagerly cooperative fourth branch, I now consider myself enlisted — politically speaking — in the militia.

As my first official act, I advise the media to take a good look at the quotation above. It's called the "Non-Aggression Principle." It's what Libertarianism is about. It's *all* that Libertarianism is about. It's all that Libertarianism was *ever* about. It's the heart and soul of Libertarianism, a lens through which libertarians view *everything*.

We've been trying to tell you this for 25 years, but you

preferred to portray us as nutsies in propellor beanies, and now, as *terrorists*. (I suspect for no better reason than that you, being products of public education, are incapable of *reading* the Non-Aggression Principle, let alone understanding it or calculating its ramifications.)

But I digress.

Does the Non-Aggression Principle look like something a terrorist believes? Or like something decent folks believe, who want a *less* violent world to live in, for themselves and their kids? Decent folks you've mocked, misquoted, defamed, misrepresented, and just plain lied about for a quarter of a century.

Who the hell are *you* to judge me or anybody else? To the last specimen, you're ignorant of history, law, economics, science; all you know is newsroom politics and competing brands of hairspray. You're fear merchants, spinning fantasies of global warming, ozone depletion, acid rain, desertification, secondhand smoke, vanishing millions of kids — each phony crisis designed as another excuse to increase government control over our lives — when you know perfectly well there isn't a shred of scientifically respectable evidence to support the least of these pseudoscientific hoaxes.

Who are you to condemn anyone — whose first political concern happens to be the Bill of Rights, who happens not to believe the liars who gave us Vietnam, Watergate, Ruby Ridge, and Waco, who happens to be dissatisfied with both established parties, who happens to be interested in guns — who are you to condemn those whose only crime is exercising their inalienable individual, civil, Constitutional, and human rights?

I'll *tell* you: a self-congratulatory gaggle of hypocritical prostitutes who believe there's only one amendment to the Constitution and that it only applies to you. Anyone who thinks there's a significant difference between *The National Inquirer* and *The New York Times*, between Robin Leach and Peter

Jennings, possesses more imagination than intelligence, and probably thinks there's a significant difference between Democrats and Republicans.

Until now, as uncritical worshippers of socialist authority in all its vile forms, your joyously self-assigned job has been to convey government lies and threats to the public, while making every individual undertaking appear stupid, crazy, or evil.

Now your whoring days are over.

There'll be a price to pay for lies you knowingly tell, whether you're the wealthiest most prestigious network anchor or the lowliest scrivener in a weekly suburban shopper. When you violate your trust as a member of the adversary media, when you sell yourself at yard-sale prices to the police state you're supposed to protect the public from, your name will appear on our "Dirty Laundry Web Page."

In your past (like everyone's), you have lovers, spouses, siblings, employers, employees, landlords, tenants, teachers, and, of course, your *victims*. Our Dirty Laundry Page will be their chance to tell 250 million of us everything they remember about you. We know the limits of libel and observe them — it won't help. You can avoid an unauthorized biography (nobody'll get mad enough to bring you to our attention) only by doing your job as it was meant to be done.

Let me help you a little. You delight in calling silly outfits like the Montana Freemen "anti-government," foolishly believing your audience will receive that as the ultimate epithet. Get real: If *you* aren't anti-government, you're not doing your job.

They didn't teach this in the state classrooms your parents were forced to send you to; you didn't learn it in the schools of tamed castrated journalism you attended, but America was *created* by intractable stiff-necked sons of bitches who hated the very *idea* of government. Everything worthwhile accomplished within its borders since has been the work of individuals of the same stripe.

That it continues to exist today as anything but the world's biggest banana republic is due neither to you nor the politicos you daily bend over and spread yourselves for, but to those that *both* of those corruptly interconnected groups despise most: the same kind of stiff-necked, intractable, *genuine* dissenters who must never be confused with *your* favorite poster kiddies, practitioners of officially sanctioned petulance on the Left.

This morning I heard some self-appointed "expert" on the radio, a would-be female Morris Dees, declare in her Bryn Mawr accent that a "resurgence" in militia activity results from America's "swing to the right." Truth is, there'd *be* no militia if George Bush hadn't broken his promise to uphold and defend the Constitution. There'd be no militia if Bill Clinton had never been born. "Brady Bill-Bob" Dole's senescent fumbling doesn't help, nor does the Libertarian Party's belly-crawling disavowal of militias.

Militias are an attempt to *communicate* by those who reasonably insist that government be limited by the first ten amendments and, as a result, find themselves rendered politically homeless by the chronically convictionless professionally unprincipled movers and money-monkeys who've conned, bribed, finagled, and threatened their way into stranglehold control over all three parties.

Any analysis of the militia that fails to center on Ruby Ridge and Waco — only the most conspicuous of many such atrocities — amounts to complicity. Why haven't you asked where somebody like Bill Clinton, who burned 82 innocents to death — 22 of them children — gets off calling anybody else a terrorist?

Ms. Bryn Mawr's a willing accomplice to a murderous

swath being cut through the Bill of Rights. She's earned her place on the Dirty Laundry Page.

Care to join her?

Who's the Wacko?
 c❧ c❧ c❧ c❧ c❧

I don't know about anybody else — that's one of the reasons I decided to write this, to try and find out — but I'm thoroughly fed up with listening to Rush Limbaugh blather, as he was doing once again just the other day, about "Wacko, Texas."

As Rush informs us smugly in the pizza commercial he's so proud of, when he's right, nobody in the Known Galaxy could possibly be more right than he is. And it's unquestionably true that we get news from him — or at least a perspective on the news — that we can't get from anybody else. Naturally, as a libertarian, I disagree with him fully half of the time. But at least it's a refreshingly *different* half than I'm accustomed to disagreeing with the mass media about. And there's always the inestimable pleasure of knowing the way he makes our mutual antagonists' blood boil, their stomachs churn, and other portions of their anatomy pucker and shrivel with even the least of his pronouncements.

But when Rush is wrong, nobody can even approach the cosmic magnitude of his wrongness. And Rush is wrong, totally wrong, embarrassingly wrong — just as he was totally embarrassingly wrong back when the whole thing happened — about Waco. It's enough to make you wonder *which* god his talent is on loan from.

I remember my frustration — and you probably remember

422

your own, as well — at the way Rush sat back on his big fat ratings, all through the despicable Branch Davidian siege, having a grand old time at the expense of the dozens of innocent helpless men, women, and children whose religious beliefs failed so feloniously to coincide with his own, and whom the United States government was working up its microscopic courage to obliterate with a callousness and brutality seldom witnessed even at the height of the Third Reich's malevolant sway.

It's all too easy to lose hold of the ugly facts, sometimes, too easy to let the hated memories fade, of a hundred individual human beings surrounded, threatened, tortured, shot, gassed, and burned to cinders by a State whose one and only reason for existing was the protection of their lives, liberties, and property. God — or somebody — forbid that any of us ever get protected the same way.

Protected to death.

The reason, one is forced to presume, for the big man's inappropriately jocular indifference to the Waco atrocity is that Jackboot Janet and her orcs were only following through — pretty damned stupidly, as it turned out — on a plan conceived, approved, and rehearsed by their predecessors in the Bush Administration.

I remember how Drug/Education Czar William Bennett, the authoritarian bully-boy Rush toadies up to so disgustingly — a philosophical thug who amounts to little more than Pat Buchanan with a vocabulary — helped to get the whole mess started by having his staff write up the first version of the so-called "Clinton" rifle and magazine ban for introduction by Newt Gingrich in the House and Phil Gramm in the Senate, proposing to strip millions of otherwise blameless gun-owning citizens of their social respectability and turn them into criminals overnight with the stroke of a pen, setting the stage for what happened at Waco and for a thousand incidents just like it still to come.

I remember, too, how the revered and beloved Nancy Reagan was chosen to cut the ribbon on the war on drugs — which we all know now was really a war against the Bill of Rights — that made something like Waco thinkable. And doable.

What disturbs me almost as much as these appalling lapses of Republican morality and courage is my perception (correct me if I'm wrong) that, in this context, the Great Mouthpiece speaks pretty much directly for the current party establishment, which has missed the boat again by failing to comprehend the significance of what history will come to regard as the definitive event of our times. If so, it means the changes last November and a future change of Presidential regimes will bring us no relief, not from unconstitutional gun laws, not from the likelihood that something a lot like Waco will happen again.

So what to do? I won't try to boycott Rush or his sponsors (proving that I'm smarter than the average liberal). But if you share my concerns and you agree with me that the easiest way to change the course of the Republican Party may be to change the mind of its *real* leader, then join me in writing to him at:

Rush Limbaugh
2 Penn Plaza, 17th Floor
New York, NY 10121

Even better, for the individuals most likely to be reading this, Rush's Internet address is <mailto:rush@eibnet.com>.

Tell him he was dead wrong about Waco and that he's been dead wrong ever since. Tell him that, if he ever used *both* halves of his brain, he'd know he's wrong. (And he'd probably be a libertarian, to boot!) Tell him that if he's honest, when he finally figures it all out, he's going to be more ashamed of himself than words can adequately express. And if you can't think of anything better or you haven't got the time for anything else, forward this essay to him.

Think of it as an experiment in integrity, Rush.

Your integrity.

A Maple-Leaf Rag
ော ော ော ော ော

As the Libertarian movement's most widely published and prolific living novelist (there — I finally said it, and I'm glad!), I don't usually respond to what's referred to (too politely, if you ask me) as "literary criticism."

In fact, I don't even read the stuff.

However, since an obscure Canadian magazine recently decided to make it personal, to smear me by association in a manner that anyone who knows me, or my work, will unquestionably regard as the most impossibly absurd, I suppose it's time to take the metaphorical gloves off and humiliate them in precisely the way they deserve most — with a high-tech "secret weapon" they've clearly never heard of: the truth.

You will notice I haven't named them. I don't intend to; they don't deserve the publicity. When I tried to get a copy of their publication in this university town of more than 100,000 with its many newsstands and bookstores, the folks I called not only didn't stock it, they'd never even heard of it! And that's exactly as it should be. Short of offering them a little gratuitous advice about their circulation problem at the end of this essay, I won't do anything to change it.

What they tried, in an entire issue dedicated to attempting to link terrorism with the Internet, was to portray me, through innuendo, as a racist. This libel was so offensive to me that I couldn't help but to respond. I grew up in a household where racism was regarded as a particularly egregious form of stupidity, whether it was of the primitive but honest variety practiced by NeoNazis and Klansmen or the oilier version we now call "affirmative action" or "political correctness."

Later on in life (by way of credentials), I opposed the war in Vietnam, opposed the draft (still do — it's slavery), and campaigned for Eugene McCarthy. I'm not just "pro-choice," I'm pro-abortion, believing it to be a positive factor in our society and in individual lives. And I believe the war on drugs has to be ended if we're to have any society left at all.

A simple phone call or five minutes' research into my work would have told the feebs and moral cripples at this maple-leaf rag all they needed to know to avoid embarrassment. The article of mine they quoted, an essay I wrote for the Net called "Bill Clinton's Reichstag Fire," carried, as all my Internet essays do, a tag paragraph crassly touting five of my books and containing three separate ways to get in touch with me.

But instead, since they asked for it, let's do what they were too stupid or lazy to do, and look at one minor aspect of my record as a novelist.

Edward William Bear, the hero of my first novel, *The Probability Broach*, and my second, *The Venus Belt*, is a full-blooded Ute Indian (by the way, there *are* no "native Americans" — we're *all* immigrants here, right back to Folsom Person) whose wife Clarissa is a freckled strawberry blonde and whose best friend is Lucille Conchita Gallegos Kropotkin, the 137-year-old Mexican widow of a famous Russian prince.

These are the books that also introduced sapient chimpanzees, gorillas, orangutans, gibbons, porpoises, and killer whales to science fiction, all of them full participants in a unique civilization called the "North American Confederacy," an amalgam of the United States, Mexico, and Canada.

Remember that, as it may prove important later on.

Agot Edmoot *Mav*, the valiant and intelligent protagonist of my third novel, *Their Majesties' Bucketeers*, is a meter-high, hairy, nine-legged, three-eyed, crab-like firefighting detective whose species has three genders. And yes, it *was* a pretty interesting book to write.

No dirty bits, though.

Bernie Gruenblum, the viewpoint character of my fourth novel, *The Nagasaki Vector*, is Jewish, although he doesn't keep kosher as far as I know (I never asked him) and he speaks with a decidedly West Texican accent. He's followed around by three tiny freenies, caffeine-addicted aliens who think he's God. And his flying saucer has fallen in love with him.

I honestly don't know the racial background of YD-038, the hero of my fifth novel, *Tom Paine Maru*. As you may be able to judge from his "name," he's an escapee from the kind of world that the socialists who call themselves liberals have spent the last 60 years trying to build for us, and his ethnicity just didn't seem important at the time. Sorry.

With *The Gallatin Divergence*, my sixth novel, we're back to Win Bear, the Ute Indian again, who gets time-traveled to the 18th century by Ooloorie Eckickeck P'wheet, a physicist who also happens to be a *Tursiops truncatus* — that's bottle-nosed dolphin, for those of you who run Canadian magazines.

Somewhere in there, I also wrote three books — recently combined and reprinted as *The Lando Calrissian Adventures* — about the guy in *Star Wars* who owned the *Millenium Falcon* before Han Solo did. You may remember him; he's the fellow who blew up the second DeathStar, and he was played by Billy Dee Williams.

Now in my tenth novel, *The Wardove*, we have a rock band in the distant future, one of whose girl singers is having an affair with an alien who looks like a cross between a helium balloon and an umbrella. You tell me whether that's racist, sexist, or open-mindedly enlightened. She probably just couldn't resist that long curved handle.

Okay, so the mighty Sedrich Sedrichsohn, the hero of *The Crystal Empire*, my eleventh novel, is a white guy, I confess. And he's even an unabashed sort of sword-swinging, Nordicoid, semi-Viking, make what you will of that. The three loves of his life are a voluptuous blonde, a beautiful Indian, and finally a Moslem princess (it's a long book) who helps him battle an alliance of Renaissance Aztecs and Ming 2.0 Dynasty Chinese. Note that even my *villains* are equal-opportunity employers.

I never knew what race the hero of my twelfth novel, *Brightsuit MacBear* was (it never occurred to me — sorry), although he's the great-grandson of that Ute who started the whole thing, way back when. His best friend is one of those nine-legged crabs, and they team up with a critter who — no, no, I'd better not. I don't think you're quite up to that, yet.

Lucky thirteen, *Taflak Lysandra*, concerns Elsi Nahuatl, a young lady of Australian Aboriginal extraction and her father, G. Howell Nahuatl, the American coyote with a cybernetically augmented brain who adopted her. Elsie starts off being unhappy (like many adolescents are), because she doesn't have blue eyes, freckles, or a turned-up nose, but learns to be happy with her looks because, as she discovers in the end, compared to the kind of person she is inside, those things are basically unimportant.

Now admittedly, except for the occasional alien, *everyone* in my fourteenth novel, *Henry Martyn*, is white. That's because they're descended (900 years removed) from the last remaining guilt-ridden middle-class liberals in the Solar System, who were exiled to a faraway star cluster when everybody else finally got thoroughly fed up with them.

Otherhandwise, in numbers fifteen, sixteen, and seventeen — *Contact and Commune, Converse and Conflict,* and *Consent and Cosmos*, respectively — hardly anybody's white, because of an especially nasty kind of "affirmative action" carried out by the American Soviet Socialist Republic. I have talking molluscs. These books, by the way, collectively known (by their proud author) as the "Forge of the Elders Trilogy," proved so politically incorrect that the publisher canceled the third volume!

Which brings us to my eighteenth novel, *Pallas,* in which Emerson Ngu, a little half-Cambodian, half-Vietnamese boy refugees out of a UN agricultural commune. Over the course of his long productive life, he loves three white women (one, for complicated reasons, with a Sikh surname), while battling a White American Male former U.S. Senator you may recognize, although I assure you that the resemblance is purely coincidental.

The hero of *Lever Action*, my nineteenth book, is ... *me*! It's a collection of two decades' worth of essays, articles, and speeches, and *my* race and ethnic background are none of your frigging business.

My twentieth (and favorite) novel, *Bretta Martyn*, takes us back to the strange far-off universe of Throwaway White Liberals I mentioned earlier.

Finally, in my twenty-first novel, *The Mitzvah* (with Aaron Zelman), half the characters are Roman Catholic and the other half Jewish. The hero, Monsignor John Greenwood, happens to be both, which is what the book's all about.

Now look: Thirty-odd years ago, I took an oath never to initiate force against another human being for any reason, nor to advocate or delegate initiated force. That, plus my deep lifelong regard for the First Amendment — I forgot, they don't have one of those in Canada, do they?

Make it my deep regard for free speech — oops, they don't really have that, either.

What I'm *trying* to say is that I value the liberty to say what you want so highly that I won't sue these cretins no matter how much they deserve it.

I admit, I thought about it for a while.

I've no way of proving it, but since they seem to monitor the Net, I suspect what this is really all about is a speech I gave at an Arizona Libertarian Party convention a few years ago in which I promised — when my wing of the party comes to power — that we'll offer statehood to any Canadian province that ratifies the Bill of Rights. That promise is still good (some Canadians are working on it right now) and nothing this slimy little magazine can do will stop it, or even slow it down.

What they might try instead, if they really want to increase their microscopic readership, in my country, or in that future portion of the United States of America they live in, is to give up their obsolete ideology (or leave it at home when they come to work) and — I know it's unprecedented in conventional mass media — try telling the truth.

It's like sex — it might hurt a little the first time.

Stop the Nagging
ᴄᴈ ᴄᴈ ᴄᴈ ᴄᴈ ᴄᴈ

I guess it all began for me in 1952 when we had our first TV in McQueenie, Texas.

I was about six years old and the national preoccupation, at least in early broadcast circles, seemed to be smoking in bed, which, judging by what I saw and heard, constituted a threat, not only to Western Civilization, but to Life on Earth As We Know It. All of those "public-service announcements" (or PSAs as they're called today) must have solved the problem — everybody must have stopped smoking in bed — since you don't see or hear spots about it any more.

Or maybe it was even earlier than that, in Denver when I was about four, lying in my crib, listening to *The FBI in Peace and War*, which took time to admonish me, at the end of every program, to "drink plenty of beverages." I didn't have a clue what "beverages" was, but even then, it was clear that if the anal-retentive sado-masochistic fascists in Our government (who claimed to be protecting us from the anal-retentive sado-masochistic fascists in Their government) asked me to do something, it almost certainly wouldn't be good for me.

More to the point, it made me feel pushed around, and I didn't like it a bit. I've always been nag-resistant (my mother says the first word I uttered was "No!"), a sensation I experience at the visceral, rather than the cerebral, level.

I listen to PSAs cleverly placed between segments of Rush Limbaugh's show, or Ken Hamblin's (I wonder who the American Anti-Vivisection League think they're gonna convince in *that* audience), and ask myself the same question I ask you now: Would you permit a stranger, a neighbor, even a family member, to barge into your living room or office and browbeat you over the least details of your life? Would you let them lecture you about fat, salt, sugar, cholesterol, calories, nicotine, registering for the draft, beating your wife, or recycling garbage? Or would you pitch them right out in the street on their ear?

Mark me down for the latter — and tell me why you let a little box with speakers on the front, or a bigger one that pretends to be a window, do the same thing you wouldn't tolerate from a stranger, a neighbor, or a family member.

Much of the time, these do-gooders don't know what they're talking about, either. Somewhere in between beverages and bed-smoking it was, "Only you can prevent forest fires." Only it turned out, 30 years later, that forest fires are a good thing and perhaps *shouldn't* be prevented quite so energetically. It seems forests are considerably healthier — and maybe a bit less dangerous — when an occasional fire sweeps through them and does a little of Darwin's work.

Which is what we get, I guess, for listening to a bear wearing a silly hat.

Not long ago it was "vitamin supplements are unnecessary and basically a scheme by evil capitalism to callously steal the hard-earned money the IRS doesn't take from you." Now, however, doctors advise you to take anti-oxidants like Vitamin C and tell me that my habitual consumption of Vitamin E is what prevented any lasting damage when I suffered two heart attacks back in 1993.

Remember when evil video-arcade games were going to despoil American youth?

Lately it's been, "Wear the Gear" (in short, negate every reason you ever bothered to learn to use roller blades, ride a bike, or do whatever people do on a skateboard) because the safety Nazis worry themselves sick with the fear that the thrill of taking a worthwhile risk, the exhiliration of sheer velocity and personal freedom, might spread like cancer to the rest of your life — to your job, to your school, to your voting pattern — and then where would they be? Certainly not making and airing subsidized, tax-deductible, FCC-compulsory PSAs.

PSAs are "the hand that rocks the cradle" in the Nanny State and if Republicans were serious about eradicating socialism in America (which they decidedly are not — they're merely offering a competing brand of the stuff), this is where they'd concentrate their not-so-friendly fire. Each and every one of the damned things is an advertisement for the underlying collectivist philosophy of the Democratic National Committee (such as it is) and they should each and every one be summarily jerked off the air during election years.

Perhaps Republicans could begin, in their typical timid way, with a few questions that desperately need asking. Who or what is the "Ad Council," anyway?

And what's a country with a First Amendment to its Constitution doing with an armed federal bureaucracy that calls itself the Federal Communications Commission?

For that matter, what's a country with a Constitution doing with armed bureaucracies?

Meanwhile, I have some nagging of my own to do, aimed at the Ad Council, the American Heart and Bladder Association or whatever they call themselves who made quitting smoking so much harder for me, and all the rest of you radio nannies:

Shut up.

Go away.

Don't come back.

Ever.

And go to hell, Valerie Yarborough, whoever you are.

Lemme tell you, if they'd really do it, I'd consider *that* a public service.

Unanimous Consent
and the Utopian Vision

Presented at the Future of Freedom Conference
Culver City, California, November, 1987

The continued relative invisibility of Libertarianism in America, after forty years of back-breaking heart-breaking labor, has nothing to do with any lack of money, ideas, personnel, or anything else we Libertarians continually whine about. It isn't the fault of any evil Northeastern conspiracy. Nor, as the timorous, timid, and trembling among us often recommend, is it any reason to tone down our rhetoric, to soften our principles or their expression, or to make it more "conservative" or "practical" in approach. All of that has been tried, over and over again in the history of the movement, and by now its miserable abject failure is self-evident to everyone but a blind, deaf, and, particularly dumb handful of seminar schlockmeisters and Libertarian Party "pragmatists."

What we Libertarians sometimes lack in our own hearts and minds, what we often fail to communicate to others, is a vision of the new civilization we intend to create. It may be sufficient — for Libertarians — that America today is politically, economically, and socially repulsive. It may be sufficient — for Libertarians — that what we propose represents a moral imperative. *It is not enough for others*. Most people require a concrete realization of the future, a picture that will motivate them to learn what Libertarians mean by "right" and "wrong," and inspire them to work toward its fulfillment.

It may appear contradictory that the achievement of practical ends must rely on what seems to be a fantasy — but nothing could be further from the truth. What we Libertarians need is a foot in the door. There's no conflict between flights of imagination and political realism, any more than there is between "radical abolitionism" and "moderate gradualism." Each has a role in the creation of progress. Neither can afford to try operating without the other. Division-of-labor is more than an abstract economic principle, it's a matter of life or death for the cause of individual liberty. Utopianism, far from being a hindrance or embarrassment, is a vital effective means toward that goal.

We Libertarians take our philosophy too much for granted. Our concepts of what it can accomplish are too abstract. We wrongly assume that others can see its potential as clearly as we do. We often fail to see it ourselves. As a remedy, we must begin to ask ourselves, now and each day for the rest of our lives, certain fundamental questions. Why are we Libertarians? What do we wish to accomplish? What constitutes success? By what signs will we know that we've won? What's in it for us? What's in it for me? What do I really want?

Our present collection of answers seems to range from the negative to the obscure:

"Well, *you* know ... "

"Because I want to see that bastard [insert the bastard of your choice] get what's coming to him!"

"Because what's going on now is wrong and I want to stop it."

"Because I'm afraid that civilization is going to collapse unless we do something."

A common variation noted by Our Founder David Nolan is, "Because I *know* that civilization is going to collapse, and I want to be around to say 'I told you so'!"

I first heard the best of this rather unsatisfactory lot from English Libertarians who told me, "Because, even if I were absolutely convinced that my efforts would come to nothing, I can't honestly imagine doing anything else."

I'd like to share with you some of my answers. Before I began spreading them around through my novels, they were somewhat different from those of most Libertarians. To the extent that I'm a fanatic, they are what's responsible. They are what drives and motivates me. They are the reason I'll keep right on "disturbing the peace" until I'm hauled off to some 21st century Super-Dachau and lasered to death, or pigeons begin paying respects to my statue in a private city park.

One of them, of course, comes from an adolescence of filling my head with "garbage" — pulp science fiction stories in which I witnessed cultures, societies, whole galactic empires being created, tinkered with, torn down, and built up all over again by talented (and some not-so-talented) yarn-spinners who, just like me, were obsessed with finding out what makes civilization tick. They taught me that the future is *malleable*, sometimes even by a single individual standing at a sensitive-enough leverage point. I have been looking for that leverage-point ever since. I have an idea of what I want the future to look like. What's more, I want to have a principal role in its making. In short, I have a Utopian vision of my own, rooted in the Libertarian philosophy of Unanimous Consent. I want to see that vision realized, not just for my daughter's sake, but soon enough to enjoy it myself. That's what *I* really want.

Thirty years ago, singer and social activist Joan Baez smugly observed that there are no right-wing folk songs. I'd noticed the same thing myself, but as a professional guitar player busily compromising his newly fledged Objectivist principles to the Barry Goldwater campaign, I was disinclined to gloat about it.

There are no right-wing Utopias, either, not one spellbinding adventure novel of the colorful William F. Buckleyite future. The conservative's view of heaven is the *status quo ante*

— a dead, flat, black-and-white daguerreotype of a past that probably never existed. And any *status quo* will do, as long as it isn't a *Communist* status quo. If its victims are tortured in banana-republic jails, that's perfectly acceptable as long as they're not *Marxist* jails. If a long train of abuses and usurpations are visited on liberty in *this* country, that's fine, as long as they're not *left-wing* abuses and usurpations — and even better if they're in the name of Moral Rectitude or National Security.

Traditionally, Utopia is the territory of the Left. Imaginative stories gave ordinary people images of what had previously only been abstractions for pasty-faced intellectuals, and this — the work of men like H.G. Wells and Edward Bellamy — had more to do with the progress of socialism than anything Karl Marx, Friederich Engels, Vladimir Lenin, or even Geraldo Rivera ever accomplished. The dictionary, in a burst of unusual candor, defines Utopia as "the ideal state where all is ordered for the best, for mankind as a whole, and evils such as poverty and misery do not exist"; not only have we learned the hard way that this is self-contradictory in practice, but it is more than sufficient reason why Utopia is a province populated, almost exclusively, by the enemies of liberty.

The word "Utopia," however, only came to be synonymous with "impossible dream" when the internal inconsistency, the inherent cynicism, and the utter emptiness of socialism became unmistakable to whoever happened to be watching. In some instances, its sterile no-exit character was already visible in the pages of otherwise upbeat Victorian novels decades before it became political reality — Utopia bored itself to death. More frequently, socialist victories in the real world turned into disaster all by themselves, generating economic, social, and military devastation, and incidentally smashing the Utopian promise along the way.

Lever Action

Utopian novels fell out of fashion only when the idealists on the Left ceased to believe in their own fairy tales. Dispirited, disoriented, beaten in a way they could never understand, reduced to a petulant nihilism, they couldn't *dream* anymore. Rather than being exceptions, today's few, sad, threadbare left-Utopias make the case. Read Skinner's *Walden Two* for its constipated lack of scope. Examine LeGuin's *The Dispossessed* for its injured perplexity. Try Clarke's *The Songs of Distant Earth*. He's peddling shopworn goods and he knows it. He ought to, living in Sri Lanka! Socialism's time has run out on this planet because the credibility of its Utopian vision self-destructed.

The tragedy is that, when leftist Utopias fell into dishonor, they took all the rest with them. Shattered socialist dreams discredited any dreams at all of a rational, humane social order. Libertarianism was born an orphan in an age of negative Utopias like *Brave New World*, *1984*, and *We*. Ayn Rand wrote disUtopias, *Anthem*, *Atlas Shrugged*, *We The Living*, admirably showing us the dirty, bloodstained underside of collectivism's brilliant promises, but she and others like her made too few promises of their own. She pointed out a great deal to avoid, but gave us little to aspire to, which, I submit, is poor motivational psychology.

Before I began writing, there were semi-Libertarian Utopias, glimmers in the works of Robert A. Heinlein and Poul Anderson, the stories of Eric Frank Russell — brighter more explicit pictures drawn by H. Beam Piper and Jerome Tuccille. But somehow — perhaps the fault was mine — they failed to stick to my philosophical ribs.

Nor were our "basic" Libertarian works much better. Where most Utopian fiction failed to be Libertarian enough, most Libertarian non-fiction failed to be Utopian at all. Where was the softly glowing promise in John Hospers' *Libertarianism*,

Murray Rothbard's *For A New Liberty*, Roger MacBride's *A New Dawn*, or David Friedman's *The Machinery of Freedom*? Where was the excitement and adventure in Paul Lepanto's *Return to Reason*, Harry Browne's *How I Found Freedom In An Unfree World*, or Robert LeFevre's *This Bread Is Mine*? Where was the color in Hazlitt's *Economics in One Lesson*? Where was the *fire* in any of them? Was it enough only to be satisfied that most of our "beginner's books" weren't too boring?

If Rand had written *The Moon Is A Harsh Mistress* or edited its cynical and pessimistic ending, if Heinlein had written *Atlas Shrugged* and paced it like *Door Into Summer*, John Hospers would have made it to the White House and auctioned off the furniture, because we'd have captured people's *imaginations*. Their hearts and minds, their money and votes would have followed faithfully behind.

Ordinary people *want* Utopia. They've watched *Star Trek* until the emulsion wore off the celluloid, and helped *Star Wars* outgross World War II, because Jim Kirk, Mr. Spock, and Luke Skywalker assure them that there *is* a future, one worth looking forward to, at that, in which human beings (and other critters) will still be doing fascinating dangerous things. *Having a good time*.

It says here, eighty-four percent of us first-generation Libertarians got hooked by reading *Atlas Shrugged*, which I've just described as disUtopian. Now I'll contradict myself. It *wasn't* just to watch civilization crumbling down deservedly around Dagny Taggart's ears that I waded through that kilopage of *magnum opus* at the tender age of fourteen. Its fascination for me was in that all-too-brief glimpse of a small, working, slightly kinky, Libertarian society. *Atlas Shrugged* is mainly disUtopian, but in the end, it's every bit as cheery as Piper's *A Planet For Texans*, and almost as delightfully bloodthirsty.

Lever Action

Those among my audience who haven't read my novels may well ask what kind of Utopian vision I think we Libertarians ought to communicate. Well, once, in a moment of mixed premises and moral depravity, I defined it in terms of "freedom, immortality, and the stars." No, I didn't dig that out of the pages of *The National Enquirer*. I meant individual freedom in the Libertarian sense of society totally without coercion; immortality as a logical scientifically foreseeable extension of that freedom into time; and the stars as an equally logical and foreseeable extension of that freedom into outer space — as human beings reach out for what has always seemed to me to be their evolutionary Manifest Destiny.

I do have a more specific dream, a more detailed vision. It's expressed in the Covenant of Unanimous Consent, which I first wrote as a kind of moral substitute for the Constitution and the Bill of Rights, and later included in my novel of the Whiskey Rebellion, *The Gallatin Divergence*. The Covenant has circulated in more than forty countries and has Signatories in a majority of the states and provinces of North America. I wouldn't be surprised if the dreams and visions expressed in the Covenant are similar to your own. If we differ at all, it's because I've never believed it pays to be bashful about visions. We must share our vision with others, so that they'll begin to work toward its fulfillment, too.

For practice, let's try building a "Utopia of Unanimous Consent" right here and now. You already know the rules. Morally, in a future Libertarian society, each individual is free to live his or her own life as an end in itself and defend it against anyone who would compel otherwise. Ethically, this is accomplished by adopting a single law or custom: individuals are forbidden — the specific mechanism, as we all appreciate, is still being debated — to initiate force against others. Socially and economically, a voluntary exchange of values, rather than force, is the basis for all human relationships.

H.G. Wells used to start with the premise "What if ... ?" What if you could travel to the Moon in a gravity-proof ball? What if you fell asleep and woke up 200 years later? What if you found a way to become invisible? Well, I have a "what if" for you: What if one Commandment, "Thou shalt not initiate force," became the fundamental operating principle of society soon enough for all of us to see it?

For the moment, we'll skip how we get from "here" to "there," although it *is* the critical question. That's not quite the cop-out it may seem: Just now we're trying to envision a new civilization uncontaminated by any previous social order — in science this is called a "controlled experiment"; in writing it's called "poetic license" — and in any case, our Utopian vision, what it says to us and to others, is a major force itself in getting us from "here" to "there."

We'll also skip the possibility of thermonuclear war or a spectacularly unpleasant economic or civil collapse. There are reasons, as we'll see later, why I'm unconvinced of the inevitability of it all. In any case, it'll either happen or it won't. If it does, we'll either live through it or we won't, and we'll succeed in carrying off the Libertarian Millennium, with or without an introductory catastrophe — or in the long run, just like John Maynard Keynes, we'll all be dead.

A frequent error Utopia-builders make, understandably, is leaving items they're unaware of out of their extrapolation. In the surviving mutation of the leftist Utopian repertoire — Doomsday predicting — Paul Ehrlich, the Club of Rome, the Ozone Boys, and most science fiction writers make a stupid mistake amidst their orgasmic cries of disaster: They aren't figuring on Libertarians.

Before we get smug, recall that I said, back at the beginning, that this is our fault. Look how it happened; think of all those "Buy Gold, Buy Silver, Buy Irradiated Garbanzo Beans" advertisements, pamphlets, and seminars we were once so fond of. In our projections of the future, we made the same stupid mistake — and it's even stupider when we make it — we forgot about *us*! Aren't we going to affect the future? You bet your dried war-surplus fruit preserves we are!

We already have.

The shape of the future is determined, just like the present was, by two factors almost exclusively. The first is the virtually unlimited power of the individual human mind and the free-market system, which is its most monumental achievement. The second, frequently forgotten but no less important, is the inefficacy of evil.

It won't surprise anyone in this room to hear of the power of mind and market. The human mind may inhabit what one cynic called "a sort of skin disease on a ball of dirt," but its grasp encompasses the subatomic particle and the intergalactic void. The mind alone is the reason our species became dominant on this planet in a geologic microsecond. Yet, aren't we confronted each day with the victorious gloatings of evil? How can it be inefficacious when it owns the world?

Let's answer that by considering what condition humanity, its culture, technology, and economy would be in, if the villains always won. Hasn't there been overall progress in the human situation over the past several thousand years? Would there have been a Scientific Method, an Industrial Revolution, a Declaration of Independence, a Non-Aggression Principle, or even a Covenant of Unanimous Consent, if evil were all that omnipotent? In spite of the most hyperthyroid governments, the most pointlessly murderous wars, and the most disgustingly despicable badguys in all of human history, the 20th century and the United States of America offer the highest standard of living and the greatest amount of individual liberty that have ever been available to our species.

None of this is any testimony to governments, to war, or to badguys, of course, but to the human mind and the ineptitude of its enemies. Most of us have learned that mind and market always find a way. The point that liberals, conservatives, and even many Libertarians always seem to miss is that this — the highest standard of living and the greatest amount of individual liberty that have ever been available — isn't any reason to avoid asking what kind of future world could a completely uninhibited human mind create, economically, socially, and technologically? The three areas overlap, but we'll begin with economics.

The economic future will be as different from our times as ours are from the pre-industrial era of history. No one in 1636, for example, could have imagined our relative freedom from the constant threat of death by starvation, exposure, or disease that characterized those times. Few today can visualize a future of vastly greater wealth, world peace, and no bureaucrats to pry into every moment of one's daily life. Historical blindness works both ways, of course: Those born in the future will react with a mixture of embarrassment and amusement when we try explaining our times to them. The insane were once beaten, tortured, and chained, a practice that seems ludicrous and terrible to us. The IRS will seem equally barbaric to our great-grandchildren. We'll try to tell them, but they'll attribute it to senile dementia and never really believe us.

With taxation gone, not only will we have *twice* as much money to spend, but it will go *twice* as far, since those who produce the goods and services we desire won't have to pay taxes, either. In a stroke we'll be effectively *four times* as rich.

There's no equally simple way to estimate the cost of regulation. How can you estimate the cost of lost opportunities? Truckers say that they could ship goods for one-fifth the present price without it. Many businesses spend a third of their over-head complying with rules and filling out forms. The worst damage it does is to planning and innovation. Since you don't know what the whim of the legislature will be next year, how can you plan? Projects that require ten, twenty, or fifty years to mature? You might as well forget them.

Let's calculate that deregulation will cut prices, once again, by half. Now our actual purchasing power, already quadrupled by "detaxification," is doubled again. *We now have eight times our former wealth*! What kind of world will *that* result in?

Future generations won't grasp, even remotely, the con-cept of inflation, or that the government once imprisoned people for competing with its own counterfeiting operation. They'll be used to a stable diversity of competing trade commodities — gold, uranium, cotton, wheat, cowry shells — which will not only flatten a lot of wildly swinging economic curves, but give newspapers something to print besides government hand-outs: "Cowrie shells sold late on the market today at 8-1/4. Oats and barley at 4-1/2, Uranium at 87." 87 what? Sheep, gold grams, kilowatts, gallons of oil — who cares, as long as they're free-market rates, determined by uncoerced bidding, buying, and selling? Hardly anyone, of course, will carry sheep, seashells, or barrels of oil around with them. Everyone assumes that 21st century barter will be carried out on ferro-magnetic media in electrical impulses. But I suspect that a few of us surly old curmudgeons, having spent our lives being swindled with paper and plastic — and tracked by electronic impulse — will insist on having something in our pockets that jingles. Young folks will look knowingly at us and wink.

The future, as I see it, comes in segments: continuation, for however long, of things as they are, counterpointed by our increasing success — as a result of this speech, no doubt — at convincing others of the necessity and desirability of liberty.

I've said we'll skip that period, and I wish we really could.

Having sold others, we'll change what's left of what we have now into a free society: degovernmentalization of culture and the economy characterized by an eight-fold increase in individual purchasing power and an end to the importance of the State in our lives. Eight times richer, we'll be free to do whatever we wish with our new wealth. Why stick with black-and-white when you can have a color wallscreen in every room? Why drive an '84 Subaru when you can afford a brand-new Porsche? Why eat hamburger when you can have steak and lobster every night?

Increased spending appears in the economy as increased demand, leading, despite government economists, not to shortages, but to increased production. Somebody has to make all those wallscreens, Porsches, steaks, and lobsters. With all that money loose, there's new investment in established companies, as well as zillions of new ones striving to satisfy everyone's newfound consumer greed. Factories will spring up, old ones will expand, obsolete machinery will be junked and new machinery installed. More people will be working, producing all those goods and services demanded by a newly rich population consisting of themselves.

Unemployment will disappear overnight. As labor becomes scarcer, wages will skyrocket, hours will shorten, work-weeks will truncate. "Headhunters" will flourish, not only stealing managerial talent, but bribing assembly workers to desert for even better wages, conditions, and benefits. Unable to figure out what happened, unions will dry up and blow away completely. Despite increased wages and benefits (leading to more buying, demand, production, and jobs), prices will plummet as demand drives industry to even greater efficiency. Plants now standing idle half the time will operate full-blast around the clock. Society will be geared to operating 25 hours a day, eight days a week.

Against a chronic labor shortage, evil exploitive capitalists will take unfair measures like free training, free day-care,
and free health insurance. In short, everything that socialism
ever led us to expect from government at the point of a bayo-
net, the market will provide voluntarily, as companies begin to
compete ruthlessly for workers. Managers desperate for your
talents will have to change their petty coercive behavior. Their
restraints on your freedom and insults to your honesty and intelligence will vanish, simply because, for once, they *need* you,
not some anonymous, numbered, plug-in module, but *you*.

Oh, they'll resist at first.

They'll try imports and foreign labor, but it'll be their undoing, as living and working standards — and expectations —
rise abroad. Free world trade will have another effect: increased
demand, increased production, more jobs, and lower prices.

Monotonous, isn't it?

They'll try more automation, but that's another trap. It always results in more — not less — employment. For each 19th
century quill-pusher perched high at his desk, how many computer designers, engineers, manufacturers, assemblers, install-
ers, repairmen, programmers, and key-punchers are there today? For every buggy-whip maker, how many involved in automotive ignition? And automation has another side-effect: It
increases production, which lowers prices.

In a free society, the availability and quality of goods and
services increase constantly while prices drop. Wages and living standards escalate continuously. What we call a "boom" is
normal and permanent. With no State to bloat the currency,
good times have nothing to do with inflation. "Forced-draft"
advances in technology that we associate with war are a snail's
pace when people are free to pursue the buck with all ten greedy
little fingers. Which is why those future whippersnappers will

think we're hallucinating about the bad old days of price-control, strikes, inflation, tariffs, and the IRS. And they'll want to know why we didn't buy out that pest David Rockefeller with our lunch money.

Many problems *are* trivial, viewed with the proper perspective. The high-technology answer to our civilization's weird desire for "flat clothing" didn't turn out to be a bigger more complicated automated ironing-board, but simply clothing that *stayed* flat when it was washed. The wrong perspective can lead to disaster. In the 1890s, according to Bob LeFevre, the government decided — Club of Rome fashion — that mere private corporations could never bear the cost of prospecting, drilling, extracting, refining, and distributing petroleum. Therefore, oil should be a State monopoly. A kid's book I have from the '50s opines that no single government could possibly finance a mission to the Moon and it would have to be done by the UN. (If the *Challenger* disaster was a mess, think what a UN space program would be like!) These predictions should be kept in mind whenever we contemplate the inevitability of disaster or the impossibility of our dreams. The only prediction we can make *safely* about the future is that it will be far more fantastic than we can *safely* predict.

Presently, we live within a cramped, narrow, *chronically depressed* culture, largely unaware of its limitations simply because we've never seen anything better. Faced with problems, we understandably — but mistakenly — view them from the worm's-eye level to which we've always been limited by the culture we live in. Solving today's problems, however, demands a vastly wider scope. We have to learn to think big — bigger than we've ever dreamed or dared.

Take the routine objection that firing millions of bureaucrats will lead to economic disaster, or that civil servants are unlikely to support the LP if it means doing away with their own jobs. Our candidates tend to keep a low profile on this subject, but they should think big: As John Hospers once pointed out, ten million GIs were absorbed into the post-World War II economy with scarcely a ripple, despite somewhat less than laissez-faire conditions. A booming free market suffers perpetual labor shortages; nobody will be required to persuade bureaucrats to enter the private sector to enjoy the benefits of that. They will desert in hordes. The State will shrink like the little dot when you turn off your TV, and vanish.

Other problems are amenable to the same sort of analysis. For example, I'm not a very enthusiastic catastrophist, despite the fact that unfunded government liabilities currently seem to spell doom for Western civilization as we know it. Social Security alone is short by several trillion bucks, and it now looks like the early 21st century will go up in a flourish of Molotov cocktails.

In 1666, a great London fire wiped out a *third* of the total wealth of England, a cataclysmic loss amounting to some ten million dollars. Could it be we're using the wrong scale to assess our own financial problems? Trillions seems like about as much money as there ever will be — but "seems" is a very conditional word. We have in our hands the means to create a market so vast and strong that even trillions will seem trivial by comparison. The Utopian vision can hasten the day when a free economy straightens out the mess left by our predecessors.

Those inclined to Future Shock are in for a rough ride. Free trade, an end to disincentives, and steadily increasing automation will spiral living standards upward dizzily. Just as uranium was once thrown aside to get at lead and tin, we have no way of knowing what untold sources of wealth, energy, and comfort we're stumbling over now. New materials, production methods, lifestyles, and opportunities will arise by the myriad every day, if not every hour. Already in our time, a manufacturing counter-revolution is under way: High-quality investment-casting, laser and electron-discharge cutting, detonic welding, ion implantation, computer-aided design, and computer-controlled machining are all decreasing the amount of plastic and cardboard in our lives, increasing the titanium, steel, and glass. At the same time, plastics seem more like steel and glass every day, while even cardboard gets stronger and longer lasting.

Nations won't just emerge, they'll splash into the 21st century like the overripe melons Marx mentioned, but in a very different way than he intended. New territories opened by the free market will make overpopulation one of the future's biggest jokes. Antarctica, Greenland, and northern Canada will all feel the plow and deliver up their wealth. The floor, the surface, the cubic volume of the sea, the Moon, Mars, the asteroids, all of the Solar System and open space itself will be subdivided. If the total human population reaches 40 billion or 400 billion, we'll have more elbow-room than we do now, and Marshall McCluhan's one-horse Global Village of the 1960s will turn into Times Squared.

During the coming century, poverty and unemployment will become a dark half-believed nightmare of the remote past. All our elaborate discussions of private charity in a Libertarian world will be academic in a world where any basket-case who can twitch once for yes and twice for no will be desperately needed for quality control on a production line. They'll put chimpanzees and gorillas on the payroll and killer whales and porpoises will be buying split-level aquaria on the installment plan.

Pollution will be another dead issue in a 21st century America where every square inch of real estate is private property and — without any Environmental Protection Agency to "save" them — individuals are free to sue polluters. In any case, no competitive industry will be able to afford the waste of energy and material that pollution represents. Not that there won't be wilderness: When they auction off the National Forests, I'll be there, bidding with all the other hunters and fishermen. To me, heaven is being able to fire a rifle in any direction from my front porch and not hit anyone but trespassers.

As with charity, all our theoretical concern with police and security is a waste of breath. In the 21st century, peace will break out uncontrollably and cops will have to be retrained for office jobs. With victimless crime laws repealed and American cities populous and prosperous once again, 99% of the crime we presently endure will vanish. Our descendants won't understand how it ever became an issue. Middle-class values are market values. A wider regard for property, education, and long-range planning will mean less crime. A single mugging in Central Park will get four-inch headlines in New York's several dozen newsplastics. In the absence of laws against duelling, people will be more polite to each other and less inclined to offer unwanted advice. Either that or, thanks to natural selection, their grandchildren will have faster reflexes.

Lacking gun control to protect them, the few criminals left in society won't live long enough to transmit their stupid-genes. The next century will give us a welcome look at the *other* side of a familiar paradox: People who are free to carry weapons usually don't need them. Prisons will be abandoned when those who never did anything to hurt anyone are released. The rest of the convicts will be out working to restore their victims' property or health. Crimes against persons and property, including murder, will be civil offenses, with volunteer agencies acting for those without relatives or friends to "avenge" them. Restitution may even be possible for murder, given techniques of freezing corpses for later repair. Those who commit *irrevo-*

cable murder (and survive) will suffer the cruellest punishment of all: exile to a place where there's a government!

The concerns of the left with conglomerates, multinational corporations, and monopolies is as misplaced as ours with charity and crime. Before the 19th century government invasion of the market, companies had reached their optimum size and begun to shrink. Although the government keeps competition off their backs today, huge companies must divide themselves into competing subsidiaries to survive. Increased competition will doom these dinosaurs, break up concentrations of wealth and power frozen by securities and tax laws, and produce companies much smaller than those of today. The survivors will be stuck with the boring old laissez-faire task of pleasing as many customers as possible with the best quality goods and services possible at the lowest possible prices.

It's possible you're way ahead of me by now — and you may even have noticed that I haven't been following my own advice. All of these predictions I've been making are pretty general, pretty abstract, pretty impersonal. The time has come to answer the questions, "What do I really want; what's in it for me?"

The Answer? Basically, we all get to have our cake and say, "I told you so," too.

Immediately, as we've seen, the free market will boost our purchasing power eightfold, and this, of course, is only the beginning — although I hesitate to risk your willing suspension of disbelief by estimating wages and prices several decades into the era of Unanimous Consent. Let's just say that we will have eight times as much disposable wealth. Even this rather modest multiplier will offer a range and choice of goods and services unimaginable today.

One's basic material well-being will be much easier to maintain when a loaf of Grandma's Automated Bread goes for a nickel and steak for twenty cents a pound. Or how about a pair of two-dollar shoes or wristwatches for a dime a dozen? How about suits and dresses for ten bucks or disposable outfits for a dollar?

In fact, the toughest decision consumers make may be choosing between durability versus disposability: Should you drive an imposing 2087 Rolls-Rolex Fusionmobile good for generations or a plastic Mattel-Yugo easily discarded when you tire of it? Should you wear a Saville Row three-piece iron-clad business suit or a toilet-paper toga? Increased leisure time and plenty of loose cash will mean what it always has, more emphasis on expensive, hand-crafted, one-of-a-kind items. We all may wind up running second, third, or fourth businesses on the side, which means, of course, more jobs, more buying, and so on.

How about paying two to four thousand dollars for a home that's built to last, helped out by a slump in land prices when government holdings hit the market? The trend will be back to single private dwellings, on substantially larger lots, paid for in full out of this month's paycheck. If you can afford a home in the city and another in the mountains or at the beach, why not? One unhappy note for Howard Roark: Higher living-standards will encourage an unRandish human vice for embellishment. They'll bring back Baroque, Rococo, Victorian gingerbread, medieval gargoyles, and the new times will create their own elaborate forms, as well.

Aztec Modern, anyone?

For transportation, you'll choose between a five hundred dollar auto, a two thousand dollar personal aircraft, or some convertible combination. Or Laissez-Faire Airlines will fly you anywhere in the world for twenty bucks. Highways and railroads will benefit from a free market. Speed, safety, and efficiency will improve. sixty-lane, three hundred-mile-per-hour ribbons of plastic will power your electric car by induction, provide guidance if you want to read or watch TV, dissipate rain, fog, ice, and snow. Or, as I predicted in *The Probability Broach*, highways may evolve into contoured swaths of hardy grass for steam-powered hovercraft.

Or both.

Or something else entirely different.

Our grandchildren will have a good laugh over the Carter "Energy Crisis" of the last decade being revived by Clintonite reactionaries, not just because any real shortages, then or now, are political in character, but because the free market will ultimately render fossil fuels obsolete. Fusion, using water for fuel, lasers, and particle beams, or palladium for spark plugs, producing as its only byproduct inert useful helium, will be driving our civilization the day after government gets out of the way. Fusion is the nuclear reaction that powers the stars; quasars are billions of times more energetic and we don't know what powers them. When science and industry are free of government interference, we may find out. Energy will be practically limitless and virtually free.

I could go on for hours discussing the technomiracles you can read about in *Popular Science*, *Analog*, or any of the novels I've written. I've elaborated on them to this extent because I believe they're only possible under free-market conditions, which explains why we never got the picture-phones and flying automobiles that science fiction promised us in the 1930s and 1940s. Read those other publications with that caveat in mind, and you'll get the idea.

Far more important are the social and psychological effects of freedom. I can't tell you what it's like to be free, having never had the chance to try it. I'd be up against the unpredictability of human action that any Austrian economist or quantum physicist delights in lecturing about. Authoritarians who still believe in a static model of "the way things ought to be" — a model they're willing to impose at bayonet-point — work very hard to make society dull and boring. Among Libertarians, the one rule is that nobody may impose his views on anybody else, which makes for an open-ended culture impossible to describe in detail — I know, because I've tried harder than any other writer or scholar.

There's no single Libertarian future, but as many different futures as individuals to create them. For each Sunday-supplement guess I could make about who'll take care of the street lights or paint stripes down the middle of the road, coming generations will produce thousands of answers not remotely similar to mine. Our future may be weird and confusing, but it'll never be dull and boring.

So instead, try an experiment, one that'll give you a clearer picture of the future than I could draw in another hour or another hundred hours. Lean back in your chair. Relax. Imagine now that you'll never have to worry about money again. Never again for the rest of your life. You'll never waste another golden moment of your precious time tearing your hair, biting your fingernails, or shredding the inside of your mouth over paying the bills. There's no limit to what you can afford. It's no longer a significant factor in your plans.

Now, say quietly to yourself: "All my life, I always really wanted _____," and fill in the blank. Finish the sentence yourself. Only *you* know what it is you always really wanted.

"All my life I always *really* wanted _____."

You may be surprised. How many things have you denied yourself or never even acknowledged, because there wasn't enough money? Or because your dreams were being consumed to feed bureaucrats, build atomic bombs, launch nuclear submarines, construct government office buildings? Unanimous Consent will change all that. Everything you always really wanted can be yours, if you are free.

Retirement? Save it out of pocket change. Your kids' education? A new home, car, boat, plane? All of the above? Nothing more than ordinary easily accessible objectives that will hardly dent the family budget. If you are free.

"All my life, I always really wanted _____."

Is it illegal? A machine gun to mow down beer cans on a lazy country afternoon? Driving your car at 185 miles an hour? A nickel bag that really costs a nickel? An android sex-slave? A dynamite collection? A date with a one-legged jockey? It's all yours, as long as you don't hurt anyone. If you are free.

"All my life, I always really wanted _____."

The only thing that Unanimous Consent, that individual liberty, *can't* give you, the only goods it can't deliver, is *power* over the lives of others. And yet, through that one "failure," that single "sacrifice," we achieve everything else.

"All my life, I always really wanted _____."

And that, my fellow Libertarians, is the ultimate promise of Unanimous Consent, an invention so fundamental, potent, revolutionary, and unstoppable, that Scientific Method and the Industrial Revolution pale by comparison. Now you understand why I'm a fanatic, why I must make *you* fanatic, why we must create an entire nation, a whole world of fanatics. I'm fighting for everything I always really wanted! *That's* what's in it for me! That's what it's all about!

Everything.

You.

Always.

Really.

Wanted.

To the traditional strategies of our movement, education and politics, now add a third — practical Utopianism — which will break trails for the other two. While others teach and run for office, I'll continue writing science fiction. Educators and candidates will find, as they're already finding, that their students and voters came to them because of the promises I made.

They can always mess it up, of course. They can disappoint neophytes excited about the future and eager to begin creating it. They can euphemize the difficult embarrassing concepts, temporize the uncompromised positions we must take if we want to win. They can follow the chicken-livered, quail-hearted leadership of many previous LP candidates, the cowards, cravens, cringers, and crybabies whose campaigns are indistinguishable from those of Republicans and Democrats. They can emulate the weak-kneed recreants, faint-hearted, faltering, gritless, pluckless invertebrates who counsel restraint in the face of tyranny. They can accept the advice from pusillanimous milksops, gutless, spineless, spunk-deficient slinkers and skulkers, weaklings, dastards, and poltroons fearful to take an open approach with those who need to learn from us.

Or they can stop waiting for an electoral victory to bestow itself upon us, stop depending on the mass media controlled by the enemies of liberty, and instead, take big bites of the future, on their own, in sure and certain knowledge that Heinlein was right when he said, "Anything worth doing is worth overdoing."

That's the only way our future's going to happen. We're going to win as soon as we recognize, as soon as we communicate, as soon as we act on one simple fact: In order to "capture the hearts and minds" of America and the world, in order to have the major part in determining what the "shape of things to come" is going to be, we must first pull off a *coup d'etat* in the Province of Utopia.

"All my life, I always *really* wanted _____."

It's as simple as that.

It really is.

APPENDIX

The Novels of L. Neil Smith
ᝣᝣᝣᝣᝣ

FORGE OF THE ELDERS *(Baen Books, 2000)*
While most nations rejected Marxism in the 1990s, the Berlin Wall fell, and the Soviet Empire collapsed, the United States embraced Marxism wholeheartedly and dragged the whole world back down into the pit of collectivism. Now the American Soviet Socialist Republic claims the asteroid 5023 Eris, but somebody (or something) is already there! The Elders are from Earth ... sort of. They aren't human. But they're individualists and capitalists!

(Originally published as CONTACT AND COMMUNE *and* CONVERSE AND CONFLICT *by Warner Books in 1990. So politically incorrect that Warner unilaterally cancelled the third volume,* CONCERT AND COSMOS*! Now reissued as the single epic work it was always meant to be.)*

THE MITZVAH *(with Aaron Zelman, Mazel Freedom Press, 1999)*
A Roman Catholic monsignor from Chicago discovers that he's actually a Jewish Holocaust orphan and must decide, not only between the faith he was brought up in and the faith he was born to, but between his liberal pacifist beliefs and those of his real family, many of whom joined the Resistance and fought and killed Nazis.

Co-author Aaron Zelman is the founder and executive director of JPFO: Jews for the Preservation of Firearms Ownership.

THE WARDOVE *(Pulpless, 1999)*
Earth was destroyed in 2023 and only Lunar colonists survived. Nine hundred years later, in a star-spanning "nation" without conscription or taxation, Captain Nathaniel Blackburn of Coordinated Arm Intelligence must find out who's killing rock musicians raising money for the War Against the Clusterian Powers. Includes lyrics to a dozen songs written by the author. First issued in 1983.

BRETTA MARTYN *(Tor Books, 1996)*
Fifteen years after her father's adventures, Robretta Islay sails to the stars in order to expose the source of Oplyte slavery and stamp it out. Along the way she travels across half a galaxy, faces hideous perils, suffers grievously, meets many wild and wonderful characters, and eventually rediscovers the homeworld of the human race. (Also a sequel to *The WarDove*.)

THE PROBABILITY BROACH *(Tor Books, 1996)*
The book that started it all, back again to ruin the sleep and shorten the lives of socialists everywhere. In a deadly conflict with murderous federal agents, Denver homicide detective Win Bear is accidentally blown "sideways" in time, into the "North American Confederacy," where the Whiskey Rebellion succeeded in 1794 and government has grown less powerful ever since. 1980/81 Prometheus Award winner.
(Originally published by Del Rey Books in 1980. See also "The Spirit of Exmas Sideways," Alternatives, edited by Robert and Pamela Crippen Adams, Baen Books, 1989. Trying to make a place for himself in the stateless North American Confederacy, Win Bear discovers the many joys and difficulties of absolute self-ownership.)

PALLAS *(Tor Books, 1993)*

In the persons of Gibson Altman, exiled liberal United States Senator, and Emerson Ngu, a young Vietnamese/Cambodian immigrant boy who aspires to manufacture firearms, socialist "East America" and entrepreneurs of the West American "Jackelope Republic" fight for control of a whole new world, the second largest of the asteroids. Lots of action, romance, RKBA polemics, plus metallic silhouette shooting! Winner of the 1994 Prometheus Award.

HENRY MARTYN *(Tor Books, 1989)*

A thousand years from now, in the depths of interstellar space, there will be sailing ships — and pirates! Vast empires clash as young Arran Islay fights for freedom, and to regain a legacy brutally stripped from his family by the "Black Usurper."

THE CRYSTAL EMPIRE *(Tor Books, 1986)*

Moslems rule the world in this adventure of an inventor and gunsmith in an alternate universe where the Black Plague killed 999 out of 1,000, and technology — especially firearms — took the blame.

LANDO CALRISSIAN & THE MINDHARP OF SHARU
(Del Rey Books, 1983)
LANDO CALRISSIAN & THE FLAMEWIND OF OSEON
(Del Rey Books, 1983)
LANDO CALRISSIAN & THE STARCAVE OF THONBOKA
(Del Rey Books, 1983)

Youthful adventures of Star Wars' famous gambler before Han Solo won the Millenium Falcon from him. Re-released in omnibus edition titled *THE LANDO CALRISSIAN ADVENTURES*, Summer, 1994.

BRIGHTSUIT MACBEAR *(Avon, 1988)*

On Majesty, a planet covered from pole-to-pole with jungle six miles deep, Win Bear's great-grandson MacDougall battles to prevent a terrible crime and recover a lost inheritance.

TAFLAK LYSANDRA *(Avon, 1988)*

In the first of six projected sequels to Brightsuit MacBear, testing a marvelous "subfoline" craft, young Elsie Nahuatl (last seen in *Tom Paine Maru*) becomes lost amidst the bizarre collectivist cultures that lurk beneath the planet Majesty's "Sea of Leaves" with her father — a cybernetically enhanced coyote.

THE GALLATIN DIVERGENCE *(Del Rey Books, 1985)*

Win Bear travels back in time to 1794 to save Albert Gallatin, founder of the North American Confederacy, from assassins. First appearance in print of the author's "Covenant of Unanimous Consent."

TOM PAINE MARU *(Del Rey Books, 1984)*

The North American Confederacy reaches the stars at last, its Prime Directive: Search out governments wherever they are found to exist — and destroy them!

THEIR MAJESTIES' BUCKETEERS
(Del Rey Books, 1981)

On an alien world whose furry, nine-legged, crablike inhabitants are just entering their own "Age of Invention," a royal "fireman" must create the art of criminal detection from scratch, in order to solve the murder of his favorite teacher.

THE VENUS BELT *(Del Rey Books, 1980)*

How does a totally ethical culture conquer its own "final frontier"? A mysterious series of disappearances leads gumshoe Win Bear, assisted by Koko Featherstone-Haugh (a young female gorilla) and Lucy Kropotkin (a disgruntled murder victim temporarily housed in a robot body) to the asteroids, a super-villain with an all-too-familiar face, and a conspiracy stretching across whole universes.

THE NAGASAKI VECTOR *(Del Rey Books, 1983)*

Is a culture with an absolute regard for individual rights really helpless against those who would destroy it? Professional time traveler Bernie Gruenblum hires Win Bear to track down the stolen flying saucer ... who loves him.

(Based on the short stories "Grimm's Law," "Folger's Factor," and "Grandfather Clause" which appeared in Stellar Science Fiction Stories *#s 5, 6, & 7, Del Rey Books, 1980 & 1981. See also "The Embarrassment Box" in* New Libertarian *#187.)*

FORTHCOMING

THE AMERICAN ZONE

(forthcoming in 2000 from Tor Books)

Terrorists try to force a government to form in the North American Confederacy. Win Bear (hero of *The Probability Broach*), his wife Clarissa, and his friends Lucy Kropotkin and Will Sanders stalk the badguys through the self-isolated community of fresh (and frightened) immigrants to the first free country they've ever known.

TEXAS UEBER ALLES

(with Rex F. May, currently on the market)

In 1947, in an alternate version of the Lone Star Republic that was never a part of the United States — and where Richard Wagner and Scott Joplin teamed up in the east Texas city of New Orleans to write their epic opera, *Die Alamo* — an unlikely trio of Rangers race against time and foreign enemies to claim the wreckage of an unknown craft near the west Texas town of Roswell.

Rex May is the famous humorist, gag writer, and "cartoonists' cartoonist" whose work appears virtually everywhere, and who signs his work "Baloo."

ABOUT THE AUTHOR

L. Neil Smith was born in Denver, Colorado, in 1946. The son of an Air Force officer, he grew up all over North America, in places like LaPorte, Waco, and McQueenie, Texas; Salina, Kansas; Gifford, Illinois; Fort Walton Beach, Florida; Sacramento, California; and St. John's, Newfoundland. Perhaps best known for his novels (two-score and counting so far), he lives in Fort Collins, Colorado with his wife Cathy, his daughter Rylla, two orange tiger-striped cats, and a Keeshond named Greywind.

HERE'S HOW TO ORDER
ADDITIONAL COPIES

of *Lever Action*
as well as the best-selling
Send in the Waco Killers by Vin Suprynowicz

1. From the Publisher

To order directly from the publisher, send a check or money order for US$21.95 for each copy, plus $3 shipping for the first copy and $2 per each additional copy (4th-class book rate), or $6 for the first copy and $3 per additional copy (UPS ground) to: **Mountain Media, P.O. Box 271122, Las Vegas, NV 89127**

2. Credit-Card Orders and Volume Discounts

To place credit-card orders, or to inquire about international shipping rates or volume discounts for your group or store, call: **Huntington Press at 800/244-2224**

3. Via Internet

To order via the Internet, where credit-card and bulk orders are also accepted, as is payment in silver, gold, and other hard currencies, go to **http://www.thespiritof76.com/leveraction.html**